Neo-Passing

Neo-Passing

Performing Identity after Jim Crow

EDITED BY MOLLIE GODFREY AND VERSHAWN ASHANTI YOUNG

Foreword by Gayle Wald

Afterword by Michele Elam

Publication of this book was supported by funding from James Madison University and the University of Waterloo, Ontario, Canada.

1 2 3 4 5 C P 5 4 3 2 1
∞ This book is printed on acid-free paper.

Library of Congress Cataloging-in-Publication Data
Names: Godfrey, Mollie, 1979– editor. | Young, Vershawn Ashanti, editor. | Wald, Gayle, 1965– writer of foreword. | Elam, Michele, writer of afterword.
Title: Neo-passing : performing identity after Jim Crow / edited by Mollie Godfrey and Vershawn Young ; foreword by Gayle Wald ; afterword by Michele Elam.
Description: Urbana : University of Illinois Press, [2018] | Includes bibliographical references and index.
Identifiers: LCCN 2017057076| ISBN 9780252041587 (hardback) | ISBN 9780252083235 (paperback)
Subjects: LCSH: Passing (Identity) in literature. | African Americans—Race identity. | Race awareness—United States. | African Americans in literature. | Race in literature. | BISAC: SOCIAL SCIENCE / Ethnic Studies / African American Studies. | LITERARY CRITICISM / American / African American.
Classification: LCC PS169.P35 N46 2018 | DDC 810.9/355—dc23
LC record available at https://lccn.loc.gov/2017057076

For those who pass.

Centuries after, she heard the strange man saying: “Death by misadventure, I’m inclined to believe. Let’s go up and have another look at that window.”

—Nella Larsen, *Passing* (1929)

Contents

Foreword: Passing and "Post-Race" ix
Gayle Wald

Acknowledgments xv
Mollie Godfrey and Vershawn Ashanti Young

Introduction: The Neo-Passing Narrative 1
Mollie Godfrey and Vershawn Ashanti Young

Appendix to the Introduction. Neo-Passing Narratives: Teaching and Scholarly Resources 29

PART I. NEW HISTORIES

Introduction: Passing at the Turn of the Twenty-First Century 43
Allyson Hobbs

1. Why Passing Is (Still) Not Passé after More Than 250 Years: Sources from the Past and Present 49
Martha J. Cutter

2. Passing for Postracial: Colorblind Reading Practices of Zombies, Sheriffs, and Slaveholders 68
Christopher M. Brown

3. Adam Mansbach's Postracial Imaginary in *Angry Black White Boy* 84
Brandon J. Manning

4. Black President Bush: The Racial and Gender Politics behind Dave Chappelle's Presidential Drag 96
Eden Osucha

5. Seeing Race in Comics: Passing, Witness, and the Spectacle of Racial Violence in Johnson and Pleece's *Incognegro* 117
Jennifer Glaser

PART II. NEW IDENTITIES

Introduction: Passing at the Intersections 135
Marcia Alesan Dawkins

6. Passing Truths: Identity-Immersion Journalism and the Experience of Authenticity 142
Loran Marsan

7. Passing for Tan: Snooki and the Grotesque Reality of Ethnicity 158
Alisha Gaines

8. The Pass of Least Resistance: Sexual Orientation and Race in ZZ Packer's "Drinking Coffee Elsewhere" 175
Derek Adams

9. Neo-Passing and Dissociative Identities as Affective Strategies in *Frankie and Alice* 193
Deborah Elizabeth Whaley

10. "A New Type of Human Being": Gender, Sexuality, and Ethnicity as Perpetual Passing in Jeffrey Eugenides's *Middlesex* 219
Lara Narcisi

Afterword: Why Neo Now? 241
Michele Elam

Contributors 247

Index 251

Foreword

Passing and "Post-Race"

GAYLE WALD

Coeditors Mollie Godfrey and Vershawn Ashanti Young open their introduction to this volume with a citation of a 1952 *Jet* magazine article, "Why 'Passing' Is Passing Out." Penned at a hopeful moment of the incipient Civil Rights Movement, it posits the notion that passing will become "passé" as African Americans achieve political equality and full citizenship rights. The article asserts that as racial barriers to "decent employment" fall away—by means of civil rights agitation as well as state and federal nonsegregation mandates—Negroes who might have been able to pass for white will no longer find an incentive to do so. And with the erosion of workplace discrimination, *Jet* imagines, so would new opportunities for the expression of collective pride in black identity emerge and grow. The demise of passing would betoken a better future, in which color or race would no longer confer advantage or stigma.[1]

From the vantage of the present moment, "Why 'Passing' Is Passing Out" is poignant in its optimism. The author of the piece could not have foreseen either imminent civil rights triumphs—from the legal victory of the US Supreme Court decision in *Brown v. Board of Education* to the moral and political achievements of the Montgomery bus boycott—or looming civil rights tragedies—from the assassinations of Medgar Evers, Malcolm X, and Martin Luther King Jr. to the Federal Bureau of Investigation (FBI) infiltration and intimidation of black organizations and leaders. Amiri Baraka, who had been on the forefront of both the Black Arts Movement and political struggles in his hometown of

Newark, New Jersey, would reflect on the dialectical nature of progress in a 1991 eulogy for his friend the black cultural impresario and TV producer Ellis Haizlip.[2] Using a metaphor derived from Langston Hughes's 1926 *Nation* magazine cri de coeur of black artistic freedom, Baraka refers to "our jagged rise and fall and rerise and refall, up and down the racial mountain."[3] For Baraka, the Sisyphean labors of racial-freedom struggles in the United States means that history is always dynamic, victories (like defeats) always provisional.

Despite *Jet*'s optimistic vantage of early 1950s, passing, it turns out, was not quite passé in that hopeful moment—or, to put a finer point on it, was not yet obsolete as a social practice of identity and identification. As the essays in this volume make clear, passing has taken new forms and new articulations in the post-segregation era, an era that has been marked by profound racial contradiction. Barack Hussein Obama's historic election as the nation's first black president led to overeager declarations of a "postracial" America. If a multiracial coalition of voters could get behind a brown-skinned candidate of biracial heritage with an Arabic middle name conferred by his Nigerian father, then, so the thinking went, America had achieved King's dream of "seeing" beyond skin color. Of course, to riff on Mark Twain, reports of the death of racism in the United States were greatly exaggerated. Not only did what Michael Omi and Howard Winant call "the racial state" *not* disappear under Obama but the bitter election at the end of Obama's two terms also saw the renewal and expansion of white racial-identity politics and racial nativism.[4] As in the immediate post-1968 period, in the Obama era, backlash against civil rights achievements did not take the form of overt hostility to blackness—a position rendered more ridiculous by the predominance of African American culture and obvious examples of black excellence in the public sphere—but in more-insidious hostilities to "government handouts," "special preferences," and the like. As recent thinkers such as Cathy J. Cohen, Michelle Alexander, Ta-Nehisi Coates, Mark Anthony Neal, and William J. Barber II argue, we need to consider the post–Civil Rights (or for some, "postsoul") moment in terms of its production of new cleavages and new alliances, the analysis of which demands our attention to the intersectionality of identities and the profound heterogeneity of the imagined "black" collective.[5]

As *Neo-Passing: Performing Identity after Jim Crow* ably demonstrates, passing cannot be understood apart from the social and historical discourses of identity and power that condition its possibility. Although this volume includes discussions of a wide variety of passing, as a practice passing remains defined by the now-you-seen it, now-you-don't contingencies of blackness, as a fiction that has been embedded in scientific "fact" (the one-drop rule, racialized eugenics, and laws of hypodescent) and in social practice (the police state, the vulnerability of black bodies). Passing, that is to say, is a socially and historically embedded practice—which is partly why cultural narratives, with their ability to imagine possibilities and represent social worlds, are so useful in helping us understand it. This was true in the era of segregation—when passing from black to white ensured a degree of (always precarious) freedom from racial definition—and it is true in the current era of "posts," in which old expressions of state violence (e.g., de jure school segregation) take new forms (e.g., the persistence of residential segregation and the black wealth gap, the school-to-prison pipeline). So we should expect that in our current moment, passing is both passé and persistent, albeit in forms that will necessarily continue to evolve. So, too, will the social stakes of passing change, as racialized advantage and disadvantage change.

The contradictions of the Obama-era post–Civil Rights but not post-race moment were fully on display in the 2015 Broadway debut and the subsequent, zeitgeist-defining success of *Hamilton*, Lin-Manuel Miranda's acclaimed musical about "ten-dollar founding father" Alexander Hamilton, which employs cross-racial casting and sonic elements of hip-hop, rhythm and blues, and other black American musical idioms to tell its story of the founding of the nation. For many, including Miranda himself, the use of a cast that "looks like America looks now" was central to the musical's project of broadening audiences' perceptions of the racial and ethnic contours of the American story.[6] The overwhelming, cross-cutting popularity of the musical—which was lavishly praised by former first lady Michelle Obama and received enthusiastic endorsements from former vice president Dick Cheney and conservative news mogul Rupert Murdoch—combined with the lack of resistance to *Hamilton*'s nontraditional racial casting and incorporation of rapping—signaled the degree to which American culture was now, it seemed, thoroughly hybridized.

But love of black (and brown) culture, as we have known at least since the days when white slaveholders and abolitionists alike shed "ethno-sympathetic" tears at the heart-rending songs of slaves, has never been synonymous with love of black people.[7] It follows that in late 2016, the symbolic value of *Hamilton* as a Broadway high-five to multicultural, postracial America was tested by the presence in the audience of then vice president–elect Mike Pence, part of an ascendant Republican ticket that had cynically elevated a benighted coalition of white supremacists, climate deniers, Islamophobes, and others under the nativist vow to "make America great again." In a postcurtain speech directed at Pence as he was departing the theater, the multihued, multiply sexually and racially identifying cast urged him, as the number two man in the incoming

Donald J. Trump administration, to "work on behalf of all of us." This was apparently too much for the president-elect, who took to Twitter—in a hastily composed post that was later just as hastily deleted—to berate such a peaceable plea as "rude and insulting."[8] Theater is theater, Trump suggested, and should know its proper place. The headache-inducing complexities of this episode—in which a Broadway musical that overtly reimagines the white Founding Fathers in various shades of brown and black was also an occasion for a scolding of its actors by a president elect who had campaigned on a barely veiled agenda of racial *ressentiment*—are a testament to how superficial the "post" in post-race ideology can be.

From the perspective of this volume's interest in neo-passing in the post-segregation era, what is to be made from this too-real-to-be-made-up clash of art and politics? I argue that the *Hamilton*-Trump confluence is illustrative of what Daphne Brooks calls the intensification of "post–civil rights ironies."[9] As the first black president prepared to leave office, the man who helped to launch a conspiracy theory to debunk Obama's legitimacy on racialized citizenship grounds prepared to occupy his office. As *Hamilton* celebrated a cherished narrative of the United States as "a nation of [historical] immigrants" who "get the job done," a contemporary narrative of a white masculine "us" versus an amorphous multicultural and feminized "them" spurred a majority of white voters to embrace an authoritarian candidate who was more than willing to fan the flames of racism and anti-immigrant sentiments when they served his political ends.

The Civil Rights and Black Power Movements, combined with the 1960s and '70s women's movement and the movement for gay rights, have undoubtedly produced incredible possibilities for black people and women, which were unthinkable as little as a decade or so earlier. Yet, in the wake of such "openings," we also witness the continued reinvention and revivification of white supremacy, an ideology that refashions itself as opposition demands. As Omi and Winant observe in the third revised edition of their indispensable *Racial Formation in the United States*, the apogee of civil rights was followed by racial reaction and the rise of neoliberalism, prompting racial ideology to adapt to "colorblind" times.[10] And in the election of 2016, we witnessed a new turn of the post-segregation but not postracial wheel, as overt racism was renormalized and nonwhites and immigrants were broadly scapegoated as a source of American economic woes and threats to the security of the "homeland."

The relevant issue now, it seems to me, is not that passing persists but *to what end*. What motivates a woman of European descent to claim black identity and, in so doing, to covet "black" skin and hair? Why would someone want to publicly embrace and acknowledge Native American ancestry when that ancestry is not otherwise readily knowable? How and why do various practices get encoded as white or black, and how do young people negotiate their relation to these practices as they negotiate their relationship to class, gender, sexuality, and privilege? What sorts of ethical and political agency do subjects exercise when they pass, and what sorts of ethical and political judgments emerge in the "discovery" of passing? How have new media, which give people new tools to fashion avatars free from the constraints of their embodiment, given way to new forms of passing?

The United States has never been and may never be post-race, if by post-race we mean to name a future in which social distinctions of race no longer produce and align with forms of unfreedom, vulnerability, and inequality. In that sense, the United States may never be post-passing. But that doesn't mean, in the manner of *Jet* in 1952, that we do not need to imagine a different world, a world in which passing is indeed passé. A robust democratic response to the new racial crisis demands, instead of the secrecy and shame associated with passing (or the outing of passing), new intra- and interracial alliances, new crosscutting coalitions, and new political and cultural formations of identity. The essays in this volume go a long way in helping us imagine what those formations might be.

Notes

1. "Why 'Passing' Is Passing Out," 12–13.
2. Haizlip was producer of the TV show *Soul!*, which aired for five seasons during this transitional–Civil Rights to "post"–Civil Rights era. See Wald, *It's Been Beautiful*.
3. Baraka, "Soul Brother," 148.
4. Omi and Winant, *Racial Formation*.
5. Cohen, *Boundaries of Blackness*; Alexander, *New Jim Crow*; Coates, *Between the World and Me*; Neal, *Soul Babies*; Barber, *Third Reconstruction*.
6. Paulson, "'Hamilton' Heads to Broadway."
7. Cruz, *Culture on the Margins*.
8. Healy, "'Hamilton' Cast's Appeal to Pence."
9. Brooks, "How #BlackLivesMatter Started a Musical Revolution."
10. Omi and Winant, *Racial Formation*.

Bibliography

Alexander, Michelle. *The New Jim Crow: Mass Incarceration in the Age of Colorblindness*. New York: New Press, 2012.

Baraka, Amiri. "The Soul Brother." In *Eulogies*, 147–49. New York: Marsilio, 1996.

Barber, William J., II. *The Third Reconstruction: How a Moral Movement Is Overcoming the Politics of Division and Fear.* Boston: Beacon, 2016.

Brooks, Daphne. "How #BlackLivesMatter Started a Musical Revolution." *Guardian,* March 13, 2016. Accessed December 20, 2016. https://www.theguardian.com/us-news/.

Coates, Ta-Nehisi. *Between the World and Me.* New York: Spiegel and Grau, 2015.

Cohen, Cathy J. *The Boundaries of Blackness: AIDS and the Breakdown of Black Politics.* Chicago: University of Chicago Press, 1999.

Cruz, Jon. *Culture on the Margins: The Black Spiritual and the Rise of American Cultural Interpretation.* Princeton, NJ: Princeton University Press, 1999.

Healy, Patrick. "'Hamilton' Cast's Appeal to Pence Ignites Showdown with Trump." *New York Times,* November 19, 2016. Accessed December 20, 2016. https://www.nytimes.com.

Neal, Mark Anthony. *Soul Babies: Black Popular Culture and the Post-Soul Aesthetic.* New York: Routledge, 2001.

Omi, Michael, and Howard Winant. *Racial Formation in the United States.* Rev. 3rd ed. New York: Routledge, 2014.

Paulson, Michael. "'Hamilton' Heads to Broadway in a Hip-Hop Retelling." *New York Times,* July 12, 2015. Accessed December 20, 2016. http://www.nytimes.com.

Wald, Gayle. *It's Been Beautiful:* Soul! *and Black Power Television.* Durham, NC: Duke University Press, 2015.

"Why 'Passing' Is Passing Out." *Jet,* July 17, 1952, 12–16.

Acknowledgments

With the third printing of Nella Larsen's *Passing* (1929), the concluding paragraph of the novel—which we feature as an epigraph to this volume—had suddenly disappeared. *Passing* now ended with the line, "Then everything was dark," instead of the original, "Let's go up and have another look at that window." And since no evidence exists as to why the original ending was removed, subsequent editors and scholars must make a choice about which one to use, which one to discuss, which one is "real." As editors of the current volume, we present our acknowledgments in the context of *Passing*'s unstable ending—an irony that points to the indeterminacy of literary meaning, identity, and the continuing cultural phenomenon of passing itself. The lines of the competing endings anticipate possible futures of passing, futures that bring us to what we call *neo-passing* and to this present study. For instance, the line, "Then everything was dark," could mean that a lid of sorts was placed on passing, leaving it in the past; or it could mean that the future beyond passing is grim, that the past will never be behind us; or it could mean something more egalitarian—that, for once, the world must be seen through diverse American experiences, through the lenses of "darker" people, persons of color. In their foreword and afterword to this volume, Gayle Wald and Michele Elam, respectively, wade into these interpretive futures, asking what neo-passing allows us to glean and gain. We thank these two scholars, whose voices on the topic of passing and now on neo-passing continue to challenge and inspire us.

It is, however, the original conclusion of Larsen's *Passing* that best describes our attention to neo-passing in this volume. After all, the invitation to "go up and have another look at the window," and to carry out this investigation as a team—together—as indicated with "let's," perfectly describes the project we have been pursuing here. We first met at the American Studies Association (ASA) convention in Puerto Rico in 2012, a chance meeting—in passing—while waiting for the bus back from the convention center to the hotel. Striking up a conversation about our academic interests, we discovered that we were both teaching courses on passing in the new millennium that integrated classic and contemporary tales of passing. During that and subsequent conversations, we began using the term *neo-passing* to describe the newer narratives we were asking our students to read, such as Patricia Jones's *Passing* (1999), Danzy Senna's *Caucasia* (1999), Philip Roth's *The Human Stain* (2000), Percival Everett's *Erasure* (2001), and Daniel Black's *Perfect Peace* (2010).

We are deeply grateful to the ASA, not only for being an organization that brings together scholars interested in American cultures and their impact on literature, performance, politics, and the world, but also for nurturing collegial, working relationships such as ours. We further thank the ASA for accepting our panel on neo-passing in 2013, "'This Debt We Pay to Human Guile': Economies of Race in Neo-Passing Narratives," as well as our fellow panelists who supported this work in its early stage—most of whom became contributors to this volume: Derek Adams, Adrienne Brown, Alisha Gaines, and Gayle Wald. We also thank the additional contributors to this volume: Christopher M. Brown, Martha J. Cutter, Marcia Alesan Dawkins, Michele Elam, Jennifer Glaser, Allyson Hobbs, Brandon J. Manning, Loran Marsan, Lara Narcisi, Eden Osucha, and Deborah Elizabeth Whaley. We thank Dawn Durante, senior acquisitions editor at the University of Illinois Press, who expressed consistent interest and support for this project. We further thank the University of Illinois Press, its board, and the insightful and critical attention of the anonymous reviewers. The project benefited greatly from the discussions we have shared with our mentors, colleagues, and especially our students at the University of Chicago, Bates College, James Madison University, the University of Iowa, the University of Kentucky, and the University of Waterloo. Some who deserve special mention include Melissa Barton, Frankie Condon, Jacqueline Goldsby, Angelo Robinson, and Jeremy Rosen. We have also benefited from the suggestions of several readers along the way, including David Babcock, Allison Fagan, Dawn Goode, and Siân White. We are grateful for the financial support of our institutions and specifically from the offices of Dabney Bankert, Jerry Benson, Yvonne Harris, David Jeffrey, Tim Kenyon, and Doug Peers. Finally, we thank our families.

Mollie thanks her partner, Jim Bywater, and her sons, Milo and Asa, for being too wonderful for words. Vershawn thanks his parents, Dorothy Young and Richard Moore, for their constant encouragement and support, and his young daughter, Ari Zhah Young, for her happiness and laughter.

Perhaps beginning these acknowledgments with a snippet from a novel is a peculiar holdover from another connection we share. Both of us completed a PhD in English at schools in Chicago—Mollie at the University of Chicago and Vershawn at the University of Illinois at Chicago—and we studied with scholars who are also interlocutors, Kenneth W. Warren and Walter Benn Michaels, respectively. Vershawn distinctly recalls Michaels's mantra to "begin with the text," meaning that you should start and anchor your literary, cultural, or rhetorical analysis with an exemplary instance of your argument from a text. Though we are far from the years of graduate school, and we certainly recognize ourselves as intellectuals in our own right, we thank our mentors for guiding our initial practice of paying careful attention to texts, analyzing cultural patterns, and writing about literary topics that affect the lived experiences of Americans and people around world. Lastly, we thank the readers of this volume for joining us in taking "another look at that window."

Neo-Passing

INTRODUCTION

The Neo-Passing Narrative

MOLLIE GODFREY AND
VERSHAWN ASHANTI YOUNG

I

On July 17, 1952, the African American weekly *Jet* magazine featured the article "Why 'Passing' Is Passing Out." This editorial suggests that since the growing Civil Rights Movement might put an end to Jim Crow legislation and its persistent racial bias, then racial passing—the phenomenon whereby some African Americans with optically white skin choose to live as Caucasian—would also cease. Based, as it was, on nascent signs of racial progress, *Jet*'s article on the end of passing is more hope than fact: "With new and greater opportunities, the Negro is competing more and more on even terms with other men in a competitive society. The faster he becomes equally integrated into the American economy, the slower he will be to resort to the peculiar American sociological phenomenon of 'passing.'"[1] However, although *Jet* was accurate in anticipating the imminent dismantling of Jim Crow segregation and an increase in opportunities for African Americans, its prediction that passing would "pass out" has yet to occur. Instead of ending, passing has expanded. Indeed, although the term *passing* inevitably retains its conceptual link to segregation-era acts of black-to-white passing, it is now used as often to describe a white person who dupes people into believing he or she is black, a gay person who presents him- or herself as straight, a poor person who presents him- or herself as rich, a white author who uses an Asian name to get published, and so on. The aim of the current volume, then, is to understand why passing persists, why it has proliferated, and what might be gained from analyzing its transformations and unearthing the social, political, and economic conditions that spur on and stem from passing in the late twentieth and into the twenty-first centuries.

As the title to this book indicates, our primary focus is not on the classic passing experience, the kind that is presented in those novels, films, or autobiographical statements produced or written during the era of legal segregation, in which black protagonists live as white in order to escape the pains of racism. Instead, we focus on what we call *neo-passing narratives*: acts and stories of passing that recall the complex racial politics that defined classic passing narratives but that are performed or produced after segregation. As Eduardo Bonilla-Silva explains, racism in the post–Jim Crow era operates differently than it did during segregation in part because Americans are now less likely to believe that racism is a problem—a vision that reached its apotheosis with the oft-declared "post-racial" promise of Barack Obama's 2008 election.[2] Nevertheless, as Bonilla-Silva and numerous others have thoroughly documented, "racial considerations" continue to "shade almost everything in America"—from earnings, education, and housing to voting rights and criminal justice.[3] Rather than being maintained by openly discriminatory laws and discourse, these modern-day racial inequalities are enforced through covert, institutionalized means that are only perpetuated by colorblind refusals to acknowledge that they exist.[4] Although Americans' faith in the reality of postracialism or the success of colorblindness has become increasingly untenable since the deaths of Trayvon Martin and Michael Brown gave rise to the Black Lives Matter movement, the tension between colorblindness and color-consciousness as approaches to racial justice continues to dominate mainstream American discourse. Neo-passing narratives—presented in a range of fictional and nonfictional forms, in everyday life, and in the multifarious media of the new millennium—are typified by their direct engagement with just such debates, as with the idea that, as *Jet* declares, by now, passing should have passed.

By describing the range of experiences, performances, and texts under consideration in this project as "neo-passing narratives," we are deliberately aligning this effort with previous successful attempts to formulate a new cultural category out of a class of contemporary texts that take on the conventions of an important historical genre. For example, Ashraf H. A. Rushdy builds on the work of Bernard Bell in studying what Bell termed the *neo-slave narrative.* Rushdy defines this genre of narratives as mostly "contemporary novels that assume the form, adopt the conventions, and take on the first-person voice of the antebellum slave narrative."[5] Others have applied Rushdy's theorizing to other creative forms, such as film and poetry, making the term *neo-slave narrative* an inclusive rubric.

In a similar fashion, Brian Norman writes that "neo-segregation narratives are contemporary fictional accounts, often historiographic, of Jim Crow." The authors of these tales, Norman continues, "write from a post–civil rights era and its inclusive, multicultural sensibilities while their characters inhabit the terrain of compulsory race segregation." He further reports that authors of "neo-segregation narratives seek to expose systems of exclusion and disenfranchisement today."[6] Likewise, neo-slave narratives expose the relationship between American slavery and contemporary injustices by opening up underexplored or misrepresented aspects of the enslavement period and by humanizing black subjects.[7] Thus both genres, neo-slave and neo-segregation narratives, are engagements in American cultural study, with an interest in using an artistic simulation of the past to speak to current social and political conditions.

Like both neo-slave and neo-segregation narratives, neo-passing narratives also speak to contemporary injustices, asking readers to hold in mind classic and popular narratives of passing while noting distinctions between those and contemporary iterations of passing that speak to and against present social circumstances. To be sure, anthropologist Signithia Fordham does just this when she theorizes how passing has shifted away from skin color and more toward performance: for black people "becoming White . . . is not *the* issue" when passing post–Jim Crow.[8] "Acting white," or "looking white on paper—that is, behaving in ways and displaying the skills, abilities, and credentials that were traditionally associated with White Americans . . . [has] become the way to 'pass.'"[9] Fordham's assessment also comports with what we are advancing here as a notable difference between what we are terming neo-passing and the neo-slave and neo-segregation genres. The difference is that whereas slavery and segregation were legal institutions, passing was and continues to be a social phenomenon. As such, there is no locatable end to passing that one could argue there is with enslavement (about 1865) and segregation (about 1954). This difference might seem to indicate that there is nothing "neo" about neo-passing narratives. However, conventional passing narratives were always deeply grounded in the legal context of Jim Crow and the one-drop rule. Therefore, while certain facets of the genre remain bound up in America's legal past, key aspects, in addition to black people having to act white to succeed, have fundamentally transformed. For example, in such fictional depictions as Danzy Senna's *Caucasia* (1998) and Philip Roth's *The Human Stain* (2000), biracial protagonists pass as ethnic Jews during periods of intense segregation and must face the meaning of their passing in later multiculturalist moments. In memoirs, such as Gregory Howard Williams's *Life on the Color Line* (1995) and Bliss Broyard's *One Drop* (2007), children inherit a legacy of black-to-white passing from their parents and must decide for themselves whether to live as white, as black, or as both. The multiplication of identity performances available to contemporary passers are simply unavailable in classic passing narratives, where one drop of African heritage made one fully and only black.[10]

The sociological and cultural concepts of bi- and multiraciality of our present era necessarily affect the thematic development, textual construction, and production of neo-passing narratives. As a result, neo-passing narratives frequently go beyond a simple black/white binary that typified class-passing narratives in order to explore not only how identities are differently performed in relation to contemporary social norms but also how they are increasingly and explicitly intersectional—simultaneously involving class, gender, race, and sexuality. For instance, Daniel Black's *Perfect Peace* (2010) is about Emma Jean Peace, an African American mother of six sons who wants a daughter so badly that she raises her seventh son, Perfect, as a girl from birth until she is almost a teenager.[11] When Perfect learns later in life that she was born a biological boy and is forced to live as a male, she goes through emotional and psychological turmoil in trying to perform her new identity correctly.[12] The novel's setting in an African American context invites readers to draw connections between Perfect and the protagonists of Frances Harper's *Iola Leroy* (1892) and James Weldon Johnson's *The Autobiography of an Ex-colored Man* (1912), who believe that they are white until they are later forced to see themselves as black.[13] In light of Harper's and Johnson's texts, the types of questions that a neo-passing narrative like *Perfect Peace* raises are: Which identity is the one that is passing, the one before the discovery or the one after? In Perfect's case, is it the one when she was a girl who was born as a boy or the biological boy who understood himself to be a girl and is now forced to perform masculinity? In classic narratives of passing, the one drop-rule was sine qua non, so what is now the standard for gender, class, sexuality, and so forth? How do such identities get marked and forced into stasis in the post–Jim Crow moment? And what are the effects of these ideologies of identity on people's understandings of who they are and their performances of self? Neo-passing narratives such as *Perfect*

Peace remobilize passing as a trope that interrogates race through other categories of distinction, challenging static conceptions of class, sexual desire, gender identity, and racial authenticity all at once. And in some cases, neo-passing narratives build on the history of racial passing and the conventions of the passing narrative while subverting the traditional centering of racial discourse.

This broadening out of the passing narrative's thematic possibilities and concerns might lead one to question the relationship between passing and the more familiar concept of pretending. Passing, which John L. Jackson Jr. and Martha S. Jones describe as "a kind of *pretending of/with identity*," both overlaps with pretending and importantly differs from it.[14] This overlap and difference are best illustrated by performance studies theory's explanation of the difference between make-believe and make-belief. Make-believe performances are when you and your audience are conscious that you are pretending. For example, a father who is an aeronautical engineer but who comes home on Halloween dressed as a police officer—changing his manner, speech, and attitude to correspond to the performance—is not passing. He is pretending. He and his family all are conscious that he is affecting, simulating, faking. As Richard Schechner puts it, "make-believe performances maintain a clearly marked boundary between the world of the performance and everyday reality." In contrast, "make-belief performances," he explains, "intentionally blur or sabotage that boundary." For example, if the father decided to quit his job as an aeronautical engineer and become a police officer, he might feel some pressure to conceal his background and consciously change his behavior in order to better fit in at his new job. In doing so, Schechner would argue that he is "enacting the effects [he] want[s] the receivers of [his] performance . . . to accept 'for real.'"[15] He is passing. If passing is "a kind of *pretending with identity*," as Jackson and Jones argue, it is a kind that blurs the line between unreal and real upon which commonly accepted notions of pretending and identifying rely.

Because passing blurs this line, identity performances can sometimes be perceived as slipping from pretending to passing to identifying and back again. For example, if the father came home dressed as a police officer as part of an elaborate April Fools' Day joke, one could argue that because he briefly convinced his audience that his performance was real, he was—for a short time—passing. Indeed, many classic passing narratives, such as Langston Hughes's "Who's Passing for Who?" make use of reveals just such as this, as do recent reality television shows like *Black. White.*, *Joe Millionaire*, and *Undercover Boss*. And yet, in retrospect, they all know that the father didn't *really* want his family to accept his performance for real, so perhaps at that stage they might see him as only pretending. On the other end of the spectrum, the father who changed his manners and speech to fit in at his new job might eventually feel more himself in this identity performance; he may not only want others to accept the identity performance as real but he might accept it as real himself. At this point, he is no longer passing; he is identifying. Even then, others may not agree with him about this identification. His family's perceptions of which identity is real may or may not align with his; his new colleagues, were they to find out about his prior job, might have doubts as well.

In this way, passing not only disrupts the distinction between pretending and identifying but it also makes visible the complicated intersection of how one perceives oneself, how one presents oneself, and how one is received by others. Indeed, passing often represents the discord that can occur at this intersection—the possibility that these perceptions, presentations, and receptions might not always align. Take, for instance, someone who identifies as a transgender man but whose family does not perceive that identity as real. He would never describe himself as pretending or passing, nor would anyone who is supportive of trans identities; he is identifying.[16] However, because his family refuses to accept his trans identity as real, they might insist that he is only pretending, or if they notice that other people do accept his identity, they might go so far as to say that he is passing, asking the world to accept him as something they think he is not. This suggests that if passing can operate as a form of social mobility for one person, it can also operate as a form of social constraint imposed on another; it functions both as a way that individuals can move between social positions and as a way that society can police or contain their movements.

Neo-passing narratives not only broaden the concept of passing by interrogating intersectional identities but they also highlight the legacy of intersectional notions of passing within classic Jim Crow–era passing narratives. Writing in another context about this legacy, coeditor Vershawn Ashanti Young draws attention to Joseph Skerrett's short discussion of black-to-black racial passing in his analysis of *The Autobiography of an Ex-colored Man*:

> The literary critic Joseph T. Skerrett Jr. argues that James Weldon Johnson writes so well about racial passing in *The Autobiography of an Ex-Colored Man* because Johnson was drawing from his own experience. Regarding Johnson, Skerrett reports: "On several occasions, recorded in *Along This Way* [Johnson's real autobiography], his ability with idiomatic Spanish allowed him to 'pass' for some other kind of brown-skinned man than an American Negro. In these situations his goal was to avoid the potential unpleasantness

> inherent in 'a suddenly presented situation that involved 'race.'" Johnson was personally familiar, then, both with the concept of impersonation and the experience of "passing"—if not for white, then at least for some other kind of non-Negro.[17]

Neo-passing narratives frequently call attention to precisely this little-acknowledged legacy of black-to-black passing. For example, Patricia Jones's *Passing* (1999) boldly borrows the title of Nella Larsen's well-known 1929 novella about two women who pass from black to white but updates the plot for the post–Jim Crow moment by centering around a phenotypically black woman who passes not from black to white but from poor to upper-middle class.[18] When the novel's protagonist, Eulelie Giles, marries a wealthy widower, she conceals her past and refashions herself as more class privileged than she really is. This thematic shift might remind readers that Larsen's protagonist, Clare, passes not only from black to white but also from poor to middle class, thus calling attention to the intraracial class strife buried beneath the racial passing plot of Larsen's novel.

Jones's simultaneous use of Larsen's title and refusal of the conventional passing plot novel announces *Passing* (1999) as a neo-passing narrative, asserting a new trope of passing centered around intraracial class strife but fueled by the legacy of interracial tension between black and white people. One of the novel's primary concerns is with a new pervasive form of racism that is bred among black people in a post–Jim Crow context, where social class is invested with the same essentialist power once assigned to biology and is discursively and performatively deployed in a way that seems to create two races of black people, as a Pew Research Center report later described it, out of one.[19] Jones's novel thus amplifies attention to a kind of black-to-black passing, where black people can use the performance of class to pass as a member of another race of black people. What Jones's novel points up is that the post–Jim Crow era is not an era in which passing has passed out, as *Jet* magazine hoped but, rather, one in which black people can retain their dark skin but pass for a more acceptable class of black people based on their performance of racial-class. This kind of black-to-black passing presents its own dilemmas for black people, some of whom use racial-class passing to disparage other lower-class African Americans, as Jones's Eulelie Giles does, while others are wrongly accused of this kind of passing because they do not perform lower-class blackness well enough. This causes some African Americans from both classes to go through several iterations of passing in both directions in order to discover the type of black person they really are. This is the situation presented in another neo-passing narrative, the semi-autobiographical rock musical *Passing Strange* (2006) by the musician

Stew, whose black middle-class protagonist, simply called "Youth" in the play, tries to escape, by fleeing to Europe, the problems of racial-class passing and the differing expectations held out for him by his mother and friends about which type of black person he should be.[20] However, much as Larsen's biracial heroine Helga Crane found when she fled Harlem for Europe in *Quicksand* (1928), Stew finds that there is no escape from restrictive categories of identity nor from the desire to pass out of them.

Other neo-passing narratives, like Percival Everett's novel *Erasure* (2001), also highlight the often-overlooked legacy of racial-class passing, even as they turn that legacy on its head. In *Erasure*, Everett's protagonist, Thelonious "Monk" Ellison, is an elite African American writer and English professor whose dense, academic fiction languishes because it does not represent "the African American experience."[21] Ellison responds to this negation of his literary perspective by writing a satirical autobiography from the perspective of a barely literate, lower-class ex-con from the ghetto. When the book is a success, Ellison adopts the lower-class persona of his pseudonym and ultimately finds that he is unable to distinguish himself from his passing persona. Grounded in literary allusions to Richard Wright's *Native Son* (1940) and Ralph Ellison's *Invisible Man* (1952), *Erasure* not only indicates that the pressure to pass in contemporary America pushes in multiple directions but the novel also self-consciously presents that argument as an intertextual conversation with two segregation-era texts. Taken together, *Perfect Peace, Passing, Passing Strange,* and *Erasure* reveal some of the ways in which neo-passing narratives reinterpret the classic black-to-white trope in order to investigate the persistence and transformation of passing in our current moment.

The neo-passing narrative's simultaneous relationship to and difference from the conventional passing narrative also distinguishes it from broader narratives of identity transformation, which one could argue are as old as Ovid. Rather than drawing parallels between such genres, the central purpose of this collection is to delineate a broad range of texts—a bibliography of which is in the appendix to this introduction—that explore how and why race continues to matter in post–Jim Crow practices of passing. Another way to put this is to ask, if passing narratives like Charles Chesnutt's *The House behind the Cedars* (1900) or Hughes's "Who's Passing for Who?" (1952) each speak to the anxieties surrounding the establishment and dismantling of a legal color line (1896–1954), how do contemporary ethnic narratives, such as *Jersey Shore* (2009–12), or disability narratives, such as the Halle Berry vehicle *Frankie and Alice* (2010), speak to an age in which the operations of the color line have become more insidious, ambiguous, and intertwined with other categories of identity? Why is passing becoming not less but seemingly more central to discourses surrounding everyday life, as in the politics of social media, Hollywood film casting, and Halloween costumes? Given that these discourses are emerging at a time when it is largely accepted that identities are always in production and in flux, it must be asked: Why does passing persist not only in art and entertainment—as with neo-slave narratives and neo-segregation narratives—but also in the ways that we continue to think about and experience everyday life? What's more, given the seeming pervasiveness of neo-passing, what are its limits? Who can pass, who can't, and why? Perhaps the following real-life examples will help explain both the ways in which passing has changed to suit the social fictions of our times and the ways in which it remains firmly attached to the social fictions of our past.

II

In June 2015, sixty years after *Jet* proclaimed passing was passing out, the internet exploded with the news that Rachel Dolezal, a white woman, had been passing for black. Side-by-side photo spreads appeared in countless blogs, newspapers, and TV shows: one, a recent photograph of Dolezal with either braided or "natural" hair, working as the apparently black president of the Spokane, Washington, chapter of the National Association for the Advancement of Colored People (NAACP) or as an adjunct instructor of African American studies at Eastern Washington University (figure 0.1); and the second photograph, one of Dolezal as an apparently white teenager with straight, blonde hair and seemingly lighter skin (figure 0.2).[22] Commentators on both the right and the left flocked to the story, but common to their varied takes on Dolezal are two things: the sense that her story is somehow new and the sense that her story has something to tell us about the current meaning of race in America. What does Dolezal's "reverse passing," as it was called by some, tell us about the need to understand neo-passing narratives, racial belonging, white privilege, or the concept of postracialism that many have used to describe the post-Obama moment?[23]

Within two months of the Dolezal drama, two other antiracist activists were accused of a similar kind of reverse passing. First, the *Daily Beast* outed Andrea Smith, an activist and academic, as "the Native American Rachel Dolezal."[24] Smith's widely disputed Cherokee heritage had been discussed privately in Native American activist and academic circles since 2007 but only became

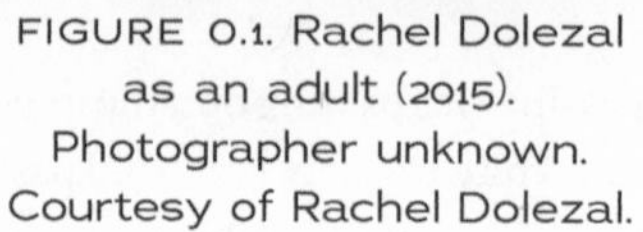

FIGURE 0.1. Rachel Dolezal as an adult (2015). Photographer unknown. Courtesy of Rachel Dolezal.

FIGURE 0.2. Rachel Dolezal as a teenager (1996). Family photo. Courtesy of Rachel Dolezal.

national news on the heels of the Dolezal scandal. Soon after, *Breitbart News* accused Black Lives Matter organizer Shaun King of "pretending to be biracial"; his wife quickly came to his defense by declaring on Facebook that he was "no Rachel Dolezal."[25] To varying degrees, all three figures drew condemnation from a variety of academic, activist, popular, and social-media sources. Many accused them of appropriating minority identities for personal gain, betraying minority communities, fetishizing nonwhite cultures, participating in a form of red- or blackface, and failing to confront their white privilege. Others, however, came to their defense, arguing that these stories exposed not the rational acts of deception of these three individuals but, rather, the irrational nature of American perceptions of race. Indeed, although Americans like to think that our current understanding of race as a social construct is more progressive than the fixed biological notions that dominated the periods of slavery and Jim Crow, the reactions to Dolezal's, Smith's, and King's stories indicate that most Americans continue to locate racial identity in exactly those fixed biological essences. Furthermore, although Smith's case might have seemed, on its own, to have little to do with the aftermath of Jim Crow, Smith's treatment in the press—both in terms of her case's emergence only in the aftermath of Dolezal and in terms of its quicker dismissal—also underlined the analytic power and interest that the black-white color line continues to assert over American identity, even in the post–Jim Crow moment. Neo-passing narratives and our complicated and contradictory responses to them help to reveal the fault lines in contemporary American racial and social consciousness.

The hyperbolic reactions to these three cases underscore what scholars have long acknowledged to be the paradoxical nature of passing. As Michele Elam notes, "two of the most common charges against or for passing" are that it "makes fake or that it makes brave—that is, that it cynically violates one's 'true' essential identity or heroically refutes social ascriptions of identity."[26] Many recent scholars of passing argue that this paradox is inescapable because of the paradoxical nature of racialization itself. What passing proves, Marcia Alesan Dawkins says, is that despite our "desire to escape racial limits . . . we cannot imagine living without racial selves."[27] Furthermore, this paradox holds on both ends of the political spectrum. Thus, where liberal antiracism requires the articulation of race in order to prevent the "deeper entrenchment of racism and racial inequality," conservative postracialism requires the articulation of race "in order to dismiss it as irrelevant."[28] Passing, Baz Dreisinger describes, "is at once a liberal and a conservative enterprise, one driven alternately by anxiety and fantasy, fear and hope."[29] Passing both requires and refutes race, underscoring in the process not only the contested nature of how we articulate our racial identities but also the contested nature of those articulations' relationships to our larger goals of racial equality and social justice.

Some scholars have tried to move beyond this understanding of "passing as paradox" by viewing "passing as synonymous with performance," such that what passing really reveals is "the degree to which all identities are constituted through routinized and repeated actions. One passes for what one purportedly is . . . everyday, in thousands of minuscule and major ways. Passing is less about faking prefabbed social identities than it is about demanding appreciation of the idea that all identities are processual, intersubjective, and contested/contestable."[30] And yet, while such formulations are theoretically appealing, they do not help us understand the intense negative reactions that Dolezal's, Smith's, and King's cases provoked.[31] In other words, equating passing with performance does not help us understand why passing identities continue to be perceived differently from other performed identities. Where performance theorists would suggest that there is no difference between what you are and what you perform—in Pamela Caughie's words, "all subjectivity is passing"—historian Allyson Hobbs insists that it is "possible to pass for something without becoming what it is that you pass for."[32] Building on Hobbs, we argue that perhaps what passing connotes is precisely that which performance hopes to obliterate or obscure: the individual or social perception of distance between the performance and the perceived reality. Passing can thus be understood as a performance of identity that—once it is described or revealed *as* passing—provokes conflict rather than cohesion with social expectations or norms, conflicts that might be felt by the passer, various portions of the passer's community, or both. As we argue above, passing is not just a matter of how identities are performed but also a matter of how identity performances are policed.

Although policing occurs in relation to all identity performances, this volume demands that we resist drawing hasty parallels or distinctions between different forms of passing in favor of understanding the anxieties from which such efforts come. In fact, one of the major fault lines that emerged in Dolezal's case concerns the quickness with which those on the left dismissed her adoption of black identity in light of the left's typical defense of transgender identities.[33] How, conservative critics asked, can the left oppose "transracial" identities while defending transgender identities, especially when the left usually describes both race and gender as social constructions?[34] The anger with which critics on the left subsequently reacted to this comparison indicates that such parallels are at the very least politically (if not also theoretically) problematic. At the same time, the ways in which critics on the left attempted to refute these parallels were equally problematic. For example, some activists on the left tried to separate transgender from "transracial" by arguing that gender unlike race *is* rooted in biology, or vice versa, claims that not only contradict one another but also oversimplify both the significance of the visible physiological characteristics that have been socially constructed as one gender or race, and the social construction of gendered and raced bodies and identities.[35]

Other activists on the left built on such distinctions to argue that the difference between someone like Dolezal and someone like Caitlyn Jenner, who announced her transition from male to female only eleven days before the Dolezal story broke, is the difference between deception and truth: Dolezal was deceiving people about her true identity, whereas Jenner was telling the truth about hers.[36] However, such arguments not only rely on biological essentialism to establish what one "really" is but they also resort to the very language of deception that was once used against transgender individuals and light-skinned African Americans to maintain transphobic and antiblack social hierarchies. For example, Brandon Teena's murderers considered their act of violence revenge for "what they considered," in Judith (Jack) Halberstam's words, "to be a grand deception."[37] Lawyers in the infamous Rhinelander case of 1925 argued that Alice Rhinelander should be denied her right to a divorce settlement because she had "deceived" her husband about her race.[38] Such cases demonstrate that, historically speaking, the language of deception has been used not to differentiate between real and unreal identity performances but, rather, to reinforce the boundaries of whichever identity category the individual's performance was calling into question.

With passing theorists becoming increasingly aware of a "gap between theory and praxis" when it comes to racial identity and passing, this volume aims to use the history of passing to articulate a theory of neo-passing that is more in tune with its contemporary praxis.[39] With this history in mind, it is easier to see why "transracial" identity has been so much harder to accept than transgender identity: historically speaking, acts of racial passing—unlike transgender transitions—have been primarily motivated by the politics of power and privilege. Historically, black-to-white passing was a way for light-skinned African Americans classified as black under America's one-drop rule to access white privilege, which meant that cases of white-to-black passing were extremely rare.[40] When white people did pass as black people, it was most often as a way of gaining access to what whites perceived as a homogenous "black experience," one that they either exoticized or pitied. Insofar as these white people were able to pass in and out of blackness at will, they maintained the dominant perception of blackness as a homogeneous other in relation to the free white subject and thus did more to maintain white privilege than to deconstruct it (even when exposing or deconstructing white privilege was their stated aim).[41] And of course, the far more common and popular form of white-to-black passing was blackface, which scholars argue gave whites access to and dominion over a homogeneous and also viciously derogatory version of black culture.[42]

While Dolezal's, Smith's, and King's cases each differ in many particulars from these precedents, it is difficult if not impossible for us to understand their identities and the controversies surrounding them without reference to the painful histories of racial passing, blackface, colonialism, cultural appropriation, white privilege, and white paternalism. Their stories thus expose both the underlying tensions within contemporary meanings of racial identity *and* the ways in which these new meanings and debates are inextricable from old meanings and debates. In these cases, the tension between our antiracist commitment to race as a social construct—borne out of our resistance to the scientific racism of the past—comes into direct conflict with our concern about white appropriations and exploitations of black culture and black people—borne out of our resistance to the long-standing operation of white privilege and power. Such "new" forms of passing demand that we attend to their newness, even as they demonstrate that forms of passing, like racial-identity categories themselves, cannot be separated from their histories; rather, such histories indelibly shape their meaning. The neo-passing narrative is a trope inescapably bound to America's Jim Crow past that yet speaks to current social and political conditions.

The quickness with which commentators both drew and refuted possible connections between "transracial" and transgender identities also indicates that any study of passing in the new millennium requires intersectional analysis. While several recent volumes on the topic of passing have presented racial and gender passing as corollaries,[43] the Dolezal-Jenner comparison demonstrates the limitations of that approach, because their cases and their reception are clearly not the same. Moreover, drawing a simple equivalency between them would make it possible to overlook the place of race in the queer community or the place of gender and sexual identity in cases of racial passing. Drawing a parallel between racial-passing narratives and narratives of closeted, gay lifestyles would make it possible to overlook the fact that media reports of "outed" gay and transgender adolescents who have been murdered or driven to suicide almost always revolve around white teens like Matthew Shepard, Brandon Teena, and Tyler Clementi rather than black youth like Sakia Gunn, Islan Nettles, and Carl Walker-Hoover. Neo-passing narratives do not make race, gender, and sexuality equivalent as categories of identity but, rather, reveal the tensions that exist at their intersections.

Just as race affects our national investment in the life and liberty of queer youth, so, too, does race affect the freedom with which individuals are able to pass as unthreatening in relation to the social status quo. For example, Sheryl Sandberg's 2013 book, *Lean In*, addresses the ways in which women in the workforce often counter the perceived masculinity of their success by passing as feminine but fails to recognize the role that race plays in perceptions and punishments of female bossiness and aggression, as evidenced by the depiction of a black woman as the "villain" in the first season of Donald Trump's *The Apprentice* (2004). Similarly, a 2014 episode of *This American Life* tells the stories of habitual drug users who pass as sober in their daily lives, but the show's sole black contributor has a very different experience: because he "look[s] like a high school jazz teacher" (i.e., he has an Afro), he is often assumed to be on drugs when really he is not.[44] In cases of mass violence, racial minorities are also more likely to be labeled terrorists, whereas white shooters are understood through the lens of mental illness, indicating that what W. E. B. Du Bois famously called the "problem of the color-line" demands to be considered through the lens of disability studies.[45] Passing in twenty-first-century America includes a variety of identity constructions and performances, but these identity constructions and performances cannot be properly understood unless we insist that passing in and out of other identity categories is always shaped and informed by racialized experience, and vice versa.

Finally, one of the things that made Dolezal's, Smith's, and King's cases seem so new is the way in which they were outed and exposed largely through social media and the internet, which both King and Smith described as "horrifying" examples of social-media "abuse."[46] For Dolezal, too, social media was not only the site of her shaming but it was also central to the way that she bolstered her black identity and to the route by which her passing became apparent.[47] Such cases of social-media shaming highlight the ways in which social media offers individuals as many opportunities to craft and shape online communities and identities as it offers the risk that the boundaries between one's social personas will break down. Shows such as *Joe Millionaire, Undercover Boss, Celebrities Undercover, Made,* and the British show *Faking It* celebrate the possibilities of passing as something you're not, at least for a little while, while shows such as *America's Next Top Model* and *The Bachelor* not only insist on the "authenticity" of their narrative arc but also protect that image by ejecting contestants who are outed as "fake," "deceptive," or "here for wrong reasons." In the marketplace of the new millennium, passing and the opposing idea of authenticity have become central to the ways in which we think about the marketability of individuals, authors, actors, and politicians, not to mention the ways in which we measure our responses as readers to various personas or texts.

So are Dolezal, Smith, and King participating in a long chain of white appropriations and exploitations of black culture and black people, or are they demonstrating that race is a complex social construction? Are ambiguously raced people exercising their white privilege when they identify themselves as nonwhite, or are they exercising white privilege when they fail to identify themselves as nonwhite?[48] Is the "policing" of identity categories necessary for minority groups to protect themselves from colonization, appropriation, and exploitation, or does the insistence on authenticity function to divide and exclude the community's rightful members in harmful or hierarchical ways?[49] Should we reject cases of cross-racial identification as white acts of violence against minority communities, or is it possible to ask, as Hobbs did in an article for the *New York Times,* what it might mean for "the larger collective goals of social justice" if more white Americans chose to identify themselves as kindred of Eric Garner, Rekia Boyd, Tamir Rice, Tanisha Anderson, Freddie Gray, Kayla

Moore, Oscar Grant, Shelly Frey, and Michael Brown—black men and women who have been killed by police officers seemingly without cause and whose deaths have brought to the fore the low value placed on African American lives in our "postracial" America?[50] How might neo-passing narratives trouble or enable such cross-racial identifications in the very presence of these new spectacles of racial violence? How do neo-passing narratives resist or reimagine the very concept of the postracial? Hobbs goes on to argue in her *New York Times* piece that whatever we ultimately think about recent cases of neo-passing, they expose a lot of our unconscious thoughts about race and force these thoughts into the open. We know that ideological concepts are defined not by their clear centers but by their ambiguous borders. It is at the borders of racial identity—the places where the visual breaks down, the places that the contributors to this volume investigate—that strong declarations about race, racism, and racial belonging can be both broken and made.

III

In order to address the major issues outlined in our discussion of the neologism *neo-passing* and recent cases of neo-passing, we organized the essays in this volume around two primary questions: First, how do neo-passing narratives reflect the racial politics of the new millennium and its relationship to the politics of prior historical moments? Second, how do racialized neo-passing narratives intersect with other categories of identity, such as class, gender, sexuality, ethnicity, criminality, and disability? Also implicit in many of the essays of both parts is a third question about the media of the new millennium: How are neo-passing narratives shaped by and how do they shape new aesthetic developments in not only literary fiction but also speculative fiction, graphic novels, film, comedy sketches, reality television, popular journalism, and even social media? While the contributors agree that the recent proliferation of neo-passing narratives exposes the contradictions of colorblind and postracial discourse, the contributors are also engaged in a vigorous debate about the specific ways in which neo-passing narratives alternatively shore up, deconstruct, or complicate our understanding of post–Jim Crow performance and identity production. We discuss each essay below with some detail in order to show how each reading helps us to understand the relationship between neo-passing narratives and our current moment, even as each essay takes its own approach to defining and articulating the meaning and significance of the concept of neo-passing.

Part 1, "New Histories," begins with "Passing at the Turn of the Twenty-First Century," an opening think piece by Allyson Hobbs to introduce the themes of this section. Hobbs compares a classic, true-life black-to-white passing story to the recent public acceptance and even fascination with racial hybridity. Rather than signaling "the realization of a 'postracial' age," Hobbs argues that "the increasing acceptance of mixed-race identities underscores just how germane race continues to be to contemporary American society" (46). Pointing to the chapters that follow, Hobbs states that the relationship between passing and neo-passing reveals that racial ideologies are simultaneously static and plastic, "quick to adapt and reproduce under new social structures" (47) and yet contain "shards of past racial regimes" (46).

Following Hobbs's opening is Martha J. Cutter's essay, "Why Passing Is (Still) Not Passé after More Than 250 Years: Sources from the Past and Present." Cutter begins our inquiry into postracial passing by looking back to the origins of the concept of racial passing in 1740s-era advertisements for runaway slaves. Using this lesser-known archive of passing texts—where individuals passed not only for white but also for free—Cutter argues that since its inception, passing has been a multivalent discourse that highlights anxiety about the construction of racial categories. Turning to classic passing texts of the twentieth century and the new millennium, Cutter asserts that racial-passing discourse continues to thrive because it allows US artists and individuals to delineate the ways in which US racial ideology is constantly "constructed, deconstructed, and reconstructed" over time (63).

In the second chapter, Christopher M. Brown turns to a range of claims that have been made about America's postracialism in order to interrogate the efficacy of beyond-ing race. In "Passing for Postracial: Colorblind Reading Practices of Zombies, Sheriffs, and Slaveholders," Brown shows that while contemporary novels that look to either the past or the future may seem to argue for our distance from the racialized past, these works are only passing for postracial. In reality, novels such as *The Known World* (2003) and *Zone One* (2012) narrate the problems that come with our contemporary fixation on effacing racial knowledge.

Brandon J. Manning enters into this conversation by proffering a more hopeful version of postracial aesthetics in his essay, "Adam Mansbach's Postracial Imaginary in *Angry Black White Boy*." In Manning's view, Mansbach's postracial imaginary is successful not because it abstracts away from material reality but because it purposefully exposes and deconstructs the white privilege that postracial narratives more typically conceal and maintain. For Manning, this more progressive vision of postracialism entails the futurist potential for "different bodies" to do "different work" not because of their break with history but because of their "understanding of sociocultural traditions and movements" (85). Mansbach's *Angry Black White Boy* (2005) thus situates itself in the tradition of the satirical passing novel typified by George Schuyler's *Black No More* (1931), using satire to articulate the distance between the postracialism of its protagonist and its creator. Manning argues that Mansbach, in doing so, lays out the groundwork for whites to perform antiracist work without reinforcing white privilege.

In "Black President Bush: The Racial and Gender Politics behind Dave Chappelle's Presidential Drag," Eden Osucha turns to another form of white-to-black racial masquerade found in Dave Chappelle's 2004 skit "Black Bush." Osucha first unpacks a genealogy of "black presidentialism" that has insisted on the insufficiency of "blackness" to ideals of national manhood. She then argues that while most millennial versions of the black president counter this genealogy by featuring presidents whose blackness is not only sufficient but inconsequential to their presidentialism, Chappelle's sketch reveals the disjunction between the racial coding of George W. Bush and "the historic race neutrality of the office, which the fictional postracial presidencies" of other millennial texts only maintain (110).

Finally, in part 1, Jennifer Glaser's essay, "Seeing Race in Comics: Passing, Witness, and the Spectacle of Racial Violence in Johnson and Pleece's *Incognegro*," continues the conversation about the relationship between present and past forms of racial oppression and violence found in part 1, while raising new questions about how new aesthetic forms have shaped the possibilities of neo-passing narratives. Glaser argues that while the 2008 graphic novel *Incognegro* is set during the US's interwar lynching epidemic of the 1930s, its use of the comics medium to expose the connections between racial violence and racial visibility directly addresses the continuing reality of violence against black bodies. Where photographs and videos of lynchings and police brutality often maintain the visibility and invisibility of black and white bodies, respectively, Glaser argues that comics offer artists a chance "to speak back to the violence being depicted" (125). Because comics encourage readers' agency "by forcing them to take an active role in making meaning from the visual and narrative text they are given" (130), Glaser suggests that the medium might have a particularly important role to play in contemporary conversations about the relationship between racial visibility and racial violence.

Part 2, "New Identities," begins with an opening think piece by Marcia Alesan Dawkins to introduce the themes of the section, called "Introduction:

Passing at the Intersections." Dawkins addresses four lessons learned from traditional passing narratives—concerning privacy, assimilation, satire, and surveillance—as they apply to contemporary cases of passing in twenty-first-century social-media contexts. Gesturing to the chapters that follow as well as a number of contemporary examples, Dawkins argues that social-media tools not only continue to encourage people to "prioritize status, visibility, and . . . carefully crafted editions of self" but they also are shaping the intersectionality and increased fluidity of neo-passing by making it "even easier for neo-passers to blend an ability to project consumable personas with a continuous address of multiple audiences," all despite our continued "obsessions with authenticity and selective disclosure" (139).

Dawkins's piece is followed by Loran Marsan's essay, "Passing Truths: Identity-Immersion Journalism and the Experience of Authenticity," which examines the phenomenon of "journalistic passing" across lines of race, ethnicity, class, and gender. Although this genre has its roots in the Civil Rights–era memoir *Black Like Me* (1961), it has proliferated in recent texts that simultaneously hinge on the performativity of the identity categories they cross even as they strive for "authentic" imitation in order to acquire and record the "real" experiences of an/Other person. Ultimately, whereas Glaser argues that neo-passing narratives in comics form may be able to destabilize our continued investments in black visibility and white invisibility, Marsan argues that these journalistic neo-passing narratives do not destabilize identity categories or construction but, rather, reinforce "the boundaries that construct these differences as opposites and Others to begin with" (144).

Alisha Gaines's examination of *Jersey Shore* focuses on the ways in which neo-passing narratives engage with the category of ethnicity amidst the contemporary obsession with "reality." In her essay, "Passing for Tan: Snooki and the Grotesque Reality of Ethnicity," Gaines compares a familiar anecdote of a young woman passing for tan in order to disguise her poverty with Snooki's claim on *Jersey Shore* that "tan" is her ethnicity. Gaines ultimately suggests that the intersection of reality television and contemporary postracial discourse has "turned the supposed trashiness of passing for tan into an enviable empire" (172). In a cultural landscape that prioritizes skin and surface, "passing for tan" enables Snooki to profit off reality television's financial investment in rescripting and reselling identity.

Derek Adams's essay, "The Pass of Least Resistance: Sexual Orientation and Race in ZZ Packer's 'Drinking Coffee Elsewhere,'" continues Marsan's and Gaines's critiques of binaristic identity categories by examining the relationship between gay rights activists and civil rights activists. Adams focuses his discussion on ZZ Packer's short story "Drinking Coffee Elsewhere," a story that both hints at and frustrates the reader's desire to know its protagonist's sexual orientation. Adams argues that the refusal by the protagonist, Dina, to "come out" is best understood as a refusal to acquiesce to the "desirability of whiteness" (187) associated with her university's lesbian community. Although Dina's indeterminacy allows her to refuse the "absence of agency" of other passing protagonists, whose identities are predicated "on adhering to terms dictated by the dominant culture" (188), Adams argues that Dina's indeterminacy still leaves her alone, an entrapment that acts as a cautionary takeaway for readers: "we risk becoming the tools of oppression we seek to destroy if we are incapable of finding creative outlets for the expression of black female sexuality without resorting to acts of passing" (189).

Deborah Elizabeth Whaley's essay, "Neo-Passing and Dissociative Identities as Affective Strategies in *Frankie and Alice*," agrees with Adams that passing is epistemologically violent insofar as it demands conformity to social prescriptions of identity but argues that neo-passing should be conceptualized as enabling the generation and occupation of multiple identities that contest rigid definitions of identity. Reading dissociative identity disorder as a version of the neo-passing narrative, Whaley turns to the film *Frankie and Alice* (2010), in which Frankie, a black exotic dancer, "struggles to negotiate alter identities: a young, precocious, and smart child named Genius, and a white, Southern, racist woman named Alice" (196). While the doctors within the film and the film itself are anxious to "fix" Frankie, to help her recover or unify her "real" self, Whaley draws on disability studies to argue that Frankie's several selves serve a "resistant and expository" purpose (214). Rather than viewing Frankie through the normative lens of the medical-industrial complex, Whaley unpacks the raced, gendered, and classed dimensions of Frankie's trauma and treatment and argues that dissociative identities and neo-passing offer ways of thinking through disability, race, gender, and sexuality in terms of affective possibilities.

Lara Narcisi concludes part 2 with the possibility of a future beyond passing. In "'A New Type of Human Being': Gender, Sexuality, and Ethnicity as Perpetual Passing in Jeffrey Eugenides's *Middlesex*," Narcissi argues that even if "society may not be ready to abandon all categories of race, gender, and sexuality, fictional space" has the potential to bring into being "multigendered subject[s] with no false façades: a person who does not have to pass" (234). Drawing on Michele Elam's insistence that we "dismiss two of the most common charges against or for passing: either that it makes fake or that it makes brave—that is, that it cynically violates one's 'true' essential identity or heroically refutes social ascriptions of identity," Narcisi argues that "the novel shifts the discourse on the topic of passing in just this way: neither fake nor brave," *Middlesex*'s numerous acts of passing—across identity categories of gender, sexuality, nation, family, ethnicity, and more—ask "what it would mean to jettison all the categorizations that render passing enticing or necessary" (234). At stake in this novel, then, is "the potential of eradicating the very categories we tend to insist upon most stridently as determinants of the self, until the very concept of passing becomes irrelevant" (220).

IV

As did the subject of passing during slavery and Jim Crow, the subject of neo-passing can evoke fear and reactionary speculation. For instance, when the Dolezal story broke, Larry Elder responded, "If racism is so pernicious, why would a white person pretend to be black?"[51] Elder's rhetorical question implies what conservatives have long insisted: that affirmative action and other anti-racist policies give African Americans an unjust advantage in an otherwise colorblind America. Our hope is that this volume points to a way beyond such attempts to use the permeable borders of our identities to re-oppress traditionally oppressed groups. Instead, we have tried to take into account the real social and economic changes that have occurred in our society, without losing sight of the ways in which we are still stymied by institutions and perspectives that value some people, yes, some races, some genders, some sexualities, some classes, more than others, and still others not at all. We present in this volume, then, analyses of neo-passing narratives and their attendant identities as potential sites of empathy and exploitation, belonging and betrayal, all for the purpose of illustrating that these borders must be interrogated if passing, in its negative iterations, is to truly pass out.

Notes

1. "Why 'Passing' Is Passing Out," 16.

2. See McWhorter, "Racism in America Is Over," Steele, "Obama's Post-Racial Promise"; Schorr, "New, 'Post-Racial' Political Era"; Bennett, "*CNN Election Center*"; Rivers, "Decision 08."

3. Bonilla-Silva, *Racism without Racists*, 2; Wise, *Colorblind*, 66–70; Alexander, *New Jim Crow*, 12–14.

4. See Bonilla-Silva, *Racism without Racists*, 4; Wise, *Colorblind*, 19. For a range of alternative scholarly opinions on the value of and/or problems with colorblindness and color-consciousness, see Omi and Winant, *Racial Formation*, 211–44; Appiah and Gutmann, *Color Conscious*; Gilroy, *Against Race*; Michaels, *Our America* and *Trouble with Diversity*; and Warren, *What Was African American Literature?*

5. Rushdy, *Neo-Slave Narratives*, 3.

6. Norman, *Neo-Segregation Narratives*, 3.

7. See Robinson, "Why Does the Slave Ever Love?"

8. Fordham, *Blacked Out*, 23.

9. Ibid., 44.

10. See F. J. Davis, *Who Is Black?*

11. Black, *Perfect Peace*.

12. According to Planned Parenthood, "[i]nstead of saying 'biological sex,' some people use the phrase 'assigned male at birth' or 'assigned female at birth.' This acknowledges that someone (often a doctor) is making a decision for someone else. The assignment of a biological sex may or may not align with what's going on with a person's body, how they feel, or how they identify" ("Gender and Gender Identity"). We have decided to use the term *biological* to refer to Perfect's assigned sex as a biological male who was then assigned the gender of girl by her mother in the novel.

13. Harper, *Iola Leroy*; J. W. Johnson, *Autobiography of an Ex-colored Man*.

14. Jackson and Jones, "Pass•ed Performances," 9.

15. Schechner, *Performance Studies*, 43.

16. Historically, some members of the trans community have used the term *passing* to refer to the degree to which they can pass as cisgender, that is, someone who identifies with the sex they were assigned at birth. For many other members of the trans community, however, the term *passing* imposes cisnormative binary standards of male and female appearance on transgender people's bodies, and risks perpetuating the conservative assumption that trans identities are not real.

17. Young, "Performing Citizenship," 18; Skerrett, "Irony and Symbolic Action," 547; J. W. Johnson, *Along This Way*, 88.

18. P. Jones, *Passing*.

19. Kohut, Taylor, Keeter, et al., *Blacks See Growing Values Gap*.

20. Stew, *Passing Strange*.

21. Everett, *Erasure*.

22. These images were provided for publication courtesy of Rachel Dolezal. In our January 18, 2017, correspondence with Dolezal for permission to use these photographs, she expressed some reluctance to being featured in a publication "which indicates 'passing' as the premise." She pressed the distinction "between identifying-as and passing-for, both in definition and historical underpinning." For more on her perspective, see her book, *In Full Color*.

23. Coker, "When Rachel Dolezal Attended Howard." Coker, writing for *Jezebel*, declares "reverse passing" a "new term," though Yoni Appelbaum and Ben Mathis-Lilley make it clear that neither the term nor the practice was new. Appelbaum, "Rachel Dolezal"; Mathis-Lilley, "Short but Intriguing History."

24. Allen, "Meet the Native American Rachel Dolezal."

25. Yiannopoulos, "Did Black Lives Matter's Shaun King Mislead"; Spargo, "He's No Rachel Dolezal."

26. Elam, *Souls of Mixed Folk*, 98.

27. Dawkins, *Clearly Invisible*, 152.

28. Hobbs, *Chosen Exile*, 278; Nerad, *Passing Interest*, 3.

29. Dreisinger, *Near Black*, 7.

30. Dawkins, *Clearly Invisible*, 6; Nerad, *Passing Interest*, 9; Jackson and Jones, "Pass•ed Performances," 11. As Wald puts it in her preface to Nerad's volume, the "late-1980s theorizing about race, ideology, and textuality/performance . . . created the conditions for 'passing' to be seen, by many of us, as a productive site of theoretical and historical exploration." However, she also claims that it has become increasingly clear since that moment that putting "quotation marks around 'race'" has not mitigated "the persistence of racism." Wald, preface, viii–ix.

31. Of the three, Shaun King has received the most public support, largely because of the perceived "authenticity" of his personal response and because of the source of the revelations: a conservative site with a clear interest in discrediting the Black Lives Matter movement. On August 19, 2015, on Twitter, King compared the exposé to the birthers' attacks on President Barack Obama. Criss and Ford, "Black Lives Matter Activist."

32. Caughie, *Passing and Pedagogy*, 4; Hobbs, *Chosen Exile*, 18. Hobbs's definition of passing is thus closer to what Nerad calls the "traditional sense" of passing theorized by Sollors (*Neither Black nor White*), Wald (*Crossing the Line*), and Sanchez and Schlossberg (*Passing*), among others. Nerad, *Passing Interest*, 9–10. However, Hobbs adds to this traditional sense the argument that "the core issue of passing is not becoming what you pass for, but losing what you pass away from." Hobbs, *Chosen Exile*, 18.

33. Melissa Harris-Perry, in particular, caught flak from Black Twitter and *The Root* for asking this question on her show. Callahan, "Melissa Harris-Perry."

34. Throughout this introduction, we use the term *transracial* in scare quotes since the term's real meaning, in use among scholars for decades, is "the adoption of a child that is of a different race than the adoptive parents." McKee et al., "Open Letter." See McKee et al., "Open Letter"; Rollins, "Transracial Lives Matter"; and Ford, "Real Meaning of' 'Transracial,'" for various accounts of the transracial adoption community's objections to the cooption of the term to describe Dolezal. Importantly, most commentators made or took this comparison not as a defense of Dolezal but as an attack on transgender identities. See Sean Davis, "If Rachel Dolezal Isn't Black."

35. For a useful analysis of this issue in the popular press, see Green, "Race and Gender."

36. For example, Meredith Talusan argues that Dolezal was "really" white and therefore lying about being black, whereas Jenner was "really" transgender and therefore telling the truth when she announced that identity. Talusan, "There Is No Comparison."

37. Halberstam, "Telling Tales," 62. Halberstam's account, specifically, of Brandon Teena's murder challenges us to think beyond deception, since that language is used primarily to shore up gender normativity. Halberstam, "Telling Tales," 80.

38. Thaggert, "Racial Etiquette," 2.

39. Dreisinger, *Near Black*, 125. See also Wald, preface, ix. A good example of this "gap between theory and praxis" emerged in the March 2017 controversy surrounding the publication of Rebecca Tuvel's article "In Defense of Transracialism" in the feminist philosophy journal *Hypatia*. Tuvel's philosophical and theoretical attempt to link transgender-

ism to transracialism provoked an angry open letter to the journal from fellow scholars who were concerned that this abstract theoretical approach had, in one critic's words, no "awareness of the context, power dynamics, or stakes of these issues for trans people and people of color." See Guenther, Facebook post; "Open Letter"; and Tuvel, "In Defense of Transracialism."

40. In contrast, cases of male-to-female transgender individuals are equally if not more common than female-to-male transgender individuals, and when transgender individuals come out, they do so despite the fact that they give up their cisgender privileges in the process.

41. For in-depth analyses of white-to-black passing, see Wald's discussions of Mezz Mezzrow and John Howard Griffin in *Crossing the Line*, 53- 81; 152–81. See also Dreisinger, *Near Black*.

42. See Lott, *Love and Theft*; Rogin, *Blackface, White Noise*.

43. In particular, see Ginsberg, *Passing and the Fictions of Identity*, 13; and Sanchez and Schlossberg, *Passing*, 3.

44. Glass, "I Was So High."

45. Du Bois, *Souls of Black Folk*, 1.

46. See King, "Race, Love, Hate, and Me"; Smith, "My Statement."

47. Jon Ronson, author of *So You've Been Publicly Shamed*, drew explicit attention to this on Twitter and in subsequent interviews and articles. See Buchanan, "Rachel Dolezal"; Larson, "Jon Ronson"; Ronson, "How the Online Hate Mob." Dolezal's online identity included Facebook posts that identified visibly black people as family members, tweets in which she described her adoption of what she later admitted was an Afro-style weave as "going natural," and an alleged childhood self-portrait drawn in brown crayon. Zavadski, "How Did White Rachel Dolezal." Gary Younge argues, "Cutting yourself off from your past is simply not possible in the internet age, where pictures of Rachel Dolezal in African head wraps, presenting herself as black, sit awkwardly with those of her as a blonde-haired teenager with two white parents. It's amazing she thought she'd ever get away with it." Younge, "Rachel Dolezal's Deception."

48. Piper, "Passing for White, Passing for Black," 26; Senna, "Passing and the Problematic," 85.

49. Johnson, *Appropriating Blackness*, 3.

50. Hobbs, "Rachel Dolezal."

51. Elder, *Fox & Friends*.

Bibliography

Alexander, Michelle. *The New Jim Crow: Mass Incarceration in the Age of Colorblindness*. New York: New Press, 2010.

Allen, Samantha. "Meet the Native American Rachel Dolezal." *Daily Beast*, June 30, 2015. Accessed September 15, 2015. http://www.thedailybeast.com.

Appelbaum, Yoni. "Rachel Dolezal and the History of Passing for Black." *The Atlantic*, June 15, 2015. Accessed August 14, 2015. http://www.theatlantic.com.

Appiah, Kwame Anthony, and Amy Gutmann. *Color Conscious: The Political Morality of Race.* Princeton, NJ: Princeton University Press, 1998.

Bennett, William. "CNN Election Center." *CNN,* November 4, 2008. http://www.cnn.com/TRANSCRIPTS/0811/04/ec.03.html.

Black, Daniel. *Perfect Peace.* New York: St. Martin's, 2010.

Bonilla-Silva, Eduardo. *Racism without Racists: Color-Blind Racism and Racial Inequality in Contemporary America.* 3rd ed. New York: Rowman and Littlefield, 2010.

Buchanan, Rose Troup. "Rachel Dolezal: 'So You've Been Publicly Shamed' Author Jon Ronson Calls for Calm over Civil Rights Leader 'Outed as White.'" *Independent,* June 12, 2015. Accessed January 27, 2017. http://www.independent.co.uk/.

Callahan, Yesha. "Melissa Harris-Perry Thinks It's Possible Rachel Dolezal Could Actually Be Black." *The Root,* June 15, 2015. Accessed August 14, 2015. http://thegrapevine.theroot.com/melissa-harris-perry-thinks-it-s-possible-rachel-doleza-1790886633.

Caughie, Pamela L. *Passing and Pedagogy: The Dynamics of Responsibility.* Champaign: University of Illinois Press, 1999.

Coker, Hillary Crosley. "When Rachel Dolezal Attended Howard University, She Was Still White." *Jezebel,* June 12, 2015. Accessed August 14, 2015. http://jezebel.com.

Criss, Doug, and Dana Ford. "Black Lives Matter Activist Shaun King Addresses Race Reports." *CNN,* August 20, 2015. Accessed January 26, 2017. http://www.cnn.com/2015/08/20/us/shaun-king-controversy/.

Davis, F. James. *Who Is Black? One Nation's Definition.* University Park: Penn State Press, 2010.

Davis, Sean. "If Rachel Dolezal Isn't Black, How Is Caitlyn Jenner a Woman?" *Federalist.* June 12, 2015. Accessed August 14, 2015. http://thefederalist.com.

Dawkins, Marcia Alesan. *Clearly Invisible: Racial Passing and the Color of Cultural Identity.* Waco, TX: Baylor University Press, 2012.

Dolezal, Rachel. *In Full Color: Finding My Place in a Black and White World.* Dallas: BenBella, 2017.

Dreisinger, Baz. *Near Black: White-to-Black Passing in American Culture.* Amherst: University of Massachusetts Press, 2008.

Du Bois, W. E. B. *The Souls of Black Folk.* 1903. New York: Penguin, 1996.

Elam, Michele. *The Souls of Mixed Folk: Race, Politics, and Aesthetics in the New Millennium.* Stanford, CA: Stanford University Press, 2011.

Elder, Larry. *Fox & Friends. Fox News,* June 15, 2015.

Everett, Percival. *Erasure.* New York: Hyperion, 2001.

Ford, Zack. "The Real Meaning of 'Transracial.'" *Think Progress,* June 17, 2015. Accessed August 17, 2015. https://thinkprogress.org.

Fordham, Signithia. *Blacked Out: Dilemmas of Race, Identity, and Success at Capital High.* Chicago: University of Chicago Press, 1996.

"Gender and Gender Identity." Planned Parenthood. Accessed October 24, 2017. http://www.plannedparenthood.com.

Gilroy, Paul. *Against Race: Imagining Political Culture beyond the Color Line.* Cambridge, MA: Belknap, 2002.

Ginsberg, Elaine K. *Passing and the Fictions of Identity*. Durham, NC: Duke University Press, 1996.

Glass, Ira, prod. "I Was So High." *This American Life*. WBEZ (NPR), Chicago, May 2, 2014. Accessed June 19, 2017. https://www.thisamericanlife.org/radio-archives/episode/524/i-was-so-high.

Green, Kai M. "'Race and Gender Are Not the Same!' Is Not a Good Response to the 'Transracial'/Transgender Question OR We Can and Must Do Better." *The Feminist Wire*, June 14, 2015. Accessed August 14, 2015. http://www.thefeministwire.com.

Guenther, Lisa. Post. *Facebook*, May 2, 2017. Accessed June 8, 2017. https://www.facebook.com/lisa.guenther.982/posts/1038183326316452.

Halberstam, Judith (Jack). "Telling Tales: Brandon Teena, Billy Tipton, and Transgender Biography." *a/b: Auto/Biography Studies* 15, no. 1 (2000): 62–81.

Harper, Frances E. W. *Iola Leroy, or Shadows Uplifted*. 1892. Boston: Beacon, 1987.

Hobbs, Allyson. *A Chosen Exile: A History of Racial Passing in American Life*. Cambridge, MA: Harvard University Press, 2014.

———. "Rachel Dolezal's Unintended Gift to America." *New York Times*, June 16, 2015. Accessed September 15, 2015. https://www.nytimes.com.

Jackson, John L., and Martha S. Jones. "Pass•ed Performances: An Introduction." *Women & Performance: A Journal of Feminist Theory* 15, no. 1 (2005): 9–16. Accessed August 17, 2015.

Johnson, E. Patrick. *Appropriating Blackness: Performance and the Politics of Authenticity*. Durham, NC: Duke University Press, 2003.

Johnson, James Weldon. *Along This Way: The Autobiography of James Weldon Johnson*. 1933. New York: Da Capo, 2000.

———. The *Autobiography of an Ex-colored Man*. 1912. New York: Penguin, 1990.

Jones, Patricia. *Passing*. New York: Morrow, 1999.

King, Shaun. "Race, Love, Hate, and Me: A Distinctly American Story." *Daily Kos*, August 20, 2015. Accessed September 15, 2015. http://www.dailykos.com/story/2015/8/20/1413881/-Race-love-hate-and-me-A-distinctly-American-story.

Kohut, Andrew, Paul Taylor, Scott Keeter, Jodie Allen, Richard Morin, D'Vera Cohn, April Clark, Juliana Horowitz, Shawn Neidorf, Allison Pond, Robert Suls, James Albrittain, and Cary Funk. *Blacks See Growing Values Gap between Poor and Middle Class: Optimism about Black Progress Declines. Pew Research Center*, November 13, 2007. Accessed August 17, 2015. http://www.pewsocialtrends.org.

Larsen, Nella. *Passing*. 1929. New York: Penguin, 1997.

Larson, Lauren. "Jon Ronson Condemns Twitter Response to Rachel Dolezal." *GQ*, June 12, 2015. Accessed January 27, 2017. http://www.gq.com.

Lott, Eric. *Love and Theft: Blackface Minstrelsy and the American Working Class*. New York: Oxford University Press, 1995.

Mathis-Lilley, Ben. "The Short but Intriguing History of White Americans Pretending to Be Black." *Slate*, June 12, 2015. Accessed August 14, 2015. http://www.slate.com.

McKee, Kimberly, et al. "An Open Letter: Why Co-opting 'Transracial' in the Case of Rachel Dolezal Is Problematic." *Medium*, June 16, 2015. Accessed August 17, 2015. https://medium.com.

McWhorter, John. "Racism in America Is Over." *Forbes*, December 30, 2008. Accessed January 25, 2017. http://www.forbes.com/2008/12/30/end-of-racism-oped-cx_jm_1230mcwhorter.html.

Michaels, Walter Benn. *Our America: Nativism, Modernism, and Pluralism*. Durham, NC: Duke University Press, 1997.

———. *The Trouble with Diversity: How We Learned to Love Identity and Ignore Inequality*. New York: Metropolitan, 2006.

Nerad, Julie Cary. Introduction to *Passing Interest: Racial Passing in US Novels, Memoirs, Television, and Film, 1990–2010*. Albany: State University of New York Press, 2014.

Norman, Brian. *Neo-Segregation Narratives: Jim Crow in Post–Civil Rights American Literature*. Athens: University of Georgia Press, 2010.

Omi, Michael, and Howard Winant. *Racial Formation in the United States*. 3rd ed. New York: Routledge, 2014.

"Open Letter to *Hypatia*." Google Docs, April 30, 2017. Accessed June 8, 2017. https://docs.google.com/forms/d/1efp9CoMHch_6KfgtlmoPZ76nirWtcEsqWHcvgidl2mU/viewform?ts=59066d20.

Piper, Adrian. "Passing for White, Passing for Black." *Transition* 58 (1992): 4–32.

Rivers, Eugene. "Decision 08 Election Night Coverage." *MSNBC*, November 4, 2008. Accessed June 19, 2017. https://www.youtube.com/watch?v=7j8QCg9R9Tg.

Robinson, Angelo Rich. "Why Does the Slave Ever Love? The Subject of Romance Revisited in the Neoslave Narrative." *Southern Literary Journal* 40, no. 1 (2008): 39–57.

Rogin, Michael. *Blackface, White Noise: Jewish Immigrants in the Hollywood Melting Pot*. Berkeley: University of California Press, 1996.

Rollins, Lisa Marie. "Transracial Lives Matter: Rachel Dolezal and the Privilege of Racial Manipulation." *Lost Daughters: Writing Adoption from a Place of Empowerment and Peace*, June 14, 2015. Accessed August 17, 2015. http://www.thelostdaughters.com.

Ronson, Jon. "How the Online Hate Mob Set Its Sights on Me." *Guardian*, December 20, 2015. Accessed January 21, 2017. https://www.theguardian.com.

———. *So You've Been Publicly Shamed*. New York: Riverhead, 2015.

Rushdy, Ashraf H. A. *Neo-Slave Narratives: Studies in the Social Logic of a Literary Form*. New York: Oxford University Press, 1999.

Sanchez, Maria, and Linda Schlossberg, eds. *Passing: Identity and Interpretation in Sexuality, Race, and Religion*. New York: New York University Press, 2001.

Schechner, Richard. *Performance Studies: An Introduction*. 3rd ed. New York: Routledge, 2013.

Schorr, Daniel. "A New, 'Post-Racial' Political Era in America." *All Things Considered. NPR*, January 28, 2008. Accessed January 25, 2017. http://www.npr.org/templates/story/story.php?storyId=18489466.

Senna, Danzy. "Passing and the Problematic of Multiracial Pride (or, Why One Mixed Girl Still Answers to Black)." In *Black Cultural Traffic: Crossroads in Global Performance and Popular Culture*, edited by Harry J. Elam Jr. and Kennell Jackson, 83–87. Ann Arbor: University of Michigan Press, 2005.

Skerrett, Joseph T. "Irony and Symbolic Action in James Weldon Johnson's *The Autobiography of an Ex-coloured Man.*" *American Quarterly* 32, no. 5 (1980): 540–58.

Smith, Andrea. "My Statement on the Current Media Controversy." Web log post. Andrea Smith's Blog. *WordPress,* July 9, 2015. Accessed September 15, 2015. https://andrea366.wordpress.com/2015/07/09/my-statement-on-the-current-media-controversy/.

Sollors, Werner. *Neither Black nor White Yet Both: Thematic Explorations of Interracial Literature.* Cambridge, MA: Harvard University Press, 1999.

Spargo, Chris. "'He's No Rachel Dolezal': Shaun King's Wife Defends Her Husband over Claims He Lied about His Race as Family Member CONFIRMS Both His Parents Are White." *Daily Mail,* August 20, 2015. Accessed January 25, 2017. http://www.dailymail.co.uk/.

Steele, Shelby. "Obama's Post-Racial Promise." *Los Angeles Times,* November 5, 2008. Accessed January 25, 2017. http://www.latimes.com.

Stew. *Passing Strange.* Music by Stew and Heidi Rodewald. Directed by Annie Dorsen. Berkeley Repertory Theatre, Berkeley, California, 2006.

Talusan, Meredith. "There Is No Comparison between Transgender People and Rachel Dolezal." *Guardian,* June 12, 2015. Accessed August 14, 2015. https://www.theguardian.com.

Thaggert, Miriam. "Racial Etiquette: Nella Larsen's *Passing* and the Rhinelander Case." *Meridians: Feminism, Race, Transnationalism* 5, no. 2 (2005): 1–29.

Tuvel, Rachel. "In Defense of Transracialism." *Hypatia: A Journal of Feminist Philosophy* 32, no. 2 (2017): 263–78.

Wald, Gayle. *Crossing the Line: Racial Passing in Twentieth-Century U.S. Literature and Culture.* Durham, NC: Duke University Press, 2000.

———. Preface, "The 'Posts' of Passing," to *Passing Interest: Racial Passing in US Novels, Memoirs, Television, and Film, 1990–2010,* edited by Julie Cary Nerad, vii–x. Albany: State University of New York Press, 2014.

Warren, Kenneth W. *What Was African American Literature?* Cambridge, MA: Harvard University Press, 2011.

"Why 'Passing' Is Passing Out." *Jet,* July 17, 1952, 12–16.

Wise, Tim. *Colorblind: The Rise of Post-Racial Politics and the Retreat from Racial Equity.* San Francisco: City Lights, 2010.

Yiannopoulos, Milo. "Did Black Lives Matter's Shaun King Mislead Oprah Winfrey about His Race?" *Breitbart,* August 19, 2015. Accessed September 15, 2015. http://www.breitbart.com.

Young, Vershawn Ashanti. "Performing Citizenship." In *From Bourgeois to Boojie: Black Middle-Class Performances,* edited by Young with Bridget Harris Tsemo, 1–38. Detroit: Wayne State University Press, 2011.

Younge, Gary. "Rachel Dolezal's Deception: Her 'Black' Identity Doesn't Make Sense—or Make Her Black." *Guardian,* June 12, 2015. Accessed August 14, 2015. https://www.theguardian.com.

Zavadski, Katie. "How Did White Rachel Dolezal Convince Everyone She Was Black?" *Daily Beast,* June 12, 2015. Accessed August 14, 2015. http://www.thedailybeast.com.

APPENDIX TO THE INTRODUCTION

Neo-Passing Narratives

Teaching and Scholarly Resources

We include here a working bibliography of neo-passing narratives, including related scholarship, that has appeared to date. The entries are divided into Comics and Graphic Novels, Creative Nonfiction, Drama, Fiction, Film, Music, Poetry, Television and Radio, Visual and Performance Art, and Scholarship.

Of course, such a list can never be comprehensive, but we offer it as evidence of the neo-passing narrative's proliferation and diversification in the post–Jim Crow period and as a resource for teachers, students, and scholars working on this topic. This resource was developed in consultation with contributors to this volume and has benefited from suggestions made by our colleagues and students.

Because the field of critical mixed-race studies both intersects with and exceeds the concerns of this volume, we have included only the scholarship from this field that addresses passing most extensively. For further work on mixed-race studies, we encourage readers to make use of such resources as mixedracestudies.org (launched in 2009) and the *Journal of Critical Mixed Race Studies* (launched in 2011).

Comics and Graphic Novels

Belton, Danielle, Yesha Callahan, and Jada Prather. "Passing: The Comic Strip." *PassingTheComic.Com*, May 15, 2014. Accessed May 19, 2014. http://passingthecomic.com/comic/gentrification/.

Duffy, Damian, and John Jennings. *The Hole: Consumer Culture*. Vol. 1. Chicago: University of Chicago Press, 2008.

Johnson, Mat, and Warren Pleece. *Incognegro.* New York: Vertigo, 2008.

Weaver, Lila Quintero. *Darkroom: A Memoir in Black and White.* Tuscaloosa: University of Alabama Press, 2012.

Creative Nonfiction

Broyard, Bliss. *One Drop: My Father's Hidden Life, a Story of Race and Family Secrets.* New York: Little, Brown, 2007.

———. "Rachel Dolezal Isn't Alone—My Family History Proves Choosing a Racial Definition Is Hard." *Guardian,* June 15, 2015. Accessed June 6, 2016. https://www.theguardian.com.

Colapinto, John. "The True Story of John / Joan." *Rolling Stone,* December 11, 1997, 54–97.

Derricotte, Toi. *The Black Notebooks: An Interior Journey.* New York: Norton, 1997.

Dolezal, Rachel. *In Full Color: Finding My Place in a Black and White World.* Dallas: BenBella, 2017.

Durrow, Heidi W. *The Girl Who Fell from the Sky.* Chapel Hill, NC: Algonquin, 2010.

Ehrenreich, Barbara. *Nickel and Dimed: On (Not) Getting By in America.* New York: Holt, 2001.

Fosberd, Michael. *Incognito: An American Odyssey of Race and Self-Discovery.* Chicago: Incognito, 2011.

Funderburg, Lise. *Black, White, Other: Biracial Americans Talk about Race and Identity.* New York: Harper, 1995.

Golden, Jamie Nesbitt. "Why I'm Masquerading as a White Bearded Hipster Guy on Twitter (Despite being a Black Woman)." *XO Jane Mag.,* April 14, 2014. Accessed May 19, 2014. http://www.xojane.com/.

Griffin, John Howard. *Black Like Me.* 1961. Boston: Houghton Mifflin, 1977.

Halsell, Grace. *Bessie Yellowhair.* New York: Morrow, 1973.

———. *The Illegals.* New York: Stein and Dy, 1978.

———. *In Their Shoes.* Fort Worth: Texas Christian University Press, 1996.

———. *Soul Sister.* 1969. Washington, DC: Crossroads, 1999.

Jones, Margaret B. [Margaret Seltzer]. *Love and Consequences: A Memoir of Hope and Survival.* New York: Riverhead, 2008.

King. J. L. *On the Down Low: A Journey into the Lives of Straight Black Men Who Sleep with Men.* New York: Broadway. 2004.

King, Shaun. "Race, Love, Hate, and Me: A Distinctly American Story." *Daily Kos,* August 20, 2015. Accessed September 15, 2015. http://www.dailykos.com/story/2015/8/20/1413881/-Race-love-hate-and-me-A-distinctly-American-story.

Kroeger, Brooke. *Passing: When People Can't Be Who They Are.* New York: PublicAffairs, 2004.

La Ferla, Ruth. "Generation E.A." *New York Times,* December 28, 2003. Accessed June 19, 2017. http://www.nytimes.com.

Leslie, Kent Anderson. *Woman of Color, Daughter of Privilege: Amanda America Dickson, 1849–1893.* Athens: University of Georgia Press, 1996.

Mansbach, Adam. "Whiteness Visible." Interview by Scott Thill. *Alternet,* May 5, 2005. Accessed January 8, 2015. http://www.alternet.org.

McBride, James. *The Color of Water: A Black Man's Tribute to His White Mother.* New York: Riverhead, 2006.

Obama, Barack. *Dreams from My Father: A Story of Race and Inheritance.* 10th anniv. ed. New York: Broadway, 2004.

O'Hearn, Claudine C., ed. *Half and Half: Writers on Growing Up Biracial and Bicultural.* New York: Pantheon, 1998.

Oluo, Ijeoma. Tweets: @IjeomaOluo. January 13, 2015, 5:27, 5:32, 5:38, and 6:47 A.M. https://twitter.com/IjeomaOluo.

Rae, Issa. *The Misadventures of Awkward Black Girl.* New York: Atria/37 INK, 2015.

Randall, Alice. *The Wind Done Gone.* New York: Houghton Mifflin, 2001.

Ross, Fran. *Oreo.* 1974. New York: New Directions, 2015.

Roth, Philip. "An Open Letter to Wikipedia." *The New Yorker,* September 6, 2012. Accessed March 5, 2015. http://www.newyorker.com.

Scales-Trent, Judy. *Notes of a White Black Woman: Race Color Community.* University Park: Pennsylvania State University Press, 2001.

Senna, Danzy. "The Mulatto Millennium." *Utne Reader,* September–October 1998. In *Half and Half: Writers on Growing Up Biracial and Bicultural,* edited by Claudine C. O'Hearn, 12–27. New York: Pantheon, 1998.

———. "Passing and the Problematic of Multiracial Pride (or, Why One Mixed Girl Still Answers to Black)." In *Black Cultural Traffic: Crossroads in Global Performance and Popular Culture,* edited by Harry J. Elam Jr. and Kennell Jackson, 83–87. Ann Arbor: University of Michigan Press, 2005.

———. *Where Did You Sleep Last Night? A Personal History.* New York: Picador, 2009.

Sharfstein, Daniel J. *The Invisible Line: Three American Families and the Secret Journey from Black to White.* New York: Penguin, 2011.

Skyhorse, Brando, and Lisa Page. *We Wear the Mask: Fifteen True Stories of Passing in America.* Boston: Beacon Press, 2017.

Thurston, Baratunde. *How to Be Black.* New York: HarperCollins, 2012.

Touré. *Who's Afraid of Post-Blackness? What It Means to Be Black Now.* New York: Atria, 2012.

Vincent, Norah. *Self-Made Man: One Woman's Journey into Manhood and Back Again.* New York: Penguin, 2007.

Walker, Rebecca. *Black, White, and Jewish: Autobiography of a Shifting Self.* New York: Riverhead, 2001.

Whitehead, Colson. "The Year of Living Postracially." *New York Times,* November 4, 2009. Accessed June 8, 2017. http://www.nytimes.com.

Williams, Gregory Howard. *Life on the Color Line: The True Story of a White Boy Who Discovered He Was Black.* New York: Dutton, 1995.

Wilson, August. "The Ground on Which I Stand." *Callaloo* 20, no. 3 (1997): 493–503.

Womack, Ytasha L. *Post Black: How a New Generation Is Redefining African American Identity.* Chicago: Hill, 2010.

Drama

America Play, The. By Suzan-Lori Parks. Directed by Liz Diamond. Yale Repertory Theater, New Haven, Connecticut, 1994.

Hamilton. By Lin-Manuel Miranda. Directed by Thomas Kail. Richard Rodgers Theatre, New York, 2015.

Incognito. By Michael Fosberg. Directed by Michael Fosberg. Bailiwick Theater Studio, Chicago, 2001.

Neighbors. By Branden Jacobs-Jenkins. Directed by Niegel Smith. Public Theater, New York, 2010.

Octoroon, An. By Branden Jacobs-Jenkins. Directed by Sarah Benson. Soho Rep, New York, 2013–14.

Passing SOLO. By Nancy Cheryll Davis. Towne Street Theatre, Los Angeles, 2015.

Passing Strange. By Stew. Music by Stew and Heidi Rodewald. Directed by Annie Dorsen. Berkeley Repertory Theatre, Berkeley, California, 2006.

Fiction

Barrett, A. Igoni. *Blackass*. Saint Paul, MN: Graywolf, 2016.

Beatty, Paul. *The Sellout*. New York: Farrar, Straus, and Giroux, 2015.

———. *White Boy Shuffle*. New York: Houghton Mifflin, 1996.

Black, Daniel. *Perfect Peace*. New York: St. Martin's, 2010.

Ellison, Harlan. "Pennies, Off a Dead Man's Eyes." *Alone against Tomorrow: Stories of Alienation in Speculative Fiction*. New York: Macmillan, 1971.

Eugenides, Jeffrey. *Middlesex*. New York: Picador, 2002.

Everett, Percival. *Erasure*. New York: Hyperion, 2001.

Johnson, Charles. *Oxherding Tale*. 1982. New York: Plume, 1995.

Johnson, Mat. *Hunting in Harlem*. New York: Bloomsbury, 2003.

———. *Loving Day*. New York: Spiegel and Grau, 2015.

———. *Pym*. New York: Random, 2011.

Jones, Edward P. *The Known World*. New York: HarperCollins, 2003.

Jones, Patricia. *The Color of Family*. New York: William Morrow, 2004.

———. *Passing*. New York: Avon, 1999.

Lester, Joan Steinau. *Black, White, Other: In Search of Nina Armstrong*. Grand Rapids, MI: Zondervan, 2011.

Macleod, Sally. *Passing Strange*. New York: Random, 2002.

Mansbach, Adam. *Angry Black White Boy, or the Miscegenation of Macon Detornay*. New York: Three Rivers, 2005.

Morrison, Toni. *The Bluest Eye*. New York: Holt, 1970.

———. *God Help the Child*. New York: Knopf, 2015.

———. *Paradise*. New York: Knopf, 1997.

———. "Recitatif." In *Confirmation: An Anthology of African American Women*, edited by Amiri Baraka and Amina Baraka, 610–24. New York: Quill, 1983.

Mosley, Walter. *Devil in a Blue Dress*. New York: Norton, 1990.

Packer, ZZ. "Drinking Coffee Elsewhere," In *Drinking Coffee Elsewhere*, 105–31. New York: Riverhead, 2003.
Prasad, Chandra, ed. *Mixed: An Anthology of Short Fiction on the Multiracial Experience*. New York: Norton, 2006.
Roth, Philip. *The Human Stain*. Boston: Houghton Mifflin, 2000.
Row, Jess. *Your Face Is Mine*. 2014. New York: Riverhead: 2015.
Senna, Danzy. *Caucasia*. New York: Riverhead, 1998.
———. *Symptomatic*. New York: Riverhead, 2005.
———. *You Are Free: Stories*. New York: Riverhead, 2011.
Whitehead, Colson, *The Intuitionist*. New York: Anchor, 2000.
———. *Zone One*. New York: Doubleday, 2011.
Zink, Nell. *Mislaid*. New York: Ecco, 2015.

Film

Associate, The. Directed by Donald Petrie. Hollywood Pictures, 1996. DVD.
Bamboozled. Directed by Spike Lee. New Line Cinema, 2000. DVD.
Big Game. Directed by Jalmari Helander. Subzero Film Entertainment, 2014.
Big Momma's House. Directed by Raja Gosnell. Twentieth Century Fox, 2000. DVD.
Big Momma's House 2. Directed by John Whitesell. Twentieth Century Fox, 2006. DVD.
Big Mommas: Like Father, Like Son. Directed by John Whitesell. Twentieth Century Fox, 2011. DVD.
Black, White, and All That Jazz. Directed by Betty Bailey. Betty Bailey and Carol Lynde, 2007.
Born in Flames. Directed by Lizzie Borden. First Run Features, 1983. DVD.
Bulworth. Directed by Warren Beatty. Twentieth Century Fox, 1998. DVD.
Chameleon Street. Directed by Wendell B. Harris Jr. Gathsemane 84, 1989. DVD.
Deep Impact. Directed by Mimi Leder. Paramount, 1998.
Devil in a Blue Dress. Directed by Carl Franklin. TriStar Pictures, 1995. DVD.
Dr. Black, Mr. Hyde. Directed by William Crain. Dimension Pictures, 1976. DVD.
Fifth Element, The. Directed by Luc Besson. Sony Pictures Entertainment, 1997.
Frankie and Alice. Directed by Geoffrey Sax. Access Motion Pictures, 2010. DVD.
Get Out. Directed by Jordan Peele. Blumhouse Productions, 2017.
Head of State. Directed by Chris Rock. Dreamworks, 2003.
House Divided, A. Directed by John Kent Harrison. Paramount Television, 2000. TV Movie.
Idiocracy. Directed by Mike Judge. Twentieth Century Fox, 2006.
Illusions. Directed by Julie Dash. Julie Dash, 1982.
It's Pat. Directed by Adam Bernstein. Touchstone Pictures, 1994. DVD.
Jerk, The. Directed by Carl Reiner. Aspen Film Society, 1979. DVD.
Man, The. Directed by Joseph Sargent. ABC Circle Films, Lorimar Television, 1972.
Mrs. Doubtfire. Directed by Chris Columbus. Twentieth Century Fox, 1993. DVD.
Slow Burn. Directed by Wayne Beach. GreeneStreet Films, 2005. DVD.
Soul Man. Directed by Steve Miner. Steve Tisch Company, 1986. DVD.
Spook Who Sat by the Door, The. Directed by Ivan Dizon. Bokari, 1973. DVD.

Trading Places. Directed by John Landis. Paramount, 1983. DVD.
Tropic Thunder. Directed by Ben Stiller. Dreamworks, 2008. DVD.
True Identity. Directed by Charles Lane. Touchstone Pictures, 1991.
2012. Directed by Roland Emmerich. Columbia, 2009.
Watermelon Man. Directed by Martin Van Peebles. Columbia Pictures, 1970. DVD.
Watermelon Woman. Directed by Cheryl Dunye. Dancing Girl, 1996. DVD.
White Chicks. Directed by Keenan Ivory Wayans. Wayan Bros. Entertainment, 2004. DVD.
White House Down. Directed by Roland Emmerich. Sony Pictures Entertainment, 2013.
X-Men. Directed by Bryan Singer. Twentieth Century Fox, 2000. DVD.
X-Men: Apocalypse. Directed by Bryan Singer. Twentieth Century Fox, 2016. DVD.
X-Men: Days of Future Past. Directed by Bryan Singer. Twentieth Century Fox, 2014. DVD.
X-Men: First Class. Directed by Matthew Vaughn. Twentieth Century Fox, 2011. DVD.
X-Men: The Last Stand. Directed by Brett Ratner. Twentieth Century Fox, 2006.
X2. Directed by Bryan Singer. Twentieth Century Fox, 2003. DVD.

Music

Aerosmith. "Dude (Looks like a Lady)." *Permanent Vacation*. Geffen Records, 1987. CD.
Big Black. "Passing Complexion." *Atomizer*. Homestead Records, 1986. CD.
Kelly, R. *Trapped in the Closet*. Jive, 2005. CD.
Scott-Adams, Peggy. "Bill." *Help Yourself*. Miss Butch, 1997. CD.

Poetry

Alexander, Elizabeth. "Race." *Antebellum Dream Book*. Saint Paul, MN: Graywolf, 2001.
Chou, Yi-Fen [Michael Derrick Hudson]. "The Bees, the Flowers, Jesus, Ancient Tigers, Poseidon, Adam, and Eve." *Prairie Schooner* 88, no. 3 (2014): 40–43. Rpt. in *The Best American Poetry 2015*, edited by Sherman Alexie. New York: Scribner, 2015.
Derricotte, Toi. "Passing." In *Tender*. Pittsburgh, PA: University of Pittsburgh Press, 1997.
Rose, Wendy. "For the White Poets Who Would Be Indian." *Lost Copper*. 1980. Banning, CA: Malki Museum, 1992.

Television and Radio

"Ally's Choice." *Radiolab*. Produced by Lu Olkowski. *NPR*, July 2, 2013. Accessed June 19, 2017. http://www.radiolab.org/story/304341-allys-choice/.
"Are You Now or Have You Ever Been." *Angel*. Written by Tim Minear. Directed by David Semel. WB, 2000.
"Believe in the Stars." *30 Rock*. Written by Tina Fey and Robert Carlock. Directed by Don Scardino. NBC, 2008.
"Black Bush." *Chappelle's Show*. Written by Dave Chappelle and Neal Brennan. Directed by Neal Brennan and Rusty Cundieff. Comedy Central, 2005.
Black. White. Written by R. J. Cutler and Ice Cube. Twentieth Century Fox, 2006.
"Black White Supremacist." *Chappelle's Show*. Written by Dave Chappelle and Neal Brennan. Directed by Neal Brennan and Rusty Cundieff. Comedy Central, 2003.

"Blood." *Law and Order*. Written by Craig Tepper and Rene Balcer. Directed by Jace Alexander. NBC, 1997.

Century City. Created by Ed Zuckerman. CBS, 2004.

"Colors." *Cold Case*. Written by Sean Whitesell. Directed by Paris Barclay. CBS, 2005.

Da Ali G Show. Written by Sacha Baron Cohen. HBO, 2003–4.

Event, The. Created by Nick Wauters. NBC, 2010–11.

"Face Wars." *The Sarah Silverman Program*. Written by Sarah Silverman and Dan Sterling. Directed by Liam Lynch. Comedy Central, 2007.

"Fireworks." *30 Rock*. Written by Tina Fey, Dan Finkel, and Brett Baer. Directed by Beth McCarthy-Miller. NBC, 2007.

"Frontline: Clayton Bigsby." *Chappelle's Show*. Written by Dave Chappelle and Neal Brennan. Directed by Rusty Cundieff. Comedy Central, 2003.

"Girl Who Is Contagious, The." *America's Next Top Model*. Written by Tyra Banks, Kenya Barris, and Ken Mok. Directed by Allison Chase. UPN, 2005.

"I Was So High." *This American Life*. Produced by Ira Glass. WBEZ (NPR). May 2, 2014. Accessed June 19. 2017. https://www.thisamericanlife.org.

"Jenny's Low." *The Jeffersons*. Written by John Ashby. Directed by Jack Shea. CBS, 1975.

Jersey Shore, The. Written by SallyAnn Salsano and Anthony Beltempo. MTV, 2009–12.

"Let's Go Surfing." *America's Next Top Model*. Written by Tyra Banks, Kenya Barris, and Ken Mok. Directed by Allison Chase. CW, 2009.

"Libertyville." *Cold Case*. Written by Kathy Ebell. Directed by Marcos Siega. CBS, 2009.

"Lyle, the Effeminate Heterosexual." *Saturday Night Live*. Written by Dana Carvey. NBC, 1989–92.

Other: Mixed Race in America. Produced by Alex Laughlin. Washington Post, May 1–5, 2017. Accessed June 19, 2017. https://www.washingtonpost.com.

"Passion of Ruckus, The." *The Boondocks*. Written by Aaron McGruder, Rodney Barnes, and Yamara Taylor. Directed by Sean Song. Adult Swim, 2006.

"Race." *Radiolab*. Produced by Jad Abumrad and Robert Krulwich. NPR. November 28, 2008. Accessed June 19, 2017. http://www.radiolab.org/story/91653-race/.

"Racial Draft, The." *Chappelle's Show*. Written by Dave Chappelle and Neal Brennan. Directed by Neal Brennan and Rusty Cundieff. Comedy Central, 2004.

"Return of the King," *The Boondocks*. Written by Aaron McGruder and Yamara Taylor. Directed by Kalvin Lee. Adult Swim, 2006.

Richard Pryor Show, The. Performed by Richard Pryor, Robin Williams, and Paul Mooney. NBC, 1977. Image Entertainment, 2004. DVD.

30 Days. Written by Morgan Spurlock. FX, 2005–8.

24. Performed by Keifer Sutherland and Dennis Haysbert. Fox, 2001–10. Twentieth Century Fox, 2002–10.

Undercover Boss. Written by Stephen Lambert. CBS, 2010–present.

"White Like Me." *Saturday Night Live*. Written by Eddie Murphy. NBC, 1984.

"Word: Blackwashing, The." *The Colbert Report*. Written by Max Werner. Comedy Central, 2009.

Visual and Performance Art

"Beauty 2010." *V Magazine*, November 2009.

"Beyonce Tribute to Fela Kuti." *L'Officiel Paris*, March 2011.

Davis, Nastassia. *Self-Portrait.* 2012.

———. *Self-Portrait.* 2013.

"Heritage Heroes." *Vogue Netherlands*, May 2013.

Kadel, Greg. "The Kid." Styling by Patti Wilson. *Numero Magazine*, October 2010.

Kim, Byron. *Synecdoche*, 1991–present.

Kim, Sebastian. "African Queen." *Numero Magazine*, February 2013.

Klein, Steven. "Individualook." *Vogue Italia*, February 2006.

———. "Lara." *Vogue Paris*, October 2009.

Lagerfeld, Karl. *Stern Fotografie Portfolio No. 60-4: Claudia and Karl.* Kempen, Germany: teNeues, 2010.

Ligon, Glenn. *Runaways.* 1993.

———. *Self-Portrait Exaggerating My Black Features / Self-Portrait Exaggerating My White Features*, 1998.

"Not Dreaming of a White Christmas." *Illamasqua Australia*, 2012.

Piper, Adrian. *Black Box / White Box.* 1992.

———. *Colored.* 1988.

———. *Cornered.* 1988.

———. *Decide Who You Are.* 1992.

———. *My Calling (Cards) #1 and #2.* 1986–90.

———. *The Mythic Being.* 1973.

———. *Self-Portrait Exaggerating My Negroid Features.* 1981.

Reljin, Dusan. "Beauty." *Vogue Italia*, July 2008.

Saar, Lezley. *Mulatto Nation*, 2003.

Schoeller, Martin. "The Changing Face of America." *National Geographic*, October 2013.

Vukmirovic, Milan. "Keep It Goin' Louder Part 1." *L'Officiel Hommes*, Spring–Summer 2010.

Walker, Kara. *The End of Uncle Tom and the Grand Allegorical Tableau of Eva in Heaven.* 1995.

———. *Gone: An Historical Romance of a Civil War as It Occurred b'tween the Dusky Thighs of One Young Negress and Her Heart.* 1994.

Scholarship

Appiah, Kwame Anthony, and Amy Gutmann. *Color Conscious: The Political Morality of Race.* Princeton, NJ: Princeton University Press, 1998.

Belluscio, Stephen J. *To Be Suddenly White: Literary Realism and Racial Passing.* Columbia: University of Missouri Press, 2006.

Bennett, Juda. *The Passing Figure: Racial Confusion in Modern American Literature.* New York: Lang, 1996.

Brennan, Jonathan. *Mixed Race Literature.* Palo Alto, CA: Stanford University Press, 2002.

Brodkin, Karen. *How Jews Became White Folks and What That Says about Race in America*. New Brunswick, NJ: Rutgers University Press, 1998.

Brune, Jeffrey A., and Daniel J Wilson, eds. *Disability and Passing: Blurring the Lines of Identity*. Philadelphia: Temple University Press, 2013.

Butler, Judith. *Gender Trouble: Feminism and the Subversion of Identity*. 2nd ed. New York: Routledge, 2006.

Carbado, Devon W., and Mitu Gulati. *Acting White? Rethinking Race in "Post-Racial" America*. Oxford: Oxford University Press, 2015.

Caughie, Pamela L. *Passing and Pedagogy: The Dynamics of Responsibility*. Champaign: University of Illinois Press, 1999.

Charles, John C. *Abandoning the Black Hero: Sympathy and Privacy in the Postwar African American White-Life Novel*. New Brunswick, NJ: Rutgers University Press, 2012.

Coronado, Marc, Rudy P. Guevarra Jr., Jeffrey Moniz, and Laura Szanto, eds. *Crossing Lines: Race and Mixed Race across the Geohistorical Divide*. Santa Barbara: Multiethnic Student Outreach (MESO) in collaboration with the Center of Chicano Studies, University of California, Santa Barbara, 2003.

Cutter, Martha J. "'As White as Most White Women': Racial Passing in Advertisements for Runaway Slaves and the Origins of a Multivalent Term." *American Studies* 54, no. 4 (2016): 73–97.

DaCosta, Kimberly McClain. *Making Multiracials: State, Family, and Market in the Redrawing of the Color Line*. Stanford, CA: Stanford University Press, 2007.

Daniel, G. Reginald. *More than Black: Multiracial Identity and the New Racial Order*. Philadelphia, PA: Temple University Press, 2001.

Davis, F. James. *Who Is Black? One Nation's Definition*. University Park: Penn State Press, 2010.

Dawkins, Marcia Alesan. *Clearly Invisible: Racial Passing and the Color of Cultural Identity*. Waco, TX: Baylor University Press, 2012.

———. "How Technology Allowed Rachel Dolezal to Pass as Black." Talking Points Memo. *TPM Media*, June 15, 2015. Accessed June 8, 2017. http://talkingpointsmemo.com/cafe/rachel-dolezal-technology-passing.

Dickey, Eric Jerome. *Milk in My Coffee*. New York: Dutton, 1998.

Dreisinger, Baz. *Near Black: White-to-Black Passing in American Culture*. Amherst: University of Massachusetts Press, 2008.

———. "Rachel Dolezal and the History of Passing for Black." Interview by Yoni Applebaum. *The Atlantic*. Atlantic Media, June 15, 2015. Accessed June 8, 2017. https://www.theatlantic.com/politics.

Elam, Michele. *The Souls of Mixed Folk: Race, Politics, and Aesthetics in the New Millennium*. Stanford, CA: Stanford University Press, 2011.

Fabi, M. Giulia. *Passing and the Rise of the African American Novel*. Urbana: University of Illinois Press, 2003.

Fordham, Signithia. *Blacked Out: Dilemmas of Race, Identity, and Success at Capital High*. Chicago: University of Chicago Press, 1996.

———. "'Those Loud Black Girls': (Black) Women, Silence, and Gender 'Passing' in the Academy." *Anthropology and Education Quarterly* 24, no. 1 (1993): 3–32.

Fordham, Signithia, and John U. Ogbu. "Black Students' School Success: Coping with the 'Burden of Acting White.'" *Urban Review* 18, no. 3 (1986): 176–206.

Foreman, P. Gabrielle. "Who's Your Mama? 'White' Mulatta Genealogies, Early Photography, and Anti-passing Narratives of Slavery and Freedom." In *Pictures and Progress: Early Photography and the Making of African American Identity*, edited by Maurice O. Wallace and Shawn Michelle Smith, 132–66. Durham, NC: Duke University Press, 2012.

Foster, Gwendolyn. *Class-Passing: Social Mobility in Film and Popular Culture*. Carbondale: Southern Illinois University Press, 2005.

Gaines, Alisha. *Black for a Day: White Fantasies of Race and Empathy*. Chapel Hill: University of North Carolina Press, 2017.

Garber, Marjorie. *Vested Interests: Cross-Dressing and Cultural Anxiety*. New York: Routledge, 1992.

Gates, Henry Louis, Jr. *Thirteen Ways of Looking at a Black Man*. New York: Vintage, 1998.

Gilroy, Paul. *Against Race: Imagining Political Culture beyond the Color Line*. Cambridge, MA: Belknap, 2002.

Ginsberg, Elaine K. *Passing and the Fictions of Identity*. Durham, NC: Duke University Press, 1996.

Glaser, Jennifer. *Borrowed Voices: Writing and Racial Ventriloquism in the Jewish American Imagination*. New Brunswick, NJ: Rutgers University Press, 2016.

Godfrey, Esther. "'To Be Real': Drag, Minstrelsy, and Identity in the New Millennium." *Genders Journal* 41 (2005): 1–18.

Godfrey, Mollie. "Passing as Post-Racial: *The Human Stain*, Political Correctness, and the Post-Racial Passing Narrative." *Contemporary Literature* 58, no. 2 (Summer 2018). In press.

Graham, Lawrence Otis. *Our Kind of People: Inside America's Black Upper Class*. New York: HarperCollins, 1999.

Gross, Larry P. *Contested Closets: The Politics and Ethics of Outing*. Minneapolis: University of Minnesota Press, 1993.

Gubar, Susan. *Racechanges: White Skin, Black Face in American Culture*. New York: Oxford University Press, 2000.

Gunkel, David J., and Ted Gournelos. *Transgression 2.0: Media, Culture, and the Politics of a Digital Age*. New York: Continuum, 2012.

Haney López, Ian F. "The Social Construction of Race: Some Observations on Illusion, Fabrication, and Choice." *Harvard Civil Rights–Civil Liberties Law Review* 29 (1994): 1–62.

Harper, Phillip Brian. "Passing for What? Racial Masquerade and the Demands of Upward Mobility." *Callaloo* 21, no. 2 (1998): 381–97.

Hobbs, Allyson. *A Chosen Exile: A History of Racial Passing*. Cambridge, MA: Harvard University, 2014.

———. "Rachel Dolezal's Unintended Gift to America." *New York Times*, June 16, 2015. https://www.nytimes.com/.

Jackson, John L., and Martha S. Jones. "Pass•ed Performances: An Introduction." *Women and Performance: A Journal of Feminist Theory* 15, no. 1 (2005): 9–16.

Jacobson, Matthew Frye. *Whiteness of a Different Color: European Immigrants and the Alchemy of Race*. Cambridge, MA: Harvard University Press, 1998.

Johnson, Charles. "A Phenomenology of the Black Body." *Michigan Quarterly Review* 32, no. 4 (1993): 595–614.

Johnson, E. Patrick. *Appropriating Blackness: Performance and the Politics of Authenticity*. Durham, NC: Duke University Press, 2003.

Joseph, Ralina L. *Transcending Blackness: From the New Millennium Mulatta to the Exceptional Multiracial*. Durham, NC: Duke University Press, 2012.

Kaplan, Carla. *Miss Anne in Harlem: The White Women of the Black Renaissance*. New York: Harper, 2013.

Kennedy, Randall. *Interracial Intimacies: Sex, Marriage, Identity, and Adoption*. New York: Vintage, 2004.

Khanna, Nikki. *Biracial in America: Forming and Performing Racial Identity*. New York: Lexington, 2011.

Lott, Eric. *Love and Theft: Blackface Minstrelsy and the American Working Class*. Oxford: Oxford University Press, 1993.

———. "White Like Me: Racial Cross-Dressing and the Construction of American Whiteness." In *Cultures of United States Imperialism*, edited by Amy Kaplan and Donald Pease, 474–98. Durham, NC: Duke University Press, 1993.

Matilda. [Matt Sycamore]. *Nobody Passes: Rejecting the Rules of Gender and Conformity*. Emeryville, CA: Seal, 2006.

Miville, Marie L., Madonna G. Constantine, Matthew F. Baysden, and Gloria So-Lloyd. "Chameleon Changes: An Exploration of Racial Identity Themes of Multiracial People." *Journal of Counseling Psychology* 52, no. 4 (2005): 507–16.

Nakamura, Lisa. *Cybertypes: Race, Ethnicity, and Identity on the Internet*. New York: Routledge, 2002.

———. *Digitizing Race: Visual Cultures of the Internet*. Minneapolis: University of Minnesota Press, 2008.

———. "Race In / For Cyberspace: Identity Tourism and Racial Passing on the Internet." In *CyberReader*, edited by Victora Vitanza. Boston: Allyn and Bacon, 1999.

Nerad, Julie Cary, ed. *Passing Interest: Racial Passing in US Novels, Memoirs, Television, and Film, 1990–2010*. Albany: State University of New York Press, 2014.

Pfeiffer, Kathleen. *Race Passing and American Individualism*. Amherst: University of Massachusetts Press, 2003.

Piper, Adrian. "Passing for White, Passing for Black." *Transition* 58 (1992): 4–32.

Robinson, Amy. "It Takes One to Know One: Passing and Communities of Common Interest." *Critical Inquiry* 30, no. 4 (1994): 715–36.

———. "To Pass//In Drag: Strategies of Entrance into the Visible." PhD diss., University of Pennsylvania, 1993.

Rockquemore, Kerry Ann. "Forced to Pass and Other Sins against Authenticity." *Women and Performance: A Journal of Feminist Theory* 15, no. 1 (2005): 17–32. Proquest.

Rogers, Jami. "The Shakespearean Glass Ceiling: The State of Colorblind Casting in Contemporary British Theatre." *Shakespeare Bulletin* 31, no. 3 (2013): 405–30.

Rogin, Michael. *Blackface, White Noise: Jewish Immigrants in the Hollywood Melting Pot.* Berkeley: University of California Press, 1996.

Sanchez, Maria, and Linda Schlossberg, eds. *Passing: Identity and Interpretation in Sexuality, Race, and Religion.* New York: New York University Press, 2001.

Sexton, Jared. *Amalgamation Schemes: Antiblackness and the Critique of Multiracialism.* Minneapolis: University of Minnesota Press, 2008.

Siebers, Tobin. "Disability as Masquerade." *Literature and Medicine* 23, no. 1 (2004): 1–22.

Smith, Valerie. "Reading the Intersection of Race and Gender in Narratives of Passing." *Diacritics* 24, nos. 2–3 (1994): 43–57.

Sollors, Werner. *Neither Black nor White Yet Both: Thematic Explorations of Interracial Literature.* Cambridge, MA: Harvard University Press, 1999.

Spickard, Paul R. *Mixed Blood: Intermarriage and Ethnic Identity in Twentieth-Century America.* Madison: University of Wisconsin Press, 1989.

Sycamore, Mattilda Bernstein, ed. *Nobody Passes: Rejecting the Rules of Gender and Conformity.* Berkeley, CA: Seal, 2006.

Thompson, Ayanna. *Passing Strange: Shakespeare, Race, and Contemporary America.* New York: Oxford University Press, 2013.

Thompson, Ayanna, and Ania Loomba, eds. *Colorblind Shakespeare: New Perspectives on Race and Performance.* New York: Routledge, 2006.

Wald, Gayle. *Crossing the Line: Racial Passing in Twentieth-Century U.S. Literature and Culture.* Durham, NC: Duke University Press, 2000.

———. "'A Most Disagreeable Mirror': Reflections on White Identity in *Black Like Me.*" In *Passing and the Fictions of Identity,* edited by Elaine Ginsburg, 151–77. Durham, NC: Duke University Press, 1996.

———. Preface, "The 'Posts' of Passing," to *Passing Interest: Racial Passing in US Novels, Memoirs, Television, and Film, 1990–2010,* edited by Julie Cary Nerad, vii–x. Albany: State University of New York Press, 2014.

Warren, Kenneth W. *What Was African American Literature?* Cambridge, MA: Harvard University Press, 2011.

Waters, Mary. *Ethnic Options: Choosing Identities in America.* Berkeley: University of California Press, 1990.

Yoshino, Kenji. *Covering: The Hidden Assault on Our Civil Rights.* New York: Random, 2006.

Young, Vershawn Ashanti. "So Black I'm Blue." *Minnesota Review* 58–60 (Spring and Fall 2002–Spring 2003): 207–17.

———. *Your Average Nigga: Performing Race, Literacy, and Masculinity.* Detroit: Wayne State University Press, 2007.

Young, Vershawn Ashanti, with Bridget Harris Tsemo, ed. *From Bourgeois to Boojie: Black Middle-Class Performances.* Detroit: Wayne State University Press, 2011.

Zackodnik, Teresa C. *The Mulatta and the Politics of Race.* Jackson: University of Mississippi Press, 2004.

PART I

New Histories

INTRODUCTION

Passing at the Turn of the Twenty-First Century

ALLYSON HOBBS

Just a few days after January 1, 1932, Lieutenant William J. French was found on a desolate road near Gilroy, California, with his pistol in his crashed car and a gunshot wound to his head. Police ruled his death a suicide. The uproar among military personnel at the Presidio in San Francisco was just beginning when a far more startling revelation appeared on the front page of the *New York Times*: "Army Man's Suicide Reveals He Is Negro." The *Times* announced that French had spent eighteen years "masquerading" as a white man. French had given the army almost two decades of "brilliant" service, reported the *Times,* and distinguished himself during World War I as a commissioned officer who led white troops. French had not heeded the warnings of his relatives, who had cautioned him against advancing too far in the military and had tried to convince him that commanding white men was far too risky. Maybe French had not expected to be promoted as quickly as he was, and once the army granted him the commission, perhaps he simply could not turn it down. Maybe French worried that to decline such a prestigious promotion would arouse suspicion. The last person to see French alive, Gertrude McEnroe, was in the car with French at the time of the crash. She claimed that French tried to kill her. McEnroe survived and later told officials that French had been on the verge of a nervous breakdown. It was McEnroe's contention that French had been driven to a state of insanity after years of fearing that his racial identity would be exposed.[1]

It is impossible to know exactly what happened in French's car before it careened and crashed into a tree on January 3, 1932. No one will ever know the nature of the relationship between McEnroe and French, who was married to a white woman. Newspaper accounts do not explain why a truck driver stopped and rescued McEnroe from the wreck but left French in the car. Reports about the case do not explain why French allegedly tried to kill McEnroe. French's mother would not comment on when he decided to pass as white, nor would she reveal any other details about his life. The *Times* notes that French visited his mother in Pasadena at Christmas and that "scores of Negroes" in that city knew that French was passing as white. But these friends and family members were uniformly silent about his personal life and his decision to pass. Most relatives protected those who passed and kept their secrets. French's family and friends were no different. Without the silence of "scores of Negroes," French's masquerade could have collapsed at any moment. But, if McEnroe's assertion is correct—that despite his family's tacit support, French's secret drove him to an acute state of mental breakdown and the desperate decision to take his own life—then the devastating and even deadly consequences of passing come into sharper view.[2]

Almost a century later, the world of Jim Crow and binary racial identities that had enveloped French has given way to new possibilities. By the late 1940s, many African Americans who had previously passed as white declared that they could no longer endure the emotional turmoil that French and others experienced. In the black press, testimonials of light-skinned blacks who disavowed passing and returned to the race registered a palpable sense of relief. African Americans described a surging race consciousness and a sense of hopefulness about the possibilities of a burgeoning Civil Rights Movement. These reports in the black press suggested that America had been made anew in the aftermath of World War II and through the early postwar period. The racial dynamics of these times might allow one to live as black and enjoy economic, political, and social freedom that had been denied to those who had been part of a previous generation. Passing had been one of a limited number of strategies that opened doors for African Americans to participate more fully in American life. Perhaps in postwar America, passing would "pass out" and no longer be necessary, especially if postwar economic prosperity extended to African Americans.[3] Perhaps African Americans could claim a black identity with pride and step out from the dark shadows that descended upon Lieutenant William J. French.

Racial passing in the American context must be acknowledged as a subset of a much-larger phenomenon that encompasses multiple disguises. Ralph Ellison characterizes disguise as an elemental aspect of American identity: "America is a land of masking jokers. . . . Benjamin Franklin, the practical scientist, skilled statesman and sophisticated lover, allowed the French to mistake him for Rousseau's Natural Man. Hemingway poses as a non-literary sportsman, Faulkner as a farmer; Abe Lincoln allowed himself to be taken for a simple country lawyer."[4] These are only a handful of examples of a sweeping phenomenon that demonstrate passing's flexibility and adaptability to various historical contexts. The poor passed as the rich, women passed as men, Jews passed as Gentiles, gay men and women passed as straight, and whites sometimes passed as black—and, of course, the reverse of each of these dyads was plausible given specific conditions and circumstances. As Ellison's quote suggests, the permutations on passing were myriad.

Given the multiple iterations of passing, it is not surprising that this phenomenon continues well after the US Supreme Court declared the legal apparatus of segregation unconstitutional. Without question, racially ambiguous people in the twenty-first century are living through a very different moment than those who lived in the 1930s or the 1830s. The racial dynamics of the new millennium have created an array of choices that were unavailable to mixed-race people in the past. In the 1920s novelist Jean Toomer wondered why he had to choose a racial identity, but his appeal for a "hybrid" identity fell on deaf ears.[5] Toomer was marked, regardless of his personal choices, as "a great Negro writer," even by close friends he assumed knew better. When he resisted this title, refused to published his poems in James Weldon Johnson's revised edition of *The Book of American Negro Poetry* (1931), moved to Greenwich Village, and became a follower of the Russian spiritual leader Georges Gurdjieff, it was assumed then (and now, among some scholars) that he had chosen to pass for white. In Toomer's time, racially ambiguous people had only two options: pass as white or live as black. Regardless of how eloquently Toomer argued for a mixed-race identity, his idea never gained traction. The racial constraints of the Jim Crow era would not allow it.

But by the late twentieth century and the beginning of the twenty-first century, the racial landscape had changed, and new choices and possibilities emerged. American society had moved toward the side of the spectrum that recognized mixed-race identities. This change was reflected not only in personal attitudes and experiences but also in federal racial classifications. In 1993 multiracial activists challenged the one-drop rule and argued that mixed-race people should be officially recognized on the 2000 census. In 1997 the US Census Bureau's policy changed for the first time in almost eighty years to allow individuals to "mark one or more" categories.[6] Suddenly, as many cultural critics and authors observe, mixed-race men and women were in vogue. A 2003 article in the Style section of the *New York Times* names a new crop of Americans "Generation E.A." (an abbreviation for "ethnically ambiguous") and notes the marketing power of this group. The article observes that casting calls for blond-haired, blue-eyed actors were replaced by calls for actors of color, such as one for a CBS soap opera: "Light complexioned African-American. Could be part Brazilian or Dominican." According to the *New York Times*, the look of racial ambiguity was especially profitable for companies that marketed products to a younger set. Linda Wells, *Allure* magazine's editor in chief, explains the fixation on the "mixed-race look": "Five years ago, about 80 percent of our covers featured fair-haired blue-eyed women, even though they represented a minority. . . . Uniformity just isn't appealing anymore."[7]

As mixed-race author Danzy Senna explains, America had entered the "Mulatto Millennium." In a futuristic parody of the same name, Senna describes her surprise when she wakes one morning to discover she is "in style . . . that mulattos had taken over. They were everywhere—playing golf, running the airwaves, opening restaurants, modeling clothes, starring in musicals with names like Show Me the Miscegenation! The radio played a steady stream of Lenny Kravitz, Sade, and Mariah Carey. . . . Pure breeds (at least black ones) are out; hybridity is in."[8] Senna had previously identified as an African American woman, "an enemy of the mulatto nation," who frowned upon those who described themselves as racially mixed. This stance on race was largely because of Senna's upbringing in the 1970s in Boston where "mixed wasn't an option. . . . No halvsies. No in between."[9] Senna chose not to claim a mixed-race identity, but she found Boston of the 1970s to be similar to Toomer's experience of Harlem in the 1920s: few Americans—black or white—were comfortable with the concept of mixed race. But by the late 1990s and the early 2000s, racial politics had changed. New marketing priorities were the result of societal and demographic changes caused by increased levels of immigration and interracial marriage. Interracial marriage increased tenfold between 1960 and 1990 (from approximately 150,000 to 1.5 million); the number of mixed-race children born to these marriages skyrocketed from approximately 500,000 to 2 million.[10]

However, the friendly embrace of hybridity in the twenty-first century does not signal the realization of a "postracial" age, nor does it support the colorblind thesis that race no longer matters. On the contrary, the increasing acceptance of mixed-race identities underscores just how germane race continues to be to contemporary American society. Mixed-race identities are still raced identities. Race continues to be reproduced all around us, at every level of society, including in our everyday lives. The long history of passing reveals that older racial formations never give way entirely; shards of past racial regimes are always visible in contemporary ones. Even in historical moments widely heralded as turning points, the past still can be seen in the present. This observation does not suggest that nothing is new or nothing has changed but, rather, that new arrangements are never wholly free of some elements of the old. Racial ideologies are plastic, and they are quick to adapt and reproduce under new social structures, but the past is stubborn.

Neo-passing narratives reveal the multiple and fluid means of racial categories while emphasizing that race and racism still persist. Sometimes racial identities are blurred or obscured; other times they remain clear and unmistakable, allowing readers and viewers to see the role of intersectionality. Even though we often think of race as a "metalanguage," to borrow historian Evelyn Brooks Higginbotham's term, that subsumes other categories,[11] the practice of racial passing relies on intertwined nature of identities of class, gender, sexuality, disability, and criminality. For example, in the neo-passing narratives of farcical depictions of black presidents onscreen that Eden Osucha discusses in chapter 4, black actors from Richard Pryor (1977) to Dave Chappelle (2005) pass by mimicking the intersectional white (raced) and male (gendered) identities of the office. But black men can only pass as president momentarily before aspects of an intersectional and stereotyped black male identity return, comically and plainly disqualifying them from the job.

Passing did not end in the 1950s when the black press enthusiastically announced that the practice had "passed out." Instead, just like race, it has taken on new forms and shapes and has adapted and adjusted to the particular circumstances, conditions, and technologies of the time period. The new histories that follow are indeed "new": they bring to life new sources, themes, and possibilities to try out different ways of living and being. Still, they have much in common with histories that we might consider "old." Most important, these new histories underscore the undeniable truth that race has become no less salient in American culture or in American lives.

Notes

1. "Army Man's Suicide." See "Black or White"; Hobbs, *Chosen Exile*, 217–65.
2. Ibid.
3. See Kingslow, "I Refuse to Pass"; Williams, "He Wouldn't Cross the Line"; "Why 'Passing' Is Passing Out"; "How Negroes Are Gaining in the U.S."; "Negroes"; Kelley, "How to Build Black Pride."
4. Ellison, "Change the Joke," 55.
5. Toomer, Letter.
6. DaCosta, *Making Multiracials*, 2.

7. Linda Wells quoted in La Ferla, "Generation E.A."

8. Senna, "Mulatto Millennium."

9. Ibid.

10. DaCosta, *Making Multiracials*, 7.

11. Higginbotham, "African American Women's History," 252.

Bibliography

"Army Man's Suicide Reveals He Is Negro." *New York Times*, January 4, 1932, 1.

"Black or White." *Atlanta World*, January 20, 1932, 1.

DaCosta, Kimberly McClain. Making Multiracials: State, Family, and Market in the Redrawing of the Color Line. Stanford, CA: Stanford University Press, 2007.

Ellison, Ralph. "Change the Joke and Slip the Yoke." In *Shadow and Act*, 45–59. 1958. New York: Vintage, 1995.

Higginbotham, Evelyn Brooks. "African American Women's History and the Metalanguage of Race." *Signs* 17, no. 2 (1992): 251–74.

Hobbs, Allyson. *A Chosen Exile: A History of Racial Passing in American Life*. Cambridge, MA: Harvard University Press, 2014.

"How Negroes Are Gaining in the U.S." *U.S. News & World Report*, June 28, 1957, 105–6.

Johnson, James Weldon. *The Book of American Negro Poetry*. Rev. ed. New York: Harcourt and Brace, 1931.

Kelley, Don Quinn. "How to Build Black Pride." *Chicago Defender*, July 24, 1968, 4.

Kingslow, Janice. "I Refuse to Pass." *Negro Digest*, May 1950, 22–31.

La Ferla, Ruth. "Generation E.A." *New York Times*, December 28, 2003. Accessed June 19, 2017. http://www.nytimes.com.

"Negroes: Big Advances in Jobs, Wealth, and Status." *U.S. News & World Report*, November 28, 1958, 90- 92.

Senna, Danzy. "The Mulatto Millennium." *Utne Reader*, September–October 1998. Accessed June 19, 2017. http://www.utne.com.

Toomer, Jean. Jean Toomer Papers, Beinecke Rare Books and Manuscripts Library, Yale University, New Haven, Connecticut.

"Why 'Passing' Is Passing Out." *Jet*, July 17, 1952, 12–16.

Williams, Richard L. "He Wouldn't Cross the Line: Herb Jeffries Cheerfully Pays the Price of Choosing His Race." *Life*, September 3, 1951, 81–94

CHAPTER 1

Why Passing Is (Still) Not Passé after More Than 250 Years

Sources from the Past and Present

MARTHA J. CUTTER

> Pass, v.: To excel or surpass. . . . To proceed, move forward, depart; to cause to do this. . . . To proceed from one existence or activity to another; spec. (euphem.) to die. . . . To give currency to; to put (esp. base or forged currency) into circulation. . . . To be accepted as or believed to be, or to represent oneself successfully as, a member of an ethnic or religious group other than one's own, esp. one having higher social status. . . . To change from one form or state to another, esp. by regular or gradual transitions; to undergo chemical, mineralogical, structural, or other gradual conversion *into [emphasis in original]*. . . .
> Pass, n.: Conjuring and Cards. An action which secretly moves or alters something, esp. cards, by sleight of hand; a conjuring or juggling trick. Also in extended use: a trick, a game.
>
> —*Oxford English Dictionary Online*

In 1845 an African American woman named Fanny ran away from her Alabama owner. Since Fanny could read and write, her owner speculates in an advertisement posted in the *Alabama Beacon* of June 14, 1845, that she might forge a pass for herself. But Fanny's master also comments that "she is as white as most white women, with straight light hair, and blue eyes, and can pass herself for a white woman."[1] Fanny can pass for white, but indeed one wonders what her owner means when he says that she is "as white as most white women." Are many "white women" not quite "pure" white? And yet, they are not subject to perpetual enslavement, as Fanny is. On the one hand, this advertisement appears to confirm the process of racialization that renders (in this time period in US history) African Americans the only groups of individuals who could be held in permanent bondage, due to their alleged racial difference.[2] On the other hand, the advertisement appears to undermine the notion of racial difference that subtends enslavement when it states that Fanny is "as white as most white woman." Her owner seems to know that nothing but "a fiction of law and custom"—to borrow Mark Twain's words in *Pudd'nhead Wilson* (1894)—keeps her enslaved.[3]

More than 150 years later, in January 1998, Danzy Senna, herself a biracial African American (daughter of a white mother and black father), published a novel called *Caucasia,* detailing the experiences of a fictional biracial (black-white) girl named Birdie who is forced by her white mother to pass as white and Jewish, while her darker-skinned sister Cole remains with her father. The novel was widely acclaimed and quickly became a favorite for classroom use. In some ways, the novel might seem to be a traditional passing narrative of racial return; at novel's end, Birdie makes the decision to stop passing for white, find her sister, and reunite with her African American father. Yet when Birdie reunites with her father, he insists, "Race is a complete illusion, make-believe. It's a costume," to which Birdie responds, "If race is so make-believe, why did I go with Mum? You gave me to Mum 'cause I looked white. You don't think that's real? Those are the facts." Birdie seems to insist on a construct of race that is real and that exists in the skin, in a cosmetic (phenotypical) difference. However, Birdie (who does not look black) ultimately affirms a black identity in the novel's ending scene, claiming her own image in the face of a black girl on a school bus: "One face toward the back of the bus caught my eye, and I halted in my tracks, catching my breath. It was a cinnamon-skinned girl with her hair in braids. She was black like me, a mixed girl, and she was watching me from behind the dirty glass."[4] There is a reclamation of blackness here (the girl is "black like me") but also an acknowledgment of race (blackness, whiteness, and mixed-race identity) as constructed behind the "dirty glass" of human perception, of the human gaze that sees and categorizes people according to perceived skin color and other racialized characteristics.

Although some scholars argue that racial passing began in earnest in the mid- to late nineteenth century, reached its pinnacle in the early twentieth century, and then abated or became "passé" by the 1930s,[5] these incidents indicate that as both a word and a behavior, passing has a longer and more extensive early history and that it continues to be a source of fascination today. In light of a recent resurgence in scholarly and popular interest in racial (black-white or white-black) passing, I consider what is at stake in this discourse, which began as early as 1747 and continues to generate—over 250 years later—a robust number of films, books, TV shows, and even graphic narratives.[6] I also make some observations about contemporary neo-passing narratives and how they broaden and recast tropes and conventions operative in earlier passing texts. I argue in this essay that passing shows us the ways in which, to borrow Barbara Jeanne Fields's terms, racial ideology must be constantly maintained and created. But we must also keep in mind that passing—as a word and a practice—has complex roots. Etymologically, dictionary definitions of the term certainly connote death, loss, and exile (passing away, passing on, passing by) but passing also demarcates other more quixotic transformations (one can pass a trick in cards or pass false coin in counterfeiting, and certain chemicals can pass from solids into liquids and then into invisible gasses).[7]

This chapter provides a broad historical overview of black-white racial passing texts in order to suggest that the most radical ones play on the multivalent possibilities of this behavior, using passing as a mirror, as a sort of "dirty" glass that is held up to the reader, one that reflects the racial preoccupation of various viewers and ultimately confuses a stable reading of the meaning of race. Such texts magically pass a trick on the reader by often *seeming* to confirm racial binaries, only to then undermine them. In so doing, these texts attempt to reveal processes of racial formation. As Ian Haney López has noted, race is "neither an essence nor an illusion, but rather an ongoing, contradictory, self-reinforcing process subject to the macro forces of social and political struggle and the micro effects of daily decisions."[8] Passing texts often elucidate processes of racial construction, even as they simultaneously query the social, legal, and ideological classifications that demarcate race—that attempt to separate blackness from whiteness as a supposedly inferior, unchanging, or hierarchical category of racial identity. Some texts try to *clarify* the meaning of race, reaffirming the passer's place within a certain racial binary (as either black or white), but others seem more committed to undermining the salience of race on a physical, legal, or social level. Furthermore, contemporary texts suggest the multiple vectors of identity at work in passing narratives—how not only racial identities but also class and sexual ones may be flexible and open, rather than static and fixed. Neo-passing narratives therefore revisit the traditional black-to-white passing trope to reexamine the meaning of other kinds of passing in the contemporary period and to reveal dialectical tensions that exist at the heart of identity categories themselves.

Reading the Prehistory of Racial Passing, 1740–1850

Early advertisements for runaway slaves who could pass for white show the complexity of this discourse and therefore provide an important prehistory to neo-passing narratives. As I have documented elsewhere, in these early advertisements, escapees are said to pass not only for white but also for free, various tradespeople, upper-class, and even assorted nationalities (such as French).[9] On the one hand, a number of these advertisements *do* affirm the idea of racial difference, forcing the escaped, near-white slave back into the category of "black" or "mulatto" (that is, nonwhite). But others seem to query the very laws, codes, and signifiers that create race, revealing a master who is in some degree of category crisis (to borrow Marjorie Garber's term) about what whiteness and blackness really mean.[10]

Some advertisements clearly state that runaway slaves who pass are "nearly white" but not "white." For example, a February 9, 1833, advertisement from the *Columbus (GA) Inquirer* by the planter Zachariah Booth reads: "Stop Mabin!! Runaway from my house in Talbot County, Georgia, on Flint River, on 25th of December last at night a man slave by the name of Mabin, about twenty years old, chunkily built, a bright mulatto, with grey eyes—hair straight and sandy—a great deal on his head and rather bushy. *He will pass for a white man where he is not known*."[11] The advertisement implies that where he is "not known," Mabin can pass for a white man, but this passing certainly does not make him white—he is still coded as "mulatto" by the advertisement. Another advertisement similarly implies that the escaped slave is not *truly* white: "Run Away . . . Mulatto, or Quadroon Girl, about 14 years of age, named Seth, but calls herself Sall, sometimes *says she is white and often paints her face* to cover that deception."[12] As read by her master, Seth is involved in a performance in which she passes for something she is not—she is a "mulatto" or "quadroon" girl passing for white. Yet, even in affirming the enslaved individual's blackness, some advertisements may query the meaning of whiteness. The *Charleston (SC) Courier* from August 4, 1820, lists an advertisement for a runaway named Jack Mason (or Jack Jones) who has "sandy, strait hair, and is *almost white*"; the owner comments that "the fellow no doubt *will attempt to pass for a white man, which by the by is nearly the fact, but not free born*."[13] Jack is "nearly" a white man but not "free born" and so is subject to enslavement. A legal status as slave trumps a white appearance, although some category crisis appears in the equivocal phrase "which by the by is nearly the fact" in regards to Jack's status as a white man.

The meaning of whiteness itself, however, was not always clear, and some slaves escaped by exploiting a connection to Native American ancestry (considered in many states to be legally free from enslavement) or by passing as a white nationality. As early as 1763, this type of racial passing was common. "RAN away from the Subscriber . . . His Mulatto Waiting Man, named Jem, about 28 or 30 years of Age," reads an advertisement from the *(Annapolis) Maryland Gazette* on October 20, 1763. The advertisement goes on to describe in detail an individual who knows how to pass for Indian, for several tradespersons, and for free:

> A well-set Fellow, wears his own black Hair, which is commonly tied in a Cue behind, or platted, and curls on each Side of his Face. Had on when he went away, a Cotton Jacket, Brown Roll Trousers, and old Shoes; but, it is supposed, he will change both his Name and Dress, as he has been seen with his Hair comb'd out straight, and an Indian Match coat on: I am informed *he intends to make his Escape in that Disguise, pass for an Indian, and profess himself a Shoe-maker*. He is well acquainted both in Maryland and Pennsylvania, and is a very handy, sly, complaisant, smooth tongued Fellow, can shave and dress a Wig as well as most Barbers, and will *(as he is a light Mulatto) probably pass for a Freeman, and profess himself of that Trade.*[14]

The discourse that seeks to reenslave Jem as a piece of property also reinforces his resourcefulness, intelligence, and knowledge. It seems that Jem could pass as Indian by straightening or braiding his hair, as a freeman by changing his clothes, and as either a barber or shoemaker by brandishing the various tools of these trades. Another man, Peter Youngblood, ran away from his owner, Captain Easterby and was advertised in the *Charleston (SC) Courier* on April 7, 1831: "Peter [has] . . . very light complexion, straight black hair, rather slim and pale. . . . When well-dressed looks very genteel, but might be taken for an Indian, or *might pass either for a free or white person*, as he can invent quite plausible stories of himself."[15] These advertisement describe resourceful, capable people who can "invent quite plausible stories" of themselves—stories that generate multiple, and mutating, identities as a free person, a white person, a Native American, a barber, a tailor, and a shoemaker.

One final example in which an enslaved man passes for free, upper class, French, and white illustrates the way these documents sometimes depict a master who has begun to question the meaning of whiteness itself. In May 1794, a "mulatto" slave named Joe Cully ran away from his master, who then advertised him in detail in the *Virginia Herald and Fredericksburg Advertiser*. Offering a twenty-dollar reward for this "very bright and much freckled . . . very genteel made, spry, active fellow," Cully's owner comments that Cully escaped with "three white shirts, one brown ditto, a pair of satinet breeches dyed purple, a pair of country jeans ditto, dyed nankeen colour, [and] one swanskin waistcoat, striped." Escaping with clothing that could mark him as an upper-class gentleman, Cully demonstrates a sophisticated awareness that not only his race but also his class could subject him to enslavement. Finally, Cully's owner notes that Cully "endeavours to pass as a Frenchman, and alters his tongue to a broken language that may be very perceivable to anyone that should converse with him." With his various sets of apparel, his light skin and freckles, his multilingual abilities, and his genteel persona, Cully can pass for a free, white, upper-class, French gentleman. Cully's master clearly admires this individual (calling him a "very genteel made, spry, active fellow") and by the very detail in which he describes Cully seems to validate him as a skillful, intelligent subject.[16] The master is in category crisis here, as whiteness is shown to be more performative than physical—and based in matters of clothing, speech, and activity. At the same time, the advertisement endeavors to reenslave Cully as an item of property and possession, an escaped slave inferior to, and lacking coequal status with, white men.

Advertisements for runaway slaves who can pass for white, Indian, or other nationalities thereby often differentiate questions about the significance, legitimacy, and construction of whiteness and blackness, as well other ethnic identities. They articulate questions about whether categories of racial identity are real and defining of an individual in some way or, conversely, are masks and roles that can be staged (or not), as the individual desires. The documents also complicate singular notions of racial identity and therefore the idea that being "true" to one's "real" racial identity is unproblematic; both the owner of the slave and the passing subject delineate the erraticism of racial identity and allegiance. Interrogations about whether the racial passer denies his or her (one) race by passing for white and whether passing troubles a black-white racial binary are still evident in contemporary debates.[17] However, it is ambiguous whether these escaped individuals who passed for white, free, Native American, or French genuinely understood themselves to *be* white, free, Native American, or French. Many deliberately changed or occluded racial and class signifiers that marked them as black and enslaved, yet in doing so they might have been articulating their sense of identity. In performing multiple sides of their identities, then, these individuals may have come to own more fully their lived, felt, or understood perception of selfhood.

Questioning Race: Passing, 1850–1930

As these advertisements reveal, *passing* is already, from its earliest incarnations, a term with many complex connotations. This multivalence continues in texts written in the latter half of the nineteenth and early twentieth centuries, where passing is often associated with dying or with racial betrayal and racial forgery, while a few texts associate it with freedom or even with simply living one's own life. For example, Frank Webb's novel *The Garies and Their Friends* (1857) primarily views racial passing as a dangerous counterfeiting of self, a passing of "false" coinage. The contrasting fates of the two children, Emily and Clarence Garie, exemplify this narrative trajectory. Emily can pass for white but does not; eventually she marries a black man and lives contentedly within the black community. Clarence, on the other hand, conceals his racial background in order to marry a white woman. The text codes this passing identity as duplicitous; Clarence describes feeling like an "undetected forger, who is in constant fear of being apprehended"; he also states, "I must shut this secret in my bosom, where it gnaws, gnaws, gnaws, until it has almost eaten my heart away. . . . No escaped galley-slave ever felt more than I do, or lived in more constant fear of detection."[18] Clarence is punished by the text for his transgression, losing the woman he loves when she finds out he is not completely white, and then dying of a broken heart. The dominant logic of the text supports an ideology in which one must be true to one's (black) race in order to be honorable and have a decent quality of life.

As critics such as Robert Nowatzki have pointed out, Webb's text does at times also query the meaning of race. However, its plot as a whole appears to reaffirm Clarence's and Emily's blackness. Other texts from this time period are not so confident on this point. J. T. Trowbridge's novel *Neighbor Jackwood* (1856) hinges on a heroine, Charlotte Woods, who is the daughter of a light-skinned slave woman and a white father. After the death of her father, her mother is remanded into slavery; Charlotte also becomes a slave and is eventually sold to a man who tries to force her to be his concubine. Charlotte escapes from slavery dressed as a white, elderly woman and ends up in Vermont, sheltered by the farmer known as Neighbor Jackwood and his family. The town's most eligible bachelor, Hector Delisle, falls in love with the beautiful Charlotte, and she eventually reveals her secret to him; after a number of plot twists, they marry. The couple then lives happily in the Vermont community, where they have a child.

This plot is unusual for a number of reasons. First, although the passer faces numerous difficulties, she never regrets passing for white (if this is indeed what she sees herself as doing). Second, although Hector at first is nonplussed by her racial background, he eventually marries her, and class (not race) seems to be the greater issue for Hector's father; moreover, few in the town appear concerned with the "one drop" of blood that would make this marriage miscegenational.[19] Furthermore, the passer is not punished by death for her racial transgression, nor does she return to her "true" race, nor does she end up in Europe—which seem to be the three dominant outcomes of the genre of the passing narrative as it often formalized in the nineteenth and early twentieth centuries. By the end of the text, Charlotte has managed to hurdle the one remaining barrier to freedom—her status as legally enslaved—as Hector buys her freedom from her former master. Finally, throughout the text Trowbridge plays with tropes of passing, masquerade, and counterfeiting, showing how passing occurs on many levels and how everyone in the text is always-already passing in some way.

Trowbridge's text was popular in the nineteenth century and even made into a play that had a long run in Boston.[20] Subsequently, however, it dropped out of the canon of nineteenth-century passing texts, perhaps because it fails to fit the thematic denunciation of passing so frequent in these works or the standard resolutions to these plots described above. Yet, Trowbridge's novel foreshadows many early twentieth-century texts, such as Charles W. Chesnutt's *The House behind the Cedars* (1900) and Nella Larsen's *Passing* (1929), in which the racial passer's identity as "black" is not always clear, and whiteness is shown to be a category constructed through geography, law, clothing, or other external signifiers, rather than through an internal or biological essence. In Chesnutt's text Rena Walden does see herself as "black" and dies following an unsuccessful attempt to pass for white. But Chesnutt's John Walden is less clear in his racial affiliation. As a young boy he wants to study the law but is told by a judge that he cannot due to his race; John proclaims: "I am white . . . and I am free, as all my people were before me. . . . I am white, and not black."[21] John's vehement advocacy of his whiteness sometimes is ignored by critics in favor of Rena's inability to truly perform a white identity, but Chesnutt here underscores race not as an essence that one must ignore to become something else but as a performative choice (at least for John). Not coincidentally, perhaps, John does not die at novel's end.

Like Chesnutt's novel, Larsen's *Passing* primarily views racial identity as a choice, instead of a physical essence, one that *might* lead to freedom, rather than a lasting sense of racial betrayal, as Rena Walden and Clarence Garie seem to feel. Yet, what is most intriguing about Larsen's novel is not only that Clare Kendry configures racial passing as a mode of finding identity but also that at the center of the text there is a mystery: does Clare view herself as black, white, both, or neither? At times Clare manifests a longing for her (African American) "people," but at other times she claims to have no alliance to anyone or anything: "Why, to get the things I want badly enough, I'd do anything, hurt anybody, throw anything away."[22] How Clare views her racial identity is never (to use a bad pun) clarified, but what is clear is that others project a racial essence onto her. Irene, for example, describes Clare as having "Negro eyes" that are given to her by her "grandmother and later her mother and father."[23] But it is never particularly evident what makes Clare's eyes "Negro eyes," and apparently her racist white husband, Jack Bellew, never detects this "racial" trait. Through Clare, then, as I have argued elsewhere, Larsen complicates the idea of blackness and whiteness as anything more than performative, even as she shows the ways that characters like Irene cling to the idea of color as being manifested on some level through racial "difference."[24] Larsen's novel, like Trowbridge's, shows the ways in which race functions as a sliding signifier into which individuals project racial fantasies and ideologies. To borrow terms from Judith Butler, we must wonder if for writers such as Trowbridge, Chesnutt, and Larsen, acts and gestures create the illusion of an interior and organizing racial core, but race itself can be "neither true nor false, but only produced."[25]

Passing in a "Postracial" World?

In the early twentieth century, then, *passing* is no longer exclusively named as a term associated with racial forgery or disguise but also as one that potentially creates a certain type of performative freedom and transformation. This performative freedom and transformation are sometimes evident in terms of class and sexuality; for example, in Larsen's *Passing,* Clare also exhibits fluidity in her class identity (moving from working class to upper class) and sexuality (flirting with both men and women). Of course, Clare still ends up dead at novel's end, but she seems to have transformed herself (prior to her death) in some way and cut all ties to any normative form of racial and sexual self-identification, and this makes Larsen's text revolutionary in its treatment of the racial-passing genre. One definition of (nonracial) passing from the *Oxford English Dictionary* perhaps clarifies this difference: passing can also mean "to undergo transition from one form or state to another, to be changed by regular gradations; to undergo chemical, mineralogical, *structural,* or other gradual conversion."[26] These changes may be permanent; some solids, when they become gasses, cannot pass back into the material from which they came. Clare seems to have transformed herself into a creature who flouts *all* racial, class, and sexual conventions, because she no longer (or perhaps never did) believe in them.

Such might also be the case in Philip Roth's novel *The Human Stain* (2000), the first post–Civil Rights neo-passing narrative discussed here; in this novel, passing becomes entirely liberating to the protagonist, an example of what Randall Kennedy might call an individual's "racial self-determination," his or her "ability to revise stated racial identities."[27] The central passing act of the novel is Coleman Silk's decision to pass for white in order to obtain what he considers to be freedom. Coleman Silk comments that "all he'd ever wanted, from earliest childhood on, was to be free: not black, not even white, just on his own and free. . . . The objective was for his fate to be determined not by the ignorant, hate-filled intentions of a hostile world but, to whatever degree humanly possible, by his own resolve."[28] For Coleman, then, passing is about creating a "free" and autonomous self, and a racial status as "black" (he presumes) hinders this freedom. Of course, what Coleman sees as freedom his family and friends see as loss: "Many things vanish out of a family's life. . . . To vanish, as they used to say in the family, 'till all trace of him was lost.' 'Lost himself to all his people' was another way they put it."[29] But, clearly, for Coleman the freedom of passing overrides such considerations of loss and finally transforms him into a new entity. Sociologist Brooke Kroeger's book on passing chronicles the stories of six modern-day passers and claims to show that "people . . . pass to be more truly themselves."[30] People pass, Earlene Stetson comments, in order to assert that they are "a human person with all the rights and privileges thereof."[31] Although this is certainly true at times, this ideology is maintained in only a few passing texts.

Coleman does construct a "new self" and "new life" in the novel and (it seems) permanently transform himself into a white person, to the extent that he cannot go back to being "black," even when he is accused of racism and it might save him his job and his reputation to do so. In an analysis of the real-life individual that many critics believe Roth alludes to in his portrayal of Coleman Silk (Anatole Broyard, who died in 1990),[32] Henry Louis Gates Jr. makes a similar point: "Broyard passed not because he thought that race wasn't important but because he knew that it was. . . . But the ideologies of modernity have a kicker, which is that they permit no exit."[33] Having chosen to be "white," Coleman feels that he cannot go back. Therein lies the fundamental conservativism of the central passing act that constitutes *The Human Stain*. Whiteness, once passed into, becomes a "true" racial identity out of which the protagonist cannot pass, at least from the point of view of the novel's narrator, Nathan Zuckerman.

Yet, Roth's novel is a neo-passing narrative, and as such it also plays up a more performative quality not only of race but also of identity itself. Here, for example, is Faunia (a white woman) contemplating her desire to become a black crow: "All that blackness. Nothing but blackness. . . . I think I sometimes believe that I already am one [a black crow]. . . . Why not? There are men who are locked up in women's bodies and women who are locked up in men's bodies, so why can't I be a crow locked up in this body?"[34] Faunia, it seems, is only passing for a human being. This is a complex image that metaphorically links racial passing (blackness) with gender dimorphism but also suggests that no one can really be a nonpassing self; from the narrator's point of view, we are all constantly performing some sort of identity: as human, as black, as white, as Jewish, or as something else. Roth's novel here picks up on a radical performative strain embedded in earlier passing narratives: the way these narratives sometimes envision human identity in its entirety as a performance, and work to destabilize all fixed categories of what we "know" ourselves to be. Therefore, finding an identity that matches who we "really" are does not lead to freedom; instead Roth's novel seems to validate the performance, the transformation of the self on an open stage. Perhaps this is the most radical quality present in neo-passing narratives—the idea that beyond racial categorization, identity itself is always-already performative, always being created and re-created in the eye of human perception and on the stage of culture itself.

A similar mode of racial performativity is also present in another millennial text—Spike Lee's film *Bamboozled* (2000), in which a contemporary television minstrel show is created by an African American television producer named Pierre Delacroix (played by Damon Wayans) who is (allegedly) trying to create a satire. However, the show becomes incredibly popular, as both white audience members and African American performers take on blackface and perform stereotypical modes of blackness. In the movie, there is also a white man named Thomas Dunwitty (played by Michael Rapaport) who claims to be "blacker" than Pierre Delacroix: "You got your head stuck so far up your ass with your Harvard education and your bullshit pretentious Buppie ways. Brother man, I'm blacker than you. I'm keepin' it real. I'm bad as bad. I got the role. You're just frontin', trying to be white." Dunwitty blatantly links whiteness with education and an upper-class status, while blackness is associated with "keepin' it real" and being "bad as bad." Dunwitty also rejects any scripts that Delacroix creates concerning the black middle class because such shows would only portray "white people with black faces."[35] To complicate phenotypical readings of race even more, Lee's movie includes a white-looking member of a rap group called the Mau Mau, who is named 1/16th Blak (played by real-life rapper M. C. Serch, alongside members of the group played by other real-life black hip-hop artists such as Mos Def). When the Mau Maus are attacked by the police at the end of the film, every single member is killed except the white-looking 1/16th Blak (who may or may not actually *be* 1/16th African American), suggesting that although he has *claimed* a performative blackness, the police still refuse to move beyond epidermal demarcations of race.

Throughout this film, Lee indicates that racial identity is always in process and constantly re-created around the dialectical poles of racial essence and/or appearance and racial performance. Cultural mulattos—individuals who pass as white *and* black—as Meredith McCarroll has noted, are present in the film and may threaten both individual identity and the idea of cultural authenticity.[36] In this sense, we can read *Bamboozled* as a neo-passing text—one that tries to move beyond the trope of black-white (phenotypical) racial passing. Still, Lee takes pains to show the ways in which narrow (epidermal) definitions of "whiteness" and "blackness" still exist, prompting the continued presence of various forms of racial passing, even in the "postracial" era. The dizzying array of racial performances and the overlap between "real" and "fictional" characters may destabilize a viewer's ways of reading race, even as the film indicates just how entrenched racial binaries remain. This is not to say that race is meaningless in this film, for skin color ultimately does determine (quite literally) who lives and who dies. But Lee also emphasizes that just what race is—and what blackness and whiteness are—remain vexed and unstable in the contemporary moment. Furthermore, race is not only associated with skin color but with other variables, such as education and socioeconomic class.

Even more recently, Toni Morrison's novel *God Help the Child* (2015) opens with a brief discussion of racial passing. A character named Sweetness comments on the first page of the novel, "You should have seen my grandmother. She passed for white and never said another word to any one of her children. . . . Almost all mulatto types and quadroons did that back in the day, if they had the right kind of hair that is. Can you imagine how many white folks have Negro blood running and hiding in their veins? Guess. Twenty percent I heard." Morrison's novel—which shows the ways passing can lead to a type of freedom but also, as Allyson Hobbs phrases it, a chosen exile—begins in the 1990s, with the birth of the very dark-skinned child named Bride, and it indicates that racial passing has not ended if one has "the right kind of hair" or skin. One of Morrison's characters comments much later in the novel, "Scientifically there's no such thing as race . . . so racism without race is a choice. Taught, of course, by those who need it but still a choice."[37] Taken together, these comments suggest that in this novel, racial passing and colorism (negative views of darker-skinned individuals) offer an opportunity to explore racial construction, racial performance, and racial discrimination.

As we see, then, scrutiny of how the racial passer might undermine society's construction of a racial binary takes place in fictional "postracial" texts. Nonfictional neo-passing memoirs also take up similar questions about the salience of racial categorization and the significance of racial binaries. For example, in Gregory Howard Williams's popular and descriptively named book *Life on the Color Line: The True Story of a White Boy Who Discovered He Was Black* (1996), Williams learns while growing up in the 1950s that his father, Tony, is not a "swarthy Italian" but from a black family, making Williams himself "black." What is perplexing, still, is that Williams is continually coded as white by his father, while his brother Mike (who has the same skin color) is coded as black. After Tony makes his sons fight each other, saying that his white son Billy (Gregory Williams) will fight his "nigger son" Mike, Williams's young persona says, "I'm not white. And Mike's not a nigger," to which Tony responds: "[Mike's] gonna be a no-count black bastard just like me. Oh hell, he's gonna learn how to hustle and make a buck. I'll teach him that, but he's never gonna climb to the top of the mountain. You need to be a white boy to do that. Mike's already too much of a hustler to change. . . . You're a white motherfucker, whether you like it or not."[38]

In this neo-passing text, then, racial identity seems to be allied not only with skin color but also with temperament, ability, perceived intelligence, and economic progression, the ability to "climb to the top of the mountain." All this appears to mean that ultimately Mike cannot pass for white, but Billy/Williams can—and indeed must—pass for white. While Tony's logic is muddled, it does speak to the question of why racial passing might continue into a "postracial" era: Whiteness becomes associated with upper-class status, social movement, and economic mobility, whereas blackness is often allied with poverty, social immobility, and economic instability. In some neo-passing texts, passing comes to signify not so much an escape from skin color but an elision of pejorative economic and social assumptions that remain tied to constructs of blackness through processes of racialization.

The nonfictional representation of the vagaries of racial identity and racial construction is also present in Danzy Senna's even more recent text about her family's history *Where Did You Sleep Last Night?* (2009), parts of which take place in the years between (roughly) 1990 and 2005. Despite her attempt to claim a black identity, Senna finds herself being continually forced into the category of whiteness. Married to a darker-skinned man (the writer Percival Everett) and pregnant in California, she comments that "it strikes me that my husband and I are only passing as an interracial couple. I wonder if these same people will be disappointed when they find out, if they find out, that we are in actuality something far more old-fashioned—a redbone black man with a high yellow woman." When she is traveling with her father, people take her as the white half of an interracial couple or "a young white woman with her older black boyfriend." At one point she even passes as the Puerto Rican wife of her father, a child bride who speaks no English. Carl Senna (her father) believes that "many white people he met were actually black people passing as white." At the same time, he maintains a racial essentialism in which he is obsessed with the idea that "black music was coded and that white people would never understand it."[39]

Senna's text does not resolve these contradictions, and it is never really clear why Senna herself is always taken for white, even when she is with her black husband or black father. As a neo-passing narrative, however, her memoir sets these paradoxes out so that a reader can *see* them, and it uses them to point to the ways that race, although a construction, endures over time and is constantly made and remade in the dirty mirror of human perception, recognition, and (perhaps most important) misrecognition. After Senna gives birth to a son, she notices that people continually try to gauge his race, reading their own racial preoccupations into him: "People see my baby, and in the face of his racial ambiguity their own past hurts, desires, fears, and fantasies rise to the surface. He—the baby—becomes the Rorschach inkblot upon which all of their own projections come to the surface."[40] People see what they want to see in the mirror of the passing persona or in the Rorschach of a racially ambiguous infant child. Ultimately, Senna's narrative does not so much clarify *what race is* but depicts the process whereby race is perpetually made and unmade in the eye of human perception.

Conclusion: The Persistence of Passing

As this brief survey of racial passing texts from the mid-1750s to the contemporary era has shown, passing has played multiple roles in the history of racial formation in the United States. Passing texts do sometimes affirm racial essence—the idea that one has a true (biological) race to which one should adhere, as well as the idea of race as primarily a physical aspect of one's being (skin color, eyes, or hair); they may also at times reinforce a rigid racial binary in which one must be "white" to succeed in US society. Yet, simultaneously, they often explore the unstable and plural ways that race is created, performed, and maintained, as well as the ideological constructs that subtend racial formation. This is particularly the case with neo-passing narratives, which tend to show that not only race but also class, gender, and sexuality are performative and fluid, rather than static and fixed.

Finally, passing discourse allows artists and writers to excavate questions that remain at the center of US racial ideology. People still will pass, and literature, film, and memoir still will continue to explore this subject, even as the new millennium advances, because passers often push back against the ideological underpinnings of constantly re-created yet still salient theories of racialization. Neo-passing texts in particular also illustrate how whiteness becomes constellated with a whole set of values that are not in and of themselves racial (such as success, freedom, economic mobility, intelligence, and wealth) but *become racialized* within a society that cannot move beyond a stark black-white binary. In portraying the plethora of ways that identity itself is constructed, deconstructed, and reconstructed, neo-passing texts sometimes explode the very idea that we can locate racial, sexual, or class identity within some definitive physical, mental, economic, or social vector. In some neo-passing texts, then, identity exists solely within the dirty glass of human perception, a flawed mirror that only replicates our most intimate fears, fantasies, obsessions, and desires.

Notes

1. *Letter to Louis Kossuth*, 12.

2. Fields argues that the laws that marked African or African-descended slaves as subject to the condition of perpetual slavery did not come into being until 1661 and that Euro-Americans "resolved the contradictions between slavery and liberty by defining Afro-Americans as a race" sometime between the time of the American Revolution (1776) and the ratification of the Constitution (1788). Fields, "Slavery, Race, and Ideology," 104, 116. Ira Berlin is more sensitive to the ways the idea of perpetual enslavement was negotiated in different parts of the United States due to disparate labor systems but still sees a new order based in permanent African slavery developing in the last decades of the eighteenth century; see Berlin, *Many Thousand Gone*, chap. 5. David Brion Davis has also examined the profound ways that, during the era of the American Revolution, individuals who opposed slavery were complicit with those who favored it and settled on race as an explanation for the existence of slavery; in so doing both groups coalesced racist ideologies of blackness. See Davis, *Problem of Slavery*, chap. 1.

3. Twain, *Tragedy of Pudd'nhead Wilson*.

4. Senna, *Caucasia*, 391; 393; 413.

5. According to Werner Sollors, Nathan Irving Huggins coined the phrase "Passing is passé" as the title of an essay written in the early 1970s and ultimately published in his book *Revelations*. See Sollors, *Neither Black nor White*, 408. The phrase has also been used more recently in texts such as Spickard's *Mixed Blood*. For studies that view passing as

primarily occurring from 1850 to 1940, see Bennett, *Passing Figure*; Belluscio, *To Be Suddenly White*; Zackodnik, *Mulatta and the Politics of Race*; and Dreisinger, *Near Black*.

6. The earliest reference to racial passing I have found is from the May 25, 1747, *New-York Weekly Journal*: "Made his escape from on board the Privateer Brig, Pollux, on the 20th inst, a Mulatto man named Storde, a Bermudian Born, aged about 23 years, pretty tall and pock broken, but not very much, but pretty large pits in his face, pretty fair, with his *Head commonly shaved in order to make himself pass for a white man*." Hodges and Brown, "*Pretends to Be Free*," 21–22, emphasis added. Racial passing continues to be represented in novels, memoirs, television shows, films, and movies today. For a discussion of recent postracial passing texts, see Nerad, *Passing Interest*, as well as chapter 3 of Elam, *Souls of Mixed Folks*.

7. *Oxford English Dictionary Online*, s.v. "pass."

8. Haney López, "Social Construction," 7.

9. Cutter, "As White."

10. I borrow here Marjorie Garber's construct of category crisis, which she develops in terms of transvestism but also believes is applicable to other binary categories: "By 'category crisis' I mean a failure of definitional distinction, a borderline that becomes permeable, that permits of border crossings from one (apparently distinct) category to another: black/white, Jew/Christian, noble/bourgeois, master/servant, master/slave." Binary categories are sometimes put in question or under erasure by such definitional failure. Garber, *Vested Interests*, 16–17.

11. Proctor, "Slavery in Southwest Georgia," 6, emphasis added.

12. *New York Royal Gazette*, March 15, 1783, emphasis added, in Hodges and Brown, "*Pretends to Be Free*," 282.

13. "America's Historical Newspapers: Early American Newspapers," emphasis added.

14. Windley, *Runaway Slave Advertisements*, 2:51, emphasis added.

15. "America's Historical Newspapers."

16. Costa, "Geography."

17. See, for example, Kroeger's misleadingly titled study *Passing: When People Can't Be Who They Are* or Pulley, *Blacks Who Pass for Indian and White*. Also see Hobbs's discussion of racial passing as "an exile" and her statement that "the core issue of passing is not becoming what you pass for, but losing what you pass away from" (presumably, a black identity). Hobbs, *Chosen Exile*, 4, 18. Yet, for many individuals, racial identity may often be in flux, changing, or unstable in different periods of their lives or even on a day-to-day basis. For studies that confirm this observation, see Miville, Constantine, Baysden, and So-Lloyd, "Chameleon Changes"; and Dineen-Wimberly and Spickard, "It's not that simple."

18. Webb, *Garies and Their Friends*, 306; 304.

19. Trowbridge, *Neighbor Jackwood*, 263.

20. S. N. Roth, *Gender and Race*, 170.

21. Chesnutt, *House behind the Cedars*, 113.

22. Larsen, *Passing*, 119, 149.

23. Ibid., 46.

24. Cutter, "Sliding Significations."

25. Butler, *Gender Trouble*, 186.

26. *Oxford English Dictionary Online*, s.v. "pass," emphasis added.

27. Kennedy, *Interracial Intimacies*, 333.

28. P. Roth, *Human Stain*, 121.

29. Ibid., 144.

30. Kroeger, *Passing*, 2.

31. Stetson, "Mulatto Motif," 45.

32. Roth denies that Coleman Silk is based on Broyard, whom Roth had met but did not know well. See P. Roth, "Open Letter."

33. Gates, *Thirteen Ways*, 208.

34. P. Roth, *Human Stain*, 169.

35. Lee, *Bamboozled*, 9.16–9.40.

36. McCarroll, "Consuming Performances."

37. Morrison, *God Help the Child*, 3, 143.

38. Williams, *Life on the Color Line*, 34, 156.

39. Senna, *Where Did You Sleep*, 18, 50, 59, 139–40, 129.

40. Ibid., 165.

Bibliography

"America's Historical Newspapers: Early American Newspapers Series 1–6, 1690–1922." *Readex.com*. Accessed March 12, 2013. http://www.readex.com/content/americas-historical-newspapers.

"America's Historical Newspapers: Hispanic American Newspapers, 1808–1980." *Readex.com*. Accessed March 12, 2013. http://www.readex.com/content/americas-historical-newspapers.

Belluscio, Steven J. *To Be Suddenly White: Literary Realism and Racial Passing*. Columbia: University of Missouri Press, 2006.

Bennett, Juda. *The Passing Figure: Racial Confusion in Modern American Literature*. New York: Lang, 1996.

Berlin, Ira. *Many Thousands Gone: The First Two Centuries of Slavery in North America*. Cambridge, MA: Harvard University Press, 1998.

Butler, Judith. *Gender Trouble: Feminism and the Subversion of Identity*. 2nd ed. New York: Routledge, 2006.

Chesnutt, Charles Waddell. *The House behind the Cedars*. 1900. New York: Penguin, 1993.

Costa, Thomas, comp. "The Geography of Slavery in Virginia." *University of Virginia*, 2005. Accessed September 27, 2012. http://www2.vcdh.virginia.edu/gos/.

Cutter, Martha J. "'As White as Most White Women': Racial Passing in Advertisements for Runaway Slaves and the Origins of a Multivalent Term." *American Studies* 54, no. 4 (2016): 73–97.

———. "Sliding Significations: Passing as a Narrative and Textual Strategy in Nella Larsen's Fiction." In *Passing and the Fictions of Identity*, edited by Elaine K. Ginsberg, 75–100. Durham, NC: Duke University Press, 1996.

Davis, David Brion. *The Problem of Slavery in the Age of Revolution, 1770–1823*. Ithaca, NY: Cornell University Press, 1975.

Dineen-Wimberly, Ingrid, and Paul Spickard. "'It's not that simple': Multiraciality, Models, and Social Hierarchy." In *Multiracial Americans and Social Class: The Influence of Social Class on Racial Identity*, edited by Kathleen Odell Korgen, 205–21. New York: Routledge, 2010.

Dreisinger, Baz. *Near Black: White-to-Black Passing in American Culture*. Amherst: University of Massachusetts Press, 2008.

Elam, Michele. *The Souls of Mixed Folk: Race, Politics, and Aesthetics in the New Millennium*. Stanford, CA: Stanford University Press, 2011.

Fields, Barbara Jeanne. "Slavery, Race, and Ideology in the United States of America." *New Left Review* I, no. 181 (1990): 95–118.

Garber, Marjorie. *Vested Interests: Cross-Dressing and Cultural Anxiety*. New York: Routledge, 1992.

Gates, Henry Louis, Jr. *Thirteen Ways of Looking at a Black Man*. New York: Vintage, 1998.

Haney López, Ian F. "The Social Construction of Race: Some Observations on Illusion, Fabrication, and Choice." *Harvard Civil Rights–Civil Liberties Law Review* 29 (1994): 1–62.

Hobbs, Allyson. *A Chosen Exile*. Cambridge, MA: Harvard University Press, 2014.

Hodges, Graham R., and Alan E. Brown, eds. *"Pretends to Be Free": Runaway Slave Advertisements from Colonial and Revolutionary New York and New Jersey*. New York: Garland, 1994.

Huggins, Nathan Irvin. *Revelations: American History, American Myths*. Edited by Brenda Smith Huggins. New York: Oxford University Press, 1995.

Kennedy, Randall. *Interracial Intimacies: Sex, Marriage, Identity, and Adoption*. New York: Vintage, 2004.

Kroeger, Brooke. *Passing: When People Can't Be Who They Are*. New York: Public Affairs, 2003.

Larsen, Nella. *Passing*. New York: Knopf, 1929. *Open Library*. Accessed April 30, 2015. https://openlibrary.org.

Lee, Spike, dir. *Bamboozled*. 2000. Los Angeles: New Line Cinema, 2001. DVD.

Letter to Louis Kossuth, concerning Freedom and Slavery in the United States. Boston: Walcutt, 1852.

McCarroll, Meredith. "Consuming Performances: Race, Media, and the Failure of the Cultural Mulatto in *Bamboozled* and *Erasure*." In *Passing Interest: Racial Passing in US Novels, Memoirs, Television, and Film, 1990–2010*, edited by Julie Nerad, 283–306. Albany: State University of New York Press, 2014.

Miville, Marie L., Madonna G. Constantine, Matthew F. Baysden, and Gloria So-Lloyd. "Chameleon Changes: An Exploration of Racial Identity Themes of Multiracial People." *Journal of Counseling Psychology* 52, no. 4 (2005): 507–16.

Morrison, Toni. *God Help the Child: A Novel*. New York: Knopf, 2015.

Nerad, Julie Cary, ed. *Passing Interest: Racial Passing in US Novels, Memoirs, Television, and Film, 1990–2010*. Albany: State University of New York Press, 2014.

Nowatzki, Robert. "Blurring the Color Line: Black Freedom, Passing, Abolitionism, and Irish Ethnicity in Frank J. Webb's *The Garies and Their Friends*." *Studies in American Fiction* 33, no. 1 (2005): 29–58.

Oxford English Dictionary Online. Accessed March 30, 2015. http://www.oed.com.

Proctor, William G. "Slavery in Southwest Georgia." *The Georgia Historical Quarterly* 49, no. 1 (1965): 1–22.

Pulley, Clyde. *Blacks Who Pass for Indian and White*. Chicago: Adams, 1978.

Roth, Philip. *The Human Stain*. New York: Vintage, 2001.

———. "An Open Letter to Wikipedia." *The New Yorker*, September 6, 2012. Accessed March 5, 2015. http://www.newyorker.com.

Roth, Sarah N. *Gender and Race in Antebellum Popular Culture*. New York: Cambridge University Press, 2014.

Senna, Danzy. *Caucasia: A Novel*. New York: Riverhead, 1999.

———. *Where Did You Sleep Last Night? A Personal History*. New York: Picador, 2009.

Sollors, Werner. *Neither Black nor White Yet Both: Thematic Explorations of Interracial Literature*. Cambridge, MA: Harvard University Press, 1999.

Spickard, Paul R. *Mixed Blood: Intermarriage and Ethnic Identity in Twentieth-Century America*. Madison: University of Wisconsin Press, 1989.

Stetson, Earlene. "The Mulatto Motif in Black Fiction." PhD diss., State University of New York Buffalo, 1976.

Trowbridge, J. T. *Neighbor Jackwood*. 1856. Boston: Tilton, 1865. *Hathi Trust*. Accessed March 3, 2013. https://catalog.hathitrust.org.

Twain, Mark. *The Tragedy of Pudd'nhead Wilson: And the Comedy Those Extraordinary Twins*. Hartford, CT: American, 1894. Google Books. Accessed June 3, 2012. https://books.google.com.

Webb, Frank. *The Garies and Their Friends*. 1857. New York: Arno, 1969.

Williams, Gregory Howard. *Life on the Color Line: The True Story of a White Boy Who Discovered He Was Black*. New York: Plume, 1996.

Windley, Lathan A., comp. *Runaway Slave Advertisements: A Documentary History from the 1730s to 1790*, Volume 2, *Maryland*. Westport, CT: Greenwood, 1983.

Zackodnik, Teresa C. *The Mulatta and the Politics of Race*. Jackson: University of Mississippi Press, 2004.

CHAPTER 2

Passing for Postracial

Colorblind Reading Practices of Zombies, Sheriffs, and Slaveholders

CHRISTOPHER M. BROWN

In the second episode of the hit television series *The Walking Dead,* a survivor of the zombie apocalypse fires his rifle indiscriminately from the rooftop of an Atlanta office building at the "walkers" below. The shooter, Merle, is a caricature of a Southern racist: profane, violent, contemptuous of authority, indiscriminate in his prejudice. When one of his fellow survivors insists that he stop drawing attention to their location, Merle balks at taking orders from a "nigger" and attacks the lone black member of the group. Amid their fighting, Sheriff Rick Grimes intervenes, subduing and handcuffing Merle and pronouncing the new racial order of their postapocalyptic world: "Look here, Merle. Things are different now. There are no niggers anymore. No dumb-as-shit-inbred-white-trash-fools either. Only dark meat and white meat." This opening gambit in *The Walking Dead* suggests the kind of totalizing postracial narrative that has come to be familiar in our twenty-first-century moment: with the election of President Barack Hussein Obama, many Americans seem to believe that discrimination, prejudice, and raced subjectivities have become things of the past.[1] According to many critics, the series' ostensibly postracial (or colorblind, as some prefer) aesthetic is of a piece with a broader trend in today's culture, epitomized by the president himself, where racial difference goes unnoticed and audiences demand diverse casts and characters.[2] Shows like *The Walking Dead, Scandal,* and *Sleepy Hollow* arguably celebrate black characters without fetishizing race, seeming to suggest that skin color is a distinction without a difference.

But can it really be that the survivors in *The Walking Dead* are freed from their racialized ontologies and materialities? Or might it be that everyone's favorite zombie show embodies a different kind of racial ethos? Zombie stories, after all, often play on our anxieties about the loss of our humanity in the face of, well, you name it: nuclear Armageddon; political discord; daunting scientific progress; and the alienating effects of modernity, capitalism, the postmodern, and globalization (to name just a few). Could it be that a principal anxiety that motivates *The Walking Dead* is precisely the *loss* of racial identity? And that the loss of the particular knowledges that race affords us in interpreting the narratives of our lives—crucial epistemologies that tell us as much about where we have been as a nation as they do about where we are headed—risks a new order in which political commitment to substantive and systemic change is trumped by a superficial attention to form?

Another zombie text, Colson Whitehead's 2011 *Zone One,* seems to suggest as much. Whitehead is, of course, no stranger to the politics and obligations of racial representation; his loosely autobiographical novel *Sag Harbor,* which recounts the coming-of-age summer of a black teenager in an all-black enclave in the Hamptons, seemed to capture the promise—and ambivalence—of "postblack" fiction in the minds of many critics.[3] And we might be forgiven for mistaking *Zone One* to be a kind of doubling down on the colorblind aesthetic. Recounting the immediate aftermath of a zombie-spawning virus and the government's attempts to reestablish order in Manhattan, the novel follows the travails of its chief protagonist, a racially unmarked survivor known to his fellow "sweepers" by his nickname, Mark Spitz. (Sweepers rid the island of zombie corpses.) Indeed, no one in the novel bears any racial designations or identifiers. *Zone One* is what Toni Morrison might call "an experiment in the removal of all racial codes from . . . narrative." (Morrison's own twinned texts—"Recitatif" (1983) and *Paradise* (1997)—are, of course, exemplars of the form.) The attentive reader suspects that something is being withheld, wonders whether Whitehead could really write a novel that flatly ignores race.[4] And in the only break in a text that seems to completely inhabit its commitment to colorblindness, our protagonist shares with Gary, his sweeper colleague, the story of how he came to be christened Mark Spitz. Trapped with another group of survivors by zombies, with the East River at their back, he chooses to battle his way through the crowd of undead rather than join his compatriots as they jumped into the water. He escapes, and as he tells Gary, his astonished friends mistakenly assume that he fought because the alternative was to drown:

> Here was one of the subordinate ironies in the nickname: He was anything but an Olympian. The medals awarded to Mark Spitz were stamped from discarded slag. Mark Spitz explained the reference of his sobriquet to Gary, adding, "Plus the black-people-can't-swim thing."
>
> "They can't? You can't?"
>
> "I can. A lot of us can. Could. It's a stereotype."
>
> "I hadn't heard that. But you have to learn how to swim some-time."
>
> "I tread water perfectly."[5]

Whitehead allows us only this single moment of recognition: our narrator is a black man but one whose racial identity has been stripped of its meaning in the face of the new zombie order. Gary's stark construction—"They can't? You can't?"—makes the disassociation of postapocalypse politics plain. But Mark Spitz is unconvinced; in 336 pages, only in this moment does he reveal any hint of his racial markedness, and yet

> [Mark Spitz] found it unlikely that Gary was not in ownership of a master list of racial, gender, and religious stereotypes, cross-indexed with corresponding punch lines as well as meta-textual dissection of those punch lines, but he did not press his friend. Chalk it up to morphine. There was a single Us now, reviling a single Them. Would the old bigotries be reborn as well, when they cleared out this Zone, and the next, and so on, and they were packed together again, tight and suffocating on top of each other? Or was that particular bramble of animosities, fears, and envies impossible to recreate? If they could bring back paperwork, Mark Spitz thought, they could certainly reanimate prejudice, parking tickets, and reruns.
>
> There were plenty of things in the world that deserved to stay dead, yet they walked.[6]

Signifiers of race are withheld from us, and yet the protagonist's ostensible surrender of his blackness to the new postracial order is belied both by the racial knowledge embedded in his nickname and by his abiding faith in the "undead"-ness of these racial epistemologies. In other words, what I suggest here is that both Whitehead and Mark Spitz are merely performing their particular inhabitations of colorblindness.

I begin with zombies because they are such perfect vessels through which to imagine the negation of difference. In both *The Walking Dead* and *Zone One*, the post–zombie apocalypse enables an effacement of racial knowledge that—depending on one's politics—reads as either ironic or aspirational. And as a critic with a particular interest in the racial epistemologies of the law, I'm intrigued by the analogic potential afforded by the genre, where zombies are to postracial politics what colorblind jurisprudence is to the realization of racial justice in the United States. The zombies in these texts, to put it more plainly, seem to assuage our racial anxieties, to quiet the histories and logics and affects that linger from an earlier moment, to reassure us that the fictions by which we now order our lives are somehow different. So, too, with the legal rationales that have, in short order, banned the consideration of race in college admissions, gutted the Voting Rights Act, and turned a blind eye to the violence done to black bodies at the hands of the state. As *The Walking Dead* and *Zone One* seem to suggest, perhaps the law, too, is only passing as postracial. And in this chapter I encourage us to think about contemporary neo-passing narratives such as these as offering some of the sharpest rebuttals—both formally and tropologically—to contemporary colorblind reading practices, particularly those that are proliferating in the law.

I start with Ken Warren's *What Was African American Literature?*, which I think is a terrific example of the kind of colorblindness that we see ascendant in both literary and legal criticism in recent days.[7] Warren's claim goes like this: because what we now call "African American literature" was born out of a socio-legal-political crisis for blacks as to how to respond to the age of constitutionally sanctioned racial discrimination known as Jim Crow, the undoing of that legal regime and its attendant "problem of the color line" mean that today's texts written by African American authors no longer confront that same problem and as such can no longer be a part of that earlier literary tradition. Warren argues that texts by black authors written since the Supreme Court's 1954 decision in *Brown v. Board of Education* lack any unifying racial theme or form and that as the political impetus behind "African American literature" as a genre fell away, so, too, has the efficacy of reading such texts through the lens of race. Read in the context of Warren's claim, the argument of this chapter is quite simple: by reading *without* attention to race, we—literary and legal critics alike—lose an extraordinary insight into the histories and identities that shape the narratives we tell about ourselves and our nation.

So what, Warren asks, "is the contemporary vitality of race?" And to put it in terms of the literature that Warren is reading, what is the contemporary vitality of a text like *Invisible Man*, a novel whose political urgency, to Warren's mind, evaporated just a few years after its 1952 publication with the Court's landmark ruling in *Brown*? Now Warren's book is compelling for my purposes on several levels. First, he explicitly positions the resonance of the African

American literary project as *legal* and asks us to think about the continuing vitality of black literature in terms of the law. And, second, while one can disagree with Warren's conclusions about the political and historical status of the black subject and the black literary text in the post–Jim Crow moment—and this is where most critical responses to Warren's argument have resided—he also implicitly suggests a genuine aesthetic break between the African American literary texts of the long Jim Crow era and those of today. But it is precisely in the terms of the aesthetic that some of today's most politically engaged African American literary texts challenge Warren's thesis and the logic of postracialism more broadly. The racial formalism that marks *What Was African American Literature?* would not seem to be able to account for the recent proliferation of neo-passing narratives, stories about the performance of racial identity that invoke what our editors' introduction describes as "the complex racial politics that defined classic passing narratives" but which seem to take as their point of departure precisely the politics of the present moment and the vexed question of the ways in which race might still matter.

Colorblind Justice

Like our zombie texts, Edward P. Jones's 2003 Pulitzer prize–winning novel *The Known World* constructs a quintessentially postracial passing narrative—with a twist.[8] Jones tells the story of Henry Townsend, an ambitious antebellum Virginia planter whose dynasty is quickly undone by the hubris of his curious passing conceit: he is a black man who imagines that the law will protect his right to own slaves just as it would a white man's. Joining legal and literary hermeneutics around the question of just what it means to be "colorblind," *The Known World* interrogates the efficacy of beyond-ing race. And while so many of the texts of our postracial moment ask us to consider the ways in which race is no longer relevant to how we understand the world around us, I'd like to suggest that Jones's novel poses precisely the opposite query. Indeed, *The Known World* narrates the spectacular *failure* of a colorblind experiment, wondering what is lost to readers—of literature and of the law—when one pledges fidelity to the politics of the postracial. Reasoning that "I ain't done nothing no white man wouldn't do," the paradox of Jones's protagonist's ambition to own slaves propels the illogic of mid-nineteenth-century racial formalisms into our present moment. The law's racial formalism in *The Known World* professes to treat black owners of slaves the same as white owners, maintaining the distinction between master and property notwithstanding the master's race. What's more, by allowing free blacks to own slaves, the law conforms to its own sense of itself.

It provides the illusion of an integrity and an internal consistency that a fuller vision of the law's reality would undermine, and the protection of an abstract idea—colorblindness—in the face of the absurdity of its consequences.

Jones's formal passing conceit, which relies on a black character's faith that he won't be read as black, joins his novel with works like Danzy Senna's *Caucasia,* Toni Morrison's *Paradise,* Richard Powers's *The Time of Our Singing,* and Colson Whitehead's *John Henry Days* as texts that insist we interrogate the loss attendant to an interpretive praxis that eschews race, and it seems difficult to read *The Known World* as something other than a response to *legal* colorblind reading practices, in particular. What kind of knowledge is the law interested in, the novel asks, if it closes itself off from this particular way of knowing?

The Known World explores precisely this epistemology: the kinds of knowledge that the law and race can share and the kinds of knowledge that remain hidden, unavailable, indecipherable. Jones's novel leverages the trope of blindness in exploring how enslaved African Americans find themselves the unlikely property of black masters and how both the law and its subjects—black and white—"learn" to see some things but not others. Its many narrative threads connect through Townsend, whose plantation collapses following his early death. *The Known World* imagines the law's omnipresence in the life of southern blacks, free and enslaved: from the local figures of the sheriff and the slave patrollers to the 1806 Expulsion Act that required freed slaves to leave the state within twelve months of manumission or their condition would revert to property (because "freed Negroes lack the 'natural controls' put on a slave")[9] to the stunning consequences of the 1840 census for Jones's fictional Manchester County (where the children of white men and Indian women are labeled slaves because they were "too dark" to be considered anything other than black). And yet, at the same time, the book explores those aspects of the life under slavery that the law cannot, or will not, see: a sheriff's lust for the black slave he raised as a daughter, the sanity of a mad woman, the motivations of the many blacks who flee from their "homes" to escape to the North, the kidnapping of free blacks to be sold back into slavery. The juxtaposition of these two kinds of knowledge reveals the institutional blindness of the law, an inability—or a refusal?—to see how color functions in a world ordered by race.

This unintelligibility—what we might even call an incommensurability—appears again and again in *The Known World* as a kind of blindness, one that is embedded in the law. Henry Townsend—born a slave to William Robbins, the county's most esteemed white man, but bought out of slavery by his father, Augustus—remakes himself in his master's (rather than his father's) image: as an ostensibly benevolent owner of thirty-three of his own slaves, his race ignored in the eyes of the law so long as he can manage his property like a white man. Robbins tells Henry after he buys Moses, his first slave, that

> "The law will protect you as a master to your slave, and it will not flinch when it protects you. That protection lasts from here"—and he pointed to an imaginary place in the road—"all the way to the death of that property"—and he pointed to a place a few feet from the first place. "But the law expects you to know what is master and what is slave. *And it does not matter if you are not much darker than your slave. The law is blind to that. You are the master and that is all the law wants to know.* The law will come to you and stand behind you. But if you roll around and be a playmate to your property, and your property turns around and bites you, the law will come to you still, but it will not come with the full heart and all the deliberate speed that you need. You will have failed in your part of the bargain. You will have pointed to the line that separates you from your property and told your property that the line does not matter."[10]

Here one might recall the "baseball umpire" analogy offered by Chief Justice nominee John G. Roberts Jr. during his 2005 confirmation hearing: "Judges are like umpires. Umpires don't make the rules; they apply them. The role of an umpire and a judge is critical. They make sure everybody plays by the rules. But it is a limited role."[11] But the decision to exclude race from one's rubric of interpretation is, of course, a political decision in its own right. Where colorblind rhetoric, perhaps most famously in the polemics of Justice John M. Harlan's *Plessy* dissent and Martin Luther King Jr.'s I Have a Dream speech, once sounded a righteous rejoinder to the injustice of white supremacy and demanded racial progress, today it seems to echo in the public consciousness as an empty signifier, a politics that draws its force precisely from its disassociation from the term's historical origins.

The very first cases interpreting the meaning of the Fourteenth Amendment following its enactment in 1868 invoked the broad hermeneutic question of what to do with race as a jurisprudential question. Notwithstanding the legislative history of the Civil War Amendments, the Court rejected the notion that federal legislation might be enacted specifically for the benefit of blacks. Indeed, in *The Civil Rights Cases* in 1883, the Court struck down as unconstitutional the criminalization of discrimination in privately owned "public accommodations," holding that the Fourteenth Amendment applied only to official state conduct and prohibited governmental interference with private contractual relations. Justice Joseph P. Bradley's majority opinion in *The Civil Rights Cases* articulated, for the first time, the Court's antipathy to legislation extending protections to black people in the wake of the country's quite recent history of slavery. Not even twenty years had passed since the Emancipation, yet Bradley wrote: "When a man has emerged from slavery and by the aid of beneficent legislation has shaken off the inseparable concomitants of that state, there must be some stage in the progress of his elevation when he takes the rights of a mere citizen and *ceases to be the special favorite of the law* and when his rights as a citizen or a man are to be protected in the ordinary mode by which other men's rights are to be protected."[12] The tortured history of "colorblindness" in the rhetoric of the Supreme Court begins with these words, which, incredibly and prematurely, declared the effects of state-sanctioned discrimination to have passed. Moreover, Bradley's brand of interpretation makes plain the debilitating isomorphism of formalism and colorblindness: not only are colorblind reading practices the paradigmatic formalism but all interpretive formalisms also necessarily implicate the racializing consequences of colorblindness.

The dissent of Justice Clarence Thomas in *Grutter v. Bollinger*, the Supreme Court's 2003 opinion addressing the constitutionality of the University of Michigan Law School's race-conscious admission policy and the first opinion by the Court to address affirmative action in the university context since 1978, could well have been written by Bradley. Thomas's dissenting opinion asserts that the majority affords undue deference to the state's justifications for its policies, and he begins with a quote from a speech given by Frederick Douglass in 1865:

> The American people have always been anxious to know what they shall do with us. . . . I have had but one answer from the beginning. Do nothing with us! . . . Let him alone! . . . Your interference is doing us positive injury.[13]

With these words Thomas positions Douglass as an ally in the colorblindness debate. Of course, Douglass was no such thing. Thomas's ellipses disingenuously mask the import of Douglass's entreaty. Far from forbidding the state to take remedial action for the harms suffered by blacks, Douglass was asking for an end to the virulent discrimination and bias that continued to be prevalent in the wake of emancipation:

> Let him alone! If you see him on his way to school, let him alone, don't disturb him! If you see him going to the dinner-table at a hotel, let him go! If you see him going to the ballot-box, let him alone, don't disturb him! If you see him going into a work-shop, just let him alone—your interference is doing him a positive injury.[14]

Douglass continued that without freedom from such discrimination, without the franchise, without true equality, the black race's "liberty is a mockery."[15]

His refusal to accept the guarantee of a formal liberty, a liberty in name only, lays bare the dramatic deficiency of a formalist interpretive methodology that would equate emancipation with freedom.

And yet, Thomas goes on, a century and a half later, to argue:

> The Constitution abhors classifications based on race, not only because those classifications can harm favored races or are based on illegitimate motives, but also because every time the government places citizens on racial registers and makes race relevant to the provision of burdens or benefits, it demeans us all.[16]

Here, Thomas relies on the "colorblind" rationale of Harlan's famous *Plessy* dissent, which is oft quoted by racial formalists, not least of all Justices Antonin Scalia and Thomas, for its formulation of a constitutional rule that would forbid any differentiation in the law premised on race: "Our Constitution is color-blind, and neither knows nor tolerates classes among citizens." Seldom acknowledged by those who would rely on such language is its very historicity. Borrowing the notion of colorblindness from the petitioner's brief, authored by Albion Winegar Tourgée—a noted civil rights proponent, lawyer, and author—Harlan ignores the pedigree of Tourgée's phrase. Tourgée himself first used the term in his 1880 novel *Bricks without Straw,* characterizing the trope of colorblindness as a "defect that does not allow people to see the actual condition" of blacks.[17] Tourgée, anticipating and rebutting Justice Bradley's reasoning in *The Civil Rights Cases* that blacks had been elevated to the status of equals by virtue of the Civil War Amendments, proclaims, "Right he had, in the abstract; in the concrete, none. Justice would not hear his voice. The law was still color-blinded by the past."[18] The signature phrase of Harlan's dissent, relied upon by today's racial formalists, makes precisely the opposite point they intend.

The law's colorblindness in *The Known World* professes to treat black owners of slaves the same as white owners, maintaining the distinction between master and property notwithstanding the master's race. What does this colorblindness accomplish? First, the law allows and even protects Henry in his reproduction of the order of the plantocracy. Property rules established racial hierarchy, and even property ownership that "transgressed the customary boundaries of race" reinscribed the hegemony of capital.[19] Indeed, Robbins petitions the state assembly to allow Augustus Townsend to remain in the state following his manumission, if only because the graceful furniture and elaborately carved walking sticks Augustus composed were prized possessions for the county's elite. And Henry's own emerging skill as Robbins's groom and as a shoemaker reveals the dark counterpoint to capital's prominence, Henry's increasing value as a slave: "The cost of [Henry's competence] was not fixed and because it was fluid, it was whatever the market would bear and all of that burden would fall upon" Henry's parents, impeding their ambition to buy Henry's freedom. And just as it remains unremarked upon by the narrator, Henry's own labor as a slave—standing in the cold rain awaiting Robbins's morning returns from his liaisons with his black mistress—is unacknowledged by his master, and "[i]f the horse recognized the boy from all the work he did, it never showed."[20]

The ostensible "fairness" of the law of Manchester County—and its "equal" treatment of black and white—is metaphorized in the figure of John Skiffington, William Robbins's handpicked sheriff. A pious man whose wife, Winifred, was raised a Philadelphia Quaker and an abolitionist, Skiffington's own sense of the law's justice is continually compromised—and occasionally blinded—by his fidelity to the people he is tasked with protecting and by the juxtaposition of the peculiar institution with the dictates of his conscience. After his brother, Counsel, gives John and Winifred a black servant as a wedding gift, the newlyweds struggle with how to negotiate the competing knowledges of North and South, free and slave, fairness and injustice:

> Despite vowing never to own a slave, Skiffington had no trouble doing his job to keep the institution of slavery going, an institution even God himself had sanctioned throughout the Bible. Skiffington had learned from his father how much solace there was in separating God's law from Caesar's law. . . . As long as Skiffington and Winifred lived within the light that came from God's law, from the Bible, nothing on earth, not even his duty as a sheriff to the Caesars, could deny them the kingdom of God. "We will not own slaves," Skiffington promised God, and he promised each morning he went to his knees to pray. Though everyone in the county saw Minerva the wedding present as their property, the Skiffingtons did not feel that they owned her, not in the way whites and a few blacks owned slaves.

But, of course, they do own Minerva, and the decision about how to handle "the wedding gift" reveals precisely the kind of rationalizations that undo aspirations toward justice: "She might be better off with us than anywhere else," Skiffington consoles Winifred when she confesses her discomfort on their wedding night. Here his concern for the young black girl's future is undermined by his attention to his own, as he wonders "not only about what would happen if they sold her into God knows what but what their neighbors might say if they gave her to Winifred's people for a life in the North: Deputy John Skiffington, once a good man, but now siding with the outsiders, and northern ones at that. Skiffington asked his wife, 'Are you and me not good people?'"[21] Minerva remains their servant—and increasingly the object of Skiffington's desire—until she escapes from Winifred and assumes the life of a free woman of color in Philadelphia.

The Known World contrasts these two Skiffingtons to great effect: one a wise sheriff, politically attuned and deft at managing those both above and below his class and rank; the other increasingly mired in the unfurling collapse of Henry Townsend's—and, indeed, the antebellum South's—halting attempts to reconcile the competing logics of law and race. In legal matters uncomplicated by race, Skiffington demonstrates the law's potential for equity and its oft-unrealized capacity to see beyond the self-imposed limits on its vision. Adjudicating a dispute between two neighbors over the sale of a cow—a cow the seller knew produced no milk—Skiffington tells them, "I take no side but the right one."[22] Skiffington knows the seller to be a cheat and a liar, suspects the seller tried to swindle the buyer, and is quietly tickled by the cow's sudden and newfound supply of milk, which has the seller demanding the cow back. Skiffington's resolution is Solomonic: the sale stands, but the seller can fill two buckets twice a week with the cow's milk. "There would be no more trouble with the cow," the narrator assures us. Without the complexities and complications of race, the law—Skiffington—confidently and successfully resolves a dispute that was nearing violence, and he does so by looking outside the four corners of a contract and to fuller notions of equity.

Sheriff Skiffington's turn to confront the problem of runaway slaves, then, is complicated by an inversion of the usual scenario, one in which the law is both complicit and at the same time wholly impotent to redress: the kidnapping of Augustus Townsend, a free black man. Three of Skiffington's slave patrollers meet Augustus and his wagon on the road in the dark of the evening. Offended at Augustus's attempt at small talk, one of the patrollers invokes the authority of his position—"This ain't no damn church social. . . . This is the law's business"—and rejects the old man's free papers, though he had seen them many times before: "You ain't free less me and the law say you free." These three men, though agents of the law, have already rejected the legalistic paradox at the novel's center, in which Henry Townsend's race is ignored in the service of the law's veneration of property as an abstract right. "This is what happens," they say among themselves earlier in the story while confronting another runaway, "when you give niggers the same rights as a white man." And as Augustus Townsend stands before them, they reject it again, one of the patrollers eating Augustus's free papers and then selling him to a passing slave trader. When another patroller protests that the whole town knows Augustus to be free, the first replies, "Don't tell me what I know and don't know."[23] The poor white slave patroller here makes a doubled claim. First, he revels in the difference between the law's knowledge and other competing knowledges, in this instance prioritizing legal form over local truth. Second, he articulates a larger claim that appears in the novel again and again: what the law can know is delimited by its failure to understand the anxieties of race.

And it is perhaps not surprising that it is in the novel's own form that we find explicit comparisons between what and how the law knows (and doesn't know) the black characters that populate the story. *The Known World* repeatedly introduces extratextual artifacts—statutes, academic texts, historical documents, and business ledgers—the kind of seemingly objective textual evidence that informs legal reasoning. And then it deconstructs them. The census that taxonomizes many of the novel's characters, for example, reveals that the law is interested only in counting who lives in what house and who is mother or father to which and how many children. It cannot tell us, as Jones's narrator does, "that black children were [a white man's] flesh and blood and that he traveled into Manchester because he loved their mother far more than anything he could name and that, in his quieter moments, after the storms in his head, he feared that he was losing his mind because of that love."[24] The law is unable—or unwilling—to invest itself in this kind of affect. As a result, the law's consequences, or, more aptly, the subjects who suffer those consequences, become, in a very real way, unintelligible to the law, and, of course, the law is rendered similarly unintelligible to those same people.

If it is indeed true that the law lacks a vocabulary, and even a logic, for recognizing the ways in which justice and equality and freedom fail for African Americans and if it is also true that the failure of colorblind legal praxis has been an insidious fact of life for blacks in the United States, then it seems essential for any understanding of the literature of the African American experience that we theorize how this fundamental disjuncture has come to shape its texts: both in thinking about what that aesthetic relationship might look like and indeed the politics suggested by the very form of these neo-passing narratives and in how literary figures of incommensurability signify on the seeming impossibility of bridging the distance between the law's idea of itself and the black writer's representation of it. Does *The Known World* suggest to us that the incommensurable is a kind of foil to colorblind reading practices?

If that's so, can the incommensurable help us to understand the relationship between law and the tradition of African American letters, in particular, and the structure of racialized subjectivity, more generally? The incommensurable—what historian and philosopher Thomas S. Kuhn calls knowledges that live "in different worlds"—then, is revealed in the collision of inapposite perceptions, singular axes of experience, unparalleled philosophies.[25] It is the distance between two languages that, more than simply signifying differently, fail even to recognize a common referent. Commensurability lies at the heart of the law. Commensurability, in many ways, is exactly the object of any system of law and may indeed even be the object of contemporary colorblind reading practices. The universal language of law—its formal properties, its proportionality, its objectivity—professes to make competing particularities commensurable and then compares them. Yet, race and its attendant complications—its subjectivities, its histories, its own competing logics—so often resist what literary critic Wai Chi Dimock has called the law's ratios and equivalences and exchanges.

Now if it's the case, as I've suggested, that the registers of the two fields of law and literature simply do not operate on the same terms, then it also seems to me that this particular incommensurability has produced a richly productive tension in the tradition of black letters and offers a way to understand many of the predominant but under-read thematic in its texts: madness, betrayal, the absurd, and, of course, blindness. The law's tortured history with race in the United States is marked by a certain kind of incommensurability: the illogic of the commodification of the enslaved body, the division of the antebellum nation into separate free and slave states, caste laws that meant a person was white in North Carolina but a slave in Georgia, the legal fact of Jim Crow. And the double character of the law—its professed neutrality and impartiality in the face of two centuries of legally sanctioned racial apartheid—testifies to the folly of such a thing as separate but equal.

But what of the literature? I think that the law has contributed in a profound way to how racial difference is represented in cultural production, and the texts of the African American literary tradition—and, in particular, the neo-passing narratives that are the subject of this volume—find themselves again and again taking up the paradoxes and contradictions of our racialized legal history. In its encounters with the law is where the literature most often takes on a madness of its own. It is the inability—and, indeed, the impossibility—of assimilating the twisted logics of racialized law into the narratives of their lives that so often lead black narratives and black protagonists to this kind of madness. Embedded in the idea of the incommensurable is a fundamental disjuncture between legal and literary narratives—competing implications about property and hermeneutics and liberty and justice. Legal and literary critics are surely interested in decidedly different things about it, but in that comparison lies the source of a richly productive literary rendering of the incommensurability of law and of black life under the law.

Edward Jones invests the trajectory of such a world in the character of Alice Night, an enslaved woman on the Townsend plantation who people said lost her mind after being kicked in the head by a mule. Henry leverages her madness, recognizing that she's a good worker and "a woman of half a mind had been so much cheaper to buy than one with a whole mind." But he is blind to the efficacy of her madness and to how Alice leverages it to transgress the order of slavery. The patrollers explain it as a failure of law: "This is what happens, they said among themselves, when you give niggers the same rights as a white man." But Alice's madness enables her to invert the received logic of a world ordered by legally sanctioned slavery: she is able to wander at night without a pass (learning every nook and cranny of the land in anticipation of her eventual escape), speak truth to whites (God would "toss them into hell with no more thought than a woman dropping strawberries into a cup of tea"), and reverse the sexual violence of slavery (she grabs the patrollers' crotches and threatens to take them away with her).[26] Jones embeds in Alice the anxiety of proslavery whites (and blacks) that the rationality of their racial order can be undone. Alice flaunts her disregard of the conventions of the antebellum South, a fool speaking truth to power.

Henry Townsend's brother-in-law Calvin, another black owner of slaves, finally discovers Alice in Washington, D.C. She has crafted two tapestries after her escape that are displayed in an exhibit hall; each captures, in devastating detail, the history of Manchester County and of the Townsend plantation, a vision of "what God sees when he looks down."[27] Calvin recollects his role in building the Townsend plantation and confesses to his sister Caldonia that Alice's art leaves him chastened: enslaving his own people, he realizes, perhaps means he is more culpable for the crime of slavery than even someone like William Robbins. It is through Alice and her art that Calvin—and we—can apprehend the extraordinary constraint that this kind of blindness entails, and the difference between what Alice can see and the law can see. Rather than a negation, *The Known World* concludes with a hermeneutic knot, a text within a text that demands to be judged precisely through the lens of race.

Notes

1. Even President Obama himself has steadfastly refused to be defined in racial terms. Cillizza, "Obama's Vision."

2. Blake, "Post-Racial Revolution."

3. Whitehead was in good company: the sometimes ambiguous racial politics of novelists as accomplished as Zadie Smith and Percival Everett often leave critics untethered. Touré, "Visible Young Man."

4. Anyone who has read Whitehead's perfect satire of our self-congratulation following the 2008 election knows the answer before the question is even asked. Whitehead, "Year of Living Postracially."

5. Whitehead, *Zone One*, 231.

6. Ibid.

7. Warren, *What Was African American Literature?* Warren argues that what we now know as African American literature was in fact a political and historical enterprise "that gained its coherence as an undertaking in the social world defined by the system of Jim Crow segregation" (1). It "took [its] shape . . . [in response to] the enforcement and justification of racial subordination and exploitation represented by Jim Crow," and it was only in response to the political exigencies of Jim Crow that nineteenth-century texts by black writers were assimilated into an African American canon. "[W]ith the legal demise of Jim Crow, the coherence of African American literature has been correspondingly, if sometimes imperceptibly, eroded as well" (2). As such, what we still *mistakenly* call African American literature refers to a now-defunct historical enterprise rather than "the ongoing expression of a distinct people" (8). The turn to other critical frames besides race—the diasporic, transatlantic, global—evidence an awareness that the distinctiveness of African American literature has waned. What's more, African American literature, in Warren's view, was never a "transhistorical" enterprise but only constituted itself as "a literary practice responsive to conditions that, by and large, no longer obtain" (9). The necessary condition of a tradition of African American literature was white skepticism of black competence, a premise that can no longer anchor a political project; and the paradox of African American literature was always that in accomplishing its political ends it would render itself obsolete (17, 18).

8. Jones, *Known World*.

9. Ibid., 15.

10. Ibid., 123, emphasis added.

11. Weber, "Umpires v. Judges."

12. *Civil Rights Cases*, 25, emphasis added.

13. *Grutter v. Bollinger*, 349–50 (J. Thomas, dissenting), ellipses in original.

14. Douglass, "What the Black Man Wants," 4:59, 68.

15. Ibid., 70.

16. *Grutter v. Bollinger*, 354.

17. Thomas, "*Plessy v. Ferguson*," 45, 62.

18. Tourgée, *Bricks without Straw*, 35.

19. Bassard, "Imagining Other Worlds," 408.

20. Jones, *Known World*, 17, 21.

21. Ibid., 43, 34.

22. Ibid., 358.

23. Ibid., 211, 13, 211.

24. Ibid., 21.

25. Kuhn, *Structure*, 149.

26. Jones, *Known World*, 13, 13, 12.

27. Ibid., 384.

Bibliography

Bassard, Katherine Clay. "Imagining Other Worlds: Race, Gender, and the 'Power Line' in Edward P. Jones's 'The Known World.'" *African American Review* 42, no. 3–4 (2008): 407–19.

Blake, John. "The Post-Racial Revolution Will Be Televised." *CNN*, March 23, 2014. Accessed October 20, 2014. http://www.cnn.com/2014/03/23/showbiz/sci-fi-post-racial/index.html.

Cillizza, Chris. "Obama's Vision of a Post-Racial America Looks Even More Distant Than Before." *Washington Post*, August 17, 2014. Accessed January 19, 2015. http://www.washingtonpost.com/.

Civil Rights Cases, The. 109 U.S. 3 (1883).

Douglass, Frederick. "What the Black Man Wants." In *The Frederick Douglass Papers*, edited by John W. Blassingame and John R. McKivigan, 4:59–70. New Haven, CT: Yale University Press, 1991.

Grutter v. Bollinger. 539 U.S. 306 (2003).

Jones, Edward. *The Known World*. New York: Amistad, 2004.

Kuhn, Thomas S. *The Structure of Scientific Revolutions*. 4th ed. Chicago: University of Chicago Press, 2012.

Thomas, Brook. "*Plessy v. Ferguson* and the Literary Imagination." *Cardozo Studies in Law and Literature* 9 (1997): 45–65.

Touré. "Visible Young Man." *New York Times*, May 3, 2009. Accessed October 31, 2014. http://www.nytimes.com/.

Tourgée, Albion W. *Bricks without Straw*. New York: Fords, Howard, and Hulbert, 1880.

Warren, Kenneth W. *What Was African American Literature?* Boston: Harvard University Press, 2011.

Weber, Bruce. "Umpires v. Judges." *New York Times*, July 12, 2009. Accessed October 31, 2014. http://www.nytimes.com/.

Whitehead, Colson. "The Year of Living Postracially." *New York Times*, November 4, 2009. Accessed October 31, 2014. http://www.nytimes.com/.

———. *Zone One*. New York: Anchor, 2012.

CHAPTER 3

Adam Mansbach's Postracial Imaginary in *Angry Black White Boy*

BRANDON J. MANNING

In the fall of 2014 I went to the Renegades of Rhythm concert that featured DJ Shadow and Cut Chemist, two white disc jockeys, who played and scratched Afrika Bambaataa's personal record collection. I had recently moved to the Las Vegas area with my family, and this was the first trip to a show on the strip as a local. The concert was in a venue that served gourmet Southern cuisine ($25 fried chicken). I stood there feeling the bass vibrate through the soles of my feet, looking at two DJs mixing up Bambaataa, who at the time was a visiting professor at Cornell University. The DJs mixed on six turntables for a Las Vegas crowd that was mostly white, middle, and upper class—an audience that excitedly yelled when the music said, "It all began in Africa." The DJs began to create a sonic space that historicized and contextualized Bambaataa's influences and, by extension, the influences for hip-hop. This sonic genealogy began with James Brown as digital images of graffiti scrolled across the jumbo screen behind the DJs. These images were followed by album art for the records they were playing as well as an assortment of subway trains and pictures of how-to pop-and-lock manuals—it was a postmodern pastiche of hip-hop culture. The scene reminded me of hip-hop's far-reaching impact as the music was sonically contorted, respected, commodified, and jammed by a younger whiter audience.

The experience prompted me to question if the afrofuturism embedded in Bambaataa's drums and vision revamped George S. Schuyler's *Black No More*

(1931) into a 2014 "white no more" or whether this was the progeny of Langston Hughes's "when the negro was in vogue."[1] All the while, I questioned what the convergence of deference, commodity, authority, and authenticity meant in this space—what it meant for the DJs or for Bambaataa. For the majority of the audience, I realized that this was merely a show, something to go to, something to consume, when they visited Las Vegas. The DJs recognized this point when they repeatedly asked the crowd to do their own research. However, I was more interested in the two white DJs and how they performed this deference, authority, and authenticity over the turntables. They played Bambaataa and the Soulsonic Force's "Looking for the Perfect Beat," the fifth track on *Planet Rock: The Album*, and I wondered what the perfect beat was for this audience in this moment. What bass, synthesizer, 808, or offbeat could capture the rhythm and the breaks of different bodies attempting to do different work because of their understanding of sociocultural traditions and movements? Was this a postracial groove?

By way of further examining these questions, I turn to Adam Mansbach's satirical novel *Angry Black White Boy or the Miscegenation of Macon Detornay* (2005).[2] Mansbach's novel takes place over the course of a year and follows the protagonist, Macon Detornay, a white freshman at Columbia University from the Boston suburbs. Macon identifies himself as a hip-hop head, graffiti artist, and black radical/militant. Mansbach's interest in exploring the interplay between identity formation and cultural appropriation with Macon Detornay creates a critical line of inquiry that echoes E. Patrick Johnson's opening questions in *Appropriating Blackness* (2003), "What happens when 'blackness' is embodied? What are the cultural, social, and political consequences of that embodiment in a racist society? Or, alternatively, how are the stakes changed when a 'white' body performs blackness?"[3] Most critical perspectives like that of Eric Lott in *Love and Theft* (1993) cite the legacy of minstrelsy as an early white expressive form that attempts to embody and perform blackness.[4] While this critical approach yields insightful analyses around the potentiality of such performances for black and white subjects alike, I question what it might mean to locate Mansbach's novel as a neo-passing narrative, instead. By neo-passing narrative, I mean a narrative that contemporizes the historical legacy of black bodies passing into the realm of whiteness as a means of negotiating and surviving the white-supremacist racial hierarchy of American racism. Devon W. Carbado and Mitu Gulati give a more contemporary understanding of passing by asserting that one can "partially pass . . . by affirmatively identifying or associating with institutions, cultural practices, and social activities that are stereotypically perceived to be white."[5] Although Carbado and Gulati focus on the traditional notion of passing as an act where the "outsider," to use their expression, is a person of color trying to pass into whiteness, I am choosing to use it in a broader context to think about Macon's desire to transcend whiteness into blackness and no longer be understood as "a white devil."[6] I reimagine this historical and literary trope, at the center of works like Nella Larsen's *Passing* (1929) and James Weldon Johnson's *The Autobiography of an Ex-colored Man* (1912), to consider how neo-passing narratives incorporate the nuance and complexities of the new millennium to the racial ideology of American passing.

In this chapter, I argue that Mansbach's novel serves as an exploration into a postracial imaginary that thinks about the future of resistance and race in America. Mansbach creates this postracial imaginary by juxtaposing the neo-passing site of Macon's identity formation with the racial logic and history of black people passing for white during the late nineteenth and early twentieth centuries. Mansbach's attention to Macon's white privilege makes this a post-racial project. Mansbach utilizes popular tropes from black satirists such as an investment in destabilizing the idea of race, an intraracial self-reflexivity that allows Mansbach to critique whiteness, and an awareness that the idea of race is both socially constructed as well as a sociocultural and political reality with real stakes for people of color. Thus, similar to DJ Shadow and Cut Chemist, *Angry Black White Boy* is Mansbach's performance of deference, authority, and authenticity to a black satirical tradition and as such functions as an aggregate of Schuyler, Fran Ross, Ishmael Reed, Percival Everett, Paul Beatty, and others in a nonappropriative, nonconsumptive, and nonexploitative way.

After a successful presidential campaign in 2008, the iconicity of the Obamas in Grant Park on election night engendered an American postracial imaginary that sought to look beyond race or, more aptly, in spite of race to a homogenous future free from the wounds of racism. Barack Hussein Obama's successful campaign marked a moment in history that sought to erase or resolve a racist past and to decentralize race and American racism from social, cultural, and political conversations for a utopic racial future. Within this formulation, the presidency, as an office, serves as a symbol of the highest success or actualization of the Civil Rights moment. Legal scholar Terry Smith succinctly defines postracialism as "one in which racial disparity persists but race as national issue falls out of vogue."[7] Smith's pragmatic definition of postracialism highlights an American racial ideology that at its core is hostile toward issues of race in a post–Civil Rights America and that uses Obama's presidency as a signpost of racial cohesion. Similarly, legal scholar Kimberlé Crenshaw plays with the utopic notion embedded within the rhetoric and ideological underpinnings of postracialism by referring to it as "the postracial Promised Land."[8] Crenshaw, a leading legal scholar, defines the phenomenon as "the idea that our basic quest for social justice is complete."[9]

Whereas Smith's and Crenshaw's definitions of postracialism, while different, both speak to dominant culture's similar utopic conclusion about the future possibility of race being a nonfactor, Mansbach's novel provides an alternative to thinking about postracialism in America—a way that centers those on the margins. For Mansbach, telling Macon's story and critiquing him at specific moments throughout the narrative allow Mansbach to conceptualize an understanding of postracialism that contradicts contemporary formulations of the term, and while Mansbach never specifically uses the term *postracial* in the novel, Macon consistently tries to and, arguably, succeeds in provoking a "racial apocalypse" in the form of a race riot and destabilizes whiteness through his own racial performance and political ideologies.[10]

For Macon, hip-hop serves as a conduit into black history, rage, and antiracist activism. For example, early in the novel as Macon is driving his taxicab, "The light clicked green and Red switched up the soundtrack, segueing into 'Days of Outrage, Operation Snatchback,' X-Clan's song about being assaulted by cops at the Yusef Hawkins rally on the Brooklyn Bridge."[11] Here, Mansbach uses X-Clan's song as a sonic space of legitimacy and authenticity for himself and for Macon. In addition, the song's history in telling the story of police brutality at a rally decrying police brutality and the wrongful death of Yusef Hawkins illustrates how resistance and rage serve as a central concept in hip-hop music and culture. In doing so, Mansbach embraces a history of conscious hip-hop that performs and encourages black rage. For bell hooks, there is political work in rage as "a necessary aspect of resistance struggle" and "as a catalyst inspiring courageous action."[12] By adopting that rage, Mansbach demonstrates how Macon's conception of racism and white privilege and desire for other white people to be critical in the same ways could potentially usher in a type postracial utopia.

In other words, by reading Macon's use of rage and self-reflexivity as neo-passing and as a precursor for a postracial imaginary, Mansbach combats the contemporary hegemonic notion of postracialism by attempting to represent a different kind of postracialism—one that interrogates the adoption of blackness as neo-passing. He is able to accomplish this by having Macon adopt a black cultural identity as a way of resisting white privilege. Indeed, there are pivotal moments throughout Mansbach's novel where Macon considers himself black or at least blacker than other characters. When attending a meeting held by a black student organization at Columbia, Macon thinks to himself, "He was blacker than each and every last one of these bourgeois motherfuckers," referring to the black students at the meeting.[13] Macon's treatment of blackness in the novel oscillates from deference to indignation depending upon how black characters fit into his fixed, overdetermined understanding of blackness. The illusion of blackness, for Macon, is that it is monolithic in its commitment to antiracism and the disenfranchised.

Mansbach's critique of Macon demonstrates that white people's proximity to black cultural production, as a form of neo-passing, is not inherently postracial. The liminal racial space that the title gestures toward—the angry "black" white boy—is one that Macon wants to claim as solely his own. For instance, Macon's authority, authenticity, and understanding toward blackness is something he feels that only he can claim: "He went to work constructing a rhetorical framework that would allow him to embrace the Five Percenter's truths without capitulating his soul: *White people aren't evil, but evil is white people.* There it was. Simple. Elegant. True. It bought Macon space to live in, to be special, angry, the exception, the crusader. The down whiteboy."[14] Mansbach outlines the possibility and failings of Macon's turn toward hip-hop and his "down-ness" as an act of resistance to white privilege when Mansbach says in an interview, "White kids trying to absolve their guilt over their whiteness by getting into hip hop is an interesting thing, and a moment fraught with possibility: They're getting involved in black culture . . . precisely because they understand the problematic nature of whiteness. But there are pitfalls . . . where you think you're the downest white boy ever and no one can tell you shit."[15] Although Mansbach demonstrates the dangers of neo-passing especially as it pertains to white performances of racial authenticity, he also suggests that this form of neo-passing does begin some of the work of acknowledging the presence and problems of whiteness.

Other white characters' ability to misrecognize Macon as black typifies the meticulous way that he shapes and performs his identity and also serves as a more direct way to imagine Mansbach's novel as a neo-passing narrative. In the first half of the novel, Macon drives a cab in New York City and robs some of his white wealthy passengers. However, it is also this moment, a moment where Macon is so enraged—presumably with a "black" rage—that he acts criminally to distance himself from other white people. The turning point for Macon is when he realizes that the white people that he has robbed thought that he was black. Unfortunately, his actions reinforce a stereotypical understanding of blackness for these white patrons whose conversations demonstrate their white-supremacist thinking. Mansbach's narration is worth quoting at length:

> He'd done it: found some kind of worm hole in the white psyche, some uncharted reflex, and here he stood, divorced from his own color by the violence and conviction of his actions. Those fools hadn't seen white knuckles gripping that gun. They couldn't. Their brains weren't wired to link whiteness to the words Macon had hurled at them, the fear he'd made them feel. It had to be a nigger. Macon was invisible. . . . Did the world merely call traitors to whiteness black? What was the turning point, the secret password, the moment when you were no longer recognized, the instant when your picture faded from the ferry pass and you had to stay on the island of Blackness forever or swim back on your own?[16]

Although Mansbach allows the reader to know that the white riders think Macon is black before Macon finds out, his narrative choice to portray this moment through a third-person narrator that ventriloquizes Macon's tone and unmediated thoughts is helpful for the reader. The choice to use the words *divorce* and *had to,* in the abstract, are equally as telling as the use of the *n*-word. Indeed, the choice to articulate Macon's assumed separation from whiteness and the force with which it is happening informs the way the reader understands Macon's anxiety around "leaving" whiteness. Similarly, the use of the *n*-word seems to be a sign of his departure of whiteness and his full ascension into blackness. In addition, the imagery of being marooned solidifies Macon's racial binary and his own anxiety toward performing race.

If we believe Mansbach's title to be true, then Macon is angry—very angry. Furthermore, the centrality of anger coupled with the liminality of Macon's racial performance suggests that anger is operating in two different ways in the text. On the one hand, Macon demonstrates that through his understanding of history and hip-hop, he can perform a sort of pseudoblack rage, and on the other hand, he is an angry, discontented white youth—an anger and, more important, the public performance of that anger that are symptomatic of his white privilege. bell hooks describes the variations of rage: "The rage of the oppressed is never the same as the rage of the privileged. One group can change their lot only by changing the system; the other hopes to be rewarded within the system. Public focus on black rage, the attempt to trivialize and dismiss it, must be subverted by public discourse about the pathology of white supremacy, the madness it creates."[17] Similarly, in *Angry White Men* (2013), Michael S. Kimmel locates anger as the underlying affective position of contemporary white masculinity. By analyzing the centrality of white men in American mass killings, the marketability and anger of political punditry, and other highly visible sites of white masculine hostility, Kimmel suggests, "It's that aggrieved entitlement that fuels their rage: once they were in power, they believe, but now they've been emasculated, their birth-right transferred to others who don't deserve it."[18] Macon's "aggrieved entitlement" is important to his adaptation and performance of a hip-hop masculinity.

Returning to that moment before Macon robs his first passengers, he is reminded of one of his high school tormentors, Scott. Macon's memory retells a moment in high school when Scott corners Macon because Macon hangs out with the black children at school: "[Macon] wanted to kill Scott Cartwright, hated himself because at that moment he cared what Scott Cartwright thought of him—felt ridiculous, ashamed. And yet Macon knew he'd courted this. He wanted his defection from whiteness and his acceptance by black people to be public, the subject of wonder and envy, anger and scorn."[19] Here, Macon's psyche suggests to the reader why he wants black people to accept him. If this moment is emblematic of a larger childhood narrative that situates his performance and acceptance of blackness as both a site of protection and derision, then the anger and zeal in which Macon appropriates this pseudoblackness is meant to protect him from the threat of white masculine violence. Miles White speaks to the cultural capital for white men performing a black masculine subjectivity: "In this new street theater of the racially absurd, the physical power, sexuality, and ability to inspire fear that black male bodies have historically conveyed become transferred onto white bodies in ways that usurp agency of the black body, exploits it as a site of social anxiety, and perpetuates its demonization."[20] For Macon, it is precisely this need to capitalize on the cool poses of black masculinity to help him through his adolescence as well as his own racial and historical consciousness and guilt. For instance, Macon thinks at one point, "Just being down with the brothers gave him a bigger dick by association, swelled his masculinity like it did that of every kid thugging it up in front of his bedroom mirror, rhyming along to a rap song."[21] Macon's commitment to antiracist activism is undone by his exploitative relationship to blackness.

Whereas Macon fails to acknowledge his white privilege and how it informs his antiracist activism and thereby fails to actualize Mansbach's idea of postracialism, Mansbach succeeds in performing his vision of postracialism by being critical of Macon's white privilege. In an interview, Mansbach states, "The main thing that Macon does that I want to be critical of is this idea that blackness is the opposite of white privilege. Because the true opposite of white privilege is the dismantling of white privilege."[22] Throughout the novel, Mansbach uses narration as a tool to critique Macon's white privilege, referring to him as "Flyboy raceman asshole" in order to demonstrate the failed potential of his antiracist activism.[23] Mansbach's omniscient third-person narrator both echoes Macon's problematic understanding of himself—one that occasionally uses the *n*-word and describes the extent to which Macon performs black authenticity but allows for this same narrator to refer to him as an "asshole." In this way the novel's narration is markedly different from Macon's first-person-narrator prologue, "Letter from a Birmingham Bus," in which his petulance and egotism are unmediated by a third-person narrator. Mansbach utilizes Dre and Nique, Macon's two black associates, to illustrate how Macon's white privilege is antithetical to his desire to transcend whiteness. Dre, who is characterized as "a stoic, amiable receptacle into which fake-empathetic whiteboys dumped their views, a priest who heard confessions and smoked joints with the sinners to absolve them," serves as a site where Mansbach critiques Macon's white guilt and misguided notions of authenticity.[24] Mansbach's strategic uses of the narrative voice and of Dre and Nique illustrate for the reader that Macon's neo-passing falls short of Mansbach's concept of a postracial imaginary.

Unlike Macon's inability to create coalitions, Mansbach's use of signifying and intertextuality makes the antiracist work of *Angry Black White Boy* conversant with broader African American literary and satirical traditions. In the prologue Macon says, "I was hoping someone would call me the white Bigger Thomas, but nobody had the nutsack even though it's an obvious comparison, what with Bigger being a chauffeur and me a cabbie. I talked a lot more shit than Bigger ever did, though. And I did what I did on purpose."[25] Here, Mansbach evokes Bigger Thomas, the protagonist of Richard Wright's *Native Son* (1940), through the only moment of first-person narration in the novel: the prologue. The use of Bigger is then twofold: for the reader, it signifies that both the writer and protagonist are well versed in an African American literary tradition, and for Mansbach, it serves as a way to characterize Macon's white privilege by appropriating a literary genealogy of black rage. It was Bigger's lack of privilege that Wright foregrounds in *Native Son*, thus when Macon evokes Bigger and says, "It's an obvious comparison," he does so without realizing how white privilege operates within America's racial landscape.[26] Similarly, the prologue's title, "Letter from a Birmingham Bus," demonstrates Macon's appropriation of Martin Luther King Jr.'s incarceration to juxtapose it with Macon's celebrity and people misunderstanding him. Furthermore, Macon's remark at the end of the prologue, "The question is not how I got this way, but how the rest of y'all didn't," demonstrates that his ignorance of white privilege is not limited to the specificity of his own neo-passing and misguided antiracist work but reveals a broader ignorance of the systemic nature of whiteness.[27]

African American satirists throughout the twentieth century and beyond have created a blueprint for troubling monolithic notions of race. Mansbach's use of satire and his engagement with a black satirical tradition in *Angry Black White Boy* signal his use of this blueprint to critique whiteness in the same ways that black satirists have provided social commentary about whiteness and blackness. Later in the novel, when asked on a television show who his favorite authors are, Macon responds, "Gunnar Kaufman, Raven Quickskill, and Daniel Vivaldo."[28] All three of these "authors" are characters in African American novels, two of them as protagonists in satirical novels. Gunnar Kaufman is the protagonist in Paul Beatty's *The White Boy Shuffle,* Raven Quickskill is the protagonist in Ishmael Reed's *Flight to Canada,* and Daniel Vivaldo is a main character in James Baldwin's *Another Country.* Here, Mansbach is signifying on the black satirical and literary traditions by evoking writers in metanarratives. "Signifyin(g)," as Henry Louis Gates Jr. articulates it, is a process of "repeating received tropes and narrative strategies with a difference . . . an extended commentary on the history of the black novel" and is an apt way to describe the work that Mansbach's intertextuality is doing in the novel.[29]

Mansbach's postracial signifying practices return to the ideological underpinnings of Schuyler's *Black No More*—specifically, Schuyler's nascent idea that blackness and, more broadly, race are socially constructed and not intrinsically tied to biological determinates.[30] *Black No More* is a satirical, science-fiction novel that demonstrates the allure of white privilege when a scientist, Dr. Crookman, creates a serum to turn black people white, thereby decimating vibrant black communities across America during the height of the Harlem Renaissance. Indeed, in the third and final section of *Angry Black White Boy,* Mansbach "repeats" and "extends" the theoretical framework about race in *Black No More* when Macon is introduced to a psychiatrist that is able to rid people's racial anxieties and identity formations. Whereas Dr. Crookman in *Black No More* creates a serum to turn black people white, Donner in *Angry Black White Boy* is a psychiatrist that uses "a combination of hypnosis, therapy, psychodrama, various re-acculturation techniques, to alter an individual's self-image."[31] By contemporizing Schuyler's disruption of essentialist notions of race, Mansbach is able to criticize Macon's attempt at black authenticity and his self-centered, white privileged form of antiracist activism. If *Black No More* is the quintessential passing narrative for the ways that it foregrounds passing at the epidermal level during Jim Crow, then Mansbach's psychological turn serves as an exemplary postracial neo-passing narrative for the ways that Mansbach extends the conversation on racial essentialism, authenticity, and privilege for the de facto racism of today.

Ultimately, Mansbach's postracial imaginary is realized by his authorial critique of Macon. In this way, Macon's neo-passing acts as Mansbach's cautionary tale for his reader. By centering Macon's failed potential, Mansbach intimates that the impetus and execution of antiracist work have to be a nonappropriative, nonconsumptive enterprise. In essence, Mansbach echoes Audre Lorde's claim that one cannot dismantle the master's house with the master's tools. Mansbach's tropological use of African American satire as a blueprint to critique America's racial ideology allows for Macon to be conversant with Stephen Jorgenson in Wallace Thurman's *Infants of the Spring* and other satirical critiques of white liberalism and antiracist work.[32]

Similar to Mansbach's use of hip-hop as an antiracist mechanism, it's the permanency of hip-hop in the Renegade of Rhythms concert that evokes this same conception of postracialism. By beginning the concert with "It All Began in Africa," DJ Shadow and Cut Chemist demonstrated that they were going to keep Bambaataa's politics central to the sonic space they were re-creating. On the tour's website, DJ Shadow states, "Bambaataa as artist, exploring the influence of his classics like 'Planet Rock'; Bambaataa as collector, and the genre-defining breaks he discovered; and Bambaataa as peacemaker and force for social change. He influenced an entire generation worldwide, so we feel a great obligation to get it right."[33] Furthermore, it is Afrika Bambaataa's afrofuturism that parallels the future potential of Mansbach's conception of postracialism. They exuded a deep knowledge, love, and respect for the music and for Bambaataa. Through the haze of a smoky stage, strobe lights, and scrolling hip-hop images on a giant screen, DJ Cut Chemist and DJ Shadow performed a postracial subjectivity for their audience while "Looking for the Perfect Beat."

Notes

1. Hughes, *Big Sea*, 228.
2. Mansbach, *Angry Black White Boy*.
3. Johnson, *Appropriating Blackness*, 2.
4. Lott, *Love and Theft*.
5. Carbado and Gulati, *Acting White?*, 29.
6. Ibid., 17.
7. Smith, *Barack Obama, Post-Racialism*, 1.
8. Crenshaw, "Racing to Post-Racialism."
9. Ibid.
10. Mansbach, *Angry Black White Boy*, 207.
11. Ibid., 18.
12. hooks, *Killing Rage*, 16.

13. Mansbach, *Angry Black White Boy*, 123.

14. Ibid., 18. The Five Percenters is a concept in the Nation of Islam that states only 5 percent of the population knows the truth about God and that all humankind derives from black people. Mansbach writes earlier in the novel, "Before he joined the five percent nation and gained Knowledge of self and realized that the Original Asiatic Black Man was the Maker, the Owner, the Cream of the Planet Earth, Father of Civilization and God of the Universe. Before he became part of the Five Percent of the population who overstood the Supreme Mathematics and threw off the shackles of mental slavery to become Poor Righteous Teachers." Ibid., 14.

15. Mansbach, "Whiteness Visible."

16. Ibid., 109.

17. hooks, *Killing Rage*, 30.

18. Kimmel, *Angry White Men*, 277.

19. Mansbach, *Angry Black White Boy*, 20.

20. White, *From Jim Crow to Jay-Z*, 105.

21. Mansbach, *Angry Black White Boy*, 180.

22. Mansbach, "Whiteness Visible."

23. Mansbach, *Angry Black White Boy*, 195.

24. Ibid., 31.

25. Ibid., 2–3.

26. Wright, *Native Son*.

27. Mansbach, *Angry Black White Boy*, 3.

28. Ibid., 196.

29. Gates, *Signifying Monkey*, 217.

30. Schuyler, *Black No More*.

31. Mansbach, *Angry Black White Boy*, 292.

32. Thurman, *Infants of the Spring*.

33. DJ Shadow, "Announcing Renegades."

Bibliography

Carbado, Devon W., and Mitu Gulati. *Acting White? Rethinking Race in "Post-Racial" America*. Oxford: Oxford University Press, 2015.

Crenshaw, Kimberlé. "Racing to Post-Racialism: Critical Race Theory, Constitutional Law, and Sustaining Communities." Lecture, California State University, Los Angeles, April 14, 2011.

DJ Shadow. "Announcing Renegades of Rhythm Tour This Fall w/Cut Chemist." *DJ Shadow*, June 16, 2014. Accessed February 16, 2015. http://djshadow.com.

Gates, Henry Louis, Jr. *The Signifying Monkey: A Theory of African-American Literary Criticism*. Oxford: Oxford University Press, 1988.

hooks, bell. *Killing Rage: Ending Racism*. New York: Holt, 1995.

Hughes, Langston. *The Big Sea*. 1940. New York: Hill and Wang, 1993.

Johnson, E. Patrick. *Appropriating Blackness: Performance and the Politics of Authenticity.* Durham, NC: Duke University Press, 2003.

Kimmel, Michael S. *Angry White Men: American Masculinity at the End of an Era.* New York: Nation, 2013.

Lott, Eric. *Love and Theft: Blackface Minstrelsy and the American Working Class.* Oxford: Oxford University Press, 1993.

Mansbach, Adam. *Angry Black White Boy or the Miscegenation of Macon Detornay: A Novel.* New York: Three Rivers, 2005.

———. "Whiteness Visible." Interview by Scott Thill. *Alternet,* May 5, 2005. Accessed January 8, 2015. http://www.alternet.org.

Schuyler, George S. *Black No More.* 1931. Boston: Northeastern University Press, 1989.

Smith, Terry. *Barack Obama, Post-Racialism, and the New Politics of Triangulation.* New York: Palgrave Macmillan, 2012.

Thurman, Wallace. *Infants of the Spring.* 1932. Boston: Northeastern University Press, 1992.

White, Miles. *From Jim Crow to Jay-Z: Race, Rap, and the Performance of Masculinity.* Urbana: University of Illinois Press, 2011.

Wright, Richard. *Native Son.* New York: Harper, 1940.

CHAPTER 4

Black President Bush

The Racial and Gender Politics behind Dave Chappelle's Presidential Drag

EDEN OSUCHA

Before the election of 2008 made the first African American president a historical reality, black presidents were an established trope of US popular culture. This figure belongs to an archive of national fantasy that charts a history of dominant discourses of the present, including the deep ambivalence, antipathy, and contradictory racializations that attend the public image of President Barack Hussein Obama. Its earliest notable instance is the 1933 Warner Brothers musical short *Rufus Jones for President,* in which the black-president trope operates on behalf of some of the crudest caricatures of the era's white-supremacist political imaginings.[1] Later in the twentieth century, the 1964 Irving Wallace novel *The Man* and its 1972 made-for-TV adaptation again present the black president as an emblem of impossibility. Whereas the incongruence of an African American president in *Rufus Jones* expresses the racist suppositions that shape its narrative and diegesis, in the book and the TV movie *The Man,* it is the insufficiency of the nation itself that finds expression through the trope. Since the 1990s, the trope has been refigured once again to convey "postracial" understandings of the politics of the present. For example, in the Fox television series 24, which aired from 2001 to 2010, David Palmer's nonchalance about his racial identity marks him as the president who just *happens* to be black. Now reinflected by the historic event of the Obama presidency, this fiction has helped construct "the black president" as the preeminent sign of the postracial in popular media.[2]

From Rufus Jones to David Palmer, the lineage of fictional black presidents that precede the Obama presidency outlines a history of presumptive racial progress. However, comedian Dave Chappelle's 2004 sketch "Black Bush" illuminates a very different history of the black president.[3] In the second season finale of his self-titled sketch comedy series, which ran from 2003 to 2006, Chappelle's performance as Black Bush reimagines then President George W. Bush as African American, mapping different aspects of black masculine vernacularities onto Bush's Iraq War policy and its justifications.[4] Invoking an exaggerated black hypermasculinity, Chappelle's provocative use of racial masquerade to portray the self-proclaimed "war president" mobilizes the black president as a figure of social critique, even as the era's postracial manifestations would seem to foreclose the trope's critical possibilities. Most obviously, this performance targets the Bush administration and its now discredited justifications for invading Iraq. However, it can also be read as a critique of the prevalent understanding of the black presidency of Obama as a postracial production, identifying the racial and gender logics that subtend this formulation. The black president, as a popular culture trope, is an ideal figure through which to reconsider the place of gender in the traditional passing narrative and its unsettling in the various representations of neo-passing studied in the current volume.

As I argue below, the Chappelle sketch exposes how popular culture's discourse of black presidentialism—which extends from fictional depictions to media treatments of Obama even prior to his election—variously trades upon the idea of racial passing. Traditional literary and cinematic treatments of the passing experience depend on the disjunction between the whiteness of the subject's bodily appearance and what the dominant culture's "one-drop" ideology construes as its "true" racial identity. Even though these passing narratives depend for their very coherence on a clearly demarcated, stable, and transparent color line, they suggest how through the very authority of its territorializations the color line gives rise to its own transgression,[5] enabling the light-skinned body's performed reification of whiteness to stand in for a concealed black identity. As clear examples of what this volume of essays terms *neo-passing* narratives, the post–Civil Rights era fictional black presidents examined in this essay invoke what the traditional passing narrative understands as the constitutive disconnect between its protagonist's appearance and presumed essence of their identity. In the case of the black-president trope, that dualism is recoded as the tension between the abstracted whiteness of the office of the presidency and black racial particularity. These post–Civil Rights fictions offer a distinct variation of the traditional passing narrative by interrogating the idea that in order to be legible as the president in the post–Civil Rights era, the invariably male black president must transcend his racial identity, such that his racial blackness is made to serve as the sign of its suppression.

The figure of the black president is apotheosized in its "postblack" archetype, which *24*'s Palmer exemplifies. The president's embodied blackness is presented, in such instances, as something of a visual catachresis; as in the conventional black-white construction of racial passing, here the *surface* of racial appearance chafes against the assumed *depth* of racialization. Played straight, the persona resolves this tension through its gendering, adopting codes of masculinity that emphasize the black president's incommensurability with popular tropes of blackness. Popular tropes that identify the black male body in visual culture with hypermasculinity, criminality, and social deviance provide the compositional elements of Chappelle's satirical portrait of Bush. And these tropes are explicitly eschewed in the characterization of Palmer, as played by actor Dennis Haysbert. In short, gender transacts the black president's pass, transforming racial identity from collectivized difference to a form of exceptionalism. His masculinity's articulation outside of popular codes of blackness signals the *not*-blackness that traditional depictions of racial passing convey through white embodiment. This marks an additional sense in which contemporary popular culture's black presidents participate in the neo-passing genre's broader revision of the traditional passing narrative. As Valerie Smith points out, the light-skinned, phenotypically ambiguous body—a "sig[n] of the inescapable fact of miscegenation"—grounds the intersections of race and gender in these earlier depictions, in which the freedom to pass, for female subjects, is associated with a dangerous sexual freedom and lack of domestic constraints.[6] By contrast, the texts I discuss all tie the visibility of race itself to sexual and gender performances that differently locate black male subjects in relation to the ideal of "presidentialism."

In a trenchant, black feminist critique of popular fictions featuring black presidents, Erica Edwards describes the contradictory political impulses that inscribe this figure in post–Civil Rights US culture as "a solution to the racial rift of the nation and as the dangerous reminder of that rift . . . as messianic figure who embodies the nation's most sacred ideals of liberty, brotherhood, and equality, while either banishing the threat or fulfilling the promise of black social protest."[7] At the turn of this most recent century, the black president most often serves as evidence that institutional racism has been overcome and that race is now politically irrelevant. Thus, in the case of Palmer of *24*, the precise point of his being written as black is that his *being* black is beside the point, an argument that also accounts for the great bulk of the media discourses surrounding President Obama's blackness.[8] In the public discourse of presidentialism, what Dana Nelson and Michael Warner variously describe as the mass iconicity of the body of the president projects white masculinity as the signature of national political authority. The racialization of the presidency establishes the grounds by which the African American president, in fiction and in real life, is interpellated as engaging in a form of racial passing, inasmuch as his identity as president is produced as a dissimulation of his blackness.

Although the postracial presidencies of contemporary popular culture—so ably decoded by Edwards—are well-known to contemporary viewers, less well-known is the *first* "first black president," played by a seven-year-old Sammy Davis Jr. in *Rufus Jones for President*. The genealogy of the black-president trope that extends from James Earl Jones's portrait of Douglass Dilman in the 1972 TV movie *The Man* through the contemporary postracial presidencies of *24* and films such as *Deep Impact* and *2012* seems discontinuous with this unambiguously racist text, in which the infantile President Rufus Jones conveys a "blackness" congenitally insufficient to the ideal of (white) national manhood that underlies the presidency. However, the logic of passing that underlies later popular depictions can be linked to *Rufus Jones*'s parodic treatment of black masculinity. Masculinity is the naturalized sign of presidentialism, but in *Rufus Jones*, it is thoroughly evacuated.[9] Not only is the first black president a frail and diminutive child (introduced, on screen, as a bawling victim of neighborhood bullies) but, once inaugurated, he cedes his putative political authority to his mother. The film effectively uncouples the black (male) presidency from black *masculinity* and its ascribed threat to the existing racial order.

The opening scene invokes this early musical revue's minstrel-stage affinities to frame the titular concept of President Jones as farcical. Rufus's mother, in headscarf and apron, looks the part of the archetypal mammy, an association the film reinforces by referring to her as such. And when we first see Rufus, he is wearing white cake frosting over the entire lower half of his face, courtesy of his tormentor, who complies with the mother's instruction to "give Rufus back his cake" (though not in the way she'd intended). The high-contrast stock used in this film makes Davis's skin look especially dark against the whiteness of the frosting. His mother comforts him with the promise that he will one day transcend his victim status by becoming a man no one can bully: the president. Rufus is incredulous until she explains that "as the book says"—meaning, the Constitution—"anyone who is born here can be president." "Ain't that some'in!" declares Rufus. The "darky" dialectic employed in the script of their extended exchange signals the difference between what "the book says" and what, in a still segregated United States, actually "is" and also the naïveté that precludes mother's and son's understanding this disparity. Dialect is also an aural signifier of blackface-performance tropes, inviting the audience to read in his incongruous appearance a form of inadvertent racial masquerade. A black president, Rufus's white "mask" suggests, is possible only as an absurd burlesquing of the real thing.

The entire sequence of performances that elaborate the dawn of the first African American presidency, from the election through his first meeting with Congress, is, literally, a child's fantasy—a dream that comes to Rufus while he dozes in his mother's lap. Comprising mostly song-and-dance routines, the extended dream sequence shows the state of the American nation when the "natural" arrangements of race and power as imagined by this film are inverted, and Rufus Jones becomes the first African American president. Rufus's campaign promises, "Two pork chops every time you vote!" and his mother personally offers voters fried chicken. The president is sworn into office with his hand on a telephone book, the conventional inauguration ceremony replaced by a song-and-tap-dance number in which the president is asked to uphold a series of what the film brazenly reputes to be African Americans' political aspirations: free pork chops, reduced tax on razors, padlocks removed from all chicken coops, and replacing the national anthem with "The Memphis Blues." Next we see legislators playing dice in the halls of an all-black Congress and members of the Senate searched for razors upon entrance. Rufus Jones's administration oversees the creation of new offices, such as a poultry commission entrusted with removing the locks from the nation's chicken coops. Collectively, these scenes indicate this short film's indebtedness to *Birth of a Nation* (1915) and its infamous portrait of the Reconstruction-era South Carolina statehouse as a haven of barefoot, chicken-eating, whisky-swilling, black legislators, lolling in their seats and leering at white women in the visitors' gallery.

Within the diegesis, Rufus Jones's youth and stature go unremarked, but their singularity in the film is a point of visual emphasis. In the alternative nation conjured by *Rufus Jones for President,* the whole of the civic culture and government offices are African American, but only the presidency is infantile. This symbolic infantilization is echoed in how presidential authority is subsumed within maternal authority as Rufus's mother appoints herself the nation's "presidencess." Transformed from the peasant archetype clad in headscarf and apron to an elegant, bejeweled figure in a sparkling evening gown and headpiece, it is she who becomes the face of the presidency, serving as the vehicle for the film's ugly jokes about loaded dice, chicken stealing, and watermelons, which she articulates as the central policy concerns of a black presidency. The president himself is given a fashion makeover that instructs the audience to read the presidencess's glamour as instrumental in the film's racial burlesque. In the dream, Rufus Jones's urchin rags are replaced with a formal tuxedo and top hat. Like other major studio productions of the era featuring African American performers, *Rufus Jones* transposes the black dandy from the minstrel-stage tradition of dressing blacked-up white performers in the vestiges of privilege and authority in order to naturalize the whiteness of the social offices invoked by its stock character.[10] As embodied by the diminutive Davis, the figure of the nouveau riche dandy simultaneously invokes the grandeur and propriety of the presidency and the absurdity of Rufus Jones's aspirations. Dandyism functions here in concert with Davis's short stature and singularity as the sole child performer in the political set pieces and with the towering presidencess's deformations of power. All are visual markers of the incommensurability the film's myriad racist jokes convey.

Although racial blackness is the defining trait of the trope of the black president, gender is key to the coherence of these representations because of the historic and naturalized maleness of the presidency.[11] What is perhaps most striking about Rufus Jones, when considered within the context of this genealogy, is how the character presents a black male president without imagining a black *man* as president, reflecting the film's provenance in a historical moment in which antiblack, often sexually motivated lynchings were still accepted practice in the South. The utter dissimulation of black manhood in *Rufus Jones for President* contains the perceived threat of black masculinity its inverted racial order would seem to invoke. Ironically, this overtly racist film in this way anticipates the postracial ideal contemporary media depictions promote, which construct "the black president" largely in isolation from the hyperbolized masculinities that otherwise figure in popular representations of black men and black male bodies. In repressing the black masculine, *Rufus Jones* inadvertently reveals the anxiety that attends even the fantasy of a black president in US popular culture in the historical moment of its production. It is from this vantage that the fiction of the black president looms on the horizon of political life—not as the final promise of American democracy but as a threat to that democracy.

Rufus Jones for President laughs at the election of a black president because to consider it seriously would be unbearable.[12] The black presidents that emerged in popular culture in the later twentieth century and early twenty-first century all in different ways engaged in aspects of passing—reconfiguring and/or interrogating gendered codes of "race," if not always racial hierarchy itself, and drawing attention to the historical function of the US president as an ur-symbol of white supremacy. Rufus Jones, by contrast, ascends the presidency without crossing or even troubling the color line. Indeed, through the film's dark farce, the color line seems only more deeply entrenched; in keeping with this message, the refrain of the mother's lullaby that precipitates Rufus Jones's presidential dreaming is, "Stay on your own side of the fence." The film thus presents an emblem of the unimaginable, exorcising through the crude comedy of its visual invective a phantasm of black political and symbolic power that vexes the white imagination. It's hardly surprising, then, that a black president does not resurface in the nation's popular culture until 1972—nearly four decades after the release of *Rufus Jones for President*. A somber political drama, the made-for-television film *The Man*'s historic remove from its predecessor is registered in how starkly its tone and style contrast with the earlier film's musical comedy of stale racial caricatures. Made in the wake of the Civil Rights Movement's most celebrated gains, *The Man* uses the trope of the black presidency to highlight the persistence of racial strife and inequality beyond the formal dismantling of Jim Crow segregation. Postracial fictions conceive the black presidency as repairing the national rift of race, but that salvific promise is predicated on the electoral process—that is, an African American president having been elected to the office. With its unusual premise that has an African American senator succeeding rather than elected to the office, *The Man* constructs a black president as a critique of the pervasive and systemic racism that would have precluded his election. This president, in other words, is both a sign of racial division and of the potential for reconciliation. In its ambivalence, black presidentialism in the novel (and, likewise, its televisual adaptation) echoes the traditional passing narrative, in which the individual passing subject's transgression of racial caste both subverts the color line and reinforces it.

As in Wallace's 1964 novel, the movie *The Man* dramatizes an unlikely turn of events whereby the president pro tempore of the Senate, Douglass Dilman, assumes the office of the presidency after the US president and Speaker of the House of Representatives are killed in a freak accident and an elderly and infirm vice president decides he is too disabled and ill to serve.[13] Dilman's leadership position in the Senate is itself a product of tokenism, intended by his colleagues to appease activist demands without achieving meaningful political change; "president pro tempore" sounds impressive but is a largely ceremonial title, designating an alternate to preside over the Senate in the absence of the vice president and third place in the line of presidential succession. No one is more surprised than Dilman himself when—quite reluctantly—he becomes the nation's first African American president. The book's title deploys a once-popular slang term for institutional or state authority; as the tenant of the nation's highest office, the US president is The Man personified. In postwar African American vernacular, *The Man* also denotes whites' collective domination and social privilege, a meaning that specifies the whiteness and the maleness of political authority. As the title of this novel and its adaptation, *The Man* thus ironically comments on Dilman's raced and gendered distance from the presidentialism he is called upon to inhabit.

By the logics of American racial hegemony that *The Man* seeks to expose, the black president of this text remains an incoherent figure, an occasion of crisis for both the nation and himself. Both versions stage this as, specifically, a crisis of masculinity, which finds resolution through what Jeff Smith, in his analysis of the book, describes as the "remasculation" of the protagonist.[14] As penned by Wallace, Douglass Dilman is an unmanly bundle of nerves, from the first morning of his presidency. The book is replete with instances in which Dilman is represented as anxious or queasy, easily living up to his general reputation among Washington insiders as a "stodgy, frightened Negro," a temperamentally conservative politician who "shiver[s]" at the news of the terrorist tactics of militant black nationalists in the United States. In the narrative, these affects, as Smith's reading demonstrates, align with a racialized rhetoric of manliness.[15] Dilman tells his closest confidant that in the public life of the nation, he is "not a human being . . . but a black man, meaning a half man."[16] Throughout, the mark of that mismeasure is what the text construes as an "unmanly" emotional style.

By the novel's conclusion, Dilman has triumphed over his political foes, the decisive "no" vote cast in his impeachment proceeding by a Senator who defends his choice by proclaiming, "President Dilman has shown us he is a man." Dilman himself affirms this pronouncement in his own self-description, following the proceedings, as "a person who only recently found out he has the right to perform as a man and not just a colored man." That the fate of his presidency would turn on his ability to "perform as a man" is presaged earlier in the text when at the height of the impeachment crisis, a garrulous but sage former president counsels him to "stand up on [his] hind legs like a man." Quoting Lyndon B. Johnson's famous statement that until African Americans enjoy full equality of opportunity in the United States, "emancipation" will remain merely a "proclamation," the ex-president (fittingly named "the Judge") exhorts Dilman to "make [emancipation] a fact . . . not as a Negro who is President but as an American man who is President."[17] This progression subtly reframes Johnson's thesis of American history within the ideological framework of colorblindness, suggesting that emancipation for twentieth-century African Americans means not freedom from the long shadow of American slavery but from racial identity itself.

In other words, for Dilman to embody the presidency, he would need to achieve a semblance of manhood that supersedes his racialization. That he cannot is implicit in his decision to ultimately forsake the pursuit of a second term, in spite of the restoration, at the climax of the novel, of his now politically legitimized manhood. In referring to himself as "a person who . . . has the right to perform as a man and not just a colored man," Dilman invokes a masculine performance that remains circumscribed by racial boundaries unassimilable to the abstracted whiteness of the presidency. It is *as* "a Negro who is President" that Dilman fulfills Johnson's mandate for equality of opportunity, and yet his presidency simultaneously falls short of that mandate as long as Dilman remains identified with his blackness.[18] If to the nation and himself he is no longer dismissible as "just a colored man," neither is he ever—as the text makes clear—fully legible as "just" the president. Although he has proven as "full" a manhood previously deemed "half," this remasculation does not escape the ambit of his racialization.

Whereas the book's protagonist experiences the nation's first black presidency as a testament to the impossibility of his position, insofar as he makes no plans to run for reelection, the televised film imagines an initially reluctant President Dilman, who ultimately embraces the office and appears at the Democratic convention to seek—and, presumably, win—his party's nomination. Dilman's transformation in the film versions raises two linked questions. How does the film depict and account for this shift in the character's self-understanding, from seeing himself as wholly unsuited and improbable, to believing that he's the best person for the job? How does this shift then resolve the tensions between racial and national identity that in the historical moment of *Rufus Jones for President* marked the black presidency as a stark contradiction in terms? In this version of the text, Dilman's remasculation is linked to his distancing from certain signifiers of blackness, a displacement that enables the protagonist to come into view as a markedly more presidential figure. In effect, Dilman approximates the performance of presidential passing that lies at the heart of contemporary postracial ideations of the trope so brilliantly repurposed in Chappelle's satirical Black Bush.

The revised plot turns on the attempted assassination of the South African minister of defense in which an African American college student stands accused. Initially convinced of his innocence, Dilman refuses the apartheid regime's request for extradition. Even his black congressional allies urge a different course, viewing the extradition agreement as a way of cultivating an electable image of black leadership. Film footage then surfaces that implicates the American student—and also provides Dilman's political opponents with grounds for impeachment. Defying the anti-apartheid American Left, religious and other advisers, and Wanda, his activist daughter, Dilman holds a press conference announcing his plans to hand the student over to South African authorities before heading to the Democratic National Convention where he plans to announce his candidacy for the upcoming presidential election.

The film's uncoupling of Dilman's image from his racial identity and hence the denaturalization of the "whiteness" of the presidency derives from this plot, which internationalizes the book's depiction of violent black radicalism. This shift scrambles the defining codes and positions of US racial hegemony as the American student's supporters talk about his potentially being lynched by the South African government—language that globalizes white-supremacist violence—and anti-apartheid demonstrations in front of the White House feature primarily white activists. The racial script of this crisis is further complicated by the role of African American congressional leaders, who, in contrast to the student's white activist supporters, advocate for extradition. Through the controversy, Dilman asserts disidentification with the era's prevailing styles of political black masculinity: the moderate accommodationism of the black congressional leadership and the militant machismo of the accused, whose politics are also implicated in his characterization as volatile, duplicitous, misguided, and immature. Dilman's refusal of these polar positions on what the film treats as the available spectrum of politically engaged black masculinity places him outside the categorical delimitations of "race" by which his presidency is initially defined.

Passing conventionally relies on visual cues, yet the drama of passing in which *The Man* participates is largely invisible. Triumphing over political adversaries and adroitly negotiating an international political crisis, Dilman becomes a viable contender for the presidential nomination, which is to say he comes to "pass" at what he already, ostensibly is—the president. This also means that by the symbolic logics that historically construct the figure of the US president as the nation's (white) father, Dilman comes to pass as what he is not—racially unmarked. In contrast to the book and set in a later historical moment, within a political landscape defined as much by intraracial as interracial conflicts, the film offers a version of the character that brings new coherence to the black-president trope by staging that presidency as a variation on the racial pass. What this entails, however, is a depiction of passing that does not rely on the visual optics of race. Instead, Dilman's racial identity is transcoded as racialized gender. The "unmanly" emotional style ascribed to the character in the book in his first days in office is conveyed, on film, by body language. Meek-voiced and stooped, incessantly ringing his hands, the newly appointed president is so tremulous that he needs both hands to hold the glass of scotch he's poured to calm his nerves but then drops it anyway.

This scene closes with an image that brings to life the metaphor of "half man" deployed in the book. Alone for the first time that evening, Dilman pauses his worried pacing next to a decorative mirror hanging in what appears a private library in the White House residence. The camera zooms to focus on Dilman as he turns to address his reflection. Dilman himself is facing away from the camera as the gaze of his reflection, seen in three-quarters profile, looks toward it. The two Dilmans take up the frame of this shot. With a mock gesture of obeisance, Dilman addresses his mirror image, "Mr. President." He immediately bursts into tears and, convulsively sobbing, leans against the mirror. The camera continues to move closer until that the mirror's frame lies beyond the shot, giving the illusion of two sobbing Dilmans leaning against one another's heads. The crying continues for several more seconds until the scene cuts to black. What the history of this fictional trope deems the incoherence of a "black president" translates, at the level of subjective experience, into Dilman's feeling quite undone—or by the logics of Wallace's story, *unmanned.*

This image literalizes the idea that Dilman's sudden political ascension has him "beside himself" with grief—a gendered reaction that indexes this new president's insufficiency. As well, the accompanying dialogue displaces the identity of "Mr. President" from Dilman's own person, making his reflection—and not himself—the holder of the title. Such visual and verbal punning conveys what the book terms a "halved" masculinity. Showing Dilman as effectively emasculated by the contradictions that construct the concept of the black presidency in *The Man*'s historical moment, this scene has its antithesis in the film's final image, frozen under the rolling credits: a low-angle shot of Dilman at the DNC podium, backdropped by a massive American flag. This image is the culminating shot in a sequence of crosscuts between Dilman's face as he surveys his supporters, the vertically hung flag, what appears to be documentary footage from the actual party convention, and a visibly moved Wanda gazing adoringly at her father and thereby restoring via embodied spectatorship his formerly diminished patriarchal authority. By this tableau, black presidentialism is made congruous with what Dana Nelson describes as the white confraternity of the presidency. The newly monumentalized image of Dilman serves the party's broader interest in reproducing, through the convention, its symbolic capital. These radically divergent images—from weeping into his reflection to looking triumphantly presidential at the convention podium—foreground how, over the course of the film, the character achieves the racial pass refused in Wallace's novel. Jones's President Dilman transcends his initial racially delimited status as the accidental first black president to realize something like the abstracted iconicity that the office of the presidency presumes as its natural deictic.

The style of black political masculinity performed by Jones in *The Man* reverberates in the postracial presidencies of more-recent film and television, investing what Edwards describes as "the sentimental sci-fi apocalyptic narrative" in *Deep Impact* (1998), or the more recent *2012* (2009), with somber authority. In these films, as Edwards notes, a black president serves to aestheticize neoliberal statism's ideal of global humanity.[19] The trope does similar work in *24* and the more recent action film *White House Down* (2013) on behalf of the post-9/11 global security state. This ideological topography seems far afield from *Rufus Jones for President* and even *The Man,* in which the first African American president is no longer, as the earlier film would have it, an intrinsically farcical notion but, instead, a limit case for the national project of racial inclusion. In these more recent genre entertainments, this trope serves as a sign of an alternative reality to the pre-Obama present, a reality in which the problem of the black presidency, as the problem of its challenge to white hegemony, has already been resolved. Or, in the wake of the Obama era, it projects an expansion of the new historical reality of black presidentialism beyond the singular figure of the forty-fourth president. For these popular texts, if the black presidency poses a "problem" at all, it is a problem for characters in the diegesis—as individual racists—rather than something political that the narrative understands itself as obligated to address. Seemingly the denouement in the shifting inflections of black masculinity that characterize the earlier history of the trope, the postracial black president archetype proliferates across a variety of genres and forms—from science fiction to political thrillers and action, in both film and television.

Chappelle's Black Bush derives much of its comedic torque from what the postracial instantiation of the black president would seem to repress: an explicitly black masculine performativity. In Edwards's analysis, this take on the trope indexes a second genre of contemporary black presidency narratives: that of black-authored comedy. In this genre, a vernacular presidency, debased in the racist *Rufus Jones,* is recuperated as the critical race-conscious rejoinder to the sober postracial presidency, embodying what Edwards describes as a "commonsense black nationalist misogyny." Paradigmatic in this regard is Chris Rock's 2003 film *Head of State.* Rather than a bland universalism, contemporary black popular culture's comedic black presidents emphasize racial particularity and masculine swagger, to offer what Edwards "calls[s] black vernacular fraternity as an answer to an American political culture structured in the power and privileges of whiteness, on the one hand, and as a curative to an inauthentic, bourgeois, post–Civil Rights blackness, on the other."[20] As Edwards explains, these formally opposed registers are ideologically congruent in their common interest in recuperating by reformulating black political masculinity in the post–Civil Rights era.

In its broadest gestures, Black Bush can be read to resonate with Rock's performance and, perhaps, invite the feminist critique *Head of State* warrants. And yet, the political common sense Black Bush channels is not a populist appeal to a vernacular confraternity but the actual foreign-policy agenda of the Bush presidency. Likewise, the primary referent for Chappelle's character is not the crisis of political black masculinity that, in Edward's critique, underwrites both postracial and comedic iterations of black presidentialism but, instead, a crisis for the white national manhood traditionally embodied by the US presidency. As the sketch makes clear, in linking the war in Iraq to the 9/11 terrorist attacks, the administration's political rhetorics framed the invasion as resolving a crisis in masculinity that, as the sketch underscores, Bush's own oratory personalized.

Chappelle's Black Bush recasts the logics and behavior that characterize the Bush presidency *through* the figure of a "street" black guy, revealing an equivalence between the reality of our forty-third president and the hypostatized "black president" that the dominant culture still fears, our society's postracial self-image to the contrary. The gestures of this performance are essentially deconstructive. Throughout its history, the trope of the black president has operated to preserve a fantasy of the competency and authority of the "white president"; the germinal instance of Douglass Dilman suggests that, even in the post–Civil Rights era, the trope continues to perpetuate this fantasy under the veil of putative "race neutrality."

Chappelle's burlesquing of presidential authority carries the opposite intention. The performance calls into question a specific white president's competency and authority by transcoding Bush's white masculinity as black hypermasculinity. Chappelle, as himself, introduces the sketch before a studio audience. "If our president were black, we would not be at war right now—not because a black person wouldn't have done something like that but because America wouldn't let a black person do something like that without asking them a million questions." His comment sets up the sketch that follows as doubly counterfactual, imagining a black president in George W. Bush's place and an America that actually *would* "let a black person do something like that." What Chappelle says next provides an additional lens on the performance and its reference points. The comedian refers to "minorities"' famous mistrust of government, saying to the whites in his audience, "You don't understand what this looks like for us." Bambi Haggins describes the premise of the sketch as "facetiously educational: making it clear to nonwhites why they wouldn't trust the government either if it was being run by 'Black Bush.'"[21] But Chappelle's comments about "what this looks like for us" suggests an additional premise aimed at his white audience, essentially: Let me show you the kind of guy African Americans see when they look at Bush.

What follows is a faux documentary that interweaves press conferences, media interviews, and, as with the film adaptation of *The Man*, actual news footage. In sections "The Lead Up to War," "British Intelligence," "Proof," "Oil," "U.N.," "Invasion," "Victory," "Civil Unrest," and "Saddam Captured," the sketch revisits the presidential rhetoric that mediated the Bush administration's foreign policy on Iraq before the invasion and in its aftermath. A journalistic voice-over frames the opening "lead up to war" press-conference clip: "President Bush continues to make his case for an invasion of Iraq." The character identified by an onscreen caption as "President Black Bush" explains to the press corps, "After carefully examining the region, me and my cabinet agree that the area is definitely ripe for 'regime change,'" using the Bush administration's favored euphemism for invasion and colonial occupation. Black Bush then quickly drops his mannered political persona, switching from the rhetorical conventions of statecraft to those of the street vendetta. Getting, in his words, "real" with the gathered journalists and, by extension, the American people, Black Bush lays out the true rationale for his war effort: "He tried to kill my father, man. I can't play that shit." Egged on by his White House counsel, played by *Chappelle's Show* regular Donnell Rawlings, who interjects, "Say Word. He tried to kill your father," Black Bush then dramatically grabs the boom mic, in the manner, as Haggins notes, of an angry MC. "The nigger tried to kill my father," he shouts at the camera.

Haggins points out that like other moments in the sketch, the comedy in Chappelle's abrupt abandonment of the pretense of "presidential" behavior trades on how "the image of Black Bush and his Pentagon posse getting ready to roll, replicates any number of moments in black gangsta–inflected films—from *Menace II Society* to *Baby Boy*."[22] As with the hip-hop allusions that run elsewhere throughout the sketch,[23] Black Bush's cultural blackness amplifies the racial masquerade. His "blackness" is not just, like the postracial president's, phenotypical but steeped in references to black cultural production that provide particular pleasures to members of this crossover comedy audience who "get" Chappelle's jokes.

But the conflation of race and culture here also has an ideological valence. It reprises the comedian's earlier point that African Americans mistrust George W. Bush because they "get" *him*—that is, are able to read him and his rhetoric about Iraq, its dangerous leader, and fabled weapons of mass destruction via familiar cultural scripts of the "gangsta" and "hustler" that inform Chappelle's performance. Black Bush remains, at every turn, an interpretation of George W. Bush, as Chappelle draws from the latter's actual claims and rhetoric. Even what seems a clear departure from presidential form, the claim, "That nigger tried to kill my father," reproduces actual Bush discourse. At a 2002 fundraising event for Republican Senate candidate John Cornyn, President Bush gave a speech in which he described Iraqi President Saddam Hussein as posing "a much graver threat than anybody could have possibly imagined." With reference to a failed assassination attempt on George H. W. Bush as proof, he maintains that Hussein's "hatred is mainly directed at us"—seeming to mean both the United States as a whole and the Bushes themselves: "There's no doubt he can't stand us. After all, this is a guy that tried to kill my dad at one time."[24]

This character President Black Bush is thus at once a reference to an amalgam of black hypermasculine archetypes and to the actual George W. Bush. Bush's public image contradictorily straddles two divergent ideals of white masculinity—the WASP and the cowboy. The joke lies in the isomorphism between Bush's country-club machismo and the "thug" mentality of Chappelle's Black Bush. This character's hyperbolic black masculinity and vernacularized bluster reveal the effective *whiteness* of Bush's rhetorical style and public posturing, a racial specificity otherwise kept invisible by symbolic structures that make white manhood the cultural general and thus the unmarked but given race of the presidency itself. Chappelle's counterburlesque in this way derives further torque in distinguishing between the racial coding of this president and the historic race neutrality of the office, which the fictional postracial presidencies of Palmer and his ilk maintain.[25] Chappelle's performance thus illuminates how the black presidency only coheres, in the national imagination, as a kind of implicit racial pass. That is the legacy of the long prehistory to Obama's presidency that US popular culture provides and what ultimately enables the black-president trope to function as a sign of the postracial.[26] Black Bush also shows how that pass turns on a specifically gendered logic of race. In fiction, as in real life, the black president does not pass by suppressing his race—the singular traît linking all these representations—but, rather, by suppressing a racialized gender identity.

In using the performance venue of the presidential press conference to expose and explode the passing inherent to the black-president trope, the Black Bush sketch recalls a performance by comedian Richard Pryor on his short-lived 1977 television series, *The Richard Pryor Show*. In its first episode, Pryor satirized the racist anxiety that a hypothetical African American president's ruse of race-neutral presidentialism would actually conceal an essential, threatening "blackness." The sketch concerns a presidential press conference that begins with a sober discussion of Middle East policy. By the conclusion of the sketch, roughly seven minutes later, the press conference has devolved into chaos: white and African American journalists brawling and the secret service attempting to constrain a pugilistic president, furious over a white Southern reporter's insulting comments about (what else but?) his mother.

The humor and political significance of all this lie in the turn that Pryor's performance takes midway through when what the sketch imagines as, essentially, this fictional president's racial masquerade starts to slip, in response to an African American newspaper reporter's question about the space program of the National Aeronautics and Space Administration (NASA). Importantly, this is a topic not conventionally framed as relevant to conversations about race, which gives the black president an opportunity to show his "real" agenda. Asked if his recent increases to the NASA budget reflect plans to recruit more African Americans, the president goes on to critique the whiteness of the astronaut program as an implied extension of the US's traditionally racialized imperialism, arguing not only for the hiring of black personnel but also transforming the culture of life in space. Instead of the European classical music the astronauts reputedly listen to in flight, this president's spacemen will listen to Miles Davis and Charlie Parker. "We're gonna have some different kinda things in there, that's right," he affirms, speaking, for the first time, in a looser, louder, distinctly vernacular voice. As Pryor's black president's formal English gives way to the racialized inflections of the African American urban slang of the era, his body language follows suit, relaxing its gestures, which now seem animated by an unconcealed masculine bravado. In short, with the space-program question, his persona becomes increasingly "black" and therefore, by the logics of the sketch, less "presidential"—which is to say, Pryor's nameless president becomes, essentially, President Black Bush.

The reporter who asks the space question is also implicated in the tension between the black masculine and presidential manhood Pryor's performance begins, at this point, to explore. Embodying the image and voice of black bourgeois "respectability," utterly uninflected by linguistic or sartorial vernacularities, the journalist's professional manner belies the race-conscious politics behind his question. An echo of the very contradictions Pryor's comedy mines, between the black president's *form* and his imagined *content*, the journalist is followed by another colleague—representing *Jet* magazine—whose appearance, demeanor, and question for the president signal even greater affiliation with black politics, culture, and identity. A third African American journalist from *Ebony* is even more forthright in his identifications; clad in the Black Panther uniform of beret and blue jeans, he invokes the black power salute by raising his fist instead of his hand to ask a question and addresses the president directly as "Brother." Correlatively, the president's own identity becomes even more racialized with each of these subsequent exchanges, in which he vociferously aligns his policy agenda with pro-black initiatives in areas of public life even beyond the purview of presidential power—such as the racial composition of National Football League team ownership and coaching staffs.

In its steady deformation of the black president's pass, this sketch enacts as satire the racist anxiety that for an African American man to be president, he would have to perform falsely a version of race neutrality, expressed as self-sameness with an idealized "white" president but that behind that ruse would exist an *essential* "blackness." The black president, in this racist fantasy, is in effect a form of the racial pass. The a priori failure of that pass is the heart of Pryor's comedic exposition of the fantasy. Following that deceptively "bourgie" reporter's initial question about the space program, his voice, body language, and political agenda are increasingly inflected as black, by way of prevailing stereotypes about the black male body and the body politics of black nationalism. This performance can be read as anticipating the postracial "black president" of the post–Civil Rights era by exposing what the sketch suggests whites project as being its racial unconscious. In its critical and performative dimensions, Pryor's sketch, like Chappelle's, is paradigmatic for how neo-passing narratives, in addition to their intersectional conception of identity, foreground the persistence of racial norms in the era of formal equality, exposing the underlying ideological investments of liberal race neutrality.

Chappelle's performance builds upon Pryor's. "Black Bush" shows how a logic of the street impersonated in Pryor's sketch had, through the presidency of George W. Bush, become the logic of the nation's diplomacy. The earlier performance, by staging the president's failure to suppress "blackness," sends the message to Pryor's white audiences: This is what you think a black presidency would be like. Chappelle takes this fear of a black president and the racist suppositions about this then still-hypothetical figure's belligerence, narrow partisanship, croneyism, low-mindedness, and general unfitness for office and says to America in 2004: What you're afraid you would get with a black president, you already have.

Notes

1. *Rufus Jones.*

2. Indeed, *24*'s depiction of the first African American presidency so closely resembles the neoliberal hues of the actual forty-fourth presidency that, in interviews, the actor who portrayed Palmer has characterized Obama's "performance" as historically related next to his own. Sonner, "Dennis Haysbert."

3. "Black Bush."

4. Each bit of the sketch reprises a specific Bush administration claim—from those elusive weapons of mass destruction to the USS *Abraham Lincoln* mission-accomplished speech. For critics of contemporary television satire, Chappelle's skewering of the Bush presidency is an exemplary instance of political parody. See Haggins, "In the Wake," 245–49; Willett, *Irony*, 108.

5. Wald, *Crossing the Line*, 5.

6. Smith, "Reading the Intersection," 45.

7. Edwards, "Black President Hokum," 33. Film and television in this genre include *Rufus Jones for President* (1933), *The Man* (1972), *Born in Flames* (1983), *The Fifth Element* (1997), *Deep Impact* (1998), *24* (2001–10) *Head of State* (2003), *Century City* (2004), *Idiocracy* (2006), *2012* (2009), *The Event* (2010–11), *White House Down* (2013), and *Big Game* (2014).

8. The close relationship between Obama's racialization in media coverage of his first presidential run and the racial tactics of his campaign strategy suggests the discourse of Obama as the specifically "postracial" black president reflects a carefully managed performance of that identity. See Tesler and Sears, *Obama's Race*, especially the introduction and chapters 7 and 8, for an insightful analysis.

9. Nelson, *National Manhood*, 225.

10. For a discussion of the complex historical roots of this minstrelsy trope, see Miller, *Slaves to Fashion*, 96–98.

11. The exceptions that prove the rule are the independent 1983 feminist science-fiction art film *Born in Flames*, which imagines a black female president, and the short-lived 2004 TV series *Century City*, in which Oprah Winfrey herself is president. Oprah is also imagined as president in a 2006 episode of *The Boondocks* called "Return of the King."

12. Many of the song-and-dance numbers in *Rufus Jones* have no discernible diegetic function, indicating that the main purpose of the film is simply to give its outrageously talented African American stars an opportunity to perform popular tunes—Sammy Davis Jr. singing "You Rascal, You" in imitation of Louis Armstrong, and Ethel Waters, in her gorgeous presidencess guise, performing two of her signature songs, "Am I Blue?" and "Underneath a Harlem Moon."

13. The vice president is depicted as, in his words, already "close to death" and arrives at the emergency cabinet meeting the night of the president's death, in a wheelchair pushed by an attendant. The vice president refuses to assume office, stating that two presidential funerals in one term would be too traumatic for the country. This plot point departs from the book, in which the veep is also killed. Perhaps, the change in the screenplay is intended to give the audience a chance to reflect on the racist logics by which the presidential advisers and congressional leaders charged with managing the succession insist that a black president would be more traumatic for the country than would the potential grief over another dead president. Wallace, *Man*.

14. Smith, *Presidents We Imagine*, 186.

15. Wallace, *Man*, 489, 274.

16. Ibid., 251.

17. Johnson, "Remarks"; Wallace, *Man,* 758, 764, 547, 547. The quote in full: "Until justice is blind to color, until education is unaware of race, until opportunity is unconcerned with the color of men's skins, emancipation will be a proclamation but not a fact. To the extent that the proclamation of emancipation is not fulfilled in fact, to that extent we shall have fallen short of assuring freedom to the free." Ibid., 547.

18. The conundrum of the (late) Civil Rights–era black presidency as revealed in this passage indexes a logic of "racechange," to borrow Susan Gubar's term for representations of race that conceptualize the mutability and instability of its borders. Gubar, *Racechanges,* 5.

19. Edwards, "Black President Hokum," 33.

20. Ibid., 33, 34.

21. Haggins, "In the Wake," 242.

22. Ibid., 243.

23. Among the members of Black Bush's "coalition of the willing" are the nations of Stankonia (a popular album by the hip-hop group *Outkast*) and Afrika Bambaataa and the Zulu Nation (important early progenitors of hip-hop music).

24. Bush, "Remarks."

25. I take the term *counterburlesque* from Eric Lott, who uses it to characterize parodic imitations of white officialdom and wealth in performance practices of eighteenth- and nineteenth-century African American festivals and pageantry in the northern US states. Lott, *Love and Theft.*

26. According to Catherine Squires, who analyzed the use of "postracial" throughout all sectors of the news media from 1990 through 2010, usage of the term exploded exponentially in the years 2008 and 2009 in connection with the candidacy and election of the nation's first (nonfictional) black president. Her analysis shows how the meaning of the term shifted dramatically, too: whereas in prior usage, "postracial" when it appeared in the news referred to a future after the end of racism, in the era of the term's explosion in popularity, it was intended as a description of the present moment or of certain figures who emblematize the present, such as biracial celebrities, depictions of multiracial families, and, especially, Obama himself. Squires's analysis makes clear that, in the popular imagination, the 2008 Obama campaign and presidency are incontrovertibly linked to the narrative of the postracial nation. Squires, *Post-Racial Mystique,* 37–40.

Bibliography

Big Game. Directed by Jalmari Helander. Subzero Film Entertainment, 2014. Anchor Bay Entertainment, 2015. DVD.

Birth of a Nation, The. Directed by D. W. Griffith. David W. Griffith and Epoch Producing, 1915. Image Entertainment, 1998. DVD.

"Black Bush." *Chappelle's Show: Season 2.* Written by Neal Brennan and Dave Chappelle. Directed by Neal Brennan and Rusty Cundieff. Comedy Central, 2005. Paramount, 2005. DVD.

Born in Flames. Directed by Lizzie Borden. First Run Features, 1983. First Run Features, 2006. DVD.

Bush, George W. "Remarks by the President at John Cornyn for Senate Reception." Speech, Hyatt Regency, Houston, Texas, September 26, 2002. Accessed May 15, 2015. https://georgewbush-whitehouse.archives.gov.

Century City. Created by Ed Zuckerman. CBS, 2004.

Deep Impact. Directed by Mimi Leder. Paramount, 1998. DVD.

Edwards, Erica R. "The Black President Hokum." *American Quarterly* 63, no. 1 (2011): 33–59.

Event, The. Created by Nick Wauters. NBC, 2010–11.

Fifth Element, The. Directed by Luc Besson. Sony Pictures, 1997. DVD.

Gubar, Susan. *Racechanges: White Skin, Black Face in American Culture*. New York: Oxford University Press, 2000.

Haggins, Bambi. "In the Wake of the 'Nigger Pixie': Dave Chappelle and the Politics of Crossover Comedy." In *Satire TV: Politics and Comedy in the Post-Network Era*, edited by Jonathan Gray and Jeffrey P. Jones, 233–51. New York: New York University Press, 2009.

Head of State. Directed by Chris Rock. Dreamworks, 2003. DVD.

Idiocracy. Directed by Mike Judge. Twentieth Century Fox, 2006. Twentieth Century Fox, 2007. DVD.

Johnson, Lyndon B. "Remarks of Vice President Lyndon B. Johnson Memorial Day." Gettysburg, Pennsylvania, May 30, 1963. Accessed May 15, 2015. http://www.usmemorialday.org/Speeches/President/may3063.txt.

Lott, Eric. *Love and Theft: Blackface Minstrelsy and the American Working Class*. New York: Oxford University Press, 1993.

Man, The. Directed by Joseph Sargent. ABC Circle Films, Lorimar Television. 1972.

Miller, Monica L. *Slaves to Fashion: Black Dandyism and the Styling of Black Diasporic Identity*. Durham, NC: Duke University Press, 2010.

Nelson, Dana D. *National Manhood: Capitalist Citizenship and the Imagined Fraternity of White Men*. Durham, NC: Duke University Press, 1998.

"Return of the King." *The Boondocks*. Written by Aaron McGruder and Yamara Taylor. Directed by Kalvin Lee. Adult Swim, 2006. Sony Pictures, 2006.

Richard Pryor Show, The. Performed by Richard Pryor, Robin Williams, Paul Mooney. NBC, 1977. Image Entertainment, 2004. DVD.

Rufus Jones for President. Directed by Roy Mack. Warner Bros., 1933. Black Boogie Woogie Blues Vol. 1: 1930s–1950s. VideoBeat, 2004. DVD.

Smith, Jeff. *The Presidents We Imagine: Two Centuries of White House Fictions on the Page, on the Stage, Onscreen, and Online*. Madison: University of Wisconsin Press, 2009.

Smith, Valerie. "Reading the Intersection of Race and Gender in Narratives of Passing." *Diacritics* 24, nos. 2–3 (1994): 43–57.

Sonner, Scott. "Dennis Haysbert: I Helped Pave Obama's Way." *Huffington Post*, July 9, 2008. Accessed May 11, 2015. www.huffingtonpost.com.

Squires, Catherine R. *The Post-Racial Mystique: Media and Race in the Twenty-First Century*. New York: New York University Press, 2014.

Tesler, Michael, and David O. Sears. *Obama's Race: The 2008 Election and the Dream of a Post-Racial America*. Chicago: University of Chicago Press, 2010.

2012. Directed by Roland Emmerich. Columbia, 2009. Sony Pictures, 2010. DVD.

24. Performed by Keifer Sutherland and Dennis Haysbert. Fox, 2001–10. Twentieth Century Fox 2002–2010. DVD.

Wald, Gayle. *Crossing the Line: Racial Passing in Twentieth-Century US Literature and Culture*. Durham, NC: Duke University Press, 2000.

Wallace, Irving. *The Man*. New York: Simon and Schuster, 1964.

White House Down. Directed by Roland Emmerich. Sony Pictures, 2013. DVD.

Willett, Cynthia. *Irony in the Age of Empire: Comic Perspectives on Democracy and Freedom*. Bloomington: Indiana University Press, 2008.

CHAPTER 5

Seeing Race in Comics

Passing, Witness, and the Spectacle of Racial Violence in Johnson and Pleece's Incognegro

JENNIFER GLASER

Probably no medium more clearly dramatizes the dialectic between seeing and being seen—the twin registers of visual culture—than that of comics. Until recently, little scholarly attention has been given to the ways in which comics construct race.[1] This chapter addresses this absence by analyzing Mat Johnson and Warren Pleece's *Incognegro* (2008), a neo-passing narrative about race, lynching, and (mis-)recognition in America. Johnson and Pleece's depiction of race in *Incognegro* troubles assumptions about visual typology and racial identification while making a strong case for the importance of bringing conversations about comics into the discourses of both critical visual studies and critical race theory. The author-artist duo make it clear that portrayals of racial passing shed light on the constructed nature of race and the importance of the visual to how we uphold and undermine racial essentialisms. Moreover, although *Incognegro* is set in Harlem and the South during the 1930s—the height of the US's interwar lynching epidemic—its use of the comics medium to expose the connections between racial violence and racial visibility reverberate with our own contemporary moment. Johnson and Pleece's exploration of the various forms of media used to represent race and the violence committed against black bodies places their graphic narrative firmly in our current culture of surveillance, racial profiling, and cell phone–video representations of police violence.

Incognegro intervenes in these debates by using the visual vocabulary of the comics medium to open up a conversation about the long-running primacy of the visual in American racial discourse. Ian Haney-Lopez's pivotal work on the social construction of race opens with a vignette that precisely demonstrates the importance of the visual realm to discussions of both passing and the larger imagination of race in America. He narrates the story of three generations of women, members of the Wright family, who sued for their freedom from slavery in 1806. Although the women argued that they deserved freedom because of their purported predominance of white and Native American blood, the question of whether they would remain slaves hinged on their physical appearance and their capacity to pass for white. As Haney-Lopez puts it, "the fate of the women rode upon the complexion of their face, the texture of their hair, and the width of their nose. Each of these characteristics served to mark their race and their race in the end determined whether they were free or enslaved."[2] He uses this vignette not only to point out the oppressive vagaries of the American legal system and its role in maintaining slavery and systemic racism but also to highlight the mutability of racial definitions in American culture.[3] Ideas about what constitutes blackness and whiteness are shifting, a fact made painfully clear by those, like the women in the Wright family, who can pass between the supposedly ironclad poles of the racial binary.

Like the women Haney-Lopez describes, Zane Pinchback, the "incognegro" protagonist of Johnson and Pleece's graphic narrative,[4] experiences his racial identification as a matter of life or death. *Incognegro* focuses on the travails of Pinchback, a journalist from Harlem who travels to the Jim Crow South to report on the epidemic of lynching. His light skin and putatively white-identified features make it possible for him to pass for white, allowing him to personally witness and record scenes of graphic racial violence. Johnson's story and Pleece's drawings work in tandem to make the complexities of race in 1930s America visible. At the same time, their depiction of passing and the fate of those who can't pass during this time period provides a meditation on the dangers of black visibility and the political possibilities of invisibility for African American subjects that continues to have weight for readers in today's racial landscape. Johnson and Pleece's representation of lynching (and their suggestion that the reader is complicit in the violence as a witness and spectator), as well as their exploration of Pinchback's canny ability to pass in and out of a deeply compromised whiteness, dramatize the intersection of race and visibility in the novel and in our wider culture.

Incognegro's primary contribution to conversations about race and visibility comes through its representation of racial passing. As a neo-passing narrative, the graphic novel self-consciously participates in the genre of the passing narrative by alluding to a number of its most famous figures and the conditions experienced by black Americans during the Jim Crow era. As Johnson mentions explicitly in his author's note, *Incognegro* is based in part on the story of early National Association for the Advancement of Colored People (NAACP) leader Walter White, who passed in order to observe lynchings in the South. The graphic novel also manages to invoke a number of twentieth-century passing narratives from James Weldon Johnson's *The Autobiography of an Ex-colored Man* (1912) to Nella Larsen's *Passing* (1929), John Howard Griffin's *Black Like Me* (1961), and the complicated mutual passing of Jean Toomer and Waldo Frank emblematized by *Cane* (1923) and *Holiday* (1923), respectively.[5] *Incognegro* owes a particular debt to Toomer, whose exploration of the complexities of race in his fiction and poetry arose from the writer's own complicated pedigree. Toomer was the grandson of white-appearing P. B. S. Pinchback, son of a plantation owner and slave, whose "one drop" of African American blood did not keep him from becoming a prominent state senator (and, almost, governor) in Louisiana during Reconstruction. The graphic novel takes its protagonist's name from Toomer, whose original name was Nathan Pinchback Toomer.

Although Johnson and Pleece's tale follows a racially indeterminate character not unlike those found in the more canonical passing narratives of Toomer, Johnson, and Larsen, it departs from earlier stories of passing in fundamental ways. Borrowing its visual and narrative vocabulary from film noir and superhero comics, *Incognegro* is a self-reflexive text distinctly aware of its own participation in and capacity to play with the genre of the passing narrative. Chief among its interventions is to use an explicitly visual medium to explore racial passing—and its reliance on visual recognition and misrecognition to support the particular story it wants to tell about the constructed nature of racial categories. As Scott McCloud points out in his pivotal *Understanding Comics*, comics provide a particularly apt vehicle for encouraging both reader identification and reader interpretation.[6] Comics artists make a number of decisions that affect what to show and what not to show, on one end of this spectrum of participation, to how realistically or cartoonishly to represent their characters and how to use the gutter spaces that exist between panels, on the other. Johnson and Pleece are deeply engaged in using these and other aspects of the comics medium to allow themselves and their readers a space to "write" against conventional narratives of race in America. The graphic novel's success as a neo-passing narrative comes precisely from this ability to borrow from, while simultaneously rewriting, the racial scripts of the past.

Among other things, Johnson and Pleece use Pinchback's role as a writer (of his column and his identity) to provide a metacommentary on passing as a process that draws attention to questions of racial legibility and performance, as well as to the repercussions of being a bad reader. After all, passing is itself about reading in a dual sense: both the passing subject's canny ability to read the semiotics of white performance in order to effectively enact whiteness and the white world's inability to *see* race when it is not being performed in what that world perceives to be a legible manner. Pleece's illustrations dramatize the tension between legible and illegible racial performances by drawing all the characters in the novel with similar coloring and facial features that require interpretation from the reader—and, by extension, from the other characters in the graphic narrative. This refusal to clearly mark race in visual choices parallels and extends novelist Johnson's narrative decisions in *Incognegro*. From the first pages of the text, he makes it clear that racial identification is messy and often imperfect, relying, as it does, on deciphering behavioral and speech cues whose meaning shifts over time.

Johnson provides a look at the vagaries of racial identification, in part, through the integration of his own story into that of Pinchback. *Incognegro* begins with a foreword that narrates Johnson's own ability to pass, suggesting that his commentary on racial politics and passing is a contemporary one, despite the novel's early twentieth-century setting. He writes about growing up "a black boy who looked white." Later, he relates that he became the father of twins, "one of whom is brown-skinned with black Afro hair, the other with the palest of pink skins and more European curly hair . . . two people with the exact same ethnic lineage destined to be viewed differently only because of genetic randomness." He emphasizes that the interpretation of these random attributes is historically specific, however, noting that "in a predominantly African American neighborhood, during the height of the Black Power era, . . . I stood out a bit." He "started fantasizing about living in another time, another situation, where my ethnic appearance would be an asset instead of a burden." The idea that appearance, not to mention the shifting meaning of that appearance in different times and places, can dictate fate is the jumping-off point for Johnson's meditation on identity and recognition in *Incognegro*, as well as a direct link to canonical passing narratives of the Jim Crow era.

Perhaps for this reason, the graphic novel takes the form of a classic whodunit, the staples of its visual and narrative vocabulary borrowed, as mentioned, from the conventions of film noir. A photograph of a racially indeterminate man in noir-ish dress adorns the cover of the book (Johnson in disguise?), suggesting that the question of identity and the identity of the author are at the center of the text (figure 5.1). Pleece illustrates the tale in stark black and white with menacing shadows everywhere, while Johnson's narrative follows the traditional formula of the gumshoe detective on the hunt for the truth. The

FIGURE 5.1. Front cover, *Incognegro* (New York: Vertigo, 2008).

mystery at the heart of the story, however, is not who killed whom or how to collect the requisite insurance money after the deed is done. Instead, *Incognegro* provides an exploration of the complexities of identity, ideology, and recognition in an America obsessed with race. The novel is filled with cases of mistaken identity and people whose lives differ radically depending on "genetic randomness." Tired of putting himself at risk, Pinchback plans to retire from his role as "incognegro" but is convinced to venture back to the South for one last expedition precisely because he feels guilty about the results of phenotypical randomness: his dark-skinned brother has been beaten and imprisoned for a crime he did not commit, while Pinchback lives comfortably in Harlem. The whites in the South see Pinchback's brother's dark skin as a mark of potential criminality from which he cannot escape. Moreover, he is suspect because he has transgressed against local racial mores; the woman he is accused of killing is a white woman with whom he was having a romantic relationship. Here, Johnson and Pleece make it clear that *Incognegro* is not simply about the role of the visual in imagining race in America but also how the visual culture of the Jim Crow South functioned to police race. Jim Crow worked through a politics of the visual—both in terms of the literal signs that segregated blacks from whites but also in those more figurative semiotics that African Americans had to be adept in reading in order to stay alive. Chief among them, as the tragic story of Emmett Till's murder would illustrate twenty years after the events of *Incognegro*, were the taboo against black male desire and the so-called miscegenation to which it was purported to give rise.

Johnson and Pleece also explore the role of visual culture in what we might now call racial profiling. Their representation of race and passing emphasizes that cultural assumptions allow us to see and interpret only certain aspects of a situation or a person. Passing and other instances of mistaken identity become a rich possibility in the text because the upper-class whites who identify (or, often, misidentify) Zane Pinchback and his friends so often can't see or read African American identity, believing all African Americans to be interchangeable. As Johnson and Pleece make clear, the white characters in the text can't recognize an individual as passing. Often, they can't tell one African American person from another. At one point, it becomes clear that this blindness extends to their reading of class and gender, as well. One of the story lines in *Incognegro* centers on a poor white woman, a member of what the townspeople call the "Jefferson whites," who effectively passes as a man and works as a deputy sheriff because no one in town looks closely enough to decipher exactly who she is.

Like the woman deputy, the mostly African American characters in *Incognegro* are deeply engaged with the instrumentality of passing. Can passing have more than one use? Does passing simply aid in Negro acculturation or class mobility? Zane's equally light-skinned friend, Carl, sees passing as a means to infiltrate white business establishments to consort with wealthy patrons. Zane, instead, explores the political possibilities of passing as a powerful tool in the act of witness. Johnson and Pleece suggest that skin color itself is political. As they demonstrate, light-skinned African Americans like Zane and Carl provide uncomfortable reminders of America's history of often-violent miscegenation. Zane himself sees his countenance as a materialization of the hypocrisy of the South. In one panel, the rape of an African American slave by her white master is superimposed on Zane's figure, literally and figuratively shadowing both Zane and the American culture that produced and interpreted him. Just a few panels later, an American flag is similarly placed on his body. Ironically, it is at this moment that Zane directly addresses the readers of the graphic narrative, asking that they "watch [him] go *invisible*. Watch [him] step outside of history."[7] Passing relies for its success on invisibility—the passing subject's ability to melt into whiteness and, as Zane puts it, "step outside of history." At the same time, as Johnson and Pleece make abundantly clear, the act of passing is often steeped in history—to be precise, the history of white, male sexual violence that was so common during the time of slavery.

Nonetheless, to Zane, "assimilation [is] revolution" precisely because it allows him to see without being seen in white culture.[8] Zane is able to don and doff whiteness so effectively because he recognizes that "race is a strategy."[9] As he points out, the white people who surround him think they are raceless, universal, invisible—the norm against which racial difference must be measured. Zane's racial "strategy" relies on his ability to make whiteness visible. In order to effectively pass for white, black people have to be able to see whiteness and the strategies that uphold it as a performance. This form of reading race as performance not only undermines the biological essentialism at the heart of racial categorization but it also participates in the deconstruction and denaturalization of whiteness. After all, one of the central tenets of critical whiteness studies, cousin to critical race theory, is making white identity visible so as to denaturalize it.[10] Zane points out, "That's what white folks never get. They don't think they have accents. They don't think they eat ethnic foods. Their music is classical. They think they're just normal. That they are the universal, and that everyone else is an odd deviation from form. That's what makes them so easy to infiltrate."[11] The language Johnson uses in this section matches perfectly with the images employed by Pleece, as both construct an image of Pinchback as a kind of spy whose features become increasingly indistinct as he dons the costume of "incognegro," a subversion of the superhero figure so common in mainstream comics.

Zane is a superhero of sorts because he illuminates truths about America that many would rather not see. The radicalism of *Incognegro* comes from its insistence on the continuing reality of violence against black bodies—the danger of being seen, surveilled, and, often, murdered by agents of the law or so-called vigilante justice. It is clear that visibility, for a black man, often ends in death, a fact made tragically manifest in the lynchings that Pinchback infiltrates. It is hard not to read this history of violence without it being shadowed by the contemporary moment and the rash of police shootings of black men that have made headlines since Ferguson, Missouri, in 2014. The medium of comics has a unique ability to dramatize the ethics of representation—particularly visual representations of violence. *Incognegro* begins with an iconic image of a lynching.

Pleece's full-page drawing is at once unique and synecdochic for the archive of lynching photographs disseminated during this era in the form of family keepsakes and postcards. Over five thousand people were lynched in the United States from the late nineteenth century to the mid-twentieth. As Anthony W. Lee suggests in his introduction to *Lynching Photographs,* most disquieting about the many photographs taken of lynchings was that they "often pictured not only the mutilated and dangling bodies of the lynched victims, but also, all too frequently, the proud, laughing, self-righteous crowds who attended and participated in the lynchings."[12] When these photos began to be shown as part of art shows and museum exhibitions during the latter years of the twentieth century, they were advertised as documents that recorded the atrocities of an earlier era. Spectators to galleries and museums were told that their viewing of the photographs was part of an ethical act of bearing witness. However, as Lee points out, the visitors who thronged to these exhibitions "replicated the crowds that attended the original events, both groups of onlookers brought to the scene because of the spectacle of the lynched body."[13] Johnson and Pleece use the medium of comics to pose uncomfortable questions about viewer fascination with spectacular violence and the abject black body. These questions have a disquieting resonance in our own era—when images of dead or dying black men go viral on an almost-daily basis. Writing after the 2015 police killing of the unarmed Walter Scott in North Charleston, South Carolina, after a routine traffic stop, Sheena Howard points out, "Today, the thought of watching a person hanging from a tree at a lynching party sounds grotesque, yet people across the nation and the media cannot get enough of watching Walter Scott being shot to death, which is no different than voluntarily attending a slave auction or lynching party."[14] Anticipating these arguments about the ethics of watching violence against black bodies in the internet age, Johnson and Pleece use the medium of comics to shrink the distance (literal, emotional, and ethical) between the reader and the viewers of early twentieth-century lynchings. Doing so forces us to think about the role of visual desensitization in allowing such state-sanctioned violence to continue unabated.

After all, lynching, like the hegemony of whiteness, more generally, has become natural, neutral, and taken for granted in the South of Johnson's narrative. *Incognegro* seeks to defamiliarize this familiar violence. From the first page of *Incognegro,* Johnson and Pleece make it clear that they will intervene in the order of things by disrupting the spectacular nature of violence and taking it into their own visual and narrative vernacular. As mentioned, the first page of the novel is a full-page panorama of a lynching in progress. Pleece's images are drawn in a stark black and white, with no shades of gray to be seen. Rather than focus in on a small number of onlookers, whose eyes directly meet those of the viewer, as most lynching photographs do, Pleece's drawing zooms out to show the gaggle of faceless onlookers who are participating in the lynching and the circus-like atmosphere that prevails during the violence (a vendor is selling snacks and booze as the photographer sets up his equipment).

The narrative constructed in this single image emphasizes the differences between comics and photography (not to mention video) at the temporal and spatial levels as media used to record violence. The lynching Johnson and Pleece portray is not static, not an act of violence already completed. Since comics are, by definition, sequential art that tells stories through juxtaposed images, as both Will Eisner and McCloud have argued, comics allow the authors to show the reader a lynching in progress and make him or her feel more responsible for its outcome.[15] This technique also permits the lynching victim to become a subject, rather than simply the object of a viewer's gaze. In Pleece and Johnson's depiction, the lynching victim is begging for his life and speaking to the crowd. He is not always already dead—as he is in lynching photographs. Zane provides the victim with a backstory, relating that he is a former soldier who was stripped of his uniform and placed in a clown costume in order to further his humiliation. This individuation of the lynching victim stands in direct contrast to the often unidentified and unidentifiable corpses featured in photographs from the period.

Johnson and Pleece seem to offer comics as a more productive medium for visualizing race and, particularly, African American identity, than photography, which has for so long had a complicated relationship to African American experience due to its role in violently taxonomizing race or (often) taxonomizing racial violence. So often, photography has been used to record violence against African American bodies—whether in lynching photographs or in other records of the aftermath of violence, such as photographs of assassinated black leaders, depictions of the physical scars left behind by slavery, powerful photographs of the beaten bodies of black males, like the teenager Till, or, more recently, the cell-phone videos that have been circulating online of police violence against black men.[16] Comics offer the comics artist—and the reader—a chance to speak back to the violence being depicted.

In *Incognegro*, speech is literally superimposed on the panels. The image of the lynching is overlaid with boxes framing Zane's conversation with his friends back in Harlem. Zane explains to his naïve companions that he uses his light skin to fit into the scene at the lynching. The juxtaposition between word and image here is ironic, as Zane's conversation with his friends is calm and somewhat distant from the scene he is narrating. As Zane attempts to draw a picture of the lynching in words, Pleece provides other images from the lynching. These drawings focus on the stark violence of the act, borrowing cinematic tools, such as the close-up and the montage, to magnify the tortured face and body of the lynching victim. Increasingly, Zane is questioned about his own complicity in the violence. When one of his friends, Mildred, asks why he didn't "try and stop them," he replies, "By the time I show up, the man is already long doomed." Instead of directly intervening in the violence (as would have been largely impossible), Zane, like Johnson and Pleece, punishes participants at the lynchings by taking control of the picture they are seeing. Zane pretends to work with the photographer hired to capture images of the lynching and asks for the spectators' identifying information, claiming to need their names and addresses in order to send them a photographic keepsake. He then publishes the witnesses' identities, exposing their depravity to the gaze of readers in the North. He suggests that his role as witness is powerful precisely because it disallows lynching from being invisible in American culture. As he puts it, "most of the white papers don't even consider [the lynchings] news. To them, another nigger dead is not a story."[17]

Throughout this and other lynching scenes, Johnson and Pleece emphasize the complicity of the viewing public or spectator and the complexity of the act of witness. They ask, Do the spectators at the lynching—and, by extension, the spectators of Johnson and Pleece's representation of the lynching—get a perverse thrill from seeing violence? Later in the text, Johnson and Pleece make these connections among sex, violence, and the gaze explicit by juxtaposing images of lynching cards (playing cards with photographs of lynchings) with pornographic images. The text also questions Zane's complicity in the lynching and questions his "whiteness" when he witnesses the lynching. Like other neo-passing narratives, *Incognegro* recalls the themes of earlier passing narratives and their commentary on racial indeterminacy in the United States. In this case, Zane's act of witness invokes a similar scene of complicity that occurs near the end of *The Autobiography of an Ex-colored Man*. When the unnamed, biracial narrator of Johnson's 1912 novel witnesses a lynching, he, too, can do nothing to stop it. However, it is witnessing the lynching that catalyzes his decision to live out his life passing as a white man. He decides that he cannot be "identified with a people that could with impunity be treated worse than animals."[18] Why and how does this act of witness as a "white man" catalyze his refusal to identify with the person being lynched? If the narrator refuses identification with "a people that could with impunity be treated worse than animals," isn't he tacitly agreeing to identify with a people who could with impunity treat others as animals?

While *Incognegro* poses these complex, and largely unanswerable, ethical questions about passing, it also suggests that passing can be a fundamentally subversive act precisely because it allows those who are usually looked at to gaze back at those in power. In her work on what she calls "the oppositional gaze" in African American culture, bell hooks explores the potency of the "look back":

> Spaces of agency exist for black people, wherein we can both interrogate the gaze of the Other but also look back, and at one another, naming what we see. The "gaze" has been and is a site of resistance for colonized black people globally. Subordinates in relations of power learn experientially that there is a critical gaze, one that "looks" to document, one that is oppositional. In resistance struggle, the power of the dominated to assert agency by claiming and cultivating "awareness" politicizes "looking" relations—one learns to look a certain way in order to resist.[19]

The gaze that hooks describes is not only "critical" but also documentary in nature; it sees so as to witness and record. Although she is not referring directly to the type of looking (or "looking back") that Pinchback does, her discussion of the gaze as site of resistance provides an entryway into thinking about how we might view passing in *Incognegro,* as well as, perhaps, how we might start to use the contemporary witnessing of violence against black men to political use. The invisibility of the marginalized here carries an unexamined power to see—and eventually, as in Pinchback's case, expose the casual violence and oppression of white Southern culture in the 1930s. How might we humanize the often-dehumanizing gaze of the camera in order to encourage activism around police violence? Are other forms of media more apt to provide a voice for—as well as an image of—those who are victimized?

Johnson and Pleece are acutely aware of these questions of medium. In their hands, the graphic narrative itself functions as an analogue for Pinchback's role in *Incognegro*. Like journalist Zane, Johnson and Pleece act as witnesses, (sometimes literally) illustrating the repercussions of racism and racial essentialism for their readers. Like Zane, their choices place them in a profoundly complicated position from the purview of ethics. Also like Zane, they are forced to contend with an uncomfortable history—in this case an aesthetic or representational one. Comics and comics artists have long had a vexed relationship to race. Traditionally, the medium of comics has been associated with racial caricature. As Sander Gilman points out in his analysis of anti-Semitic caricature,[20] the traditions of comics and caricature blossomed in tandem with a post-Enlightenment figuration of difference that often took pictorial or graphic form. Along with a growing interest in scientific racism as a basis for inequality, many artists used visual media to concretize perceived racial difference and emphasize the boundaries between insider and outsider in the national imaginary. Frantz Fanon notes that comics (and, particularly, the jungle adventure stories favored by many comics readers) were also complicit in the romanticization of the colonial enterprise and the hegemonic racial project at its heart.[21]

Johnson and Pleece, like many comics artists before them, grapple with this complex inheritance of racial caricature in their depictions of racially marked bodies in *Incognegro*. Art Spiegelman, one of the most prominent composers of the graphic narrative, faced similar issues when constructing *Maus*, a tale that directly engages with Europe's history of grotesque Jewish caricature.[22] Among other things, Spiegelman's choice to represent his Jewish characters as mice in *Maus* invokes the frequent depiction of Jews as vermin in Nazi illustrations and film of the time period in order to interrogate the racial essentialism that undergirded the Third Reich. Although Spiegelman challenges racial stereotype in his drawings, he suggests that some form of caricaturing is unavoidable in comics. Writing about the cartoon Mohammed scandal in 2006, he asserts, "Cartoon language is mostly limited to deploying a handful of recognizable visual symbols or clichés. It makes use of the discredited pseudo-scientific principles of physiognomy to portray character through a few physical attributes and facial expressions."[23] Johnson and Pleece must contend with an equally pervasive tradition of visual caricature and exaggerated physiognomy—postbellum illustrations of African Americans that borrow their storehouse of racist imagery from the dramatis personae of the minstrel show. Pleece's photorealistic drawings defy the flattening iconicity of caricature and refuse easy identification between reader and character. As McCloud points out, the comics artists' decision to draw their characters photorealistically instead of cartoonishly forestalls the possibilities of easy reader identification and projection.

Johnson and Pleece's complex role as comics artists trying to negotiate the thorny history of race in America is not dissimilar from the difficult time the characters in the narrative have moving through the racial landscape of the United States in the 1930s. For the characters in *Incognegro*, passing is a double bind. Too-successful passing occasions a loss of self, while the failure of the passing subject often brings death, as it does for so many black subjects who become visible to the white gaze. Remaining unseen, as Zane needs to do in order to report on lynching and survive while doing so, undermines his connection to his family, as well as to his identity as a writer. Although Zane recognizes the value of his undercover reporting, he also resents being a faceless "incognegro" writer during an era of literary celebrity in Harlem. As his editor insists, Zane's power arises from his dual invisibility. A light-skinned black man, he is able to pass for white in the South. At the same time, the important work he does is also invisible. His editor asks him, in order to protect his safety and mobility, to do his work in secret, keeping his real name and photograph from appearing in the pages of the black newspapers in which his reports appear. Zane's desire to show himself at the same time that he recognizes the danger of being seen (particularly, for black men) is a metaphor for the ambivalent fate of the passing subject. The passing subject exposes the ideological strictures of race and denaturalizes whiteness at the expense of not only their families but also their very selves.

Despite the existential dangers of passing too successfully, failing is even more perilous. Many passing narratives hinge on the eventual failure of the passing subject and his or her punishment for not remaining within the boundaries of his or her position (whether that position be defined by race, gender, sexuality, or something else entirely). In *Incognegro,* acts of passing are not without repercussions. Being reminded of their own blindness enrages the white citizens whom Zane and his friend Carl encounter. Carl accompanies Zane south and poses as an Englishman. His passing is successful at first because he mimics the sound of British English he's heard on the radio and plays to the stereotypes the Southerners associate with England (namely, class and wealth). When he is found out, however, another, far more disastrous act of misidentification occurs. The white citizens of the unnamed Southern town have been told that a black man has been coming south to report on violence and lynching. They take Carl for this man—for Zane. To them, he is just another "incognegro," and this is how he ends his life—lynched with a sign saying "incognegro" around his neck.

Although Johnson and Pleece end the novel on this terrible note, they also provide an ironic coda that suggests the possibilities available to writers and artists who want to inscribe a new racial narrative atop this tragic one. Zane takes a photo of the Ku Klux Klan elder who has organized Carl's lynching and publishes it in the paper under the headline "Negro Race Spy's Identity Revealed." With this act, Zane uses his photographic and narrative prowess to disrupt the fixed image of race and power relations held by the men who killed Carl. Zane also suggests, again, that being a bad reader is dangerous; the Southerners who see this headline and the photograph beneath it unquestioningly set out to attack the man who was once their leader. Zane Pinchback's use of word and image to probe at the thorniness of race, violence, and identity is an analogue for the unexplored power of comics and graphic narrative to do the same.

If, as many comics-studies scholars suggest, comics encourage readers' agency by forcing them to take an active role in making meaning from the visual and narrative text they are given, might the medium have a particularly important role in contemporary conversations about race and racial violence? On a daily basis, critics from all corners of the political spectrum decry the ways in which American culture has become saturated by images that have desensitized us to the tragic weight of violence on the lives of those who suffer it. In *Incognegro*, Pleece and Johnson illustrate the power of images to critique violence, as well as to passively portray it. They suggest a way forward for those, like Pinchback, who recognize the complicated ethical position of the witness but simply cannot (and perhaps should not) look away.

Notes

1. Frederick Luis Aldama's edited collection on this topic, Michael Chaney's work in *Graphic Subjects*, and Derek Parker Royal's volume of MELUS on multiethnic comics are some of the other recent work that looks at race in comics. See Aldama, *Multicultural Comics*; Chaney, *Graphic Subjects*; and Royal, "Coloring America."

2. Haney-Lopez, "Social Construction."

3. Critical race theory (CRT) began as a movement of legal theorists seeking to expose the ways in which the law, while purportedly colorblind, was anything but.

4. I use the terms *graphic narrative* and *graphic novel* to describe *Incognegro* to mark the continuing terminological tension that exists in comics studies, where some scholars use the designation of *graphic novels* to refer to fictional and highly literary longform works, such as *Incognegro*, and others see the term as primarily a marketing one that creates unnecessary boundaries between "high" and "low" comics.

5. *Incognegro* is not the only work in which Mat Johnson manifests this interest in responding to earlier narratives about race. His novel *Pym*, published in 2011, is a rewriting of Edgar Allan Poe's only novel, *The Narrative of Arthur Gordon Pym of Nantucket*, which focuses on the story of a shipwreck on an imaginary island filled with black natives.

6. McCloud, *Understanding Comics*.

7. Johnson and Pleece, *Incognegro*, 18.

8. Ibid., 18.

9. Ibid., 19.

10. I can't help but see a correlation between this deconstructive methodology and earlier existential writings of Simone de Beauvoir about the problematic naturalization of man in the gender binary system.

11. Johnson and Pleece, *Incognegro*, 19.

12. Lee, introduction, 4.

13. Ibid.

14. Howard, "Lynchings."

15. Eisner, *Comics and Sequential Art*; McCloud, *Understanding Comics*.

16. Photographs were not the only way that violence and the visual were joined in the exercise of power on African American bodies. Saidiya Hartman notes the role of visual spectacle in slavery—the fearsome power of whippings not only in disciplining the slave who was being punished but also in disciplining the gaze of those who were witnessing the punishment. See Hartman, *Scenes of Subjection*.

17. Johnson and Pleece, *Incognegro*, 8, 7.

18. Johnson, *Autobiography of an Ex-colored Man*, 187.

19. hooks, "Oppositional Gaze," 116.

20. Gilman, *Jew's Body*.

21. Fanon, *Black Skin, White Masks*, 124–25.

22. Spiegelman, *Complete Maus*.

23. Spiegelman, "Drawing Blood," 45.

Bibliography

Aldama, Frederick Luis. *Multicultural Comics*. Austin: University of Texas Press, 2011.

Chaney, Michael. *Graphic Subjects*. Madison: University of Wisconsin Press, 2011.

Eisner, Will. *Comics and Sequential Art: Principles and Practices from the Legendary Cartoonist*. New York: Poorhouse, 1985.

Fanon, Frantz. *Black Skin, White Masks*. New York: Grove, 2008.

Frank, Waldo. *Holiday*. 1923. Champaign: University of Illinois Press, 2003.

Gilman, Sander. *The Jew's Body*. New York: Psychology, 1991.

Griffin, John Howard. *Black Like Me*. 1961. New York: Signet, 2010.

Haney-Lopez, Ian. "The Social Construction of Race: Some Observations on Illusion, Fabrication, and Choice." *Harvard Civil Rights–Civil Law Review* 29, no. 1 (1994): 1–62. Accessed January 16, 2017. http://scholarship.law.berkeley.edu/ facpubs/1815.

Hartman, Saidiya. *Scenes of Subjection: Terror, Slavery, and Self-Making in Nineteenth-Century America*. Oxford: Oxford University Press, 1997.

hooks, bell. "The Oppositional Gaze." In *Black Looks: Race and Representation*, 115–32. Boston: South End, 1992.

Howard, Sheena. "Lynchings to Walter Scott: The Public Display of Black Death." *(Trenton, NJ) Trentonian*, April 16, 2015. Accessed January 16, 2017. http://www.trentonian.com/.

Johnson, James Weldon. *The Autobiography of an Ex-colored Man*. New York: French, 1912.

Johnson, Mat. *Pym*. New York: Spiegel and Grau, 2011.

Johnson, Mat, and Warren Pleece. *Incognegro*. New York: Vertigo, 2008.

Larsen, Nella. Quicksand *and* Passing. 1928. New Brunswick, NJ: Rutgers University Press, 1986.

Lee, Anthony W. Introduction to *Lynching Photographs*, edited by Dora Apel and Shawn Michelle Smith. Berkeley: University of California Press, 2008.

McCloud, Scott. *Understanding Comics*. New York: Morrow, 1994.

Parker Royal, Derek, ed. "Coloring America: Multiethnic Engagements with Graphic Narrative." *MELUS* 32, no. 3 (2007): 7–22.

Spiegelman, Art. *The Complete Maus*. New York: Pantheon, 1996.

———. "Drawing Blood." *Harper's*, June 2006, 43–52.

Toomer, Jean. *Cane*. New York: Boni and Liveright, 1923.

PART II

New Identities

INTRODUCTION

Passing at the Intersections

MARCIA ALESAN DAWKINS

> I don't remember the first time I typed to a stranger.
> It wasn't monumental for me.
> But it did speak to a desire to escape . . .
> I could be anyone I wanted to be online.
>
> —Issa Rae, *The Misadventures of Awkward Black Girl*

As actress and *New York Times* best-selling author Issa Rae expresses with these poignant lines, passing is not always deliberate, purposeful, or even eventful in its first stages.[1] Over time, however, passing exposes our concerns with the way things are and our curiosities about the way things ought to be. As a passer like Rae, I certainly carry my own concern with and curiosity about life's limitations and possibilities. I learned to pass, and hence to craft, present, and preserve a carefully "edited self," when I needed to attend all-day elementary school in a New York City neighborhood different than the one in which I lived. Like so many before me who were "Negro by night" and "white by day," I, too, was passing.[2] I was an age passer, a four-year-old by night passing as a six-year-old by day, in a reality that existed completely offline but was nevertheless imbued with media and technology.

Among other things I had to remember a different year of birth and different address, each made available to me because of the resources to which my parents had access (i.e., telephones, automobiles, Xerox machines, and word processors). I had to learn how to appropriate and dole out other pieces of personal information to appear authentic to my classmates. My teacher was always watching, always concerned about my performance in class because I did not have the motor skills and physical abilities of my peers. Not only did I become painfully shy because my parents and I could not share my secret without the risk of my expulsion but also I learned to work twice as hard as my peers in order to meet expectations and earn the access to a better education passing granted me. Though my passing into the first grade was serious business, my parents and I also learned to have a sense of humor about the situation. We joked often and congratulated ourselves with strawberry milkshakes when I did well.

In the end my passing was productive despite the anxiety and intrigue it created. From it I developed a work ethic that served me well beyond elementary school and through my doctoral studies when I was diagnosed with cancer. Once again I passed. Rather than share my health status with colleagues, students, and professors and run the risk of failing to complete my degree, I became an ability/health passer. I kept my diagnosis private and continued with treatments while maintaining the appearance and workload of a full-time, healthy graduate student. Looking back on my experiences with and research on passing and forward to the essays in part 2 of the current volume, I realize that while conventional passing is often considered an ephemeral performance across a fixed binary line,[3] neo-passing is an "elastic," intersectional, and ever-present state of being.[4] Whether along the axes of race, class, gender, religion, age, health, sexual orientation, (dis)ability, criminality, or something else entirely, the acts of neo-passing explored here represent as much a set of practices as they do a way of life. The hallmark of this lifestyle is the "edited self" that is a carefully crafted, presented, and preserved profile unit to be promoted in exchange for recognized social status. What is more, I realize that when the edited self is made meaningful in economies based on commodification, the appearance of the commodity (particularly, in media) is the measure of its social value.[5] And for many marginalized identities, value and status are equivalent, calculated relative to that of the dominant culture.[6] The idea that value and status are equivalent means that even in the wake of Jim/Jane Crow segregation, there are still lessons to learn about how today's neo-passers figure out how to enact new identities and update their profiles. In what follows, I briefly describe these lessons—about privacy, assimilation, satire, and surveillance, or PASS—as they shape and are shaped by the new identities and technologies of our historical moment.

The first lesson concerns *privacy*. In the social media–driven marketplace of the new millennium, identity is often reduced to a "profile" and considered private property worth protecting.[7] But the logic for this conception of identity harkens back to an act of racial/class passing and the infamous 1896 US Supreme Court *Plessy v. Ferguson* decision, which upheld the constitutionality of state laws requiring racial segregation in public facilities under the doctrine of "separate but equal."[8] The Court used law as a technology to create a concept of (white) identity as a form of private property that needed to be protected from invasion by nonwhite others.[9] That ruling meant racial passers were treated as identity thieves and "privacy pirates" rather than as human beings and "hacktivists" who strove to return autonomy to those from whom it had been eliminated by institutionalized racism.[10] This privacy-oriented perspective on passing helps to contextualize today's concerns with privacy and identity protection, revealing an obsession with individuals and individual harm and an absence of attention to structural inequities.[11] Conceived thus, neo-passing narratives reveal that privacy only protects those who inhabit the spaces in which they appear to "belong."

The second lesson that can be updated from passing's performance narratives to neo-passing's "edited selves" regards *assimilation*. While many critics argue that passing is always an attempt to assimilate, passing like Homer Plessy's actually represents the profound failure of an assimilationist project.[12] As evidence for the persistent truth that neo-passing is also about a failure to assimilate, take the contemporary case of African American journalist Jamie Nesbitt Golden. In April 2014 Golden penned an article for *XO Jane* explaining why she passes 2.0-style as "a white bearded hipster guy on Twitter."[13] Golden argues that she is trolled less and respected more for her opinions when she attaches a white male avatar to her profile:

> The number of snarky, condescending tweets dropped off considerably. . . . I had suddenly become reasonable and level-headed. My racial identity no longer clouded my ability to speak thoughtfully, and in good faith. It was like I was a new person. Once I went back to Black [and female], it was back to business as usual.[14]

Golden's experience as a passer reminds us that in a culture whose values and opportunities are reserved largely for the bodies of "white bearded hipster guys," it is often necessary to take on the characteristics of such bodies to become more valuable. Put differently, Golden shows us that "the problem of appropriation, 'the making of a thing one's own property,' stands at the very center of the problem of passing."[15] Passers know that when assimilation fails, appropriation takes its place.

The next lesson learned from traditional narratives of passing that can be applied to neo-passing concerns *satire*. In a traditional passing narrative like

George Schuyler's 1931 novel *Black No More,* passing satirically reveals that differences between people who are differently raced are not essential but structural, experiential, and socially constructed. The satirical function of the traditional passing narrative reemerges in recent neo-passing narratives, such as Seattle-based writer Ijeoma Oluo in several tweets in January 2015 in response to one that informed her, based on a photo she had posted to her Twitter profile, that she was not a woman of color but was white.[16] Oluo immediately responded to this "helpful stranger" with a thread of satirical tweets about the "life changes" she would now have to undergo. For instance, Oluo would no longer have to "care about this equality stuff anymore" and could now focus on important things like borrowing "a polo shirt" instead. She then asked, "So is this where I get mad about not being able to say the 'n' word?" followed by, "Where does one buy Uggs?" and "Does this mean that now if I go missing y'all are going to look for me?" Perhaps most poignant was her final exclamation, "Wow you guys. I just tried to not see color for the first time and it's AMAZING." Oluo's tweets are both a powerful critique of racist and postracial discourse and an example of immediate, visible, and sharable storytelling that can engage community building, personal brand management, and social resistance through social media. Through satire, neo-passing narratives can critique the notion that the social-media age, or any age before it, promotes an egalitarian society or provides meritocratic opportunities for success. Indeed, the very fact that people take such great pains to pass—to curate and edit selves for public consumption—is opposed to the stated ideals of equality, meritocracy, and collaboration that permeate mainstream discourses of politics, entertainment, and technology.[17] Like the social-media outlets through which identities are currently projected, neo-passing teaches us about ourselves and about how to create inhabitable worlds both online and off.

The final lesson an intersectional contextualization of neo-passing teaches us is about *surveillance.* The racial passing of Homer Plessy and my own age and health passing are as much about passers' surveilling possibilities and privileges afforded to others as they are about passers being surveilled by others. A key to understanding the implicit surveillance in any act of neo-passing is the myth of identity dualism, which states that passers have one true and one false persona, white or black, abled or disabled, female or male, and that someone call tell the difference.[18] This myth is pervasive and, as the authors in this part argue, leads many to assert that passing does more harm than good, is best understood as a matter of emotional loss, alienates passers from "real life," and needs to be outed at all costs. For example, in Facebook's 2014 drag-queen controversy, a single Facebook user reported several hundred drag queens' profiles, claiming the accounts were fake and belonged to "bad actors doing bad things": impersonation, bullying, trolling, domestic violence, scams, hate speech, and more. As a result, Facebook asked the drag queens to verify their identities or risk having their accounts deleted. Although the outrage that followed finally resulted in Facebook apologizing and updating its gender options to include a drop-down menu of fifty-six options and a space to type in answers, the controversy reveals how deeply this dualistic claim has come to dominate the way many advocates, critics, corporations, and policymakers think about neo-passing's effects on our society.

The chapters featured in this section reveal a variety of justifications for shining the analytical spotlight on neo-passing. These may include exhortation, shaming, and exposing hypocrisy, or—as these chapters do—the more productive tasks of increasing the visibility of and shattering binary categories of identification and valuation. On one hand, the analyses conducted remind us of the high cost neo-passers pay for status. On the other hand, the analyses also remind us that the most successful acts of neo-passing leave few footprints. What is more, the hotly contested nature of the subject suggests surveillance might be a double-edged sword. The forthcoming chapters reveal that there might be equal pleasure in shining a light on neo-passing as there might be in colluding with neo-passers to build community in the face of discrimination. For instance, there exists the pleasure of helping neo-passers reposition those in power, "which transforms a painful scenario of collaboration into an occasion to make and remake community."[19] Of course, one's motive for analyzing, exposing, and/or colluding with passers depends on one's own social location and the status and community membership one seeks.

The chapters that follow all foreground intersectionality and update the notions of privacy, assimilation, satire, and surveillance (PASS) that are embedded in the traditional passing narrative for the identities and technologies of the present day. Media's broadcasting ability has honed and amplified passing's traditional concerns, techniques, and effectiveness, encouraging people to prioritize status, visibility, and an ability to focus audiences' attention on carefully crafted editions of self. In addition to the web, movies, literature, and journalism, social-media apps like Twitter, Facebook, Snapchat, Tumblr, Periscope, WeChat, and Instagram (not to mention content-editing tools like PhotoShop and FaceTune) have made it even easier for neo-passers to blend an ability to project consumable personas with a continuous address of multiple audiences amidst obsessions with authenticity and selective disclosure.

These updated technologies, coupled with historical concerns of privacy, assimilation, satire, and surveillance, allow neo-passing to move beyond the binaries of traditional passing to address intersectional issues of multiculturalism, multiracialism, ethnicity, gender, sexual orientation, religion, class, ability, health, crime, and punishment. The authors' analyses here expand upon on this movement and present five opportunities to learn more about the dilemmas of identification and representation in our present moment from a perspective that is grounded in experiences of the marginalized rather than of the privileged. Neo-passing confounds a culture of legibility and integrates advertising and marketing practices along with an elastic sense of self into the ways that people view their profiles, relationships, and identities.

As a passer and a scholar, it is my hope that attention to these studies will help update discourses of equality and human rights by questioning the existence of essentialist, fixed, ontological subject positions, challenging the statuses they carry and exploding the myth that collective intelligence fosters equal access to the public sphere. For all of us whose profiles and experiences are filtered through and determined by the framing of media, passing should continue to be a critical topic of conversation because it will be a way of life.

Notes

1. Rae, *Misadventures*.
2. Marwick, *Status Update*, 16; "White by Day," 80.
3. Dawkins, *Clearly Invisible*, 129.
4. Wang, "Talking to Strangers," 21.
5. Marx, *Kapital Volume One*, 144.
6. Doane, *Femme Fatales*, 22–23.
7. Dawkins, *Clearly Invisible*, 60–61.
8. Medley, *We as Freedmen*, 47.
9. Harris, "Whiteness as Property," 1720.
10. Dawkins, *Clearly Invisible*, 75.
11. Cohen, *Configuring the Networked Self*, 108–9.
12. Young, *From Bourgeois to Boojie*, 15.
13. Golden, "Why I'm Masquerading."
14. Ibid.
15. Robinson, "To Pass//In Drag," 190.
16. Oluo, Twitter posts.
17. Gunkel and Gournelos, *Transgression 2.0*, 200.
18. Gross, *Contested Closets*, 34.
19. Robinson, "To Pass//In Drag," 62.

Bibliography

Cohen, Julie E. *Configuring the Networked Self: Law, Code, and the Play of Everyday Practice*. New Haven, CT: Yale University Press, 2012.

Dawkins, Marcia Alesan. *Clearly Invisible: Racial Passing and the Color of Cultural Identity*. Waco, TX: Baylor University Press, 2012.

Doane, Mary Ann. *Femme Fatales: Feminism, Film Theory, Psychoanalysis*. New York: Routledge, 1991.

Golden, Jamie Nesbitt. "Why I'm Masquerading as a White Bearded Hipster Guy on Twitter (Despite being a Black Woman)." *XO Jane Magazine*, April 14, 2014. Accessed May 19, 2014. http://www.xojane.com/issues/why-im-masquerading-as-a-bearded-white-hipster-guy-on-twitter.

Gross, Larry P. *Contested Closets: The Politics and Ethics of Outing*. Minneapolis: University of Minnesota Press, 1993.

Gunkel, David J., and Ted Gournelos. *Transgression 2.0: Media, Culture, and the Politics of a Digital Age*. New York: Continuum, 2012.

Harris, Cheryl I. "Whiteness as Property." *Harvard Law Review* 106, no. 8 (1993): 1706–91.

Marwick, Alice E. *Status Update: Celebrity, Publicity, and Branding in the Social Media Age*. New Haven, CT: Yale University Press, 2013.

Marx, Karl. *Kapital Volume One*. Translated by Ernest Mandel. 1867. New York: Vintage, 1977.

Medley, Keith Weldon. *We as Freedmen:* Plessy v. Ferguson. Gretna, LA: Pelican, 2003.

Oluo, Ijeoma. Twitter post @IjeomaOluo. January 13, 2015, 5:27, 5:32, and 5:38 A.M. https://twitter.com/IjeomaOluo.

Rae, Issa. *The Misadventures of Awkward Black Girl*. New York: Atria, 2015.

Robinson, Amy. "To Pass//In Drag: Strategies of Entrance into the Visible." PhD diss., University of Pennsylvania, 1993.

Wang, Tricia. "Talking to Strangers: Chinese Youth and Social Media." PhD diss., University of California, San Diego, 2013.

"White by Day . . . Negro by Night." *Ebony*, April 1952, 31–36. Rpt. in *Ebony*, November 1975, 80–83.

Young, Vershawn A., with Bridget Harris Tsemo, ed. *From Bourgeois to Boojie: Black Middle-Class Performances*. Detroit: Wayne State University Press, 2011.

CHAPTER 6

Passing Truths

Identity-Immersion Journalism and the Experience of Authenticity

LORAN MARSAN

John Howard Griffin's *Black Like Me* holds a unique place in the history of passing narratives. Published in 1961 in the midst of the Civil Rights Movement and desegregation—after *Brown v. Board of Education* (1954) and the Montgomery bus boycott (1955–57) and before the Civil Rights Act of 1964—*Black Like Me* was unlike the conventional passing narratives that preceded it. Where conventional passing narratives focus on black individuals passing as white, Griffin's text focuses on a white individual passing as black. And where those conventional texts usually depict passing as an individualistic act carried out for personal gain, often at the expense of the community, Griffin's text depicts passing as a selfless act carried out for the sake of the public good. *Black Like Me* went on to become the reference point for a recognizable genre of identity-immersion journalism that includes Grace Halsell's *Soul Sister, Bessie Yellowhair,* and *The Illegals*; Barbara Ehrenreich's *Nickel and Dimed: On (Not) Getting By in America*; Norah Vincent's *Self-Made Man: One Woman's Year Disguised as a Man*; and the 2006 FX channel reality TV series *Black. White.* While these texts present many different modes of boundary crossings across lines of race, ethnicity, citizenship, gender, and class, they all follow Griffin by positioning themselves as experiments designed to gain "authentic" knowledge about people different from themselves for the purpose of creating empathy and understanding across those lines of difference.

Written during the period of large-scale protest, unrest, and violence (by whites against blacks) that led up to the passing of the Civil Rights Act of 1964—*Black Like Me* marks the beginning of a new subgenre of passing narratives, one that claims to be committed to the humanist goal of healing the divide between the races. Gayle Wald and Baz Dreisinger both include *Black Like Me* in their seminal works on passing literature, placing Griffin's temporary white-to-black passing on a continuum with a variety of real and fictional passing narratives that go in "both" directions (as it is often marked within the black/white binary).[1] I draw from Wald's and Dreisinger's arguments about white-to-black passing narratives in order to further interrogate how passing narratives function in the realm of journalism, which (according to journalists, at least) has its root in truth, objectivity, and the real.[2] As a journalistic text explicitly devoted to promoting cross-racial understanding, *Black Like Me* departs from what Kathleen Pfeiffer describes as the individualism of earlier passing narratives.[3] This more heroic goal also places *Black Like Me* in conversation with other neo-passing narratives addressed in the current volume because the "experiment" that it proposes to undertake speaks directly to the dissolution and aftermath of Jim Crow.[4] The subsequent emergence of an entire genre of journalistic experiments following in the footsteps of *Black Like Me* reveals the neo-passing narrative's reinvention of the passing narrative in the service of post–Jim Crow calls to make our society more inclusive and understanding of diversity not only in terms of race but also in terms of gender and class.

And yet, despite the popularity and proliferation of this neo-passing subgenre aimed at knowing and understanding the "Other," passing as the Other is clearly an odd way to gain authentic knowledge about the Other, given that passing is defined as the performance of a nonauthentic identity. Linda Schlossberg argues that "the passing subject's ability to transcend or abandon his or her 'authentic' identity calls into question the very notion of authenticity itself. Passing, it seems, threatens to call attention to the performative and contingent nature of all seemingly 'natural' or 'obvious' identities."[5] Likewise, Marion Rust argues that passing "mocks our melancholy, ridiculing essentialist notions of a 'true' Self preceding, and corrupted by, its subsequent enactments. In a sense, passing foregrounds what is *between*—between origin and enactment, body and gesture—calling into question all such fixed ways of determining identity."[6] Where the conventional passing narratives of the Jim Crow era typically depicted passing as evidence of racial ambiguity or deceit, identity-immersion journalism deems itself a serious inquiry into the lives of Others that works only if it can convince its readership that its acquisition of the real experiences of an/Other person is authentic. Thus, despite the fact that these neo-passing narratives often explicitly propose to help break down the barriers between identity categories in the post–Jim Crow era, their rhetorical dependence on the need to produce authentic experiences ultimately reinforces the boundaries that construct these differences as opposites and Others to begin with. As a result, although identity-immersion journalism aims at producing empathy across lines of difference, its production of objective and emotive forms of authenticity does far more to reify those lines of difference than to break them down.

Objective and Emotional Authenticity

In *Culture and Authenticity,* Charles Lindholm argues that we identify something or someone as authentic through two overlapping modes: the objective, scientific, or genealogical proof and the subjective, emotional, or interior experience. In the first mode, an object, person, place, or so forth is considered authentic if his/her/its genealogical roots can be traced back scientifically or objectively to the corresponding identity, time period, or artist. The authentication of artworks at museums or auctions exemplifies this mode. Through scientific testing of paint or techniques, or solid proof of genealogy of ownership, a work of art is deemed authentic and thus worthy of display or sale. A similar authentication process is used in some Native American and aboriginal groups to determine tribal membership through DNA—thus irrefutably confirming the "truth" of a person's "real" origins. In contrast, in the second mode, a person or event is considered authentic if what he/she/it purports to be or feel corresponds with what he/she/it really is or feels. Lindholm argues that "the dominant trope for personal authenticity in modern America is . . . the notion that feeling is the most potent and real aspect of the self."[7] Of course, the reality of one's feelings is much harder to prove, but it is often used in journalistic genres when objective authenticity is in doubt.

The rhetorical devices of reality television make use of both of these modes. Reality TV stresses its use of "real" people as participants whose "real" and "authentic" experience and emotions are caught on recordings by the fly-on-the-wall documentary style. In "Caught on Tape: A Legacy of Low-Tech Reality," Amy West argues that use of footage from amateur video or surveillance cameras is the epitome of the "real" used in reality TV, and "the intersection of amateur and accident made a special promise of authenticity."[8] The cues of authentic reality established by this camera work, as well as the confessional format, are used in reality TV to reinforce that the product is real and authentic. However, as James Friedman asserts, savvy contemporary viewers no longer accept photography and film as objective evidence, so reality TV must constantly reassert its authenticity in order to sell itself as real.[9] In many cases, reality TV shows use the authenticity of emotional experience to shore up any doubts about the objective authenticity of reality TV, pairing through narrative the objective authenticity of the visible with the subjective authenticity of emotional connection between the "real" people on screen and viewers.

Likewise, the emphasis on personal, lived reality in identity-immersion journalism reveals the ways in which this genre draws together scientific and/or objective registers and emotional registers of authenticity in order to create the real of the participants' experiences. Indeed, most pieces of identity-immersion journalism begin with a description of the scientific nature of their projects. In *Black Like Me*, Griffin writes, "This began as a scientific research study of the Negro in the South, with careful compilation of data for analysis when a so-called first-class citizen is cast on the junkheap of second-class citizenship."[10] Griffin later refers to the project as his "experiment," just as Halsell later does when she wonders in *Soul Sister* what "this experiment" will do to her body and mind.[11] Ehrenreich also references her book as an experiment: "In the end, the only way to overcome my hesitation was by thinking of myself as a scientist, which is, in fact, what I was educated to be."[12] Griffin, Halsell, Vincent, Ehrenreich, and the producers of *Black. White.* all utilize the rhetoric of the real to authenticate their passing experiences, citing a quest for real knowledge as the thing that makes it not only okay but necessary for them to pass and write about it objectively. Griffin asks, "How else except by becoming a Negro could a white man hope to learn the truth? . . . The Southern Negro will not tell the white man the truth. He long ago learned that if he speaks a truth unpleasing to the white, the white will make life miserable for him."[13]

Academics have found this supposition of scientific study problematic in its assumption of unbiased access to an/Other's lived reality. In addressing Griffin's text, Wald argues his experiment and methodology are troubling because of "his implicit perception that as a white male intellectual he is entitled to the cultural knowledge of others; his assumption that he can willfully transcend the conditions of his own social formation; [and] his conviction that passing affords the only means of authenticating racial oppression."[14] This was the largest critique of Griffin's work and one he eventually acknowledged, taking himself off the lecture circuit and saying that he could no longer be a voice for African Americans. Nevertheless, the identity-immersion texts that follow Griffin's continue his "conviction that passing affords the only means of authenticating . . . oppression."[15] The authors of these texts may try to temper the problems associated with Griffin's assertion that he is "becoming" black by emphasizing that they are only "being treated as" or "received as" rather than "being." They may even explicitly admit, as does Vincent, that one can never get the full experience of an/Other because of the built-in escape hatch of returning to one's real identity or because of not being raised with a lifetime of that Other's experience. Ultimately, however, even the most recent identity-immersion narratives quickly dismiss these limitations in favor of the altruistic intent of going in search of a Truth—a Truth that the very proliferation of these texts erroneously suggests cannot be found by simply talking with those Others about their experiences.

Even when identity-immersion journalists do admit the scientific or objective limits of their experiments, they often do so in order to describe them as more truthful as a result of their personal and emotive content. After his assertion that his experience "began as a scientific research study," Griffin describes, "But I filed the data, and here publish the journal of my own experience living as a Negro. I offer it in all its crudity and rawness. It traces the changes that occur to heart and body and intelligence."[16] Halsell similarly writes that she wanted to "get the facts of a situation and use them in a manner that would go beyond mere data to some kind of 'truth.'"[17] And while Vincent admits that "to say that I conducted and recorded the results of an experiment is not to say that this book pretends to be a scientific or objective study," she argues that her experience was no less real as a result: "I did partake in my own experiment, live it and internalize its effects. Being Ned changed me and the people around me, and I have attempted to record those changes."[18] Formally, too, these texts mirror this twin commitment to the two modes of authenticity. Griffin's and Vincent's works consist entirely of journal entries that "attempted to record" the emotional and personal change resulting from the experiment, and Halsell's and Ehrenreich's works loosely follow this trend. The use of journal entries in these texts conveys the emotional truths of the writers in the objective form of daily records; the authors present themselves as anthropologists who are "torn between these two positions: the empiricist observer and the romantic participant."[19] Likewise, in every episode of *Black. White.*, participants are shown talking directly to the camera about the episode's events and experiments. The show carefully edits out the interviewers' questions in order to mimic the impression of intimacy and immediacy provided by a video confessional. These interjections often contain venting about the emotional difficulty of the experiment—how they are scared, worried, excited, hurt—thus shoring up the objective authenticity of the experience by insisting, repeatedly, on its emotional authenticity.

Difficulty and Essentialism

These journalistic narratives strive to depict emotional authenticity precisely in order to rectify the dissonance that their performances of an inauthentic identity might otherwise provoke. As Lindholm comments, "the notion that feeling is the most potent and real aspect of the self" is a major tenet of authenticity.[20] Authenticity is threatened by the taking on of inauthentic identity, and emotion is used to shore up authenticity in multiple ways. What the writers and/or participants feel throughout the process is foregrounded as what makes their experiences real. Bussing into Mississippi and encountering hatred by whites, Griffin "felt the insane terror of it" and later "felt disaster."[21] Both he and Halsell write of "feeling" black. Halsell relates, "I feel myself most black when I see white cops cruising by," and Griffin says he "felt more profoundly than ever before the totality of my Negro-ness, the immensity of its isolating effects."[22] Vincent as well talks of how wearing the mask of masculinity made her feel like it was an uneasy fit but that this, in the end, is what men experience. When perceived as a black person or a man, the authors reacted with genuine feeling, and, thus, according to them, their experience is authentic.

However, while these texts frequently use emotional intimacy to reinforce the perceived authenticity of writers' experiences, they as often use that emotional intimacy to stress its difficulty. In a scene previewed at least six times throughout *Black. White.*, Rose in black makeup is seen from a distance, shot through the door of her trailer, with her hand to her head, crying, "I don't want to be in makeup anymore!"[23] The repetition of this emotional scene shows the toll that playing another race takes on an individual. It is preceded by Halsell's and Vincent's breakdowns at the close of their experiments. Vincent explains her "mental collapse" before checking into a mental hospital was because disguising herself as a man opened a "fault line" in her mind.[24] Halsell was "terror-stricken" while in Mississippi disguised as a black woman.[25] Griffin's first experiences as a black man are emotionally authenticated through the physical pain he feels after walking all day, Halsell's are marked by multiple medical emergencies including infected feet, and Ehrenreich's are focused on the physical toll of working for low wages. These emotions and physically felt experiences work in two ways: to authenticate their emotional reality of their passing experiences and to insist that they were extremely difficult to withstand and continue. For example, Vincent ultimately argues: "If I'd known then what I know now, I could never have embarked on the project. Yet . . . I wouldn't trade the experience for anything. The knowledge was absolutely worth the pain. . . . The lesson I can apply to my next project is that I can never again try to be someone else, someone that I'm not."[26] The message is clear—only in the search of knowledge is passing a good thing, but it is so difficult and harrowing that no one should or could do it for long periods of time. Identities are simultaneously "authentically" experienced and kept in their appropriate boxes. Boundary crossings are simultaneously made and depicted as dangerous, if not impossible, to enact and sustain.

By asserting the difficulty and enormous effort of passing, these texts not only purport to inhabit "otherness" but they also seek to both acknowledge and reify the perceived dissonance between the authenticity of the experience and the inauthenticity of their performed identity. It is significant that no mainstream journalist or documentary-style racial-passing text focuses on mixed-race individuals who need no technological miracles to successfully "pass" one way or the other in a society that, until recently, demanded singular identification. While there are many memoirs written by such individuals, they do not purport to be objective experiments but, rather, subjective accounts of a person's life. These are valuable in their own right but are not part of this journalistic documentary genre. Valerie Rohy comments, "In matters of race as well as sexuality, passing both invokes and unravels the logic of primary and secondary, authenticity and inauthenticity, candor and duplicity, by placing in question the priority of what is claimed as 'true' identity. The discourse of racial passing reveals the arbitrary foundation of the categories 'black' and 'white,' just as passing across gender and sexuality places in question the meaning of 'masculine' and 'feminine,' 'straight' and 'gay.' Racial passing is thus subject to an epistemological ambiguity."[27] Mainstream neo-passing texts seem terrified of this epistemological ambiguity and strive to nullify it—primarily through ignoring mixed-race or genderqueer people and histories of passing that required no makeup, medicines, or experts. *Black Like Me* and *Soul Sister* passages reveal the tedious courses of doctor visits, skin pigment–changing pills, and long tanning sessions necessary to become black. Vincent's *Self-Made Man* also underscores through seven pages of description that the "switch" from one side of a binary to the other is not done easily.[28] And *Black. White.* includes lengthy sections on how difficult it is to make black people look white, and vice versa. At least a third of the first episode focuses on the difficulty, time, and expertise involved in the transformation.[29] Episode 4's commentary is solely on makeup. Every episode shows each participant in the makeup chair, and all the participants in their own commentaries record the large number of hours spent there: anywhere from five hours for Rose's hair and makeup to eight hours for Brian's first makeup experience.[30] The impossibility of passing without makeup or medical technology reinforces the show's idea of completely separate and static identity categories with boundaries that are not—and should not—be easily crossed. Unlike recent autobiographical memoirs that focus on identities that more comfortably occupy spaces of duality, multiplicity, mimicry, and artifice,[31] these neo-passing journalistic texts reinforce the idea that passing *should* be hard because the identity categories represented are so fundamentally opposed.

In its ultimate reassertion of these binaristic categories, identity-immersion journalism is much more like conventional passing narratives than one might expect, despite the multiplicity of identity categories that it now represents. Like conventional passing narratives, identity-immersion journalism frequently focuses on the difficulty associated with the deception and inauthenticity necessary when passing. Feelings of guilt plague these passers as they fret about not presenting their true selves. Significant parts of these texts address not only their feelings of guilt at lying but the occasions when their passes are revealed to a select few. This emphasis on the difficulty of deception results in reifying the status quo ideology invested in refuting the possibility of passing while reaffirming both their emotive authenticity (being true to themselves) and their true identity (by revealing themselves). Vincent describes this: "The difficulty lay in the consequences of passing, and that I had not even considered. As I lived snippets of a male life, one part of my brain was duly taking notes and making observations, intellectualizing the raw material of Ned's experience, but another part of my brain, the subconscious part, was taking blows to the head, and eventually those injuries caught up with me. . . . I paid a higher emotional price for my circumstantial deceptions than any of my subjects did."[32] Although she admits that physically passing was easier than she thought it would be, she negates this by saying the emotional toll was extremely hard, she was punished for it, and not being true to herself—not being authentic—led to this punishment. In an interesting gendered dynamic of *Black. White.*, all three women but no men express guilt and regret about their deception once they become close to someone.[33] Rose is first in the show to make connections with people while in makeup and first to express regret at deceiving members of a poetry group: "The hardest part about this is keeping the lie. The poetry classes are so honest. I just cannot stand lying to them anymore. I am not going back there pretending anymore. These are the people I wanna be real with. I really need to tell them the truth."[34] The use of close-ups cue the viewer in to the emotional content and authenticity of this statement by showing her facial expressions in detail and literally getting closer to her.

Just as quickly as participants feel guilt at lying about their true selves, they reveal themselves—bringing the story back into the fold by authenticating true identities and feeling, lending authenticity to the pass through the "truth" of the revelation. The inauthenticity of passing is resolved by the interpersonal authenticity of the reveal. In all these texts, scenes of revelation are documented in great detail, including the lead-up, the actual reveal, and the minutia of the passed-to person's reaction. Rose's revelation to her poetry class is fraught with emotion as she tells them, "I'm actually a white girl in black makeup. I live in Santa Monica, I've told you the truth from the beginning except for the fact that I've walked in here in makeup, and that is the lie."[35] This is followed by reaction shots of poetry club members and three of them commenting on it, two whom are supportive because of the education aspect of the project and her truthfulness. One student's disgust is rooted in an inability to "see" Rose's true self and thus an inability (reiterated three times) to know who Rose is. Rose responds that she appreciates his honesty (his authenticity). This is followed by a party where the student makes peace with her—presumably because now he knows who she "really" is, a white girl.

The reveal is an essential part of any conventional passing narrative,[36] and these neo-passing narratives reveal their indebtedness to the static notions of identity that dominated the Jim Crow era by relying on this generic trope. Regardless of whether or how a narrative questions identity formation (if at all), every conventional passing narrative has some sort of reveal, either within the diegesis or to the audience in-the-know, that results in passers' true identities being restored. Amy Robinson argues that every passing story includes a triangular relation among passer, dupe, and in-group clairvoyant such that while there is someone who only sees the passing identity as the true identity (dupe), there is also always someone who sees the pass as pass.[37] A large part of passing is contained in the reveal—successful passing would remain unremarkable if it were unseen. The reveal is not only necessary for the audience but often for those within the texts as well—the truth must be outed, and original or real or authentic identities are always reinstated at some level of the narrative.[38]

The only text where the revelation is ultimately unremarkable (to the dupes within the story, at least) is Ehrenreich's *Nickel and Dimed*. This, though, only further reinforces hegemonic ideology about identities—some are unchangeable, but class (if only mythically) is. Ehrenreich's deception is presented as less severe, though she still enacts the guilt and reveal of the passing story: "In each setting... after much anxious forethought, I 'came out' to a few chosen coworkers. The result was always stunningly anticlimactic.... It may also be that I was exaggerating the extent of the 'deception' to myself. There's no way, for example, to pretend to be a waitress: the food either gets to the table or not. People knew me as a waitress, a cleaning person, a nursing home aide, or a retail clerk not because I acted like one but because that's what I *was*, at least for the time I was with them."[39] Ehrenreich authenticates her class experience by emphasizing that she really "was" a working-class person because she really "was" a waitress, clerk, and so on—negating the fact that she had escape hatches, such as having a car, using money she already had to pay security deposits, running home at the threat of homelessness, and others. Even though she "was" a waitress, this did not necessarily mean she was "really" living off low wages. Her claims are in step with hegemonic ideology of meritocracy, and class becomes the one passable border—the reveal becomes unnecessary because class is supposedly the only permeable boundary, but it is enacted anyway. Even though class becomes malleable, Ehrenreich remains faithful to the conventional passing narrative, and the reveal as a necessary part of the passing scene buttresses the passer's authenticity, integrity, and legitimacy endangered by the act of passing.

Becoming the Other—Splitting the Self

Identity-immersion journalism often explicitly aligns itself with a contemporary colorblind "one people" ideology, even as its rhetorical devices reify the more essentialized binaries associated with the Jim Crow era by keeping races, ethnicities, genders, and classes in opposing fields with a wide gulf between them. This colorblind sentiment is the last line of Halsell's memoir: "Strangers became just like me—when I walked in their shoes."[40] Rose says, "I'm realizing that perhaps we are just human beings, and I am just a girl. . . . Everybody is just who they are."[41] And yet, even with the overt expression of liberal, pluralist, melting-pot ideals, the strains of seeing these Others-who-are-really-just-like-us-but-most-definitely-not-like-us shines through in Halsell's reference to strangers and Rose's assertion before she says the above that the experience is one of "trying to enter a world that isn't yours."[42] This split is exemplified by the title *Black. White.* A period separates the two terms: not a slash, comma, or any punctuation that might bridge or connect the terms. A full stop separates the two in the same way that passers deem each as its own world. Vincent and the two mothers in *Black. White.* refer to their experiences as that of their "opposite," Brian Sparks is intrigued by "the other side," and many refer to their experience as Rose does—as in an entirely different "world."[43] These representations as well as ones about the "gulf," "barrier," or "wall" between the races, classes, or genders reinforce separation.[44]

These texts also contain passers who see themselves as entirely different entities when passing, separating their real selves from their Other selves and in many cases damaging their authentic identity. Griffin's oft-quoted first vision of his passing self is jarring:

> The face and shoulders of a stranger—a fierce, bald, very dark Negro—glared at me from the glass. *He in no way resembled me.*
>
> The transformation was total and shocking. . . . I was imprisoned in the flesh of *an utter stranger,* an unsympathetic one with whom I felt no kinship. All traces of the John Griffin I had been were wiped from existence. The completeness of this transformation appalled me. . . . *I became two men. . . .*
>
> I had tampered with the mystery of existence and *I had lost the sense of my own being. . . .* The Griffin that was had become invisible.[45]

Griffin is shocked by his passing self so much that he feels he is now two people and has lost his sense of being. This is reiterated in Halsell's *Soul Sister* where she says, "I will no longer be the person I've always been," "I see myself as two persons," and most dramatically after an episode of her "tan" peeling after too much sun, "As I sit looking at that face with pale, accusing eyes—self-indicted as miserable, ugly, unloving, and unlovable, not myself, not another, a no-body, a no-thing—the eyes condemn me, no longer able to see the person I have destroyed, only the unraveled, molting monster I have created."[46] Even when no physical change to the body occurs, Halsell feels disembodied and destroyed by passing as an/Other in *Bessie Yellowhair*: "I realize I am no longer *me*; *I* do not exist at all. I am now existing—*as an Indian*—but *only in the mind* of this woman. . . . I have, in a way, gotten rid of myself."[47] The act of passing causes her to exist only as she is seen and treated by others and has thus done away with her real authentic Self—at least temporarily until the pass has ended. She writes later that "the real 'me' has ceased to exist," and near the end of the book, "I had temporarily, though perhaps dangerously, lost my sense of self."[48] This is again seen in Vincent's book when she reveals that being Ned "drove the slim edge of a wedge into my sense of self. . . . A fault line opened in my mind."[49] Passing as a man has done nothing less than cause a geological catastrophe in her head. In line with Foster's argument about the invisibility of class passing, the one text that is much less invested in seeing the Other as completely different, opposite, or "alien" is Ehrenreich's about economic class.[50] But she as much as any other writer in this genre still falls into separating off that part of her that is passing regardless of how much these two selves occupy the same social world. All of these instances do two things: they reinforce the idea of passing as not only difficult but possibly dangerous, and they reify the gap between Self and Other, the essentialized binaries of hegemonic ideology. Separating the Self from the Self-passing-as-Other, these authors effectively argue that there is no

Self without its authentic race, sex, and class. Changing one of these elements attempts to leap over that fault line that separates them and causes the Self to fall into the chasm.

The taking of a new name for the Other identity in these texts further separates the Self from the Other the Self becomes. Griffin refers to his black Self in the third person. Vincent employs the third person consistently throughout the entire book in reference to Ned's experiences. Halsell relates, "As 'Bessie Yellowhair' I feel I am permanently abandoning myself; that I have to submerge, if not eradicate, all that I have been."[51] And Ehrenreich, who is adamant that class is economic and changeable, still manages to create an alter ego named Barb:

> "Barb," the name on my ID tag, is not exactly the same person as Barbara. "Barb" is what I was called as a child . . . and I sense that at some level I'm regressing. Take away the career and the higher education, and maybe what you're left with is this original Barb, the one who might have ended up working at Wal-Mart for real if her father hadn't managed to climb out of the mines. So it's interesting, and more than a little disturbing, to see how Barb turned out—that she's meaner and slyer than I am, more cherishing of grudges, and not quite as smart as I'd hoped.[52]

Even in an "experiment" that she seems to think is not passing but only an attempt to work and live on low wages, her "former self" becomes "distant," "exotic," and "strange" and is replaced by this regressed and childlike working-class "Barb."[53] This naming and distance also happens on *Black. White*. Brian Sparks becomes Brian White, Bruno Wurgel takes on the alter ego Billy Ray, and Renee Sparks names her white persona Barbara. This bolsters the idea that being a different race, sex, or class is so wholly Other that it requires its own named identity. This reifies not only essentialized binaries but also strict boundaries between them such that a change in how one or others sees oneself effects a separate identity even though all professed to be exactly the same except for changing the color of their skin, their gender, or their class.

Though produced over the span of half a century since the start of desegregation, the commonalities among these texts reflect what has and has not changed in Western ideologies about identities—and, particularly, in supposedly inherent identities like race and gender. In attempting to produce new knowledges that they profess can only be learned by becoming Other (and thus justify the pass), they all reinforce hegemonic knowledges about identity that are already in place. In these neo-passing texts, new goals and techniques are employed toward maintaining conventional ideologies. Their expressed aim to bridge gaps, understand each other, and change the way we see our Others is subsumed by their inability to acknowledge or escape the cultural constructs that inform their experiments. Ultimately, these neo-passing narratives fail to challenge ideologies of essentialized identity because they fail to address the constructed nature of both their original and their taken-on identities, not to mention the very constructed nature of authenticity itself.

Notes

1. See Wald, *Crossing the Line*; Dreisinger, *Near Black*.

2. In their books, Wald and Dreisinger include other white-passing-for-black fictional and autobiographical narratives, such as *Soul Man*, Mezz Mezzrow's *Really the Blues*, Adrian Piper's "Passing for White, Passing for Black," the 1972 *Sepia* article "How Passing Passed Out," Jeff Gerber's *Watermelon Man*, and Danzy Senna's *Caucasia*. Where fictive narratives are often more concerned with emotional, political, or personal aspects via a creative process and address, the texts addressed here are concerned with nothing less than finding the objective truth about particular identities and interactions, but this truth is found simultaneously through what all the authors label as their enactment of a lie. Both Wald and Dreisinger, as well as Eric Lott ("White Like Me"), argue that these white-passing-for-black texts say much more about whiteness than they do blackness. I tend to agree, though this is not the direction of this particular interrogation around multiple kinds of neo-passing narratives that strive for objectivity and authenticity across lines of not only race but gender and class as well. See Wald, *Crossing the Line*, Dreisinger, *Near Black*, and Lott, "White Like Me."

3. Pfeiffer, *Race, Passing and American Individualism*.

4. Wald, *Crossing the Line*, 22.

5. Schlossberg, "Introduction: Rites of Passage," 2.

6. Rust, "Subaltern as Imperialist," 22–23, original emphasis.

7. Lindholm, *Culture and Authenticity*, 15, 134, 65.

8. West, "Caught on Tape," 84.

9. Friedman, introduction to *Reality Squared*.

10. Griffin, *Black Like Me*, preface.

11. Ibid., 122; Halsell, *In Their Shoes*, 124.

12. Ehrenreich, *Nickel and Dimed*, 3.

13. Griffin, *Black Like Me*, 1–2.

14. Wald, "Most Disagreeable Mirror," 155–56.

15. Ibid., 156.

16. Griffin, *Black Like Me*, preface.

17. Halsell, *In Their Shoes*, 68.

18. Vincent, *Self-Made Man*, 16–17, 16.

19. Lindholm, *Culture and Authenticity*, 141.

20. Ibid., 65.

21. Griffin, *Black Like Me*, 68, 73.

22. Halsell, *Soul Sister*, 90; Griffin, *Black Like Me*, 109.

23. *Black. White.*, episode 6.

24. Vincent, *Self-Made Man*, 267, 270.

25. Halsell, *Soul Sister*, 156.

26. Vincent, *Self-Made Man*, 5.

27. Rohy, "Displacing Desire," 227.

28. Vincent, *Self-Made Man*, 9–15.

29. *Black. White.*, episode 1.

30. Ibid., episode 4, commentary.

31. This is evidenced by such memoirs, accounts, and volumes as Walker, *Black, White, and Jewish*; Daniel, *More Than Black*; Sanchez and Schlossberg, *Passing*; Matilda, *Nobody Passes*; and Coronado, Guevarra, Moniz, and Szanto, *Crossing Lines*. And there are many others examples of these narratives.

32. Vincent, *Self-Made Man*, 19.

33. The women are Carmen Wurgel in episode 3 of *Black. White.*, Rose Bloomfield in episodes 1, 2, and 5, and Renee Sparks in episode 5.

34. *Black. White.*, episode 2.

35. Ibid.

36. Foster, *Class-Passing*, 114.

37. Robinson, "It Takes One to Know One," 723–24.

38. Foster, *Class-Passing*, 114.

39. Ehrenreich, *Nickel and Dimed*, 9, emphasis in original.

40. Halsell, *In Their Shoes*, 252.

41. *Black. White.*, episode 5.

42. Ibid.

43. References to "opposite" are in Vincent, *Self-Made Man*, 130, and in *Black. White.*, Carmen Wurgel in episodes 1 and 3, and Renee Sparks in episode 5; to "the other side" in "Casting Video," *Black. White.*, DVD extras; and to "world" in Griffin, *Black Like Me*, 8; Halsell, *Bessie Yellowhair*, 213; Halsell, *Soul Sister*, 50, 123; Vincent, *Self-Made Man*, 285; Ehrenreich, *Nickel and Dimed*, 89; Carmen Wurgel and Rose Bloomfield in episode 1 and Bruno Marcotulli in episode 5, *Black. White.*

44. Halsell, *Soul Sister*, 142; Rose Bloomfield, *Black. White.*, episode 5; Griffin, *Black Like Me*, 8, and Rose Bloomfield, *Black. White.*, episode 5.

45. Griffin, *Black Like Me*, 11–12, emphasis added. Wald provides a Freudian analysis of this passage as well as white identity in Griffin's book as a whole. For an extended critique of Griffin's work, see Wald, "Most Disagreeable Mirror" and *Crossing the Line*.

46. Halsell, *Soul Sister*, 50, 95, 45.

47. Halsell, *Bessie Yellowhair*, 174, emphasis in original.

48. Ibid., 199, 206.

49. Vincent, *Self-Made Man*, 270.

50. Halsell, *Bessie Yellowhair*, 206.

51. Ibid., 175–76.

52. Ehrenreich, *Nickel and Dimed*, 169.

53. Ibid., 41, 101, 41.

Bibliography

Black. White. Directed by R. J. Cutler. Actual Reality Pictures. Beverly Hills, CA: Twentieth Century Fox, 2006. DVD.

Coronado, Marc, Rudy P. Guevarra Jr., Jeffrey Moniz, and Laura Szanto, eds. *Crossing Lines: Race and Mixed Race across the Geohistorical Divide*. Santa Barbara, CA: Multiethnic Student Outreach (MESO) in collaboration with the Center of Chicano Studies, University of California, Santa Barbara, 2003.

Daniel, G. Reginald. *More Than Black? Multiracial Identity and the New Racial Order*. Philadelphia: Temple University Press, 2002.

Dreisinger, Baz. *Near Black: White-to-Black Passing in American Culture*. Amherst: University of Massachusetts Press, 2008.

Ehrenreich, Barbara. *Nickel and Dimed: On (Not) Getting By in America*. New York: Holt, 2001.

Foster, Gwendolyn. *Class-Passing: Social Mobility in Film and Popular Culture*. Carbondale: Southern Illinois University Press, 2005.

Friedman, James. Introduction to *Reality Squared: Televisual Discourse on the Real*, edited by James Friedman, 1–24. Piscataway, NJ: Rutgers University Press, 2002.

Griffin, John Howard. *Black Like Me*. 2nd ed. Boston: Houghton Mifflin, 1977.

Halsell, Grace. *Bessie Yellowhair*. New York: Morrow, 1973.

———. *The Illegals*. New York: Stein and Dy, 1978.

———. *In Their Shoes*. Fort Worth: Texas Christian University Press, 1996.

———. *Soul Sister*. 30th anniv. ed. Washington, DC: Crossroads, 1999.

Lindholm, Charles. *Culture and Authenticity*. Malden, MA: Blackwell, 2008.

Lott, Eric. "White Like Me: Racial Cross-Dressing and the Construction of American Whiteness." In *Cultures of United States Imperialism*, edited by Amy Kaplan and Donald Pease, 474–98. Durham, NC: Duke University Press, 1993.

Matilda. [Matt Sycamore]. *Nobody Passes: Rejecting the Rules of Gender and Conformity*. Emeryville, CA: Seal, 2006.

Pfeiffer, Kathleen. *Race Passing and American Individualism*. Amherst: University of Massachusetts Press, 2003.

Robinson, Amy. "It Takes One to Know One: Passing and Communities of Common Interest." *Critical Inquiry* 20 (1994): 715–36.

Rohy, Valerie. "Displacing Desire: Passing, Nostalgia, and *Giovanni's Room*." In *Passing and the Fictions of Identity*, edited by Elaine Ginsburg, 218–33. Durham, NC: Duke University Press, 1996.

Rust, Marion. "The Subaltern as Imperialist: Speaking of Olaudah Equiano." In *Passing and the Fictions of Identity*, edited by Elaine Ginsburg, 21–36. Durham, NC: Duke University Press, 1996.

Sanchez, Maria, and Linda Schlossberg, eds. *Passing: Identity and Interpretation in Sexuality, Race, and Religion*. New York: New York University Press, 2001.

Schlossberg, Linda. Introduction, "Rites of Passing," to *Passing: Identity and Interpretation in Sexuality, Race, and Religion*, edited by Maria Sanchez and Linda Schlossberg, 1–12. New York: New York University Press, 2001.

Vincent, Norah. *Self-Made Man: One Woman's Year Disguised as a Man*. New York: Penguin, 2006.

Wald, Gayle. *Crossing the Line: Racial Passing in Twentieth-Century U.S. Literature and Culture*. Durham, NC: Duke University Press, 2000.

———. "'A Most Disagreeable Mirror': Reflections on White Identity in *Black Like Me*." In *Passing and the Fictions of Identity*, edited by Elaine Ginsburg, 151–77. Durham, NC: Duke University Press, 1996.

Walker, Rebecca. *Black, White, and Jewish: Autobiography of a Shifting Self*. New York: Riverhead, 2001.

West, Amy. "Caught on Tape: A Legacy of Low-Tech Reality." In *The Spectacle of the Real: From Hollywood to Reality TV and Beyond*, edited by Geoff King, 83–92. Bristol, UK: Intellect, 2005.

CHAPTER 7

Passing for Tan

Snooki and the Grotesque Reality of Ethnicity

ALISHA GAINES

From 1995 to 1999, I was touched by large quantities of white girls exactly once a year. As a token black girl in my northeast Ohio high school, I came to expect it. Aside from the ongoing microagressive questions about my hair, featuring curious white hands pulling and examining it without consent, my black girl body was always the center of attention the first day back to school after spring break. Fresh from sunny vacations mostly in Florida, white girls preened in bathroom and locker mirrors to admire their tans. However, a sun-kissed glow was not enough. For the tan to be legitimately praiseworthy, it had to be darker than my own naturally "café au lait" complexion. So, before the first bell rang for homeroom, scores of white girls would corner me either in the hall or at my locker and grab my arm to compare with their own. "Scores of white girls" might be slightly overstating it, but by the end of the day, it felt like scores. I am still unsure how my body became the litmus test for this annual "best tan" competition, but my experience is hardly unique. Black girl and women bodies, token and not, are often conscripted to be the litmus for temporary brownness. As a token, I quickly learned my experience would be far less uncomfortable if I had the forethought to wear a short-sleeved shirt that day.

Tan Like Me

Even if my family had also just met Mickey and Minnie down in Orlando, my own participation in the best-tan competition was unimaginable. Many of my high school classmates understood black skin as either fundamentally or molecularly different than white skin, puzzlingly impervious to the effect of ultraviolet rays. As outstretched white girl arms pressed against mine during those post–spring break mornings, I was often asked, "Can black people tan?" Not *do* black people tan but are we physically capable of it. Those fortunate white girls whose sun-made shade easily bested my mama-made one garnered bragging rights for days: "I'm so *dark*!" she would squeal happily. "Darker than Alisha—and she's *black*!" Clearly, these white girls did not want to be black like me. However, in the illogical paradoxes of race, they desperately wanted to be tan like me.

Likely unbeknownst to my classmates, their tan-seeking is part of a cultural history of sun worship extending far before and beyond our angst-riddled hallways. In tanning lore, the titillating shock of an accidentally darker Coco Chanel disembarking from a yacht onto the banks of the French Riviera in the 1920s ushered in a new trend, challenging the conflation of tan skin with the working class. Chanel's new body landscape, coupled with the Parisian penchant for exoticizing and eroticizing the brown body of Josephine Baker, helped resignify the tan body as one of leisure and chic celebrity rather than the unfortunate mark of an unshielded and overexposed body toiling in fields and on farms. As Chanel famously declared: "The 1929 girl must be tanned. A golden tan is the index of chic!"[1]

Two decades later, a *Collier's* editorial, "Sun-Tan Addicts," cheekily critiques this Chanel-inspired clamor for the sun:

> A coat of tan was once the badge of the outdoor workingman, and snobbery neither admired nor coveted it. You don't have to be ancient to remember the days when ladies carried parasols, and little country girls wore sunbonnets and submitted to buttermilk baths to ward off sunburn and freckles.
>
> Then, the coat of tan appeared at the other end of the economic ladder as a symbol of opulence and leisure—even as the off-season or Miami Beach tan is today. Its wearer stood out as a person who could afford to spend his summer days in or on the water, at the tennis club or on the golf course. But now, everybody seems to feel obliged to acquire a tan, even if he has to spend most of a short vacation doing it. . . .
>
> If there is any reward for all this effort, it comes when his vacation is over. He and other office tanners compare their color as if they were comparing golf scores or a day's catch of fish.[2]

Much like the temporarily bronze girls proudly showing off their new skin in the hallway, they and the white, tan-aspiring audience intended for *Collier's* critique both recognize how a tan, particularly a winter one, is a visible hallmark of class, style, fashion, and robust health. In our still-frosty, Midwest spring, even the best tan is regretfully temporary. However, to be tan for that post–spring break week signified the comfort and leisure of a family who vacationed. A tan meant money and mobility. In the already-troubled annals of adolescence, this was reinforced rather tragically when "Megan" lied about vacationing in Florida and came to school with startlingly orange skin. The sun-kissed girls with family photographs from Orlando, Hilton Head, Savannah, and Sanibel Island immediately ridiculed Megan's streaked skin as the haphazard result of a misapplication of cheap bronzer instead of the intentional "labor" of "laying out."

In the rather arbitrary and fickle racial and class hierarchies of my high school, Megan had been outed. She was outed because she tried to use her orange skin to disguise her lower-middle-class family's inability to leave northeast Ohio. The mean, southern-sunned, cool girls dictating the sociality of my high school conflated a tanned body with whiteness, privilege, class, and leisure, complicatedly disturbing logics rendering Megan's orange body as not quite good or properly brown enough. Not only did Megan's false vacation claims mark her body as "poor," a "poser," and "trashy" but also they revealed how desperately she wanted to perform the kind of whiteness embodied by those popular, upper-middle-class, sun-kissed girls.

Megan, like Nicole "Snooki" Polizzi, was passing for tan.

This chapter argues that Snooki, the unlikely star of MTV's reality television series *Jersey Shore*, passed for tan to craft her celebrity persona. Although we understand that the traditional logics of racial passing are most often motivated by explicit racial terror and/or legally and socially sanctioned disenfranchisement and segregation, Snooki's identity performance places her in conversation with discourses of passing. Further, her articulation of "tan" as an alternative or pseudoethnic category allows us to think through notions of authenticity, performance, community, and identity while reading *Jersey Shore* against the more familiar genre of the passing narrative. Snooki's declaration of a tan identity is a palpable example of the kind of neo-passing the current volume explores—a performance beyond the black/white binary, demonstrating how "new" forms of passing complicate identity beyond issues of race and Jim Crow racism. Attending to how tanning on the show signifies whiteness, the representational ideal of familial belonging, and the exaggerated performance of Italian American identity celebrated throughout the series, this chapter is also an investigation into how and why New Jersey has become the stage for how white ethnic identity, in general, and Italian American identity, in particular, are defined, refined, and understood in the cultural imagination. Enabled by a sociopolitical moment dominated by the at best naïvely hopeful, at worst reactionary mandates of postracial discourse, this chapter seeks to understand Snooki's passing for tan through the discourses of post-race, the logic of late capital, and the genre of neo-passing.

The G-Word

Aside from Coco Chanel and actor George Hamilton, no one is more famously tan than Snooki, the surprising breakout star of the stunningly popular reality television show *Jersey Shore*. As part of the most watched series in the history of MTV, Snooki and the rest of her bronzed castmates became the darlings of reality television's manufactured culture of surveillance and celebrity by following that network's pioneering formula for the now ubiquitous reality television genre of the "docusoap," a "documentary and soap opera mix."[3] A standard in the genre, the docusoap was first showcased on MTV's longest-running show and one of television's longest-running reality series, *The Real World*. However, whereas *The Real World* brought revolving casts of diverse and diametrically opposed twenty-somethings to negotiate young adulthood on the small screen, *Jersey Shore* focused on a singular, grotesque performance of ethnicity by promising to portray "the hottest, tannest, craziest Guidos."[4] As an ethnic slur, the term *guido* is waged most often against working-class Italian Americans. MTV countered the singular use of guido as a slur by employing a cast of millennials embracing and rebranding the epithet as a central part of their identity and lifestyle: Vinny Guadagnino, Ronnie Ortiz-Magro, Jenni "JWoww" Farley, Mike "the Situation" Sorrentino, Paul "Pauly D" DelVecchio, Sammi "Sweetheart" Giancola, Angelina Pivarnick, Pivarnick's third-season replacement Deena Nicole Cortese, and, of course, Nicole "Snooki" Polizzi. MTV billed the show as an inside look at "one of the tri-state area's most misunderstood species . . . the GUIDO. Yes, they really do exist! Our Guidos and Guidettes will move into the ultimate beach house rental and indulge in everything the Seaside Heights, New Jersey, scene has to offer."[5] Due to its flagrant use of those ethnic slurs, Italian American service organizations, such as Unico National, demanded MTV cancel the show. Other Italian American antidefamation organizations followed suit.

They failed. *Jersey Shore* premiered on December 3, 2009, nearly a year after Barack Hussein Obama's inauguration ushered in the hope for a postracial nation. According to Julie Cary Nerad, "part of America wants to claim that we have moved 'beyond race' and that the election of President Obama demonstrates that racism is a thing of the past. However, ironically, we can only make that claim by *emphasizing* his race. That is, we must point out the significance of his racial identity, only then to dismiss it as irrelevant or secondary."[6] In other words, the "part of America" that attempts to disavow the continued existence of racism does so by ignoring how "race *does* still matter," even to them.[7] Well before the candidacy and election of President Donald J. Trump revealed a regressive and racist "whitelash" to the eight years of the Obama administration, the claim that America had evolved past race proved unfounded. If when one considers the increasing racial polarization of American politics and the murders of unarmed black men and women necessitating the birth of the Black Lives Matter movement, the postracial devolves into the "most-racial," to borrow a phrase from Michael Tesler.[8] He explains, "*Mass politics had become more polarized by racial attitudes since Barack Obama's rise to prominence. That is, the election of President Obama helped usher in a 'most-racial' political era where racially liberal and racially conservative Americans were more divided over a whole host of political positions than they had been in modern times.*"[9] Since "post-race" overinvests in the symbolism of the first black president as the antidote to a long and complicated history of race and race relations rather than the sociopolitical realities of structural and institutionalized inequality, it is a hypothetical discourse rendered spurious by the revealing intervention of "most-racial."

This most-racial moment coupled with the naïve hopefulness of post-race discourse enabled *Jersey Shore*'s rebranding of whiteness, generally, and Italian American identity, specifically, into the televisual spectacle of the guido/guidette lifestyle. As Hunter Hargraves describes in "Tan TV: Reality Television's Postracial Delusion," "for the cast of *Jersey Shore*, Italian American identity is communicated through specific visual markers—bronzed skin and bulging muscles—that reinforce the idea of ethnicity as an ideological fiction rather than a structural relationship."[10] *Jersey Shore* stages a hyperperformance of difference, striking a deep and lucrative cultural nerve. Even as the global networks of late capital and supposedly free markets revealed their predatory disregard for working- and middle-class communities during the global economic crisis of pre-Obama 2008, *Jersey Shore* demonstrates the marketability of exaggerated notions of ethnicity and identity in the cultural imagination. Knowingly, MTV and its producers market ethnicity through individuality, allowing its cast to articulate and negotiate what it means to be guido through the seductive cult of reality TV–style celebrity and the shifting but rigorous demands of racial and ethnic "authenticity."

Although Tesler describes postracial discourse as a "dream,"[11] it troubles authenticity paradoxically in both helpful and harmful ways by making race and difference simultaneously both unimportant and hypervisible. I argue postracial discourse allows for the uneven and somewhat contradictory performances of the guido/guidette lifestyles portrayed by the cast by uncoupling performance and performativity from blood and lineage. For example, in the licentious party atmosphere of the Shore on the show's pilot episode, the castmates reveal their individual definitions of what it means to be either a guido or a guidette. First, audiences meet the overly coiffed Pauly D, a house DJ who defines *guido* as an oxymoronic relationship between lifestyle and blood: "I was born and raised a guido," he asserts. "It's just a lifestyle. It's being Italian. It's representing family, friends, tanning, gel, everything. I've got a tanning bed in my place. That's how serious I am about being a guido and living up to that lifestyle." Echoing Pauly D, Mike "the Situation" defines a guido as a "good-looking, smooth, well-dressed Italian." In contrast, viewers are then introduced to Vinny, the only self-described "generational Italian." Rather than showcasing Vinny primping and packing for his vacation like Mike and Pauly D, this "traditional Italian kid" is filmed at his large family table enjoying the culinary markers of Italian American identity. Familiar tropes of food and family visually mark(et) Vinny as simultaneously the "authentic" guido and a "mama's boy." Not to be outdone by the men on the show, the women identify themselves as "guidettes." According to Sammi, "a guidette is somebody who knows how to club it up, takes really good care of themselves, has pretty hair, cakes on makeup, has tan skin, wears the hottest heels. Pretty much you know how to own it and rock it. If you're not a guido then you can get the fuck out of my face." For these characters, guido or guidette authenticity oscillates freely between lineage and lifestyle.

However, no character pushes the association of guido/guidette authenticity with lifestyle rather than lineage further than Snooki, who has become the undisputed face of *Jersey Shore*. She occupies a paradoxical place—the least biologically Italian American on the show while its most guidette. Hers is a carefully crafted televisual persona enabled by the logics of neo-passing. A Santiago-born Chilean, Snooki was transnationally adopted as an infant by Italian American parents living in Poughkeepsie, New York, a blood "fact" never acknowledged on the show. Rather than reveal her biology against *Jersey Shore*'s ethnocentric backdrop, Snooki insists on her identity as a guidette while both she and the show skirt the "reality" of her brownness. While Snooki's Chilean origin story is ignored on the show; she is still portrayed as an Other throughout the show's pilot. For example, Mike's first impression of Snooki is that she is "a miniature Chihuahua painted with some spray-paint black." His crudely dismissive comparison of Snooki to an annoying, small, Mexican-bred dog rhetorically marks her as an outsider—a tension to which the first episode repeatedly returns. As Vinny, Sammi, and Pauly D continually misname Snooki "Snickers" and "Snookums," her other roommates dismiss and mischaracterize her, not because she might not be the Italian American guidette her last name implies but because she is "too drunk," "a stupid bimbo," and a "drama queen." To be clear, any of the other hard-partying castmates could be described in exactly the same terms and even proudly claim them as further proof of their commitment to a guido/guidette lifestyle. That they use this language to dismiss Snooki is a cover; it allows them to other her without naming the biological basis for her exclusion.

Although the pilot episode is titled "A New Family," Snooki vacillates between inclusion and exclusion. However, a moment of shocking violence is the uncomfortably generative act of her celebrity. During a typical night out on episode 4, an aggressive and drunk bar patron, Brad Ferro, viciously punches Snooki in the face for confronting his attempts to steal shots from the cast. The moment changed her relationship to her other castmates and the trajectory of the show. For example, in episode 5, Ronnie attempts to console Snooki back at the house after the attack: "We're so sorry, Snooks. You know we fucking love you, Snooks. . . . You gotta realize that." In a later confessional, he admits, "I look at her completely differently now."[12] Initially stemming from violence-induced pity, Snooki's attack moves her from ridiculed outsider to protected and vulnerable little sister. It no longer mattered she was once derided as a too drunk, bimbo Chihuahua. "Now," Snooki realizes, "I know they all love me like I love them." Even more important than Snooki's acceptance amongst the cast, the violent act transitioned those eight, strategically picked strangers from merely cast and housemates to family. "We're like one big family," Ronnie reminds Snooki while consoling her. Or as Sammi concludes, "I definitely feel, like, the whole, like 'Snooki incident' brought the housemates closer together." Now Snooki was the center of a tan, guido/guidette television family complete with obligatory Sunday dinners. In the aftermath of "the incident," the cast constructs a kinship network mimicking the Italianate ethos of family so often seen and exaggerated on and by reality television. In *The Triumph of Reality TV: The Revolution in American Television*, Leigh H. Edwards defines reality television as "a cultural site at which contemporary family politics are being negotiated" by acknowledging the genre's "special fondness for the family."[13] Without the uncomfortable spectacle of the attack on Snooki, *Jersey Shore* would never have become the family reality television often demands. Violence precipitated not just Snooki's inclusion but also the framework for *Jersey Shore*–brand kinship. The word *brand* is used strategically here since, in the logics of late capital, not just sex but violence sells. In fact, the punch Snooki faced caused a demonstrable surge in *Jersey Shore* ratings, more than doubling the viewership of its premiere episode. Snooki was now a star, and she took her new family with her.

Reality TV's Favorite State

Familial belonging is only one component to how Snooki negotiates her ability to pass for tan, and the familial logics of Italian American identity must be understood through the show's geography—New Jersey. If reality television is fond of families, as Edwards rightly claims, it has a full-blown crush on New Jersey. In the cultural imaginary, the state is a stage for class and social passing, a late capital playground of ethnic representation virtually unparalleled on television. Subsequently, New Jersey has made a cottage industry out of reality television via shows including *Jerseylicious, Jersey Couture, Cake Boss, The Real Housewives of New Jersey* (the only show in Bravo's *Real Housewives* franchise to feature an entire state rather than a particular city), *Bear Swamp Recovery, Brothers on Call, Man Caves, Split Ends, Summer Share, Shore Thing, The Apprentice, Method & Red*, and *Glam Fairy*, to name more than a few. According to Hugh Curnutt, "New Jersey has become like an industrial ingredient for reality TV," leading Lisa Rose of the *Newark (NJ) Star-Ledger* to dub this era in reality television "the Age of Jersey."[14] In the culturally dominant stereotypes of the state, New Jersey is known as brassy and loud, a bridge-and-tunnel–commuter landscape with the turnpike as its dominant feature. While New Jersey celebrates itself as "the Garden State," the rest of the country lampoons Jersey as "the armpit of America," a tacky crease in the national body overshadowed by the chic cool of New York City. With its East Coast version of Vegas-lite, Atlantic City, Jersey has a reputation for gaudy, audacious brashness coupled with an unshakable association with organized crime and financial corruption. Rose continues, "Jersey moxie has evolved into a brand, an attitude that's celebrated in shows centered on average Joes and Janes with larger-than-life-personas."[15] However, not everyone is happy the state has become the go-to geography for all types of reality television. In 2010 Governor Chris Christie specifically denounced *Jersey Shore* during a radio interview: "They parachute these New Yorkers into Seaside Heights, New Jersey. . . . They try to make the whole country think this is New Jersey. It's not. It's bad for New Jersey. It's bad . . . because it's a mischaracterization of who the people are here in New Jersey."[16] While disappointing Christie, the varied series comprising the age of Jersey teaches audiences what being from and living in Jersey means, "flaunting things we used to be ashamed of," to quote Michael Aaron Rockland of Rutgers University.[17] Defying Christie, New Jersey is a compellingly magnetic landscape for reality television.

While the Jersey brand might be a trashy one, the state's popular, televisual kitsch cannot be uncoupled from white ethnicity, generally, and Italian American identity, specifically. As Meta Gold of the *Newark (NJ) Star-Ledger* makes clear, "to be specific, one kind of Jerseyan is in: The current crop of shows all feature brassy, in-your-face characters, most of them Italian American."[18] Curnutt agrees, "[Even] if you're in California and you hear about a new reality TV show about New Jersey, you already know that it's probably about Italian-Americans, family, culture."[19] Reality television shows set in New Jersey completely obscure the racial and ethnic diversity of the state, nearly exclusively imaging it as an Italian American, immigrant, and new American geography. To fully chronicle New Jersey as a staple in reality television, we must first consider how HBO's scripted, dark comedy *The Sopranos* prepared the way for Jersey's dominance on television. The Emmy, Peabody, and Golden Globe Award–winning series about ethnic identity, family, crime, class, and anxiety debuted in 1999 and was eventually named "the best-written TV series ever" by the Writers Guild of America in 2013.[20] *The Sopranos* continues to be a touchstone in popular culture, finding much of its success in the show's thoughtfully written and nuanced characters. From Tony Soprano, the paradoxically lovable, violent, cheating, gangster, patriarchal mob boss played by James Gandolfini to the strong and vulnerable Carmela, Tony's mob wife played by Edie Falco, the show scripts murderous, conveniently convalescent grandmothers carefully against mob kids navigating the competing demands of a criminal dynasty and adolescence. *The Sopranos* brought intimacy, vulnerability, and levity to the gangster stereotypes ingrained in our cultural psyche through iconic films like *Scarface* and *The Godfather* trilogy. However, it is not only rich characterization making *The Sopranos* work but importantly its staging of New Jersey. *The Sopranos* acts as a temporal and representational bridge between the 1990s and the 2000s, crossing the geographic binary between New York and New Jersey visualized by Tony's long drive on the bridges and through the tunnels of the Jersey Turnpike during its opening credits. Writers and producers are clear, *The Sopranos* is a story about family and ethnic identity that only makes sense in New Jersey.

Along with the stereotypical templates of audaciousness and moxie making New Jersey television's favorite state, New Jersey is also a geography of passing. As Angus Kress Gillespie and Michael Aaron Rockland describe in *Looking for America on the New Jersey Turnpike*, the state is "typical of America . . . where people escaped from the cities to find a place where they might live outside history, divorced from traditions and laws."[21] New Jersey, they continue, is "the ultimate suburban state."[22] Consequently, its status as a landscape outside history allows New Jersey to have an "amorphous quality: it is a little bit of this, a little of that—not only machine and garden but hills and plain, marshes and sands, an extraordinarily diverse geography packed into a small area, with an extraordinarily diverse ethnicity and economy as well. . . . No other state provides a 'better mirror of America.'"[23] On reality television, this mirror has been distorted. It is a funhouse distortion allowing viewers to experience New Jersey as a playground of the suburban nouveau riche. Against this geography of class and social passing, Teresa Guidice and Joe Guidice of *Real Housewives of New Jersey* fame can pay for $100,000 worth of furniture in cash in the first season only to be indicted for fraud seasons later. Jersey is the place where the criminally inclined Sopranos can live comfortably amongst doctors and lawyers, downplaying their working-class roots on golf courses and in social clubs. Jersey is overly represented as the place where the white working class can aspire for the spurious all-American dream of owning a McMansion. It is a geography promising entrepreneurial opportunity and quick upward mobility. In the televisual landscape of Jersey then, the Sopranos pass as the Joneses—desperate to keep up with them. As Simon and Garfunkel croon in "America," "Countin' the cars on the New Jersey Turnpike / They've all come to look for America" to *be* American.[24] Or, in the case of *Jersey Shore*, to *be* guido.

Passing for Tan

Snooki could not craft her celebrity persona without the representational ideal of family, the guidette lifestyle, or the ripe, psychic and televisual landscapes of New Jersey. Above all, she would be unable to negotiate her identity without the affect of ethnicity, or what Thomas J. Ferraro calls "feeling Italian."[25] Feeling is Snooki's postracial opportunity, and it sutures Snooki's complicated relationship to Chilean brownness, American whiteness, and to her ability and desire to pass for tan. Feeling allows for a disavowal of the realities of blood and kinship in favor of a pseudoethnic category. We turn again to how *The Sopranos* prepared audiences for the *Jersey Shore*. Or as Rose writes, "*The Sopranos* gave New Jersey this kitschy cool image that these reality shows have run with."[26] How *The Sopranos* negotiates ethnic identity in New Jersey somewhat surprisingly links the delicate scripted genius of the series to the heavy-handed performance of Italian American identity on *Jersey Shore*. Instructively, Tony Soprano articulates his understanding of ethnicity and whiteness during a session with his therapist, Dr. Jennifer Melfi, played by Lorraine Bracco. In "A Hit Is a Hit," the tenth episode of season 1, Tony establishes himself as unquestionably Italian American but still not white *like that*.

TONY: My wife thinks I need to meet new people.
DR. MELFI: So?

TONY: C'mon, you're Italian, you understand. Guys like me, we're brought up to think that medigon are fuckin' bores. The truth is the average white man is no more boring than the millionth conversation over who shoulda won, [boxers Rocky] Marciano or [Muhammad] Ali?

DR. MELFI: So am I to understand you don't consider yourself white?

TONY: I don't mean white like Caucasian. I mean a white man like our friend Cusamano [Soprano's neighbor]. Now's, he's Italian, but he's a medigon. It's what my old man would have called a Wonder Bread wop. Ya know, he eats his Sunday gravy out of a jar.[27]

Here, Tony's rejection of Wonder Bread whiteness is an articulation of ethnicity disavowing the complicated story of how Italians became white in the United States, while recognizing how *whiteness* is a contested identity category for not just Italian Americans. In *Whiteness of a Different Color: European Immigrants and the Alchemy of Race*, Matthew Frye Jacobson writes specifically about Italians and the Jim Crow South:

> Politically Italians were indeed white enough for naturalization and for the ballot, but socially they represented a problem population at best. Their distance from a more abiding brand of social whiteness (what Benjamin Franklin might have meant by "lovely white") was marked by the common epithet "dago"—a word whose decidedly racial meaning was widely recognized at the time and was underscored by the more obviously racial "white nigger." It was not just that Italians did not look white to certain social arbiters, but that they did not *act* white.[28]

In contemporary discourse, "acting white" is a disparaging, loaded racial signifier most often used within black communities to mark the token black kid as either a racial sellout or an "oreo."[29] For Tony, acting white *like that* is about turning one's ethnic back on blood and allegiance, an unforgivable sin of enthusiastic assimilation a la the Cusamanos. Although Italian Americans are now certainly white, they are overrepresented, particularly, against the landscape of New Jersey, as a community with strong, demonstrable ties to Italy through Old World foodways and language punctuated by theatrically affective gestures. Ultimately, claiming to be not white *like that* deploys a strategic ethnocentricism attempting to separate Italian American identity from the damning histories of racism, racial terror, oppression, and discrimination associated with white supremacy. Refusing whiteness, then, attempts to obscure not just the supposed blandness of American whiteness but also still insidiously benefits from white privilege. It ensures privilege while shirking complicity with how white supremacy is both structural and institutional.

The term *guido* is certainly today's *dago*, co-opted as an ethnic performance of not white *like that*, embraced by young Italian Americans and TV producers alike. For example, on the second season of *Jersey Shore*, Snooki and JWoww rhetorically disavow whiteness in ways echoing the conversation between Tony and Melfi. The scene highlights what David Roediger concludes, that whiteness is "not a culture but precisely the absence of culture."[30] While tanning together on a beach in Miami, the setting of the show's second season, these best friends disclose their "not-whiteness" to each other in that season's seventh episode, "Sleeping with the Enemy":

SNOOKI: There's so many things I wanna do in life. . . . Bungee jump . . .
JWOWW: I call that "white-people syndrome." Only crazy white people do that.
SNOOKI: I'm not white.
JWOWW: What?
SNOOKI: I'm not white.
JWOWW: What are you?
SNOOKI: Tan.
SNOOKI (*in a confessional aside*): You're asking me what I am. I'm tan. That's what I am. Do you know when they put, um, like, "Ethnicity". . . ?
JWOWW: You put "Other"?
SNOOKI: I put "Other," and I put "Tan."
JWOWW: I've done that.
SNOOKI: I did it for a couple of job applications. That's why I didn't get the job. It was for a tanning salon.[31]

With perfect comic timing, both Snooki and JWoww admit they are "not white." For Irish and Spanish JWoww, claiming "Other" in this moment, specifically, and guidette, generally, is a strategic distancing from the kind of whiteness Tony Soprano also rejects. In the American logics of race and ethnicity, JWoww is white—in both fact and myth; however, she rhetorically attempts to avoid suffering from the "craziness" of this racial "syndrome." More than the syndrome JWoww describes, a stereotyped penchant for reckless and adrenaline-seeking behavior, she also tries to avoid both the recklessness and consequences of white privilege. Snooki's confession is different; it simultaneously obscures and highlights what remains unsaid and completely ignored on *Jersey Shore*—an acknowledgment of Snooki's Chilean nationality. Here, Snooki and JWoww both refuse whiteness by claiming "tan." In so doing they reveal their complicated relationship to a whiteness mired in class as well as their negotiation of the unevenness of identity, performance, biology, and belonging. Their confessions are even more poignant since they do so—ironically—while basking in the tropical suns of Miami, surrounded by both sun-brown and born-brown bodies.

Snooki continually disavows her Latinidad even while in Miami. Scenes later, Snooki meets an assumedly Latino guy in a club but is immediately annoyed when her partner encourages her to dance, according to Snooki, "like Spanish people." "I'm a guidette," she informs her partner on the dance floor, "I don't know this shit." That partner, later identified as Dennis, continues to irritate Snooki back at the house when he prioritizes making a sandwich instead of immediately joining her in the bedroom: "FYI," Snooki announces, "I'm *not* cooking tacos tonight." During a phone conversation after their very awkward sleepover, Dennis endearingly calls her "mami." "Ugh!" she complains to JWoww, "the worst turnoff ever. I'm a guidette! You don't say 'mami.'" Repulsed by Dennis's flirtatious overtones attempting to hail her into both rhythmically and vernacularly performing Latinidad, Snooki spuriously insists the artificial fires of the tanning bed's bulbs and the transformative mist from overused spray bottles are the sources of her brownness. While my classmate Megan deployed her bad bottle tan as an attempt to pass for leisurely whiteness, she was outed and then shamed for its obvious and streaky fakeness. On the other hand, Snooki defines tan as an identity opportunity by taking advantage of both reality television and New Jersey's possibilities for remaking, reinventing, and rescripting her biology. Rather than have anyone question her suspiciously dark, Chilean brownness, Snooki embraces the trashiness of the bottle and spray tan's ability to obscure the racial and ethnic "tells" of her skin. As an example of neo-passing seemingly skirting the black/white binary, Snooki's passing for tan recalls the absurd conclusion to George Schuyler's 1931 satirically speculative novel, *Black No More*. In it, black scientist Dr. Crookman creates a lucrative technology to turn black folks white. The process works, overwhelmingly so, but is undermined when Crookman, himself still black, reveals that those who underwent the racial change are in fact visually whiter than those born white. Schuyler describes how racial anxiety mapped onto class: "Those of the upper class began to look around for ways to get darker. It became the fashion for them to spend hours at the seashore basking naked in the sunshine and then to dash back, heavily bronzed, to their homes, and, preening themselves in their dusky skins, lord it over their paler, and thus less fortunate, associates. . . . A white face became startlingly rare."[32] *Black No More* anticipates not just the boom of the tanning industry but its ability to obscure racial, ethnic, and class tells. Mimicking the anxious desire to "get darker" as Schuyler imagines, in real(ity) life, Snooki relishes the visual alibi of Megan orange.

Like Snooki, the rest of the *Jersey Shore* cast relies on tanning as the aesthetic ethos of the guido/guidette lifestyle. However, unable to rely on blood, Snooki takes that aesthetic a step further. She collapses her caricatured performance of Italian American identity onto the subcultural idea of lifestyle. Nowhere is Snooki more forthcoming about how she negotiates her racial and ethnic identity than in her 2011, pseudomemoir, pseudo–self-help guide, *Confessions of a Guidette*. Complete with twenty-five rules on how to be a guidette, including, "Be gaudy, be tacky," "When in doubt, animal print," and ironically enough, "Always be *you*," Snooki strategically markets herself the most popular guidette guru in the country. Insisting "being a guidette has nothing to do with ethnicity," Snooki equates it with "how you look and feel. It's a lifestyle. You've got your surfers, your punks, your rockers, and your emos, and then you have your guidettes." Snooki makes guidette accessible beyond Jersey through the alibi of being tan. Even when Snooki discloses her Chilean origins in her book, she still insists on marketing herself tan, provocatively declaring, as she did on that Miami beach, "Tan is my friggin' ethnicity." "Be tan," Snooki admonishes her readers. "Be brown. Be friggin' orange. Be anything other than pale!"[33] In Snooki lexicon, being pale is equivalent to being a Wonder Bread wop, unremarkable in the blandest and most generically American sense.

Interestingly, Snooki's neo-passing for tan flies in the face of how one would historically and traditionally pass from black to white. For example, in Lawrence Otis Graham's exposé on the secrets of the black upper class in *Our Kind of People*, he details a seventeen-point litany of tips for racial passing, garnered through his conversations with the black folks closest to the methodology of black-to-white passing. Graham offers advice like, "Passing will be easier if you attempt it while away at college—preferably on a campus that is predominately white and is located in a small rural town," and "Change your last name to one that is not associated with black family names." Notably, his eighth tip encourages would-be passers: "Recognize the physical features that can undermine your new identity. Avoid getting tanned at the beach."[34] While passing for white for black bodies requires blending in by being as Wonder Bread as possible, passing for tan is about defiantly standing out. Snooki ignores Graham's advice, making "being tan" an accessible way for millennials to establish identity and acceptance in the ever-growing pantheon of supposedly postracial options. Snooki created an empire based on passing for tan. Along with her surprising, *New York Times* bestselling novel, *A Shore Thing*, a line of fluffy slippers, the boring *Jersey Shore* spinoffs *Snooki and JWoww* and *Snooki and JWoww: Moms with Attitude*, and her participation on ABC's career-resuscitating, competitive dance show, *Dancing with the Stars*, and NBC's *The Celebrity Apprentice*, Snooki has most poignantly lent her name to a line of "black bronzer" called Snooki Ultra Dark, a product promising "the deepest, darkest tan imaginable."

Megan was merely a casualty of her times. She attempted to pass for tan in order to disguise her poverty. She attempted to pass for tan before the supposed twilight of ethnicity and before postracial discourse enabled passing for tan an accessible lifestyle option. She attempted to pass for tan before Snooki's celebrity turned the supposed trashiness of passing for tan into an enviable empire. Snooki knew what Megan could not. Passing for tan, bolstered by geography, constructed kinship networks, celebrity, performance, and the logics of reality television, can be possible—even popular—particularly, when green trumps any color.

Notes

1. Quoted in McCright and Vannini, "To Die For," 229.
2. "Sun-Tan Addicts," 74.
3. Edwards, *Triumph of Reality TV*, 47.
4. Quoted in Kaufman, "'Jersey Shore' Castmember Defends Show."
5. Quoted in Erb, "Here's the Situation."
6. Nerad, *Passing Interest*, 3, emphasis in original.
7. Ibid, 5.
8. Tesler, *Post-Racial or Most-Racial?*
9. Ibid., 3, emphasis in original.
10. Hargraves, "Tan TV," 292.
11. Tesler, *Post-Racial or Most-Racial?*, 3.
12. *Jersey Shore*, season 1.
13. Edwards, *Triumph of Reality TV*, 87.
14. Rose, "New Jersey Becomes a Mainstay."
15. Ibid.
16. O'Neil, "Chris Christie Says."
17. Gold, "New Jersey Steals the Show."
18. Ibid.
19. Rose, "New Jersey Becomes a Mainstay."
20. "WGA Names Sopranos Best-Written." Television critics, fans, and connoisseurs could make a strong argument that the HBO, Baltimore-based show *The Wire* deserves that title.
21. Gillespie and Rockland, *Looking for America*, 8, 7.
22. Ibid., 8.
23. Ibid.
24. Simon, "America."
25. Ferraro, *Feeling Italian*.

26. Rose, "New Jersey Becomes a Mainstay."

27. *The Sopranos*, season 1, episode 10. The closed captioning translates *medigon* as *Americani*. Both often mean generically white but not ethnic.

28. Jacobson, *Whiteness of a Different Color*, 57, emphasis in original.

29. *Oreo* is a racial epithet waged against mostly black kids and young adults who are "black on the outside but white on the inside." Other racial equivalents are *banana* for those deemed not Asian enough and *coconut* for those not Latin enough.

30. Roediger, *Towards the Abolition*, 13.

31. *Jersey Shore*, season 2.

32. Schuyler, *Black No More*, 221–22.

33. Polizzi, *Confessions of a Guidette*, 4, emphasis in original; xiii; xiii; 20; 4.

34. Graham, *Our Kind of People*, 380, 381.

Bibliography

Edwards, Leigh. *The Triumph of Reality TV: The Revolution in American Television*. Santa Barbara, CA: Praeger, 2013.

Erb, Kelly Phillips. "Here's the Situation: Call to Block 'Jersey Shore' Tax Credit." *Forbes*, September 16, 2001. Accessed June 19, 2017. www.forbes.com.

Ferraro, Thomas J. *Feeling Italian: The Art of Ethnicity in America*. New York: New York University Press, 2005.

Gillespie, Angus Kress, and Michael Aaron Rockland. *Looking for America on the New Jersey Turnpike*. New Brunswick, NJ: Rutgers University Press, 1989.

Gold, Matea. "New Jersey Steals the Show." *Los Angeles Times*, April 21, 2010.

Graham, Lawrence Otis. *Our Kind of People: Inside America's Black Upper Class*. New York: HarperCollins, 1999.

Hargraves, Hunter. "Tan TV: Reality Television's Postracial Delusion." In *A Companion to Reality Television*, edited by Laurie Ouellette, 283–305. Malden, MA: Wiley, 2014.

Jacobson, Matthew Frye. *Whiteness of a Different Color: European Immigrants and the Alchemy of Race*. Cambridge, MA: Harvard University Press, 1998.

Jersey Shore. Directed by Brad Kreisberg. 2009–12; Hollywood, CA: MTV Networks, 2010–13. DVD.

Kaufman, Gil. "'Jersey Shore' Castmember Defends Show against Detractors." *MTV News*, December 1, 2009. Accessed November 20, 2010. http://www.mtv.com.

McCright, Aaron M., and Phillip Vannini. "To Die For: The Semiotic Seductive Power of the Tanned Body." In *The Body Reader: Essential Social and Cultural Readings*, edited by Lisa Jean Moore and Mary Kosut, 309–32. New York: New York University Press, 2010.

Nerad, Julie Cary. Introduction to *Passing Interest: Racial Passing in U.S. Novels, Memoirs, Television, and Film, 1990–2010*. Albany: State University of New York Press, 2014.

O'Neil, Erin. "Chris Christie Says 'Jersey Shore' Cast Members Are from New York." *Politifact*, October 21, 2011. Accessed October 31, 2011. http://www.politifact.com.

Polizzi, Nicole. *Confessions of a Guidette*. New York: Gallery, 2011.

Roediger, David R. *Towards the Abolition of Whiteness: Essays on Race, Politics, and Working Class History*. New York: Vergo, 1994.

Rose, Lisa. "New Jersey Becomes a Mainstay for Reality TV Shows." *(Newark, NJ) Star Ledger*, August 23, 2011.

Schuyler, George. *Black No More*. Boston: Northeastern University Press, 1989.

Simon, Paul. "America." *Bookends*, Columbia Records, 1968.

Sopranos, The. Directed by Matthew Penn. 1999–2007. New York: HBO Home Video, 2000–2008. DVD.

"Sun-Tan Addicts." *Collier's* 6, August 1949, 74.

Tesler, Michael. *Post-Racial or Most-Racial? Race and Politics in the Obama Era*. Chicago: University of Chicago Press, 2016.

"WGA Names Sopranos Best-Written TV Series Ever." *The Hollywood Reporter*, June 2, 2013. Accessed September 2, 2013. http://www.hollywoodreporter.com.

CHAPTER 8

The Pass of Least Resistance

Sexual Orientation and Race in ZZ Packer's "Drinking Coffee Elsewhere"

DEREK ADAMS

"Orientation games began the day I arrived at Yale from Baltimore."[1] The opening line in ZZ Packer's short story "Drinking Coffee Elsewhere" appears fairly straightforward. On its surface, the line references the getting-to-know-you series of workshops and activities incoming freshman are unrelentingly subjected to on college campuses across the nation as a way of facilitating their assimilation into an unfamiliar campus culture. Probing beneath this surface, readers discover the centrality of sexual orientation in the speaker's move from urban Baltimore to Yale. The term *orientation games* is Packer's subtle hint that her protagonist, Dina, the minute she steps onto the Yale campus, is embarking on a personal journey at the heart of which is her sexual orientation. Even as she participates in more traditional orientation games with her incoming cohort, what is really at stake for Dina is her sense of identity in the wake of possible amorous desire that defies the strictures of heteronormativity. Falling in love with the yet-to-come-out lesbian Heidi ushers in an existential crisis of identity that Packer's young protagonist contends with throughout the narrative. Yet, this is not the simple story of a young woman discovering she is lesbian. Dina's intense resistance to being labeled as either heterosexual or homosexual challenges any such casual misreading of the story. It is as though Dina is not only playing a game with the other characters but that she is becoming an orientation game that readers are invited to play as they read the story. Left disoriented and with no way to win, adept readers will most likely find themselves comfortably uncertain of her sexual orientation by story's end.

Rather than fixing Dina's "orientation," Packer seems much more focused on the second part of the term, *games,* and the multifaceted ways in which her protagonist intentionally confuses the social conventions of orientation. Dina's personal journey is full of moments where sexual orientation comes to the fore, and yet she works feverishly to divert attention away from it. Her words and actions constantly reduce the subject, which bookends the story and serves as one of its central threads, to a trivial conceit. Strikingly, her most relied upon diversion involves her racial identity. Dina utilizes her blackness and the presumed inherent alienation of entering a historically white, Ivy League world to justify her anxiety and misanthropy. The harassment and isolation she experiences are, according to Dina, a function of racial tensions between her and a white student body unreceptive to black peers, not a product of her intense feelings for another woman. This privileging of racial tension serves as her explicit attempt to disguise the importance of her sexuality beneath her racial identity but to what purpose? In light of the historically entrenched antagonisms between blacks and whites, to what end does she play up her blackness? Asked another way, why does Dina consider her (potentially homo-) sexuality as more dreaded than her race? Answering these questions involves accounting for changes in both the social perception of race in the wake of the legal dismantling of Jim Crow segregation and also the tumultuous, often homophobic relationship between civil rights activists and gay rights activists at the turn of the twenty-first century.

Blackness, Passing, and Postracial Identity Politics

Packer's decision to have her protagonist's body read as a site of blackness does not align with recent shifts in the critical treatment of race. At the end of the twentieth century during which "Drinking Coffee Elsewhere" is set, the sociocultural and institutional policing of an impermeable boundary between white and black worlds that defined Jim Crow has largely been dismantled, effectively blurring the centuries-old line of distinction around which society organized itself into distinct racial spheres. In *What Was African American Literature,* Kenneth Warren outlines the implications this has on the production of literature categorized as part of a black writers' canon, proclaiming, "African American literature itself [since the legal demise of Jim Crow] constitutes a representational and rhetorical strategy within the domain of a literary practice responsive to conditions that, by and large, no longer obtain."[2] Although reductive, Warren points to a link between literature written by black authors and recent changes in the social perception of race. The shift away from legally sanctioned segregation results in a somewhat fuller integration of mainstream culture that, though certainly not a racism-free utopia, has removed race as the primary rhetorical tool for organizing society and cataloguing citizens. The relevance of race as a category lessens through a societal investment in postracial identity politics, which correspondingly diminishes the social currency of black racial identity. By this logic, Packer's portrayal of Dina comes across as outdated and inconsequential. Kenji Yoshino similarly illustrates a collective movement toward the insignificance of racial distinction in *Covering: The Hidden Assault on Our Civil Rights*, claiming that the end of the twentieth century marks a return to the assimilationist ethos of an American "melting pot" that nullifies difference in order to promote sameness.[3] This shunning of difference, he notes, engenders "colorblind" attitudes and practices meant to signal our collective progression beyond racism, an impulse Packer resists by undercutting any effort to circumvent Dina's blackness during her orientation to Yale. Readers are set up to interpret her race through what Kalpana Sheshadri-Crooks describes as a "regime of looking," an optical mechanism through which race is visually constructed and antiblack discrimination is carried out.[4] Situating her protagonist squarely within this regime of looking by highlighting her blackness, Packer validates new conceptions of blackness and whiteness as viable social categories only to complicate their artificiality, with the meaning of either mattering primarily to the degree that they lead to insightful examinations of the convergence between Dina's racial legibility and the illegibility of her sexual orientation. The two are inextricably linked, and through their intersection Packer creates a space for the articulation of black female sexuality that openly challenges heteronormative expectations.

There resides in the concept of racial passing and neo-passing, more specifically, the language and theoretical framework to begin probing the complexities of Packer's unique illustration of black female sexuality. Much of the early discourse on racial passing is rooted in the conventional black/mulatto-becomes-white definition of racial passing Thaddious Davis outlines in her 1997 introduction to the Penguin edition of Nella Larsen's 1929 landmark novel *Passing*: "'Passing' [is] the movement of a person who is legally or socially designated black into a white racial category or white social identity. . . . When passing as white, these individuals merely relocate themselves to a space not demarcated as black, and thereby escape the association of color with inferiority that has been one of the most enduring legacies of slavery in the United

States."[5] One of the principal reasons passing narratives like Larsen's were so widely circulated in the Jim Crow world of the 1920s is that they solidify the existence of mutually exclusive, albeit artificial, racial categories. Passing stories are especially popular amongst white audiences, because, in large part at the core, the benefits of being perceived as white outweigh the consequences racial passers face at having their blackness revealed. Race is so often thought of in terms that unquestioningly privilege whiteness over blackness, and the desire of racial passers in many of the genre's cornerstones reinforces this notion. Acts of passing as defined by Davis may expose the social construction of race, yet they unintentionally valorize whiteness as they do so. Even if the white social world of Jim Crow depicted in these novels is "everything but ideal," as Mar Gallego claims, passers ensure that there is still something to be had in it that cannot be accessed in the black social world.[6] In instances when passing as white is not racially motivated, they are still described as such precisely so that whiteness will be seen as the ultimate goal.[7] As Valerie Smith points out, passers are generally motivated by class considerations, looking to partake in the educational and employment opportunities of those in power. But, Smith states, "People describe the passing person as wanting to be white, not wanting to be rich," thereby equating economic lifestyles to a specific racial identity.[8] As a result, this desire to succeed educationally and economically (Dina's choice to attend Yale can be seen as exemplary of this) becomes conflated with a desire to achieve whiteness. White heteronormativity has not been undermined because passing narratives feed into its project of maintaining the superiority of whiteness over blackness even when racial performances are based on other motivations.

Though it borrows thematically from traditional passing narratives, Packer's story is more accurately categorized as a neo-passing narrative that makes an important departure from this aspect of the genre—it resists reinforcing heteronormative whiteness. The dual nature of Dina's passing at the intersection of race and sexual orientation outside the context of Jim Crow broadens readers' understanding of the purposes and motivations of passing protagonists. In *Passing Novels in the Harlem Renaissance: Identity Politics and Textual Strategies,* Gallego posits a theory detailing the dual nature of performed identities in nearly every act of racial passing. The conventional black/mulatto-becomes-white trajectory of the genre, she asserts, is a form of "generic passing" done on the part of the author and/or text to tell a more subversive tale of moving between identity categories other than race. Gallego concludes that novels like *Passing* "[adopt] a suitable veneer . . . to tackle a very problematic topic, namely a rather unconventional critique of Eurocentric ideology and worldview from an African American standpoint."[9] Her theory challenges the notion that the genre panders to the interests of white readers, as she suggests that authors of passing narratives destabilize white institutional authority by metaphorically masking their texts through a black/mulatto-becomes-white medium the dominant culture deems acceptable. In these terms, racial passing functions as a surface narrative beneath which other categories of identity that intersect with race, such as sexual orientation, make possible critiques of racist sexual ideologies.

Deborah McDowell's analysis of Irene Redfield in her introduction to the combined volume of Larsen's novels *Quicksand* and *Passing* provides a great model for understanding generic passing in relation to the intricate ties between Dina's racial and sexual identities in Packer's story. McDowell asserts that much of the subversive nature of Irene racially passing as a white woman is invested in her potential homoerotic desire for fellow passer Clare Kendry. Larsen frequently hints at the idea of her black female protagonists as sexual beings "behind the safe and protective covers of traditional narrative subjects and conventions."[10] In McDowell's view, blurring the distinction between black and white social spheres by performing as a white woman, although certainly significant, functions as a topical layer draped over a depiction of black female sexuality considered taboo. Judith Butler poignantly argues this point in "Passing, Queering," her in-depth examination of the psychoanalytic complexities of erotic desire in Larsen's novel *Passing*. Linking psychical repression to the social constraints on black women's sexuality, Butler explains the muteness of homoerotic desire in relation to the illegibility of race, likening it to an act of passing.[11] Shaped substantially by chattel slavery and its perversions, black female sexuality has been, and in some ways remains, chained to hypersexual stereotypes. Barbara Christian argues that one black woman's desire for another is quite often perceived as a social deviancy that reflects an immorality of character, a designation many African American authors have struggled to negotiate as they contend with racial stereotyping.[12] In "The Quicksands of Representation" in *Reconstructing Womanhood: The Emergence of the Afro-American Woman Novelist*, Hazel Carby writes, "The representation of black female sexuality meant risking its definition as primitive and exotic within a racist society. Racist sexual ideologies proclaimed the black woman to be a rampant sexual being, and in response black women writers either focused on defending their morality or displaced sexuality onto another terrain."[13] Resistance to anything but tightly constrained representations of heteronormativity for black women subjects them as a whole to unwarranted public scrutiny and condemnation based on these stereotypes, creating a unique challenge for writers looking to represent black female sexuality in literature as anything other than heteronormative.

In addition to the restrictions of this discourse, Packer's project is further complicated by the prevalence of postracial sentiment declaring race to be of little or no significance. Like Larsen in *Passing*, Packer is eager to challenge heteronormativity through the creation of a character whose very identity resists the limitations imposed upon black female sexuality, following Larsen's generic passing blueprint to the extent that Packer directs the reader's focus away from the sexual orientation of her protagonist toward her racial identity. Beyond this point, however, their narratives dramatically diverge: Irene's passing takes place in a Jim Crow world where black and white could not possibly be more different, while Dina's is rooted in a postracial environment that suggests there is no difference between the two. Like many racial passers, Dina intentionally accentuates aspects of her racial identity in order to control the representation and interpretation of her race (and, in turn, her sexual orientation) upon arriving at Yale, but hers differs from that of the typical racial passer in the direction her passing takes.

Dina's passing is intraracial in that she does not cross W. E. B. Du Bois's proverbial color line in order to be perceived as white.[14] She is black, a fact emphasized through the contrasts she draws between herself and her white peers. It is also the case that her blackness is at risk of being subsumed into Yale's white cultural mainstream, an identification Dina considers not only undesirable but also personally harmful. The antagonistic black identity she cultivates in response to this pressure adheres to racial norms characteristic of a stereotypical, monolithic black experience; in other words, she is an individual black woman passing as a distinct type of black woman. Blackness is an integral component of her life experiences that is both genetically informed and socially constructed. The dark skin she inherits ensures that she appears black to others, even though her actions, such as constantly reading books and attending an Ivy League university, do not align with the social expectations for women of her race. We might say the black woman she believes others expect her to be is not the black woman she knows herself as. Yet, at Yale, she conveniently slips between these two forms of blackness as part of her game so that others will reduce her to a stereotype without ever getting to know her, therein reducing the chances of her sexuality being questioned.

Dina's performance of blackness is akin to what I have described elsewhere as *black passing*, involving the acting out of any specific set of predetermined racialized norms by an individual that undermines the desirability of heteronormative whiteness.[15] Black passing is distinct from passing as black (although the latter can certainly fit within the definition of the former) in that it does not necessitate an interracial relocation from one racial category to another.

Frederick Douglass's 1845 slave narrative provides one of the earliest examples of black passing in American literature.[16] Denied any formal education because of his status as chattel, Douglass performs black passing as a way of conning young white boys into teaching him how to write. He would profess to these boys that he knew how to spell words as well as they, something he knew himself incapable of at that time. He would scrawl onto a fence the four letters he had learned while working at a shipyard, and the white boys would rebuke him and show him his mistakes (and their assumed superiority) by spelling the words out correctly. Committing these words to memory, Douglass becomes literate by intentionally playing into stereotypes about black slaves: He feigns being the ignorant slave who believes himself to be above his station and also the humiliated slave who has been shown his place, neither of which accurately describes his true character evident in the intelligence he demonstrates. Herman Melville's infamous slave insurrectionist, Babo, from his classic 1855 novella *Benito Cereno* performs in much the same way.[17] After overthrowing his Portuguese captors, seizing control of their vessel, and assuming command of the newly freed Africans onboard, Babo is placed in a situation in which he must meet socially determined expectations for being an enslaved black. The sudden appearance of American ship captain Amasa Delano forces Babo to pretend to docility, subservience, and self-deprecation, characteristics employed to mask his power, self-sufficiency, and cunning. In both examples, the type of passing we come across is intraracial with each of the two characters performing a specific set of predetermined black norms without relocating to another racially demarcated space. Subtly mocking the supposed superiority of white individuals, the two men ensure they are perceived as stereotypically black even though their bodies are already marked as such. We might say the black men others expect them to be is distinct from the black men they know themselves as.

Dina's black passing functions similarly in form and is accomplished through her adoption of a wholly antagonistic personality she attributes to her race. The implied racial tension and animosity she employs to draw attention to her blackness are immediately apparent in the orientation games played in the opening pages. These "heady, frustrating games for smart people," as Dina terms them, include charades reinterpreted by existentialists, identifying as an inanimate object, listening to rocks, and Trust, in which one student falls freely backward into the waiting arms of other students. She does not hesitate to express her particular discomfort with Trust: "The idea [behind Trust] was that if you had the faith to fall backward and wait for four scrawny former high school geniuses to catch you, just before your head cracked on the slate sidewalk, then you might learn to trust your fellow students. Russian roulette sounded like a better way to go. 'No way,' I said. The white boys were waiting for me to fall, holding their arms out for me, sincerely, gallantly. 'No fucking way.'"[18] Dina's skepticism—"No way. No fucking way"—is entirely understandable based on her initial description of the people waiting to catch her. She identifies her four Trust-mates as "scrawny former high school geniuses" who offer no reassurance that they possess the physical ability to prevent her from falling. We understand Dina's questioning of their physical prowess in relation to their intellectual deftness. The bookishness that Dina assumes has not prepared them for the physical exertion the game of Trust demands, and they will inevitably drop her for this reason. She mentions Russian roulette as a viable alternative to comically imply that death is an almost certain outcome of trusting in their physical ability.

However, her skepticism also operates on a much-larger sociopolitical level premised on racial difference. In her second reference to her Trust-mates, Dina identifies the high school geniuses as "*white* boys [who] were waiting for me to fall." Pointing out their whiteness shifts attention away from her concern about their physical prowess and places emphasis on their racial identities in relation to the premise of the game, trust. How can she possibly trust a group of people who belong to a racial group that has systematically oppressed, disinherited, and disenfranchised an entire race of black women and men through manipulation and deceit? What possible assurance could a group of young white men provide her considering how fervently their ancestors worked to cause black individuals like Dina to fall once desegregation permitted them to enter traditionally white worlds, such as Yale? Dina is intuitively aware of this history, which explains her skepticism. Following this orientation game, she is sent to the dean's office for her snide remark that if she were an inanimate object, she would be a revolver and wipe out all mankind. While being pressed by the dean to account for her answer, Dina stares out of the window and reflects, "Through the dimming light of the dean's office window, I could see the fortress of the old campus. . . . Everything had changed when we reached those streets hooded by gothic buildings. I imagined how the college must have looked when it was founded, when most of the students owned slaves."[19] The imagery is telling. In contrast to the description of the New Haven campus's otherworldly beauty, Dina sees in its gothic architecture an unsettling darkness roiling beneath the surface of Ivy League perfection, a type of institutional passing. She perceives Yale as a fortress positioned as a symbol of war and the protection of geopolitical boundaries based on race. Moreover, the juxtaposition of "hooded" and "slaves" re-creates the tension between whites and blacks when vigilante militias spilled the blood of countless thousands to enforce the division between the two groups. Her reluctance to trust these boys because of their whiteness is principally informed by this history of violence and brutality. In this sense, Russian roulette is a metaphor for the physical and social death black individuals face when trusting white people in the wake of anxieties about slavery and integration.

The implied maliciousness of white people her reflection hints at assists her in establishing a contrast between herself and her Trust-mates that is not otherwise obvious. It is an intentional mischaracterization meant to solidify the existence of a racially contentious relationship between them and her that reflects the aforementioned history. She also describes them waiting with their arms out for her "sincerely, gallantly," indicating their genuine resoluteness to catch her as she falls. These descriptors signify qualities that should reassure her of their intentions, not cause her to question their willingness to prevent her head from cracking on the slate sidewalk. These boys are not racist bigots looking to make her a victim of some perverse racial fantasy, and Dina knows it. But she knows, too, that differentiating herself from them is necessary for maintaining an illusion that covers over her deeper concerns with being identified as a lesbian. To remain isolated and avoid questions about her uncertain sexuality, she must necessarily insulate herself as a racial outcast, a project more difficult than anticipated in a post–Jim Crow, academic environment attempting to facilitate the assimilation of all incoming students even across lines of race. Because her peers do not seem preoccupied with her visible racial identity and its relationship to theirs, she becomes the black woman she believes society expects her to become, one who feels wholly isolated from the rest of the group because of her racial identity. She performs blackness in a way that makes her stand out as an outcast while also legitimizing the attempts of the dean and the orientation counselor to pathologize her feelings of anxiety. Although care must be taken not to dispossess Dina of experiencing alienation because of her blackness, it is evident that she plays up certain aspects of it in this situation to ensure that it gets perceived in a particular manner by her white cohort. In this way, Dina's performance of blackness not only works against the traditional passing narrative arc but also offers a new way of looking at racial passing beyond the limited scope of institutionally sanctioned discrimination and the privileging of white racial norms characteristic of the genre.

Extending her racial apprehension to the female orientation counselor administering this particular game of Trust reveals Dina's hidden anxieties about her ambiguous sexuality. Her description of the counselor's physical attributes emphasizes aspects of her white racial identity associated with sexual desire: "'It's all cool, it's all cool,' the counselor said. Her hair was a shade of blond I'd seen only on *Playboy* covers, and she raised her hands as though backing away from a growling dog. 'Sister,' she said, in an I'm-down-with-the-struggle voice, 'you don't have to play this game. As a person of color, you shouldn't have to fit into any white patriarchal system.'"[20] Certainly, the irony is not lost on readers. In the middle of an exercise in which she is being conditioned to assimilate to a "white patriarchal system," she is being told by one of its white employees (who emphasizes Dina's blackness when calling her "Sister") that she shouldn't have to fit within any such system. By the very definition of her title *counselor,* this woman functions as a tool to contend with the cognitive dissonance students like Dina face when being orientated. Even more ironically, the impetus for the non-necessity of assimilating, according to the counselor, is Dina's identity as "a person of color," the one aspect of her identity she makes more overt precisely because of the long history of purposeful exclusion and disfranchisement it signifies. Were it "all cool" as the counselor suggests, then the orientation games would not be needed in the first place, and Dina would already feel right at home as a part of the campus community. Instead, the counselor comes across as someone who just doesn't understand how she feels, with her race being positioned as one of the primary reasons. Dina's focus on the blonde shade of the counselor's hair directs the attention of readers toward their racial difference. Blonde hair, in this context, is representative of the whiteness that embodies what documentary writer Jean Kilbourne describes as an ideal standard of beauty, sharply contrasting with the fetishized exoticness of black women's hair.[21] It stands out to Dina precisely because it is something she seemingly has never witnessed in person. That she has only ever seen hair this shade through a carefully edited medium (a *Playboy* magazine cover) both cheapens it and deifies it as an object of desire.

The *Playboy* cover takes on another level of importance as a metaphor for Dina's cover-up of her possible homosexuality. In offering up women's bodies for visual consumption, *Playboy* magazine symbolizes the desire to possess women as objects of aesthetic and carnal pleasure. The magazine is typically considered a heterosexual enterprise that caters to the interests of an adult male audience, one that Dina, through the association she draws between the counselor and the magazine, can be identified with. This connection with heterosexual men suggests that Dina may share their desire to consume women as objects of sexual gratification, implicitly raising questions about her sexuality. Packer so artfully manipulates readers through misdirection to see the racial distinctions between Dina and the counselor that they overlook the most significant detail of this description—viewing a *Playboy* cover. Dina's dismissive reference to the magazine causes readers to casually overlook the sexual desires it represents and how they might influence an understanding of her sexual orientation.

Passing between Gay Rights and Civil Rights

That Packer chooses Yale as the setting for Dina's black passing is no accident. Recently tagged "the gay Ivy" for its focus on nurturing a culture amenable to lesbian, gay, bisexual, and transgender, plus (LGBT+) lifestyles, Yale was notorious for being one of the last of the Ivies to establish an office of LGBT resources and major field of study.[22] In the 2009 *Yale Alumni Magazine* article "Gay at Yale: How Things Changed," alumnus George Chauncey outlines Yale's contentious history of institutional resistance to nonheteronormative lifestyles, noting a recent change, in the 1990s, in its treatment of sexual orientation. Eventually, he acknowledges, the campus culture radically transforms its attitude regarding LGBT+ concerns, making acceptance of homosexuality a campus-wide priority.[23] This collective acknowledgment is depicted in Packer's story as Coming Out Day, an event organized by students to provide a platform for openly declaring how they identify and how they would like to be recognized by others. Perhaps best thought of as the antithesis to orientation games intended to make everyone similar, the event respectfully highlights difference while aiming to create a culture of empowerment and self-affirmation. Anecdotal evidence that Yale remains less racially diverse than more urban-oriented universities like Columbia and Harvard adds an interesting sociopolitical dimension to Yale's cultural transformation. The setting, then, is primed for exploring the interplay between racial equality and LGBT+ rights. The relative invisibility of blackness on campus coupled with the newfound hypervisibility of LGBT+ identities not only epitomizes the internal tension within Dina that catalyzes her black passing but also functions as a microcosm of a deep-rooted division between civil rights groups focused on race and gay rights activists.

Providing one of the most pivotal scenes in Packer's story, Dina's reaction to Coming Out Day unfolds in a manner that symbolizes an antagonism between civil rights and gay rights struggles. Choosing not to attend and instead watch the proceedings from her dorm-room window is a way of insulating herself, and, in turn, her sexuality as a black woman from public judgment. However, it also represents much of the overt indifference communities of color have demonstrated when failing to advocate on behalf of LGBT+ communities. In the extreme, homophobia disguised mostly as religious doctrine has permeated some communities of color to the extent that they have lobbied against equal protections for LGBT+ groups—support for Don't Ask, Don't Tell; the demonization of homosexuality by figures like Michel Faulkner, founding pastor of the New Horizon Church of New York; and canvassing for the passage of Proposition 8 in California, which eliminated the right of same-sex couples to legally marry. More modestly, members of communities of color often invoke a hierarchy of oppression that diminishes the hardships LGBT+ people face in comparison to black men and women. Individuals like author and activist Ishmael Reed, for instance, argue that in never having suffered through the ravages of institutionalized chattel slavery or Jim Crow segregation, LGBT+ communities' concerns remain secondary to the needs for sustaining racial progress in black communities.[24] These notions might be traced in Dina's spatial relationship to Heidi as Heidi professes her lesbianism during Coming Out Day. Dina is in her dorm room "across the street, three stories up" situated well above the proceedings while looking down on its participants both literally and symbolically.[25] The tension between her and them in this moment parallels a wedge that has been driven between civil rights groups and LGBT+ groups when jockeying to sit atop the hierarchy of oppression. Dina's elevated position above Heidi physically symbolizes the primacy of blackness in the struggle against systemic oppression. Seen from her perspective, the concerns of Heidi and her LGBT+ cohort in working against discrimination are less meaningful than Dina's own (despite her constantly questioning her sexuality), a point emphasized by her attempts to intentionally magnify her blackness, which, in turn, give primacy to race-related civil rights struggles.

The inverse of this relationship, too, is manifest in Dina's reaction, with LGBT+ communities largely ignoring the specific concerns of women of color. The roots of this divide run deep,[26] so turning to the Millennium March on Washington, D.C., in April 2000 provides context for its more current iteration. Although analogous to Coming Out Day in its intent to promote awareness of LGBT+ issues on a national scale, the demonstration was sharply criticized by people of color for its attempts to draw direct comparisons to the Civil Rights era of the 1960s. They found the comparisons insulting because the Millennium March was considered to be white-led and to represent white gay interests at the expense of people of color. Civil Rights activist Mandy Carter, who spent three years working for the Human Rights Campaign, one of two major groups responsible for organizing the demonstration, attests, "There's a disconnect in the white-led gay organizations about the critical place of race and class in our movement. The lesbian and gay movement has been so single-focus that it fails to take into account the multiplicities of realities for lgbt people in this country."[27] Barbara Smith takes Carter's point a step further, insisting, "Lesbians and gay men of color have been trying to push the gay movement to grasp the necessity of antiracist practice for nigh on twenty years. Except in the context of organizing within the women's movement with progressive white liberal feminists, we haven't made much progress."[28] The two are describing a type of homonormativity within the movement that ignores racial, gendered, and socioeconomic complexities of intersecting LGBT+ identities, providing an incomplete portrait of their experiences. Coming Out Day reflects this white-led, singular focus on a particular type of LGBT+ identity. The participants whose identities readers can recognize are Heidi (who we know is white) and a young woman whose waist-length, bleached-blonde hair is cut, reminding us of Dina's musings on the hair of the orientation counselor whom we assume to be white. Aside from the "sepia boy" emceeing the event who readers assume is black, the participants are all female and most likely white. This public forum seemingly reflects the white assimilationist impulse of Yale generally in that it caters to white lesbians (and possibly black gays), leaving little room for examinations of nuanced black female sexuality like Dina's.

Dina's choice to forgo the event is an interesting combination of cowardice and courage reflective of the devastating effects of the civil rights–gay rights division on social progress. She sees her decision as a refusal to allow a homonormative identity (i.e., lesbian) to be imposed upon her, a courageous position, indeed. Yet, her refusal to express her potentially homoerotic desire in this moment also attests to her tacit acceptance of heteronormativity, the terms of which the event intends to actively challenge. Heidi's public affirmation of her homosexuality during Coming Out Day essentially guarantees that Dina will be labeled "lesbian" or "dyke" if she chooses to maintain their relationship, a type of guilt by association. Even more, Heidi's admission is personally unsettling for Dina because it challenges the very foundation upon which her passing performance has been built. Being white and (through her confession) becoming part of the LGBT+ mainstream focused primarily on white gays and lesbians (and even black gay men, to a degree), Heidi represents another type of assimilationist impulse tugging at Dina—the desire for whiteness. Choosing to maintain her relationship with Heidi would be to acquiesce to the desirability of whiteness she has worked against through the process of black passing as a way of avoiding being subsumed into Yale's white cultural mainstream. It would situate her as a black woman whose racial experiences are generally dismissed as part of a homonormative LGBT+ narrative and also as a lesbian woman whose race means everything as part of a white heteronormative narrative. Significant aspects of Dina's identity would be rendered both invisible and hypervisible simultaneously, with agency over how she gets perceived by others essentially vanishing.

Confronting this newfound reality, Dina once again chooses the path of least resistance by continuing her black passing and maintaining the antagonistic racial identity she pretends to. She can no longer be close to Heidi physically and emotionally while remaining categorically distant. Carrying out her orientation game in this way might tempt readers into falsely characterizing her story as simply one of heterosexual passing, an analysis that is more so incomplete than incorrect. This is not a true moment of exposure for Dina and her sexual orientation, as her performance is not a movement from one sexual category to another. The ambiguity surrounding her sexual orientation means she is never determined to be either heterosexual or homosexual at any point in the text. Even though passers frequently exist in the spaces between categories of identity that make passing possible, passers are usually designated as a member of one group (most often a marginalized one) to make possible passing into its binary opposite. Readers witness Dina's retreat to the relative safety of heteronormative assumptions and racial contention with her sexual orientation remaining intentionally illegible.

The Limitations of Black Passing

Committing fully to her orientation game prevents Dina from confronting potential reactions to her black female sexuality but comes at the cost of her and Heidi's relationship. The loss of Heidi is the painful toll Dina must pay for refusing to yield to the demands of dominant culture that come to govern the identity politics at the heart of her game. The stakes are magnified considering Heidi is the only person in the text Dina develops a substantive emotional relationship with. Heidi's insistence on Dina's vulnerability through her self-affirmation of black female sexuality undermines the possibility of furthering their intimate connection while also resisting assimilation into the white mainstream. The two work at cross-purposes. Black passing might expose the limitations of the discourse on black female sexuality, but black passing, too, suffers from the critical limitations specific to the genre. Like virtually all passing protagonists attempting to control the interpretation of their identities, Dina, through a performance of norms, whether they be heteronormative or homonormative, discovers the virtual absence of agency passers possess. Their identities as passers are predicated on adhering to terms dictated by the dominant culture, whether white or black, heterosexual or homosexual, making it all but impossible to connect with others while engaging in a socially proscribed performance of identity.

Whereas most conventional-passing narratives end with the passer returning to the black social world to reconnect with the sense of self that is lost through the process, "Drinking Coffee Elsewhere" offers no such solace. The story closes with Dina imagining Heidi knocking on her door, demanding that Dina "open up" and allow for intimacy to reenter her life. She is so wholly isolated from the world once she severs ties with Heidi that Dina even imagines herself alone behind a closed door, wishing for an opportunity to reconnect. The ending of Packer's story seemingly restores white heteronormativity with her protagonist leaving Yale without her black female sexuality having been discovered by anyone, including herself. The isolation she suffers in the closing pages, though, is much more oppressive than what she experiences during her black-passing journey. Dina's entrapment behind a closed door (closeted, if you will) at the end of the text is a cautionary takeaway, a consequence of being unable to negotiate the wedge between race, sex, and gender individually, as political movements, and as a society. Collectively, we risk becoming the tools of oppression we seek to destroy if we are incapable of finding creative outlets for the expression of black female sexuality without resorting to acts of passing. We must look inwardly, outwardly and demand of everyone involved in struggles for equal rights that we all "open up."

Dina's choice to pass is an attempt to traverse the path of least resistance in an environment hostile to certain types of identity. Racial passing in a post–Jim Crow world becomes a viable option for Dina because it allows her to discreetly travel a path that runs counter to the rigidity of heteronormative orientation, providing a nuanced depiction of black female sexuality that has proven perplexing for writers, particularly black women, to convey. Readers remain uncertain whether Dina is a homosexual, but the illegibility of her sexual orientation matters much less than comprehending her motivation to keep it hidden, the means through which she accomplishes this, and the effects this has on the individual. Although her story cannot be neatly folded into this literary tradition, many of its constituent elements are analogous to the plight of passing protagonists attempting to control how they are publicly perceived. Dina's black passing, in particular, extends beyond the governing logic of Jim Crow typically applied to accounts of racial passing and deconstructs the desirability of heteronormative whiteness and reaffirms the importance of other nonwhite identities. The particular intersection of race and sexuality at which this story operates, in which one is used to mask the other, has its roots in some traditional elements of the genre while also charting new territory into the constitution of racial and sexual categories in a shifting landscape. In *Post Black: How a Generation Is Redefining African American Identity*, Ytasha L. Womack asserts, "Politicians, organizations, business leaders, social advocates, average citizens, and the like are heavily vested in the perception of who African Americans *used* to be. How we were defined fifty, twenty-five, even ten years ago. There are those invested in who we *should* be. But there is very little understanding of who we *are*."[29] Packer's text is a creative response to this call to action, providing readers with an intimate portrait of who young black women are through her depiction of Dina. Her story moves the canon in a new direction and engenders a positive reenvisioning of contemporary African American women's identities.

Notes

1. Packer, "Drinking Coffee Elsewhere," 105.

2. Warren, *What Was African American Literature?*, 9.

3. Yoshino, *Covering*.

4. Sheshadri-Crooks, *Desiring Whiteness*.

5. Davis, introduction, viii.

6. Gallego, *Passing Novels*, 189.

7. Jessie Fauset's protagonist Angela Murray in *Plum Bun* (1928) passes to ensure her place in Greenwich Village's avant-garde artistic circle, for example.

8. Smith, *Not Just Race*, 36.

9. Gallego, *Passing Novels*, 8.

10. McDowell, introduction, xiii.

11. Butler, "Passing, Queering."

12. Christian, *Black Feminist Criticism*.

13. Carby, *Reconstructing Womanhood*, 147.

14. In *Souls of Black Folks*, W. E. B. Du Bois famously proclaims, "The problem of the Twentieth Century is the problem of the color line" (5), referring to the invisible barriers utilized to perpetuate the segregation of white and black races in all aspects of society.

15. Adams, "Black and White."

16. Douglass, *Narrative of the Life*.

17. Melville, *Benito Cereno*, 212–14.

18. Packer, "Drinking Coffee Elsewhere," 105.

19. Ibid., 107, added emphasis.

20. Ibid., 106.

21. Kilbourne's in-depth critique of popular culture in her documentary *Killing Us Softly 4* attributes the injurious psychological effects of advertising on girls and women to an ideal standard of beauty that is essentially unattainable. The ideal she describes valorizes heteronormative whiteness in much the same way it gets depicted in many racial passing narratives.

22. "Why They Call Yale the Gay Ivy."

23. Chauncey, "Gay at Yale."

24. A livestream debate about the relationship between civil rights activists and LGBT rights activists was conducted through the *Huffington Post* website.

25. Packer, *Drinking Coffee Elsewhere*, 126.

26. In "Blacklash?" Henry Louis Gates Jr. cites the appointment of A. Philip Randolph over Bayard Rustin as director of the 1963 march on Washington because of Rustin's homosexuality as one of the greatest examples of the divide between African Americans and gays.

27. Carter, "Emperor's New Clothes," 67.

28. Smith, "Blacks and Gays," 18.

29. Womack, *Post Black*, 22, emphasis in original.

Bibliography

Adams, Derek. "Black and White Both Cast Shadows: Unconventional Permutations of Racial Passing in African American and American Literature." PhD diss., University of Arizona, 2012.

Butler, Judith. "Passing, Queering: Nella Larsen's Psychoanalytic Challenge." In *Female Subjects in Black and White*, edited by Elizabeth Abel, Barbara Christian, and Helene Moglen, 266–84. Los Angeles: University of California Press, 1997.

Carby, Hazel V. *Reconstructing Womanhood: The Emergence of the Afro-American Woman Novelist*. Oxford: Oxford University Press, 1987.

Carter, Mandy. "The Emperor's New Clothes, or How Not to Run a Movement." In *This Is What a Lesbian Looks Like: Dyke Activists Take on the 21st Century*, edited by Kris Kleindienst, 60–69. Ithaca, NY: Firebrand, 1999.

Chauncey, George. "Gay at Yale: How Things Changed." *Yale Alumni Magazine*, July–August 2009. Accessed August 15, 2014. https://yalealumnimagazine.com/articles/2482.

Christian, Barbara. *Black Feminist Criticism: Perspectives on Black Women Writers*. New York: Teachers College Press, 1997.

Davis, Thaddious. Introduction to *Passing*. By Nella Larsen. vii–xxxv. New York: Penguin, 1997.

Douglass, Frederick. *Narrative of the Life of Frederick Douglass, an American Slave, Written by Himself*. 1845. New York: Penguin, 1982.

Du Bois, W. E. B. *Souls of Black Folks*. 1903. Edited by Henry Louis Gates Jr. and Terri Hume Oliver. New York: Norton, 1999.

Gallego, Mar. *Passing Novels in the Harlem Renaissance: Identity Politics and Textual Strategies*. Berlin: Lit Verlag, 2003.

Gates, Henry Louis, Jr. "Blacklash?" In *Dangerous Liaisons: Blacks, Gays, and the Struggle for Equality*, edited by Eric Brandt, 25–30. New York: New Press, 1999.

Killing Us Softly 4: Advertising's Image of Women. Written by Jean Kilbourne. Directed by Sut Jhally. Media Education Foundation, 2010. DVD.

McDowell, Deborah. Introduction to *Quicksand and Passing*. By Nella Larsen, ix–xxxi. New Brunswick, NJ: Rutgers University Press, 2011.

Melville, Herman. *Benito Cereno*. In *Billy Budd and Other Stories*, 159–258. New York: Penguin, 1986.

Packer, ZZ. "Drinking Coffee Elsewhere." In *Drinking Coffee Elsewhere*, 105–32. New York: Riverhead, 2003.

Sheshadri-Crooks, Kalpana. *Desiring Whiteness: A Lacanian Analysis of Race*. London: Routledge, 2000.

Smith, Barbara. "Blacks and Gays Healing the Great Divide." In *Dangerous Liaisons: Blacks, Gays, and the Struggle for Equality*, edited by Eric Brandt, 15–24. New York: New Press, 1999.

Smith, Valerie. *Not Just Race, Not Just Gender: Black Feminist Readings*. New York: Routledge, 1998.

Warren, Kenneth. *What Was African American Literature?* Cambridge, MA: Harvard University Press, 2011.

"Why They Call Yale the Gay Ivy." *Yale Alumni Magazine*, July–August 2009. Accessed November 30, 2016. https://yalealumnimagazine.com.

Womack, Ytasha L. *Post Black: How a New Generation Is Redefining African American Identity*. Chicago: Hill, 2010.

Yoshino, Kenji. *Covering: The Hidden Assault on Our Civil Rights*. New York: Random, 2006.

CHAPTER 9

Neo-Passing and Dissociative Identities as Affective Strategies in *Frankie and Alice*

DEBORAH ELIZABETH WHALEY

> I merely took the energy it takes to pout and wrote some blues.
>
> —Duke Ellington

> If a man does not keep pace with his companions, perhaps it is because he hears a different drummer. Let him step to the music which he hears, however measured or far away.
>
> —Henry David Thoreau

> Here's what I do baby: I close my eyes, and I let the music take me. Like I'm on the outside, just watching. Like I ain't even there.
>
> —Frankie, from the motion picture *Frankie and Alice*

Passing is a social construction. In order for a person to pass for an identity unlike the one socially ascribed, the viewer of the person must hold essentialist ideas about what constitutes and looks like a given identity. As I argue elsewhere in regards to racial passing, the language and grammars of passing require interrogation, as moving from one identity descriptor to another highlights the slippage in discourses and material manifestations of difference, challenging one to see passing as something that the viewer constructs, rather than something that the object of the gaze performs.[1] Put simply, it is the viewer that is "passing" the object of the gaze and questioning the object's ability to defy and expose arbitrary lines of identity. Agency and autonomy are lost when there is conformity to social ascriptions and prescriptions of identity. It is more productive when identity generates organically and creatively by individuals and communities who redefine race and other forms of difference to contest rigid definitions that gatekeepers create and propagate. Passing as a concept of essentialist artifice is epistemologically violent; it renders the object of the identity gaze invisible and unable to articulate multiple, self-identities or to abandon the notion of identity altogether. I define *neo-passing* as a theoretical concept that can address this problem by arguing for a reconfiguration of identities and the societal landscape that stratifies and marginalizes identities that some deem incomprehensible.

In defining neo-passing in this way, I depart from the definition of passing laid out in the introduction to the current volume by Mollie Godfrey and Vershawn Ashanti Young, which describes passing as an act of duping the looker, presenting or living as something other than what others believe the passer is; I also complicate their framing of neo-passing as constituting late twentieth- and twenty-first-centuries' iterations of passing that has expanded identity performance beyond race. Rather, I am decelerating and casting a complex and more precise frame for reconceptualizing passing through a filmic example of racial play, (dis)ability, and mental (un)wellness. My slowing down of accepted definitions of passing affirms James Clifford's advice that practitioners in cultural studies remain attuned to how identity is lived from an ethnographic framework, which centers the object of study as subject rather than as an object of the dominant hegemony. As Clifford suggests, when approaching our writing of identity, "not so fast" and "what else is there" should act as guides that encourage us to think deeply about identity as salient, lived, and plural.[2] The precision in meaning I call for between neo-passing as an analytic and passing as an accusation refers to the possibilities of the prefix to think through *felt* experiences of self-identity anew. I argue that dissociative identities can serve as useful devices to explore the cultural use of crafting an alternative self. Director Geoffrey Sax's film *Frankie and Alice* (2010) brings the concept of neo-passing and dissociative identity disorder (DID) into productive conversation, as it concerns the mental-health issues involved in creating, *passing through*, embodying, and rejecting multiple identities (figure 9.1).

In clinical terms, DID is the presence of more than one distinct personality state that recurrently exhibit identifying behaviors among those states and

FIGURE 9.1. Promotional poster for *Frankie and Alice*. Lionsgate (2010).

the condition by which one creates identities that are a coping mechanism for trauma. Formerly referred to as multiple personality disorder in psychiatric medicine and popular discourse, DID is a controversial diagnosis precisely because there is a questioning among some within and outside of the health profession regarding its existence and legitimacy as a real condition. Dissociative identity disorder as a trope in popular culture constitutes childhood and/or sexual trauma, dissatisfaction and noncompliance with gender and racial norms, and emotional fragmentation or dissonance as a coping strategy for alienation. In real life, one might consider skepticism of DID as contiguous and analogous to arguments that deny fluid racial, ethnic, sexual, and national identities. Biculturalism, bisexuality, multiracialism, and multinational identities are not semantic indulgences; these terms are lived correctives that shift discourses and the materiality of identity away from monocultural, monosexual, monoracial, and mononational constructs. Drawing from Jasbir K. Puar on the interstices (or intervening gaps) of disability and difference, I ask and answer what it would mean to think through these categories not in terms of bodies but in terms of affective possibilities. Dissociative identities and neo-passing offer a way to rethink race, gender, and sexuality as not bodily determinants of preconfigured identity or as postracial, postfeminine, and postsexual fantasies, which purport race, gender, and sexuality are not socially real and do not matter. Rather, I argue that dissociative identities and neo-passing in *Frankie and Alice* help us to think through (dis)ability, race, gender, and sexuality as what Puar describes as "assemblages of sensations, affects, and forces."[3]

Popular culture, including television, film, and fiction, illustrates examples of dissociative identity as mostly a hoax and, like the passing genre, as a deliberate attempt for a person to occlude his or her true self and responsibility for the atrocious actions of the other personalities. In medicine and psychology, dissociative identity disorder as a diagnosis has come under attack as a possible act in medical malpractice and the result of a psychiatrist's power of suggestion. Films like *The Three Faces of Eve* (1957) and the television miniseries *Sybil* (1976) purport to chronicle the true stories of women with multiple personalities. Yet, in subsequent years, there was a challenging of these filmic accounts as being nothing more than the exaggerations of female patients and an attempt among their doctors to gain monetary benefit from telling their perceived-embellished stories on the big or small screen.[4] Contemporary narratives of DID, such as the cable-television show *United States of Tara* (2009–11), moves the DID genre into new and productive spheres of cultural production by presenting DID as unresolvable and as an ongoing struggle. Despite the intervention of medical management, the protagonist is never "cured," and her competing selves are never sutured into a unified whole.[5]

I read dissociative identity as a neo-passing narrative through an examination of capacity and incapacity in *Frankie and Alice*. The film, starring actor Halle Berry, oscillates from the late 1950s to the early 1970s, showing neo-passing and DID in the '70s as a response to the social, racial, and sexual landscape of the '50s. The film's protagonist, Francine Lucinda Murdoch (mostly referred to as Frankie in the film), is a black American woman who struggles to negotiate alter identities: a young, precocious, and smart child named Genius; and a white, Southern, racist woman named Alice. Frankie works as a go-go dancer and stripper and bears the burden of the partial memories of a troubling racial and sexual past. She moves among these three identities—Frankie, Alice, and Genius—at different junctures throughout the film, revealing that each identity serves a psychological, cultural, and social purpose. Alice allows Frankie to resist the same ideologies that oppress her as a black woman by literally becoming or manifesting racial hatred. Genius allows Frankie to find solace in an innocence that is untouched by the racial trauma she experienced as a young teenager; it is also a counter to how the world sees her, that is, as an uneducated black woman. Frankie, too, is an identity phantom of racial, gender, and sexual projection. The core identity that her psychiatrist calls her to embrace, that is, Frankie, is a crafting of sexual sovereignty and a composite of Francine's rejection of sexual expectations and sexual restrictions, locating sexual expression within the intensities of affect rather than within a hailed and preconfigured identity. Thus, none of Francine's identities are necessarily authentic or inauthentic; they are an amalgam of memory screens. Purportedly based on a true story, *Frankie and Alice* challenges spectators to consider the implications of racial and sexual trauma in passing between and through alternative identities. I argue that neo-passing and dissociative identities constitute performances that generate from historical and social relations and produce psychological and material manifestations of recoded difference.

In *Black Skins, White Masks*, the psychiatrist Frantz Fanon argues that the black subject takes on disparate, racial identifications in response to the dominant culture's expectation and misconstruction of blackness.[6] Conversely, W. E. B. Du Bois and writer Ralph Ellison reveal in their separate works how black Americans may define and negotiate their identity through the distorted lens of blackness that the dominant white populace proffers.[7] Nevertheless, black women and men find ways to assert self-identifications that serve their own purposes and that are in alignment with their own lived realities and desires. In tandem with the previous core concepts of race, identity, and disability, I examine dissociative identity not as a disorder but, rather, as a reconstructive neo-passing narrative. In so doing, I explore how historical constructs and scripts of race, desire, and disparate social relations call black women to craft alternative identities; the ways medical and psychiatric discourse and practice are disenabling for the black subject; and how racial trauma and sexual projection present challenges to mental wellness. Exploring race, mental illness, and medical racism leads to the assertion that *Frankie and Alice* is a narrative and visual device that creates productive frames of reference for seeing and understanding the affective dimensionalities of multiply inscribed black feminine identities.

Francine Is Not Here: Sexual and Intellectual Affective Strategies

John Hoberman argues that disparate medical access and treatment cause a health calamity for black Americans. Hoberman writes that throughout history, the view white physicians had of black men and women was that they were unintelligent and unable to comprehend and follow instructions, were prone to obesity due to a lack of restraint, were sexually promiscuous, and were noncompliant patients responsible for the range of illnesses they experience in disproportionate numbers.[8] Erroneous ideas about racial difference thus impact black Americans' quality of treatment and their decisions to seek care for mental disabilities for fear of reinscribing ideas of racial inferiority that the medical-industrial complex (MIC) propagates.[9] An elision of social and socioeconomic class stratification, racial stressors, out- and in-group pressures results in individual and group blaming for a lack of physical and mental wellness. Although some health-care providers seek to avoid cultural bias, research indicates that the large majority of medical practitioners lack cultural competency and empathy when treating mental health disabilities among minority populations, in general, and black women, in particular. Further, Marya R. Sulsolski, Nicole T. Buchanan, and Chandra M. Donnell argue, "Nuanced depictions in popular culture, news, and research of high functioning black women who live with mental illness are rare," as are "the myriad ways in which these women successfully live."[10]

Meri Danquah, in her touching memoir about mental wellness and depression, *Willow Weep for Me: A Black Woman's Journey through Depression* (1998), similarly relates the struggle to secure mental health and the hesitance to acknowledge mental illness in the black community. "Black women are supposed to be strong—caretakers, nurturers, healers of other people—any of the twelve dozen variations of Mammy," says Danquah. As a dark-skinned African immigrant living in America, she describes her state of mind during episodes of mental illness in figurative terms, sharing that when immersed in depression, "Everything is blurry, out of focus, fading like a photograph; people seem incapable of change; living feels like a waste of time and effort."[11] Danquah indicates that an overabundance of life stressors associated with racism, classism, colorism, and sexual projection create the conditions in which mental wellness and treatment are a life challenge for women of African descent. In *Frankie and Alice*, the main protagonist experiences these stressors of race, sexuality, class, and gender, as well as the benevolent neglect of the mental health–care system. Despite the disenabling environment of exploitive and unequal social relations in which Francine resides, crafting alter identities reveals and heals her fragmented mind.

The film begins with a wide shot of a blue sky, and an overlay of white letters reads "based on true events" and then next, "Savannah, Georgia 1957." The sound of melancholy piano music is intermixed with wailing police sirens. Imaged next is a teenage Francine (played by Vanessa Morgan) in a red sports car that has apparently spun out of control and wrecked; she stares ahead through the cracked, front car window, appearing as if she is in shock. The cracked window represents the splintering of her identity from a naïve, hopeful, and lovestruck teenager to a jaded and psychologically damaged adult. Two police officers approach the car wreck to ask if she is okay, and they shine a flashlight in her face. As her eyes face the glare of the flashlight, the scene quickly transitions to present day: Los Angeles, California, 1973. Rhythm-and-blues crooner Marvin Gaye's song "Let's Get It On" plays loudly, as a camera pans the walls of a strip club. Glow-in-the-dark sketches of women drawn as sexy devils appear on the strip bar's black walls; lights in the shape of stars adorn the bottom baseboards. Scantily dressed dancers wear sheer body suits and high boots and dance atop tables—other women dance in cages as voracious men and women shout expletives and hand the dancers paper currency.

As the camera continues to pan through the strip club, it stops to focus on "Frankie" gyrating in a hanging cage. Her body moves toward the bars, she stares intensely, and then she retreats to continue dancing while she rubs her body (figure 9.2). She wears a long, straight wig; large, gold hoop earrings; a gold bra with fringe; a gold mini-skirt with fringe; and gold go-go boots. "There's nothing wrong with me loving you," says the lyrics to Gaye's song while a mostly white, male crowd in leisure suits surrounds her cage.[12] The men pant and yell for her to undress, and they throw or try to stuff bills through the cage bars. The camera follows Frankie's body in a circular motion as she twirls. She finally slinks down and slowly takes off a zebra-print pair of panties, twirls them in the air, and then offers the panties to a brown-haired, blue-eyed, white male in a baby-blue leisure suit—he responds by smiling and giving her a cluster of bills. Gaye's song continues as sexual tension builds in the scene, and Frankie places her fingers at the tip of her skirt. The crowd of men begs her to lift her skirt, while Gaye's lyrics plead:

> Don't you know how sweet and wonderful life can be?
> I'm askin' you baby, to get it on with me.
> I ain't gonna worry, I ain't gonna push. . . .
> So come on, come on. . . . Baby, stop beatin' round the bush.[13]

In unison with the lyrics "beating around the bush," Frankie finally lifts up her skirt revealing that she has a pair of gold panties underneath. She laughs and points at the men and backs away to the other end of the cage.

This erotic exchange acknowledges and legitimizes interracial desire, as underscored by the diegetic music source in which Gaye sings, "There's nothing wrong with me loving you," and the zebra-print panties, which signifies the

FIGURE 9.2. Francine as Frankie working as go-go dancer and stripper. Trailer screenshot, *Frankie and Alice*, Lionsgate (2010).

exotic otherness of Frankie and the cohabitation of black and white bodies. Frankie controls and mediates the men's pleasure, however, by, as Gaye sings, beating around the bush, or elongating and then ending her striptease. *Getting it on*, which is vernacular phrasing signifying an invitation for sexual relations, becomes a sexual, signifyin(g) practice that allows Frankie to achieve gratification through retreating away from and laughing at the men. She performs as the ultimate black feminine trickster by taking their money without revealing her "bush," so to speak. A potentially objectifying profession, that is, a stripper, is rearticulated through Frankie's control of how, when, and what the men will see of her body. While a cage might appear to confine her sexuality and stabilize it for the scopophiliac gaze, in this case, the cage protects her from the men gaining access to her body. Francine's "Frankie," then, is a performance of sexuality that allows her to feel the adoration of sexual desire by men, but she ultimately controls her and their gratification as she dances in the cage.

Frankie's labor in the sex industry is a contradictory space where mid-twentieth-century taboos of interracial desire temporarily break down, thereby allowing for a leveling of sexual, gender, and race social relations, even as her profession reifies those relations. Sex work is not a romantic or pleasurable endeavor in the film as much as the film depicts it as an economic and exploitive labor market that Francine as Frankie performs for a myriad of reasons while still being able to access moments of sexual and personal autonomy. Francine *performs* as Frankie not to reinscribe notions of black hypersexuality as created in the dominant culture's imagination; rather, she *utilizes* Frankie as a strategic financial and sexual identity. Frankie highlights the specificity of struggle for black, laboring women in the sex industry and undermines hierarchies of pleasure as she eschews the sexual and religious respectability and sanctions that the spectator later finds out were a debilitating component of her upbringing and younger life. This strategic-identity rupture coheres when Frankie retreats to her dressing room after her performance, and she sits down at a vanity, pulls off her long, straight wig that signifies her performance of white femininity, and reveals a tightly curled and coiled Afro underneath that resembles a resonating black femininity. She lights a marijuana cigarette and stares intensely into a mirror, indicating her contemplation and negotiation of feminine artifice and "monster beauty" as Frankie, with the submerged Francine.[14] When a fellow dancer who is struggling with the weight of baring her body for profit asks Frankie if stripping becomes easier, Frankie replies with an authoritative voice that slowly dissolves into a contemplative and confused tone: "Here's what I do, baby: I close my eyes, and I let the music take me. Like I'm on the outside, just watching. Like I ain't even there. Works for me." The last line of dialogue, "works for me," is an assertion that invites the following question: How does Frankie work *for* and *against* Francine?

Cynthia M. Blair posits that black, female sex workers are a productive paradox, as they bring to light and transcend "moral, sexual, and spatial divides . . . of racial politics."[15] Frankie is not *who Francine is*, she is *what Francine does* out of necessity to support herself and to engage in fantasies of cross-racial sexual desire and pleasure on her own terms. While Francine is deeply submerged in alters Frankie, Genius, and Alice, she is able to protect Frankie from the pitfalls of the sex industry that Blair alludes to in her study. One sees this later in the film when her white, male psychiatrist, Dr. Oswald (Stellan Skarsgård), queries Francine about drug use, assuming that because she is black, female, and in the sex industry, she is "strung out." Francine answers, "Frankie got rules: no coke, no smack, no speed." Frankie occasionally smokes marijuana and drinks alcohol, but as she tells her doctor in a sexually suggestive voice, her only real vice is Ding Dong pastries. Ongoing references in the film to Frankie eating or wanting Ding Dongs—a round convenience pastry that has white cream in the middle—places her as one with a healthy sexual appetite, and it insinuates cross-racial desire and pleasure in giving fellatio. Although the film engages with the precarity of labor in the sex industry and strives for sexual autonomy, the film's critique of and simultaneous embrace of the MIC speaks directly to the relationship among race, disability, neo-passing, and dissociative identities.

As the film progresses, there is a hindering of the medical management of Frankie and alters Genius and Alice, because the psychiatric team that overseas her care is indifferent to her recovery, and their actions show cultural incompetence or a lack of ability to understand the racial and sexual aspects of Francine's trauma that the film later reveals. Medical racism dissolves as Francine and Oswald gain mutual trust, but the dialogue in the film situates the treatment of Francine as being analogous to his inability to understand how the tonal complexity of jazz music can provide a window into the subconscious. Listening to jazz and switching from the music of Duke Ellington to Miles Davis provide Oswald with clues to Francine's condition. Jazz in the film is an ongoing metaphor for black culture, more generally; his stack of psychology books is race neutral, yet racially biased assumptions leave him wanting, whereas black music (and, perhaps, stereotypically so) moves him into an affective position to treat and understand Francine's alters. This prefiguring occurs before his first examination of Frankie, where Oswald says to the nurse Susan:

OSWALD: A colleague from the faculty of arts once told me that he'd had the most amazing results from listening to jazz. He claimed it allowed him full access to the subconscious state without any need for hallucinogens or stimulants. [When I listen] I don't experience anything all.

SUSAN, *sarcastic and smiling*: Well, maybe you are not listening properly.

OSWALD, *indignant*: Yes, I am. This equipment—it is absolutely state-of-the-art.

Francine's doctor does not understand Susan's response or what sociologist Stuart Hall defines as the "black" in black cultural production: expressivity, call and response, inflections toward the vernacular and the local, counternarratives, orality, elements of different and historically informed discourses of black diaspora identities, and improvised musicality and tonal rearrangements.[16] However, just as jazz represents black culture, it also represents Oswald slowly gaining cultural competence and recognizing the intelligence of the culture in which jazz music and Francine are a part.

Briggett C. Ford, in her social scientific assessment of black women and sexual and violent trauma, links the role culture plays in the treatment and comprehension of black female patients in real life. Ford concludes: "Age, race, gender, culture, ethnicity, and socioeconomic status significantly influence psychiatric diagnosis because they determine how both the therapist and client view mental illness and its symptomatology."[17] In-group and out-group perceptions of culture and, relatedly, intelligence encourage and allow Francine's alter Genius to work for Francine in ways that Frankie cannot. Genius displays an intellect that does not equal but, rather, surpasses those in her everyday life and the medical staff that seeks to treat her for DID. In so doing, just as Frankie controls men, Genius controls her treatment process and intervenes in the cultural assumptions initially made by Oswald. For example, Genius affectionately and perhaps manipulatively refers to Oswald as Dr. Oz. The nickname reveals that though he purports to have control over Francine's treatment (just as the Wizard of Oz purported to control the Land of Oz in the film *The Wizard of Oz*), it is Genius who has the upper hand and holds the key to Francine's mental wellness (similar to *The Wizard of Oz*'s Dorothy).

Genius's existence first appears when a fellow dancer, Trish, hands Frankie the crossword page of the *Los Angeles Times*.

> TRISH, *in surprise*: You did the crossword?
> FRANKIE: No, I didn't, that ain't even my handwriting.
> TRISH: Genius has done the crossword again. Whatcha trying to do, Frankie, make us look bad? You got something to prove?

The camera zooms in and quickly pans the crossword puzzle, showing the words *diesel, mishaps, creep, rabid, lurid, whacks, Adam, car,* and *knot* (figure 9.3). With a worrisome glare Frankie looks at the puzzle and reaches for a bottle of Jack Daniels and takes a swig. She looks into a mirror as if she does not recognize her reflection and then slowly bows her head (figure 9.4). The crossword

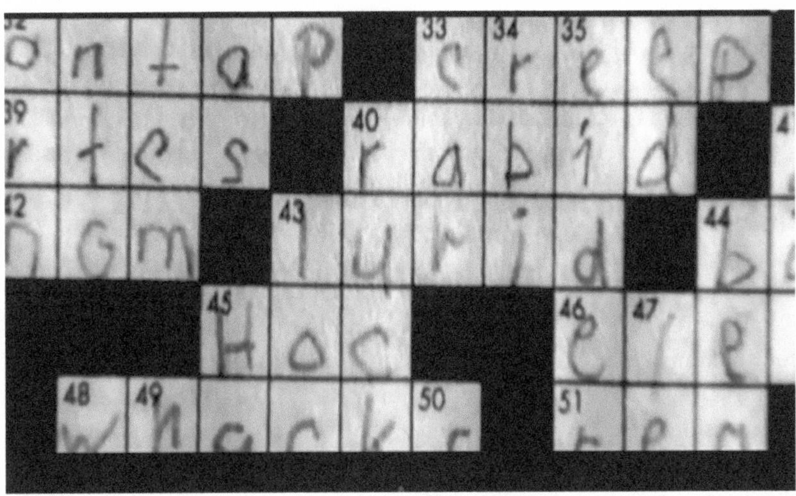

FIGURE 9.3. Genius's crossword puzzle. Trailer screenshot, *Frankie and Alice*, Lionsgate (2010).

FIGURE 9.4. Frankie in duress about the intellect of her alter Genius. Trailer screenshot, *Frankie and Alice*, Lionsgate (2010).

puzzle's words represent how Genius seeks to comprehend and knit together Francine's identities. It also represents a series of events that are responsible for her undoing: Francine's car crash that begins the film (car, diesel, mishaps, and whacks), the sexual adventures of Frankie (creep, rabid, and lurid), and, as we witness later in the film, the hyperreligious ranting of her alter Alice (Adam and knot). After there is an arrest of Alice for a violent confrontation at a childhood friend's wedding reception, Frankie calls her therapist and cries, "They fittin' to put me in jail. Because of my history, they say I don't have to go to jail if I sign myself in to the nuthouse." This moment establishes that she has had a struggle with mental wellness in the past, without resolution of the issues that she faces. Upon entering treatment, she becomes the exclusive patient of Oswald, and Genius continues to provide insight into the life and behavior of Francine and Frankie.

During her in-patient, thirty-day stay, Oswald discovers the presence of Genius by reviewing her medical record and examining her eye, hand, and body coordination. At different moments in psychiatric care, Francine's IQ varies from 132 to 156, or from above average to genius. Her eyesight oscillates from 20/20 vision to extreme farsightedness; she uses both her right and left hands to write; she smokes during sessions, but when Oswald offers her cigarettes, she claims that she never smokes; her voice passes through distinct dialects of a child, a Southerner, and an urbanite. Oswald decides to hypnotize Francine to see if he can draw out the root of the contradictions in her behavior he cannot explain. He flashes light on the exam room wall and tells her to follow the light with her eyes. The camera moves from the wall with the flashlight to close-ups of Frankie's face as tears swell in her eyes. The light on the wall becomes bigger as the camera closes in tighter. The scene transitions from the blinding light making circular movements on the wall to a round silver plate that a teenage Frankie stares into and shines.

Francine, now in a blue-and-white domestic uniform, puts down the silver plate and walks down the stairs as a group of young, white men enter the mansion where she works. Two of the men stand in the doorway; the light obscures their faces. Another young white male enters, and there is a clear image of his face; soft lighting makes him appear angelic and ethereal. He smiles and looks up at Francine. The man, who the spectator later learns is her teenage lover Pete (Scott Lyster), has dark brown hair and blue eyes (he looks similar to the gentleman at the strip club an older Frankie hands her zebra-print panties to). Francine pretends to dust the stairway; Pete walks up the stairs and discreetly caresses her arm. She turns to the side and smiles, looks down, and then looks up at him and smiles once again. His eyes glisten with excitement, he calls out to her and says, "Frankie," thus asserting their intimacy, but the spatiality of him being above on the stairs and her below visually reinscribes social inequity. Moving from a flashback of the 1950s to the film's present day of 1973, Oswald, in a voiceover, says, "Nod if you can hear me." Francine nods, and the scene transitions to a flashback of Pete appearing to say "good," but it is Oswald's voice that the spectator hears. The camera splits the image of Oswald, uses reverse shots between Oswald and Genius, and visualizes a series of flashback images in a montage (figure 9.5). Francine is splintering into Genius:

OSWALD: Now there is someone else I'd like to meet. Is that possible? (*Genius looks up, cowers in a childlike pose, looks up at him again, and his image is blurry through her farsighted eyes.*) Hi.

GENIUS, *in a precocious child's voice*: You look like that wizard from Oz. Where Dorothy fell upon that witch.

OSWALD: You like that film?

GENIUS: I read the book. I read books.

OSWALD: That's good. (*Inquisitively.*) How long are you going to keep her?

GENIUS: Who? Lucinda or Frankie? Lucinda [her middle name] from the Latin *lucidas* via *lucere,* meaning "to shine." An origin it shares with *lucid,* meaning "to think or to see clearly." (*Laughs in a childish murmur.*) Nobody ever care about Frankie. Except for momma. And Mr. Pete.

FIGURE 9.5. During Frankie's transition to Genius, her vision of psychiatrist Oswald fracturing. Trailer screenshot, *Frankie and Alice*, Lionsgate (2010).

> OSWALD: But you try to help her, don't you?
> GENIUS: When I can.
> OSWALD: What stops you?
> GENIUS: It's getting dark in here.

Genius wiggles and sits up straight: she is transitioning to the racist and anti-Semitic Alice. She says, "Good Lord," in an adult, Southern accent. Oswald asks whom he is speaking with.

> ALICE: Well, you never end a sentence with a preposition, doctor. Isn't that what we were taught in school?
> OSWALD: Perhaps Miss Murdoch can introduce me to you the next time I see her.
> ALICE, *gesturing toward the exam-room door*: That's quite slippery of you, doctor. That is a trait which is common to your race. You don't deny that you are Hebrew, do you?
> OSWALD: No.
> ALICE, *heading out the door*: At any rate, she won't be able to make an introduction. Because she won't remember a word of our encounter.

Genius's appearances are brief, and Alice repeatedly disrupts her because, as Oswald begins to decipher, Genius holds the key to the mystery behind

Francine's multiple-identity rupture, and Alice, as a manifestation of and mirror of racism, wishes to prolong Francine's suffering. When Francine transitions to Genius, she is more than intelligent, as Genius is introspective about the women Francine becomes due to the sexual and racial trauma she experienced as a teenager. Genius represents Francine as a child, and she has the ability to recall and feel empathy for Frankie's sexual indiscretions, Alice's racism, and Francine's unfulfilled potential. As a narrative tool, then, Genius brings humanity to Francine's other alters, by explaining the racial and sexual psychology and history behind their formation. To locate such introspection within the body and voice of a child simultaneously asserts the wisdom of children and reveals how if not encumbered by societal constructs of identity and lived experiences of race, gender, sexual, and class oppression and stigmas, the potential of black women is limitless: they can literally become geniuses if not weighted by these external stressors. Taken together, Frankie's autonomous sexuality and Genius's intellectual interventions reveal how historical constructs and scripts of race, desire, and disparate social relations call black women to craft alternative identities that create *remediation* and are in constant *rearticulation*.

The Fetters Tore Her to Pieces: Alice as Racial Remediation

Though the most irrational and dangerous of all alters, Alice, as a form of racial remediation, is a cultural remedy who reveals the racial social order and the sexual relations that cause Francine to splinter into multiples. Alice's affective role allows one to see at an emotional level how the racism of the dominant culture challenges mental wellness for people of African descent. Alice uses racism to reveal racism; she is a mirror reflection of Paige (Katharine Isabelle), who is Pete's racist sister, and Francine's mother (Phylicia Rashad), who, like Paige, disapproves of Francine and Pete's romantic relationship.

Affect is the "precognitive intensities of emotional, visceral, and embodied forces" that drive Alice and all of Francine's alters to "feel, transform, and act." Rather than being synonymous with emotion per se, Jasbir Puar and Ann Pellegrini propose *affect* as "the body as well as emotion's *trace effect*. Affect, from this perspective, is precisely what allows the body to be an open system, always in concert with its virtuality, [and] the potential of becoming."[18] Alice as a character of affective, racial remediation embodies an emotional composite that uncovers—through hyperreligiosity and acts of self-hatred and self-mutilation—the ways in which racial trauma and sexual trauma challenge mental wellness. Departing from the DID trope of molestation and sexual assault in childhood, *Frankie and Alice* presents how racial and sexual sanctions of black female sexuality, which disallows black females to transgress racially segregated codes of sexual interaction, can injure and leave a debilitating psychological imprint. The film does not pathologize black sexuality; it represents white fear of black sexuality and white and black fear of consensual black and white intimate and sexual relationships.

Alice is first introduced when Frankie begins to make out with a black male, Cliff, who DJs at the strip club where she dances. Cliff and Frankie stumble into his apartment, and Cliff asks, "Make you feel good?" while he gropes her breasts. Panting, Frankie replies, "Give it to me," and she walks backward toward Cliff's bed. As the two make their way closer to Cliff's bed, Frankie steps on an object that rattles—she looks down and sees that it is baby's rattle. She picks it up and appears to go into a state of shock. A diegetic sound of a baby crying heightens to a jarring screech. Frankie walks through a hallway as if she is in a trance, and the sound of a baby crying continues. She sees and walks over to a baby crib located in the rear of Cliff's apartment. A blue, quilted blanket with a white bubble print lies in the crib, and the quilt appears to cover a lumpy mass. As the sound of a baby crying continues to heighten, she removes the quilt, only to find nothing underneath but white sheets. She raises her hands to her forehead, and the sound of the baby becomes even louder as she massages her temples. Cliff assures Frankie, "It's alright. I took the baby to her mamma's on Crenshaw."

The film flashes back to the sound of a young Francine giving birth to what we later find out was her and Pete's child. Francine cries out in pain, and she asks her mother, Edna, who is delivering the baby, "Momma, what's wrong?" Returning to present times, Frankie looks up at Cliff, and his voice becomes inaudible. She kneels down and places her hands over her head again, and when Cliff tries to console her, she stands up and retorts angrily in a Southern accent, "Get your filthy nigger hands off of me!" Cliff steps back and stares at her in shock. Frankie walks toward Cliff, and she lifts her finger, scolding him and muttering a biblical reference, Colossians 3:5: "Mortify therefore your members which are on earth; fornication, uncleanness, inordinate affection, evil concupiscence, and covetousness, which is idolatry. For which things' sake the wrath of God comes on the children of disobedience." Cliff laughs and says, "Frankie, Frankie, come on, baby." Alice glares at him with hatred, with her finger still raised, and says, "Frankie is not here." She hits him with a sharp object, he falls to the ground, and he begins to bleed.

Colossians 3:5, which I interpret briefly here, calls Christians to avoid passion and desire that narratives in the Bible deem impure and do not sanction . If Alice is a white woman, sexual relations with a black man, her biblical rant insinuates, is forbidden and something to avoid, even if through death. This moment is a presage to the film's climax, when Genius tells Oswald, through a flashback sequence, that Pete died in a car crash when he and Francine made an attempt to run away. The scene in the beginning of the film, when Francine is immobile in a crashed red sport car, is not just the start to the film; this scene is the start of her alters coming to fruition to protect and sometimes hurt Francine and to help her cope with Pete's death. Genius also confides to Oswald that Francine's mother, Edna, kills Francine and Pete's baby shortly after Francine gives birth to the child in a hotel room. Indeed, upon seeing Francine's child, who has white skin and blue eyes, Edna looks at the baby in horror and watches it wiggle its hands. It cries. Edna takes the baby outside, and she disappears. Blue and white are colors that the film continually foregrounds through clothing and features (e.g., domestic uniforms, the baby blanket, Pete's and the strip club patron's appearance or clothes, the eyes and skin color of white characters and Francine's baby), perhaps signifying that whiteness causes the blues or depression. Francine's "blues" in regard to whiteness constitute a series of losses: She loses her best friend, Paige, due to Paige's closet racism and anxiety over her brother Pete and Francine's racial mixture; she loses Pete due to the violent car crash that begins the film; and she loses her baby due to Edna's reprehensible act of violence.

Francine's losses, as Alice's antics convey, result not from abstract notions of racism but, rather, from the racism of those close to Francine who declare her and Pete's union impure and socially unacceptable. Edna underscores her dislike of the teenage Francine's romantic choice when Oswald asks Edna about Pete's role in Francine's mental wellness, and a sinister and judgmental look stretches across her face. She answers, invoking the tragic mulatta narrative of yesteryear's passing literature: "They was trying to live between two worlds. Wouldn't have fitted in either one." "Are you saying that he was white?" asks Oswald. Edna coldly summarizes in a formal, Southern drawl, "It's over now." There is a further indication of the tragic mulatta trope in the film through the narrative's omission. Like the passing films *Imitation of Life* (1934; 1959) and *Pinky* (1949), Francine's father does not appear in the film, and Francine is a couple skin gradations lighter than are her mother and her sister Maxine (Chandra Wilson). The color contrasts among Edna, Francine, and Maxine may lead the spectator to wonder if part of Edna's reaction to Francine and Pete's mutual love affair and their offspring might stem from the historical legacy of slavery, in which black women were raped by white slavers, or to Francine's undisclosed paternal lineage.

Alice does not literally pass for white, other than within her own fragmented mind. Despite Francine's skin color, when Francine is dressed as and performing as Alice, her blackness is visually apparent to all through her features and through her loosely curled, though still-coarse hair texture. Yet, it is her insistence to claim whiteness as a power move to intercept social segregation, her marking of the trauma of racism by embodying racism, and her insistence to operate on equal or superior terms with other white characters (Paige and Oswald, for example) that situates her as a neo-passing subject. Oswald juxtaposes the dissimilar attributes of Genius and Alice, asserting that Alice is indeed the most dangerous—and therefore the most potent and potentially transgressive of alters—when he complains to one of his colleagues: "[Genius] is a helper, she is very smart. The other one, on the other hand, who thinks she's white—she is far too strong. She is a problem." When Alice looks into a mirror, she sees a white woman (figures 9.6 and 9.7). When she enters a room, she adopts the privilege of whiteness by navigating unencumbered by codes of segregation in public spaces, and she says the things that some may argue white people think but do not dare to say aloud. Thus, when Oswald interacts with Alice, he is interacting with his own white-skin privilege. Alice's behavior affirms that *no one is white*. Whiteness is something that people make to gain access to power.[19]

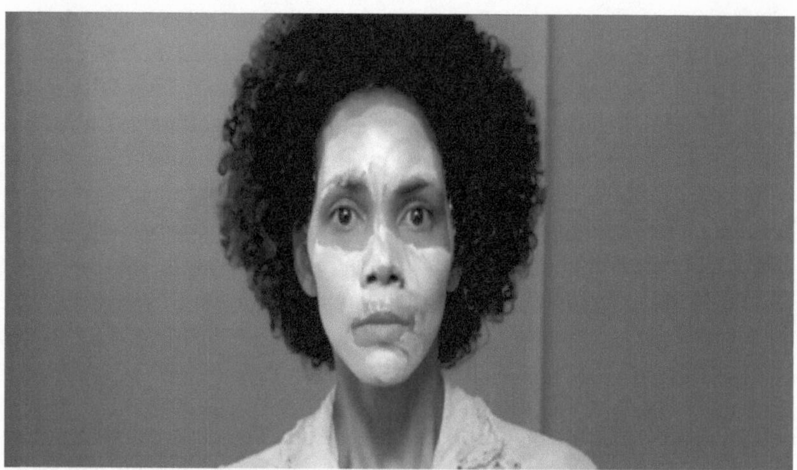

FIGURE 9.6. Frankie in whiteface, looking in the mirror, before she transitions to Alice. Trailer screenshot, *Frankie and Alice*, Lionsgate (2010).

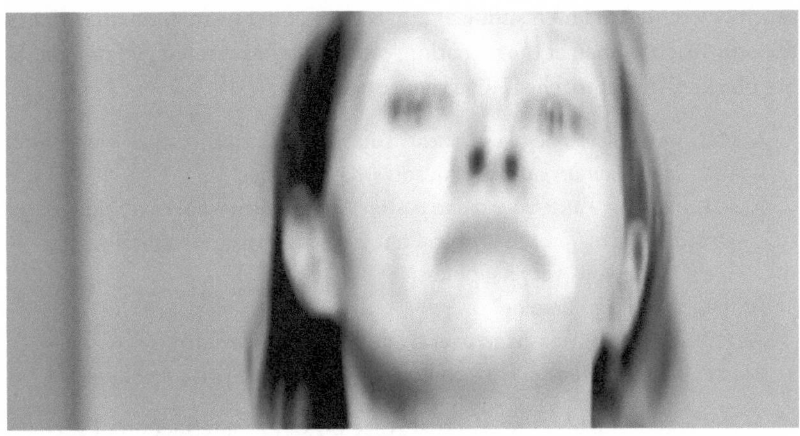

FIGURE 9.7. When Frankie sees Alice for the first time, she slams her head into the mirror. Trailer screenshot, *Frankie and Alice*, Lionsgate (2010).

Alice's character provides new ways of seeing and thinking about the psychological prospect and perils of self-identity performance and its ability to fragment onlookers' ideas of race, despite what they "see." In so doing, Alice moves spectators—both within the film and those watching the film—into an affective viewing space. Neo-passing in this productive form occurs when Alice confronts Paige in present times at Paige's wedding reception, later when Oswald realizes that Francine's third personality is a white woman, and finally, when Frankie provides the answer regarding Alice's "dominant" cultural use. *Frankie and Alice* moves to a second flashback of the 1950s and shows Paige, dressed in a pink poodle skirt and a pink blouse, open a bedroom door where she finds Francine and Pete making love. After a series of quick counter and reverse shots among Francine, Paige, and Pete, Paige retorts angrily, "Francine Murdoch! Get out, you filthy degenerate. That's my brother!" From Paige's reaction, Francine realizes Paige and Pete are not her social equals despite their proclamations of friendship (Paige) and love (Pete). Genius referring to Pete as Mr. Pete in her psychiatric sessions is a formal pronouncement of the social fact that as a young, black girl and domestic, whites, even those who purport friendship, view her as not human but as a racial degenerate and "the help." Back in present times, Frankie is at a laundromat, and in a nondiegetic voiceover, she says, "Frankie is not here." Next, Alice, in a formal dress and with her head and nose held high, walks into a ballroom; she looks around with confidence, as white women and men sitting at tables glare at her in amazement. Alice is the only black woman at the reception, only "Alice," as created by Francine, is not black. Alice approaches Paige (figure 9.8):

ALICE, *speaking in a Southern accent*: You look beautiful.
PAIGE, *in her Southern accent*: I'm sorry, have we met?
ALICE, *mocking Paige's accent and posture*: Remember, we always said we would be there for each other on our wedding days. (*Sarcastically*.) Well, I wish you every happiness.
PAIGE, *tearing up*: Frankie?
ALICE: Is that your husband over there? I'd like to see him.
PAIGE, *slapping Frankie*: How could you! Why would you come here?

At the end of the film, we find that Alice is not just a refraction of societal racism and a composite of Paige and Francine's mother, Edna; she is also the "white" child that her mother kills. There is a revelation of this when Frankie tells Oswald: "My momma killed it. All my dreams were in that baby. . . . Pete and I were going to call her . . . we were going to call her . . . *Alice*." Although a product of Francine and Pete, if she had survived, the child's appearance of whiteness, the narrative insinuates, might trigger in the "real" Alice the type of behavior and self-hate that Francine's Alice displays. Yet, the film cleverly posits that it is both the alter Alice and the real Alice that society fears most because they embody and defy socially inscribed definitions of racial identity.

FIGURE 9.8. Alice at Paige's wedding reception. Trailer screenshot, *Frankie and Alice*, Lionsgate (2010).

Oswald insists at the film's abrupt conclusion that Francine must integrate Genius, Frankie, and Alice to become whole. Musician Stevie Wonder's song "Higher Ground" plays nondiegetically, and a series of letter overlays reveals that the real-life Francine became a high school teacher and married a psychiatrist. Pictured next is a montage shot of Frankie attending college, laughing with Oswald, and complying with her psychiatric care, thereby complementing Wonder's hopeful lyrics:

> People keep on learnin',
> Soldiers keep on warrin',
> World keep on turnin',
> 'Cause it won't be too long.

Francine transforms from tortured subject to a happy object of the MIC's intervention.[20] The real Francine's normative and assumedly happy ending also knits together the messiness of alters and therefore of identity, but the most puissant aspect of Francine's story exists within the diegesis of the film, that is, the film's highlighting of medical racism and the how and the why of psychological fragmentation. In other words, *Frankie and Alice* offers to spectators that the world needs Francine and Frankie's sexual transgressions, Genius's intellect and innocence, and the racial mirror that Alice holds up to those around her and to the world.

Conclusion

It may be fine, one might argue, to point to the (re)construction of identity in film and deny its materiality in real life by cheering for the theoretical potential of mental switch points at the expense of those who experience deep and prolonged pain, because they are not what society deems mentally well. This is not the project here. Disability studies remind us that mental wellness and illness are social constructions; the definition and the power relations that arise from (dis)ability result from hegemonic and neoliberal interests. Therefore, differently able subjects can intervene in practices that purport narrow definitions of madness, biomedical intervention, and therapeutic counsel of normativity. Mad Pride is an example of this work, as it is an activist group that questions the havoc of the MIC and argues for patient-centered rather than clinician-centered care to situate disability subjects as a resource, rather than as pathological.[21] *Frankie and Alice,* though a sensational interpretation of a purportedly true story, is provocative for the film's reaccounting of the negligence and ethnocentrism of the MIC as well as a reaccounting of the source and consequences of racial and sexual trauma. *Frankie and Alice* thus works as a recuperative memoir and docudrama, and from this vantage point, Francine's alters are not necessarily mentally ill; they are *bad* (read resistant and expository) and *affective subjects*.[22] Lennard J. Davis supports such a reading of affective subjects as "abling" when he argues that normalcy speciously creates disability through Otherness and as a problem to solve; we must therefore interrogate, demystify, and argue against the normal "normal" and the normal abnormal to move theories of (dis)ability forward.[23]

For those who experience dissociation in the real world, their feelings may disrupt their ability to function in everyday life. Medical management, despite the racism of the MIC, is at times useful for people of African descent and for the general population for a range of mental health issues. Having said that, in her work on depression, Ann Cvetkovich informs that it is productive to see and understand strivings for mental health as not sensational but as mundane (i.e., something that most people experience) and as political. One can heal from additional modes of intervention outside of or in addition to the MIC. This may include moving the body and engaging in self-care and embracing psychological impasses. Cvetkovich argues, drawing from Lauren Berlant, that a psychological impasse, or feeling stuck, may seem to cripple the subject in daily life, but it may also slow one down and encourage reflection about life in ways that medication and medicalization may not through their hurried recourse and avoidance.[24] Mental wellness as it intersects with frames of identity, then, is, indeed, political. Theoretical contemplation about identity ruptures and sutures as feelings is not postmodernist solipsism. Such forms of inquiry are a political intervention that provides the grounds for mental wellness and rescripts a narrative of (un)belonging for those struggling with self-care and wellness, thereby moving subjects (or people) toward performative healing practices.

The historical moments of 1957 and 1973, which the film references, may seem like a distant past, but in contemporary times, the devaluations of blackness and of black women as autonomous sexual and life partners in (hetero)sexual life and the related stressors of racism, sexism, classism, ability, and sexual projection remain. *Frankie and Alice* asserts that in contemporary times striving for mental wellness continues, and current struggles with disability and trauma relate to past racial and sexual antagonisms. African immigrant Meri Danquah's memoir of the fight to achieve mental wellness in the racially inscribed US landscape illuminates this present-day struggle of black women. Her memoir also asks, through its title *Willow Weep for Me*, for affective resonance.[25] In the jazz standard of the same name, Nina Simone animates Danquah's and other black women's reality through her sonic interpretation of lyrics.[26] Listening to the brilliantly executed compositions of Miles Davis (a black misogynist and batterer) allows Oswald to gain insight into how to relate to and learn from Genius, Frankie, and Alice.[27] However, Simone's upbeat and tonal rearrangement and the lyrics to "Willow Weep for Me" illustrate the affective dimension of love, loss, and subsequent switch points of Francine that Davis's jazz instrumentals cannot explain with equal precision or ironic buoyancy:

> Willow weep for me
> . . .
> Bend your branches down along the ground and cover me
> Listen to my plea
> Hear me willow and weep for me
> . . .
> Whisper to the wind and say that love has sinned
> To leave my heart a sighin'
> And crying alone
> Murmur to the night
> Hide its starry light
> . . .
> Weeping willow tree
> Weep in sympathy[28]

Notes

1. Passing as a theoretical construct and reconstructive practice is discussed in early twentieth-century comics strips in Whaley, "Re-inking the Nation." 28–66.

2. Clifford, "Taking Identity Politics Seriously."

3. Puar, "Homonationalism as Assemblage," 23.

4. For a thorough discussion of DID as a narrative trope, see Schwarz, *Beware of the Other Side(s)*.

5. I work through these popular examples in my monograph in progress, tentatively titled "Feeling Her Fragmented Mind: Women, Race, and Dissociative Identities in Popular Culture."

6. Fanon, *Black Skins, White Masks*.

7. Du Bois, *Souls of Black Folk*; Ellison, *Invisible Man*.

8. Hoberman, *Black and Blue*, 22.

9. The term *medical industrial complex* (MIC) refers to the conglomeration of medical industries, practitioners, organizers, and managers; drug and equipment suppliers; and financial interests and creditors that operate in the interests of the state, business, and neoliberalism. The primary role of the MIC, therefore, is profit, with research and education being second and third in priority. Patient care is marginal, a byproduct of, or in the

interest of the MIC's financial, research, business interests, and stability. See Ehrenreich, *American Health Empire*.

10. Sosulski, Buchanan, and Donnell, "Life History and Narrative Analysis," 34. See also Spates, "Missing Link"; Wilson, "Black Woman and Mental Health."

11. Danquah, *Willow Weep for Me*.

12. Gaye, "Let's Get It On."

13. Ibid.

14. Buszek, *Pin-Up Grrrls*, 3. Maria Elena Buszek explains, "Monster beauty is artifice," as well as "pleasure/discipline" and "cultural invention." Monster beauty, then, refers to hyperfeminine appearance and performance that holds political and subversive possibilities. Buszek, *Pin-Up Grrrls*, 3.

15. Blair, *I've Gotta Make My Livin'*, 3. See also Williams, *Sex Tourism in Bahia*; Chapkis, *Live Sex Acts*.

16. Hall, "What Is This 'Black.'"

17. Ford, "Violence and Trauma," 229.

18. Puar and Pellegrini, "Affect." On theories of affect, see Gregg and Seigworth, introduction; Puar and Pellegrini, "Affect." On affect and mental wellness, see Cvetkovich, *Depression*.

19. On whiteness as a social construction, see Jacobson, *Whiteness of a Different Color*, and Roediger, *Wages of Whiteness*.

20. Wonder, "Higher Ground."

21. Lewis, "Mad Fight," 116. See also Theri Pickens, who argues that "attending to disability as another discourse of power frustrates current identity politics because it challenges the ideas of the always able ethnic body and the always abject and powerless disabled body." Pickens, "You're Supposed to Be," 30.

22. I cannot make this argument without acknowledging that like other DID narratives in popular culture that claim to depict a real-life account, Francine's story could be fictional. Additionally, an argument is that DID exists so that those who experience distinct multiple personalities can seek medical care (it has become more productive, for example, for medical practitioners to agree on and to convince insurance companies of dissociation as being real as opposed to the existence of multiple personalities). Nevertheless, I argue, the film performs recuperative work and insights into the intersection of race and medicine, racism within the field of psychiatry, and the race, class, sexual, and ability stratification that hinders black women's mental wellness.

23. Davis, "Normality, Power, Culture," 1.

24. Cvetkovich, *Depression*, 20–21.

25. Danquah, *Willow Weep for Me*.

26. This is not to say, of course, that only black women are served by or relate to the interpretation of the song by Nina Simone. "Willow Weep for Me" is powerful precisely because many have covered the song, and many relate to the song's lyrics. I agree with Barry Shank when he cautions, in regards to music, identity, reception, and politics: "The idea that groups make music that identifies the group and thereby expresses the values

of that group relies on a static concept of identity and a relatively firmly bounded notion of the group that frustrates any effort to think about the political force of music. If all music can do politically is to reinforce the already existent values of an already defined group, then music acts more as a conveyor of values constructed elsewhere than as an agent itself." My inclusion of the song aims to follow in the tradition of Angela Davis, who argues that the performative traditions of black female jazz and blues singers reenunciated the meaning of jazz standards with their tonally complex inflections, which speak to the realities, struggle, politics, and agency of black working-class women. Shank, *Political Force of Musical Beauty*, 14; Davis, *Blues Legacies and Black Feminism.*

27. For a discussion of the misogyny of Miles Davis, which fans often overlook because of his musical genius, see Cleage, "Mad at Miles," 36–43.

28. Ronell, "Willow Weep for Me." This jazz standard written and composed by Ann Ronell in 1932 is rumored to be about Ronell's unrequited love for a man.

Bibliography

Blair, Cynthia M. *I've Gotta Make My Livin': Black Women's Sex Work in Turn of the Century Chicago*. Urbana: University of Illinois Press, 2010.

Buszek, Maria Elena. *Pin-Up Grrrls: Feminism, Sexuality, Popular Culture.* Durham, NC: Duke University Press, 2006.

Chapkis, Wendy. *Live Sex Acts: Women Performing Erotic Labor.* New York City: Routledge, 1996.

Cleage, Pearl. "Mad at Miles." In *Deals with the Devil and Other Reasons to Riot*, 36–43. New York: Ballantine, 1994.

Clifford, James. "Taking Identity Politics Seriously." In *Without Guarantees: Essays in Honour of Stuart Hall*, edited by Paul Gilroy, Lawrence Grossberg, and Angela McRobbie, 94–112. Brooklyn, NY: Verso, 2000.

Cvetkovich, Ann. *Depression: A Public Feeling*. Durham, NC: Duke University Press, 2012.

Danquah, Meri. *Willow Weep for Me: A Black Woman's Journey through Depression*. New York: Norton, 1998.

Davis, Angela. *Blues Legacies and Black Feminism: Gertrude "Ma" Rainey, Bessie Smith, and Billie Holiday*. New York: Vintage, 1999.

Davis, Lennard J. "Normality, Power, Culture." In *Disability Studies Reader*, edited by Davis, 1–16. 4th ed. New York: Routledge, 2013.

Du Bois, W. E. B. *The Souls of Black Folk*. Chicago: McClurg, 1903.

Ehrenreich, Barbara. *The American Health Empire: Power, Profits, and Politics*. New York: Random, 1971.

Ellison, Ralph. *The Invisible Man*. New York: Random, 1952.

Fanon, Frantz. *Black Skins, White Masks*. New York: Grove, 1967.

Ford, Briggett C. "Violence and Trauma: Predicting the Impact on the Well-Being of African American Women with Severe Mental Illness." *Violence and Victims* 17, no. 2 (2002): 219–32.

Frankie and Alice. Written by Oscar Janiger, Philip Goldberg, and Cheryl Edwards. Directed by Geoffrey Sax. Canada: CodeBlack Films and Lions Gates Films, 2010. 2014 US release.

Gaye, Marvin. "Let's Get It On." Tamia Motown, 1973, vinyl.

Gregg, Melissa, and Gregory J. Seigworth. Introduction to *The Affect Theory Reader*, edited by Gregg and Seigworth, 1–28. Durham, NC: Duke University Press, 2010.

Hall, Stuart. "What Is This 'Black' in Black Popular Culture." *Social Justice* 20, no. 2 (1993): 104–11.

Hoberman, John. *Black and Blue: The Origins and Consequences of Medical Racism*. Berkeley: University of California Press, 2012.

Jacobson, Matthew Frye. *Whiteness of a Different Color: European Immigrants and the Alchemy of Race*. Cambridge, MA: Harvard University Press, 1999.

Lewis, Bradley. "A Mad Fight: Psychiatry and Disability Activism." In *Disability Studies Reader*, edited by Lennard J. Davis, 115–31. 4th ed. New York: Routledge, 2013.

Pickens, Theri. "You're Supposed to Be a Tall, Handsome, Fully Grown White Man: Theorizing Race, Gender, and Disability in Octavia Butler's *Fledgling*." *Journal of Literary and Cultural Disability Studies* 8, no. 1 (2014): 33–48.

Puar, Jasbir. "Homonationalism as Assemblage: Viral Travels, Affective Sexualities." *Jendal Global Law Review* 4, no. 2 (2011): 23–43.

Puar, Jasbir, and Ann Pellegrini. "Affect." *Social Text* 27, no. 3 (2009): 35–38.

Roediger, David. *The Wages of Whiteness: Race and the Making of the American Working Class*. New York: Verso, 2007.

Ronell, Ann, composer. "Willow Weep for Me." 1932.

Schwarz, Heike. *Beware of the Other Side(s): Multiple Personality Disorder and Dissociative Identity Disorder in American Fiction*. Verlag: Bielefeld, 2013.

Shank, Barry. *The Political Force of Musical Beauty*. Durham, NC: Duke University Press, 2014.

Sosulski, Marya R., Nicole T. Buchanan, and Chandra M. Donnell. "Life History and Narrative Analysis: Feminist Methodologies Contextualizing Black Women's Experiences with Severe Mental Illness." *Journal of Sociology and Social Welfare* 37, no. 3 (2010): 29–57.

Spates, Kamesha. "The Missing Link: The Exclusion of Black Women in Psychological Research and the Implications for Black Women's Health." *Sage Open* (July–September 2012): 1–8.

Whaley, Deborah Elizabeth. "Re-inking the Nation: Jackie Ormes's Cultural Front Comics." In *Black Women in Sequence: Re-inking Comics, Graphic Novels, and Anime*, 28–66. Seattle: University of Washington Press, 2015.

Williams, Erica Lorraine. *Sex Tourism in Bahia: Ambiguous Entanglements*. Urbana: University of Illinois Press, 2013.

Wilson, Melba. "Black Woman and Mental Health: Working towards Inclusive Mental Health Services." *Feminist Review* 68 (Summer 2001): 34–51.

Wonder, Stevie, composer and performer. "Higher Ground." *Innervisions*, Tamia Motown, 1973.

CHAPTER 10

"A New Type of Human Being"

Gender, Sexuality, and Ethnicity as Perpetual Passing in Jeffrey Eugenides's Middlesex

LARA NARCISI

Intersex, immigrant, incest, intertexts. In Jeffrey Eugenides's 2002 epic novel *Middlesex* are part of an ever-evolving *I*, a series of complex identity transformations. Calliope Stephanides is born an apparent girl, but her body transforms during adolescence into a masculine one.[1] This rare-but-real condition, alpha-5 reductase deficiency (A5RD), causes genetic males to appear female as children but to develop a male physiognomy at puberty. Such men unintentionally pass for women, and even their responsible gene itself may be considered to be passing, hiding recessively on the fifth chromosome until two carriers give it expression. Callie thus endures an adolescence beset by an ongoing theatrical attempt to conceal nature with nurture; upon realizing and embracing his genetic maleness, however, Cal must disguise his previous feminizing nurture with nature. From butch schoolgirl to effeminate patriarch, Cal's life is a form of passing, as he will never be man or woman. The novel questions the exclusivity not only of a binaristic gender system but also, by extension, of all such rigid categorizations. Eugenides echoes Cal's ambiguous identity in myriad others, depicting class passing, heteronormative passing, exogamous passing, and ethnic passing, along with other subtler disguises, deceits, and identity changes. Through the constant replication and refiguring of Cal's unique situation, the novel demonstrates that in a society that still insists on either/ors, we are all essentially passing. Viewing the novel through the lens of its various neo-passing narratives highlights its insistence on the potential of less clearly defined and more fluid boundaries of identification and selfhood. At stake in this novel, then, is the potential of eradicating the very categories we tend to insist upon most stridently as determinants of the self, until the concept of passing becomes irrelevant.

The many types of neo-passing found in *Middlesex* all draw attention to the impracticality and even impossibilities of identity categorization. It is easy to see why these categories exist; as Toni Morrison eloquently discusses in *Playing in the Dark: Whiteness and the Literary Imagination,* our definitions of whiteness and "American-ness" depend on ideas of blackness and otherness. Traditional racial passing has called attention to, and potentially destabilized, these categories. Of course, passing could not exist without the idea that one's race, gender, or sexuality is somehow immutable. In *Neither Black nor White Yet Both: Thematic Explorations of Interracial Literature,* Werner Sollors explains that the implication that some part of our identity (specifically, race) is stable "makes tales of 'passing' allegories of modernization that may speak to people who move toward new identifications and may experience anxieties about giving up old localities, homes, families, and belief systems."[2] Even as it relies on allegedly stable racial categories, however, passing unsettles and destabilizes such categorization;[3] it is this anxiety that *Middlesex* analyzes and critiques by showing all such binaries—not just racial ones—to be false constructs. Similarly, in *Race Passing and American Individualism,* Kathleen Pfeiffer observes that many contemporary passing narratives work to overturn easy categorizations: "It is precisely the idea of race that passing often critiques in these turn-of-the-century narratives, by complicating the segregationist's definition of white and black."[4] *Middlesex* works in the same way to overturn various segregationist categories, not just racial ones. John L. Jackson and Martha S. Jones discuss this broader definition of passing in their introduction to a special journal issue on the topic: "One passes for what one purportedly is (and, on other than bad days, actually believes oneself to be) every day, in thousands of miniscule and major ways. Passing is less about faking prefabbed social identities than it is about demanding appreciation of the idea that all identities are processual, intersubjective, and contested/contestable."[5] *Middlesex* partakes of this version of neo-passing as multifarious in contrast to more traditional ideas of passing as exclusively racial. In showing a variety of different kinds of passing, it emphasizes that all identity is a kind of performance. Judith Butler famously made this case for gender: "One is not simply a body, but, in some very key sense, one does one's body and, indeed, one does one's body differently from one's contemporaries and from one's embodied predecessors and successors as well."[6] Cal's fluctuating gender calls attention to the performative aspects of all gender construction; the normalization of Cal's experience reminds us of the constructed nature of all identities and thus questions the societal dynamics that encourage passing.

In place of binaristic systems, *Middlesex* enacts and endorses the immense potential of hybridity and change, beginning with its form. Although some reviewers found this maximalism distasteful—Stewart O'Nan of the *Atlantic Monthly* complains of the novel, "Like Cal, it's damned by its own abundance, not quite sure what it wants to be"—I contend that the myriad shifts in style are exactly what the novel wants to be.[7] Eugenides echoes or parodies Greek epics, immigrant memoirs, action movies, World War II romances, adolescent coming-of-age stories, surrealist cinema, and Americana road-trip narratives and incorporates texts ranging from mythology to William Shakespeare to James Joyce. Paralleling Tiresias, whose myth is a critical intertext for the novel, Cal celebrates his ability to see past and future, male and female, and to sample canonical great books to create a new one. The various styles are unified by the chumminess of Cal's invitational first-person omniscient narration; as *New York Times* reviewer Laura Miller observes, "the book's length feels like its author's arms stretching farther and farther to encompass more people, more life."[8] Cal's genre play and narrative fluidity, his delight in being both intertextual and intersexual, and his ability to see the comic in the tragic, all suggest the immense potential in being able to pass freely between seemingly untraversable categorizations.[9]

Cal inherits this free movement via the Stephanides family's impressive ability to transform, change, and pass, often literalized by locational shifts. Beginning with the move from Smyrna, on the Aegean coast of modern-day Turkey, to Detroit, Michigan, each spatial transition enables a new kind of passing,[10] and even the locations themselves remain fluid rather than static, often passing for what they are not. Detroit hides its darkest night beneath a surreal candy-pink sky, and its homey 1950s guise covers a radically and racially polarized powder keg that explodes into a war zone in 1967. Michael Griffith admires "Eugenides's gimlet-eyed but tenderhearted portrait of Detroit, which is exactly the kind of city Cal Stephanides is best prepared to love: raffish, troubled, heterodox, a little homely, alternating fitfully between decay and renaissance."[11] This description highlights the city's hybridity but also suggests how Detroit attempts to conceal its seedier underside beneath the image of industrial productivity. Detroit's eruption into violence parallels Smyrna's and likewise suggests a conflicted identity: Is Smyrna Turkish or Greek? Is Detroit a race-torn impoverished wasteland or All-American Motor City? They are, of course, both and neither; places, like the characters that inhabit them, only thrive if they can evolve beyond strict categorization.

It is no coincidence then that Callie's most significant relocation coincides with her own transformation: when the riots crack Detroit's façade, the Stephanides family joins the white flight from the city to the wealthy suburb of Grosse Pointe. This move involves multiple layers of passing, beginning when Cal's father, Milton, discovers that Greeks, Jews, and other "nonwhites" are "redlined": tacitly barred from owning property in the community. Against the odds, Milton gains access to Grosse Pointe when he offers to pay for an undesirable house in cash. Immigrants can be whitened by money, so the ability to pass as white enables a concomitant opportunity to pass into the middle class. Karen Brodkin makes this fascinating argument in *How Jews Became White Folks and What That Says about Race in America*, explaining how the GI Bill, post–World War II housing laws and practices like redlining, and other factors assisted Jews (and other white-appearing ethnicities like Greeks) while further subjugating black people.[12] Even paying cash, Milton likely couldn't have obtained his Grosse Pointe home and entry into the middle class if his heritage were African.[13]

The Stephanideses' new home physically embodies this passing motif. Middlesex is the name of their suburban street, but Callie applies it to the house, christening the American modernist home with the moniker of a British Victorian manor. Beginning with its very name, the house is a series of contradictions, concealing outmoded nuisances like pneumatic doors and antiteleological stairs-to-nowheres in the guise of modernist conveniences: "Middlesex! Did anybody ever live in a house as strange? As sci-fi? As futuristic and outdated at the same time?"[14] The house, embodying the notion of constant surprise via its stairway peepholes, presides over Calliope's greatest time of change; Eugenides said in an interview, "Its newfangled design accords with the unconventional nature of the book's narrator, Cal, and its conventional furnishings demonstrate the resistance Cal's family has toward anything newfangled."[15] The house, like Cal, is the untraditional dressed up as normative; both are inadvertently deceptive and ever in flux.

Cal is far from the only character to grow, change, or metamorphose, and the novel indicates that such transformations are both normal and generative for everyone.[16] As Eugenides stated in an interview, "more than making reality bizarre, I tend to make bizarre things normal."[17] The ability to pass and change is not merely normalized but valorized, as Callie suggests when describing the out-of-body experience she has when losing her virginity: "Ecstasy. From the Greek *Ekstasis*. Meaning not what you think. Meaning, literally: a state of displacement, of being driven out of one's senses."[18] Passing and other identity shifts are not merely typical but desirable; to be ecstatic *is* to be outside of one's self. Why, the novel implicitly asks, would we ever limit ourselves to something small and singular when we can, like Walt Whitman, be large and contain multitudes?

Illicit Identifications: Straight Passing

Callie spends much of her early life claiming an alternate identity to her real one, beginning with her sexuality. Believing she has been "on the freakish side" from birth, she describes her newborn self and asks, "Can you see me? All of me? Probably not. No one ever really has."[19] This mysterious identity derives in part from her closeted lesbian attractions, beginning with those toward her friend Clementine Stark at age seven. Their brief interaction is predicated on pretending and pretense; first, Callie acts the role of the man when they kiss, and then the two American girls dress up as Japanese geishas while singing the Chinese American musical *Flower Drum Song*. At first the girls are joyfully romping in the bathhouse pool: "This game is far less serious, more playful, freestyle, but we're gripping each other, trying not to let the other's slippery body go, and our knees bump, our tummies slap, our hips slide back and forth."[20] When Callie's grandfather Lefty witnesses this play, however, both girls feel immediate guilt, which amplifies when they realize Lefty has just had a stroke. Already intuiting the guilt inflicted by homophobia, Callie quickly begins "praying for forgiveness, because it was clear to me that I was responsible. It was what I did . . . what Lefty saw. . . . And I am promising never to do anything like that again."[21] Callie swears to conceal what she believes is a burgeoning lesbian identity, and, indeed, she omits the significant lesbian details of her life, even under direct questioning from gender specialist Dr. Luce, and appears to confess them only on the page, to us, a quarter century later.[22]

This self-shaming is somewhat surprising given the fact that Cal, looking back, recalls multiple examples of happy homosexuality. Callie's beloved Aunt Sourmelina lives openly with a woman for many years,[23] and even in her seventies she is proudly "a bottle redhead who drove a Firebird and wore belted denim skirts with turquoise belt buckles. After her life in the sexual counter-culture, Lina found my parents' heterosexuality as quaint as a sampler."[24] The founders of Callie's elite prep school were likely lesbians at the turn of the previous century, and, in contrast to their literary predecessors in *The Children's Hour*, no tragedy ensues; they are happily immortalized together in a school statue.[25] By the time of her adolescence, Callie observes that homosexuality "was happening more than ever in 1974. It was becoming a national pastime," yet she seems incapable of envisioning herself as openly lesbian.[26] This is due in part to peer pressure in her high school that compels her to hide how "secretly, shamefully, not entirely consciously, but for all that quite head-over-heels in love" she is with a female classmate referred to by the Luis Buñuel–inspired moniker "The Obscure Object of Desire."[27] Callie implies that this self-concealment is protective, noting that although "crushes" were deemed acceptable and intense homosocial relationships common, "the ethos of the school remained militantly heterosexual. . . . Any girl suspected of being attracted to girls was gossiped about, victimized, and shunned."[28] Despite prevalent, positive counterexamples, adolescent Callie feels obligated to hide her true identity. Although gay rights have made tremendous strides in both legislation and mainstream acceptance, a girl like Callie might experience some of the same stigmatizing today. Gabe Harper, a former student of mine, writes in *Thought Catalog* about the increasing trend among gay men toward being "straight acting," which dictates that even openly homosexual men are more desirable if they act heterosexual. Harper, whose appearance is androgynous, describes the painful contradictions of this thinking: "I finally understood that my shame had been birthed from the unconscious knowledge that who I was just wasn't good enough. I couldn't date a straight guy, and I couldn't pass for one."[29] This self-hatred masquerading as sexual preference is analogous to a black person claiming exclusive attraction to blacks who look white. The rhetoric of sexual attraction may be used to make prejudicial pressures toward a conforming appearance appear acceptable, as we see throughout the novel.[30]

Middlesex reminds us that trying to hide who you are is the norm of adolescence rather than the exception and that, therefore, Callie is not as freakish as she may feel. The natural, realistic tone of the section devoted to The Obscure Object is stylistically evocative of the traditional coming-of-age story; the setting of the woods in the summertime echoes these narratives, as well. Although Callie herself is becoming physically unique, her emotional life is relatable and normalized. She and The Object only interact sexually under the cover of night, but adult Cal reminds us that this is not abnormal: "That's the way it goes in adolescence. You try things out in the dark. You get drunk or stoned and extemporize. Think back to your backseats, your pup tents, your beach bonfire parties. Did you ever find yourself, without admitting it, tangled up with your best friend? Or in a dorm room bed with two people instead of one, while Bach played on the chintzy stereo, orchestrating the fugue? It's a kind of fugue state, anyway, early sex."[31] Eugenides's use of the second person here forces the readers to connect with Cal despite the fact that, in all likelihood, they haven't experienced the specific kind of gender confusion he has.[32] The novel's lesbian coming-of-age story is partially, as many are, a battle cry against the shameful concealment that Cal endures. It is, however, more significantly a story of how her sexuality just happens to be still-female Callie's biggest adolescent secret; as this passage makes clear, most of us at that age are trying things out in the dark.

Intersexuality: Gender Passing

While Callie begins passing as straight in childhood, she appears to be, from then until puberty, a beautiful and "normal" little girl; she passes without even knowing it. Callie appears to be the girl she believes she is, in part because gender differences between American children are so rigidly inscribed; we mark girls through dresses, pink clothing, long hair, and so on. This social construction of gender has motivated some contemporary parents, like David Stocker and Kathy Witterick, to attempt a more radical experiment in gender egalitarianism: following their first son's transgenderism, they chose to raise their third child, Storm, without any gender classification. Kathy discusses their controversial and much-publicized decision in her essay "Dancing in the Eye of the Storm," explaining that "the best evidence suggests that today's limited gender framework will have negative health and social impacts on all children—not just mine."[33] It remains to be seen whether Storm, who by the age of five had chosen the pronoun *she*, will one day come to see her upbringing as liberating or as a different kind of enforced concealment.[34] Either way, the storm of the Storm controversy, including some wild accusations that the parents were guilty of child abuse, demonstrates how strictly gendered our society remains. One of the most realistic facets of Eugenides's often-fantastical novel, then, is that in the 1960s, Callie's parents, desperately hoping for a girl, trusting their near-blind immigrant physician, and modestly avoiding close inspection of their child's elongated clitoris, persist in believing she is the normal girl they attempted to conceive through the then-new Shettles method of timing conception to influence the child's gender.[35] As a young girl, Callie is only passing insofar as her true identity would be unclear to anyone not considering the possibility of a third sex.

As an adolescent, however, Callie's body begins to change and, continuing her parents' fiction about her gender identity, to both herself and the world, becomes more of a challenge. Callie's condition, A5RD, creates the appearance of a typical female (apart from the enlarged clitoris) until puberty, when the entire physiognomy transforms to that of a typical male—though still with a vagina and with less body and/or facial hair and no balding.[36] The world discovered A5RD in 1974, the same year Callie discovers it in herself, when *Science* reported on a small Dominican village where it manifested in twelve of thirteen families.[37] Interesting, the villagers called these adolescents *guevedoces,* derived from *huevos a la doce,* which literally means "eggs at twelve" but metaphorically means "testicles at twelve." Thus even the condition's name is hermaphroditic, one thing concealed as another.

Callie's adolescence is both the beginning of her own transformation and a metaphorically significant time as all Callie's peers are trying out new roles, as well. Callie's brother goes to college and leaves behind his "science geek" self to become a "John Lennon look alike." Her popular schoolmates pretend "to be not Midwesterners but Easterners, to affect their dress and lockjaw speech, to summer in Martha's Vineyard, to say 'back East' instead of 'out East,' as though their time in Michigan represented only a brief sojourn away from home." Callie's attempts at passing are not unique but do become unusually complex. Ashamed of her increasing height and deepening voice, she feigns femininity by stuffing her bra, painfully depilating body and facial hair, and faking periods: "With Nixonian cunning, Calliope unwrapped and flushed away a flotilla of unused Tampax. I feigned symptoms from headache to fatigue. I did cramps the way Meryl Streep did accents."[38] The deceptions work but only because they confirm society's expectation of gender consistency: once a girl, always a girl.

This assumption is exactly what informs professor Peter Luce, the nurture-promoting sexologist based on the real-life Dr. John Money, likewise active in the 1960s and 1970s.[39] Money took a radical stance in the age-old nature versus nurture debate, claiming that gender was *entirely* socially constructed.[40] When baby Bruce Reimer was the victim of a botched circumcision, his distraught parents allowed the famous doctor to reassign gender from Bruce to Brenda at the late age of twenty-one months. The Reimers not only provided Money with the perfect test case but also had the ideal control subject in Bruce's twin brother, Brian, who remained male. Despite his knowledge that "Brenda" was not well-adjusted, Money touted the reassignment as a glorious success in his 1972 book, *Man & Woman, Boy & Girl: Gender Identity from Conception to Maturity.* Brenda became nearly suicidal before finally learning the truth at fifteen, when she immediately decided to have a sex change and began living as David Reimer. Tragically, both twins committed suicide before they turned forty. This sad story does not, however, prove nature the unequivocal victor. The Intersex Society of North America (ISNA), whose resources Eugenides accessed while writing, offers an interpretation applicable to Callie as well: "What the story of David Reimer teaches us most clearly is how much people are harmed by being lied to and treated in inhumane ways. We don't think we can ever predict, with absolute certainty, what gender identity a person will grow up to have. [But] . . . children who are treated with shame, secrecy, and lies will suffer at the hands of medical providers who may think they have the best of intentions and the best of theories."[41] Both David and Brian stated that they were disturbed by their repeated, mandatory visits to Money, his constant interrogations on sex and gender, and their suspicion of a major secret.[42] David could not successfully pass for female, but, most damaging, he—like Callie—did not even know he was trying to pass. Luce, like Money, lies to his patient, neglecting to tell Callie that she is genetically male and that his recommended sex-change operation will leave her with "partial or total loss of erotosexual sensation," a fact Callie only uncovers by stealing his report.[43] Callie's moment of recognition, like Reimer's, demonstrates the importance of full disclosure and the problems of trying to force anyone into a binaristic category. With greater understanding and a more open concept of gender, Callie and others like her would not have to force themselves into being what they are not.

Incest and Immigration: Ethnic Passing

Despite the novel's advocacy for allowing people to be who they are without stigma, Cal's condition has a clear and societally taboo origin: the incest of his immigrant grandparents, Desdemona and Lefty Stephanides.[44] The reviled incest origin may seem to counteract the novel's otherwise consistently positive view of intersex people. Thea Hillman, ISNA board member and author of *Intersex, for Lack of a Better Word*, praised facets of the novel but was troubled that "Eugenides unfortunately contributes to the notion of intersex people as shameful and sick, and a threat to the health of society. . . . In addition to the marriage of incest and intersex being inaccurate and misleading, it's also terribly stigmatizing. Incest is one of the last universally abhorred social taboos, with shameful, pathological and criminal repercussions."[45] In this case, the incest narrative is not inaccurate; because it is a recessive gene requiring both carriers for expression, A5RD appears only in small endogamous communities like the Smyrna village of the Stephanideses' origins. More important, however, Cal does not present his grandparents as pathological but, instead, fondly romanticizes their lifelong love. Imagining their first dance together, he writes, "The hug began to change; certain positions of the hands and strokings of the fingers weren't the usual displays of sibling affection, and these things constituted a language of their own, announced a whole new message in the silent room."[46] He evinces no anger toward his grandparents and never blames them, or anyone, for a condition he comes to embrace as self-defining.[47]

Eugenides is not the first to describe incest using language that may appear sympathetic or romantic; similar depictions appear in great American novels, such as William Faulkner's *The Sound and the Fury*, Ralph Ellison's *Invisible Man*, Toni Morrison's *The Bluest Eye*, and Vladimir Nabokov's *Lolita*;[48] incest is also the basis of the entire genealogy of Greek mythology frequently referenced in the novel. Cal's sympathetic narration of his grandparents' story makes incest appear a natural outcome of their insular community. In the novel's logic, the couple's migration to America undoes the "sin" of incest, or at least reinterprets it, as upon leaving Smyrna, the siblings begin to create and invent. This starts with their reinvention of their own relationship, as they pretend to meet and fall in love on their passage to America: "They took turns reciting Homeric genealogies, full of falsifications and borrowings from real life, and sometimes they fought over this or that favorite real uncle or aunt, and had to bargain like casting directors."[49] They succeed in passing as strangers, and their incest remains a secret until Desdemona, the one character whose life extends throughout the novel, reveals it to Cal alone as she approaches death. In contrast to Cal's dramatic uncovering of his intersex condition through subterfuge, the revelation of its derivation from his beloved grandmother is a quiet moment that brings him peace and understanding. He has already accepted who he is, and Desdemona's confession merely gives him a narrative point of origin for both himself and the novel.

Although Cal never condemns his grandparents' behavior as immoral or holds them "responsible" for his intersexuality, the act of incest does have its costs. Desdemona's fear of deformed children haunts her until she "turn(s) her marriage into an arctic wasteland" of abstinence, and so, as Debra Shostak observes, "the incestuous union that inscribed doubleness within singularity that was meant both to preserve the Stephanides' familial and cultural identity and to mark the origin of the new narratives they invent for themselves instead drives them apart. There is no inhabitable middle."[50] Shostak observes that the failed transgression of incest is one more way in which the novel shows how far our contemporary society is from a true middle ground in sexuality, ethnicity, or nearly anything else. While it is true that the novel gestures toward rather than actually depicts alternatives to traditional binary oppositions, the novel and its narrator suggest hope for the future. Incest in *Middlesex* does carry some negative symbolism of isolationism in a remote village, but while it has complicated effects for Lefty and Desdemona, as Shostak argues, it simultaneously and paradoxically acts as a conduit to the new, the different, the truly unique as embodied by Cal: the "new type of human being" and the "what was next."[51] This is what *Middlesex* has to contribute to the discourse of neo-passing: a radical reimagining of what this "new type of human being" may be and may become. While Cal himself is a fascinating depiction of gender passing, the novel's consistent unmasking of identities—in characters, locations, and even ideologies—implies a view of contemporary America that may be beyond transgender or transracial, that may interrogate and eliminate all such categories entirely.

Despite some criticism to the contrary,[52] I believe the novel's Greek immigration story is deeply interwoven with the intersex one and not only because the incest deriving from the former creates the latter. The more significant connection binding these narratives is their emphasis on self-re-creation, change, and an American hopefulness that one day no one will need to pass as anything else. Eschewing the traditional binary of old world versus new and the predictable identity crises that ensue in so many immigrant narratives, Eugenides avoids any valorization of America over Smyrna or vice versa, instead embracing the potential for change in the exchanges between the two. Cal observes, "The members of my family have always had a knack for self-transformation,"[53] and we see this crucially rooted in their history: the grandparents are Greeks but (like Homer) live in Turkey; the children are Americans, but Cal moves to Germany, wants to transfer to Istanbul, and falls in love with a Japanese American woman at a restaurant called Austria, where they talk of Barcelona. The novel acts as the antithesis of and antidote to the Ford English School pageant, which showcases Lefty and his fellow immigrants entering a giant cauldron in their individual native costumes and emerging as uniformly business-suited ("blue or gray only") American clones.[54] Eugenides's pot, in contrast, hybridizes rather than melts; it rejoices in the novelty of unusual combinations, even opining, along with Hopkins, "Glory be to God for dappled things."[55]

After Lefty is fired from the Ford plant, the novel's immigrants avoid being forced to pass as Americans and, instead, adapt in their own ways. Desdemona teaches young black Muslim girls her silk-weaving skills, stomaching her post-invasion revulsion for Turks and even claiming kinship with them: "Everybody mixed. Turks, Greeks, same same." Cal's maternal grandfather, Jimmy Zizmo, succeeds through his hybrid unpredictability: he claims to be Greek but looks Arabic and is simultaneously an "amateur herbalist; antisuffragist; big-game hunter" (and vegetarian); "ex-con; drug pusher; teetotaler." Eventually, he vanishes and remakes himself entirely, now passing as minister Fard Muhammed, a mulatto Muslim from Mecca and a real-life Nation of Islam leader with a mysterious history. Though less colorful than Jimmy, Lefty and his son Milton succeed in business by marketing their Greek heritage in American and characteristically capitalistic ways—first in Lefty's Prohibition-era speakeasy and then in Milton's Zebra Room diner, named for its African animal hide but blending myriad cultures: "Everything was hodge-podge: grandmotherly lamps stood next to El Greco reproductions; bull's horns hung from the neck of an Aphrodite statuette"; these stand alongside figurines of "Paul Bunyan and Babe the Blue Ox, Mickey Mouse, Zeus, and Felix the Cat." When the 1967 riots destroy the diner, Milton understands that "success involves adapting to new situations," and he transitions to a lucrative fast-food empire, Hercules Hot Dogs, an American food chain strengthened by its classical marketing (Greek pillars) and its ability to "be everywhere at once." Hercules Hot Dogs is the perfect business for the early 1970s, when civil rights were at the forefront of the national consciousness: a reminder to the reader that diversity is essential to our national identity, then and now. Adolescent Callie inveighs against the WASPy homogeneity of her prep school, "All of a sudden America wasn't about hamburgers and hot rods anymore. It was about the *Mayflower* and Plymouth Rock. It was about something that had happened for two minutes four hundred years ago, instead of everything that had happened since. Instead of everything that was happening now!" In contrast to the conservative perspective of her schoolmates, Cal's immigrant heritage is an integral part of the American dream; after all, even the Statue of Liberty is, like the very system of democracy, "dressed like a classical Greek."[56]

Identity Invention: Everyone Is Passing

The majority of *Middlesex* is devoted to Cal's life and history prior to the discovery of his intersexuality, lingering on the immigrant narrative and the adolescent love story. In the end Cal begins "passing" in that he attempts to make his masculine identity appear genuine rather than appropriated. This section moves rapidly, a point that Samuel Cohen criticizes, "The ending is rushed, especially for a 500-plus page novel, and simplistic; it happens very quickly, and insists too much on its not being such a big deal."[57] This insistence is, I believe, crucial, as Cal's transition does not suggest that passing between male and female is an easy enterprise but, rather, that being only one thing entirely is an impossibility. As Cal puts it, "we're all made up of many parts, other halves. Not just me."[58] Uncovering our origins, our deepest hows and whys, is the challenge: reinventing ourselves is a never-finished, always-ongoing project.

Notably, the style and allusions of the novel shift as soon as Cal adopts his masculine identity. Just as the incest narratives form the crucial intertexts for the sections on Cal's ancestry, Jack Kerouac is the primary intertext for Cal's road-trip section, which references "on the road," "beats" and "beatnik," and Kerouac himself.[59] Like Sal Paradise, Cal hitchhikes from east to west, from New York to California, surviving on large, cheap desserts and feeling "happy to be in league against the world of hypocrites and rulemongers."[60] The shift from teen-girl love story to Kerouac homage is an important one for Cal, not only because it replaces a typically feminine genre with a masculine one but also because few novels are as classically Americana as *On the Road*. As soon as Cal discovers his so-called freakishness, he normalizes, Americanizes, and owns it through the allusion to Kerouac. He links his own gender passing to all masculine posturing: "It was all a bluff, but so was it on most men. We were all walking around squinting at each other. My swagger wasn't that different from what lots of adolescent boys put on, trying to be manly. For that reason it was convincing. Its very falseness made it credible."[61] This follows the line of Butler's well-known theory of performativity: "Gender cannot be understood as a role which either expresses or disguises an interior 'self,' whether that 'self' is conceived as sexed or not. As performance which is performative, gender is an 'act,' broadly construed, which constructs the social fiction of its own psychological interiority."[62] If both straightness and masculinity are performances, then we are all essentially passing for a normalcy applicable to almost no one.

Significantly, Cal does not experience an automatic "rightness" to becoming male. The novel contrasts Cal's experience to that of transsexuals like his male-to-female (MTF) friend, Carmen: "I was like, yo! Who put this dick on me? I never asked for no dick." In contrast, Cal's transformation to a male identity is gradual and never complete; when he cuts off his long hair, he notes, "It was unquestionably a male face, but the feelings inside that boy were still a girl's. To cut off your hair after a breakup was a feminine reaction." A change of clothes does not produce automatic male feelings, either; when purchasing his first suit, Cal observes, "I didn't feel what a boy would feel. It wasn't like putting on your father's jacket and becoming a man. It was like being cold and having your date give you his jacket to wear. . . . The jacket felt big, warm, comforting, alien."[63] Cal's metamorphosis is not a transsexual one of becoming what he always already was but of discovering a new path to an identity ever in progress.

Many critics, however, persist in seeing Cal's choice of the male gender and female partner, Julie Kikuchi, as a full-stop "last stop,"[64] a disappointingly traditional and too-neat conclusion that might even presage the concerns of Eugenides's next and far less experimental novel, *The Marriage Plot*. Rachel Carroll asserts that *Middlesex* is unorthodox only in its subject matter and that it may ultimately "preserve a normative sexed identity as male and sexual identity as heterosexual. . . . A nominally transgressive narrative can nevertheless remain captive to normative discourses."[65] Samuel Cohen similarly argues that the novel falsely forecloses its tragic possibilities in a post-9/11 attempt to recapture the post–cold war American optimism: "While it is no longer common in current critical discourse to discuss works in terms of aesthetic failure or success, I believe that *Middlesex* fails aesthetically. . . . It imposes a false closure on its narrative of the main character's gender crisis."[66] I counter these and similar claims by noting that the novel does not end in a marriage plot, as Cal's relationship with Julie is only beginning rather than foreclosed, a significant distinction in a narrative of so many plot twists and open endings. Furthermore, the novel succeeds on exactly the same criteria Cohen cites as evidence of its failure: it embraces Cal's freedom to live as male in the same spirit that it celebrates choosing one's sexuality or national identity. Cal does not surgically close his vagina, which might represent a full closure of his hermaphroditic narrative and a submission to gender binaries. To say that the novel ties up neatly because Cal struts his Brooks Brothers look is to ignore Cal's own assertion quoted above that the suit never entirely suits.

Cal's complex androgyny *is* his identity and one that he celebrates. Looking back, he imagines that from the beginning, "already latent inside me . . . was the ability to communicate between the genders, to see not with the monovision of one sex but in the stereoscope of both."[67] The happiness of his love story is not due to his successful appropriation of heterosexual maleness; he will always be passing as a "real" heterosexual male. For all its rhetorical flourishes concerning biological imperatives, for all its grandiose visions of eggs and genes and fate, the novel is a narrative, not a Punnet square. What it tells us, over and over, is how Callie's rearing as a girl centrally shaped Cal's later masculine identity. Although Stephanie Hsu states that Callie "is sacrificed in the name of intersex survival, her symbolic death is not registered as a loss," Cal insists that she never disappears at all: "Suddenly there she is again, doing a hair flip, or checking her nails. It's a little like being possessed. . . . On the sidewalk I'll feel her girlish walk take over."[68] The Callie apparition never seems unpleasant to Cal; she is a part of his past and extant in the man he becomes. We see the gender sensitivity of Cal's twofold identity in comments like this one: "Society discriminated against women, no question. But what about the discrimination of being sent to war? Which sex was really thought to be expendable?"[69] Here and elsewhere Cal shows a nuanced sympathy for societal constraints on both gender roles, as he implicitly critiques the discrimination inherent both in what women are forbidden to do and what men are forced to do. In 1974, the year Callie became Cal and the real-life guevedoces were discovered, there was one more convenient convergence of the novel's chronology with reality: Sandra Bem published the results of her landmark sex-role inventory, scoring participants on traits seen as desirable in men or women.[70] Bem used the inventory to critique the inflexibility of sex roles and concludes, "In a society where rigid sex-role differentiation has already outlived its utility, perhaps the androgynous person will come to define a more human standard of psychological health."[71] Forty years later, Eugenides creates a character who can truly speak from both sides of the gender line and remind us that we all pass for something no one actually is.

Inheritance: Conclusions

The most obvious benefit of androgyny in the novel is the novel itself; the book is Cal's legacy and immortality. Cal tells the reader early on, "Despite my androgenized brain, there's an innate feminine circularity to the tale I have to tell."[72] Callie, as the daughter, is the repository of the intricate family history that forms the majority of the story; Cal, as the son, stands in traditional Greek vigil for his deceased father at the novel's conclusion. Yanoula Athanassakis, emphasizing the importance of the visual in the novel, points to certain moments when writing does not prove cathartic but, rather, the opposite: "Cal is perpetually disappointed by the written word; in a post-structuralist textual model, the signs do not signify the object world as Cal understands it. It is through writing that he finds Dr. Luce's harshest diagnoses; it is through words that Cal is categorized, pigeonholed and violated: writing is a site of trauma for Cal."[73] But trauma and cure are interrelated here; writing is both painful and palliative. Through metanarrative touches, Cal consistently reiterates the importance of the story itself, reminding us: "That's how people live . . . by telling stories. . . . Stories are everything," or, "I, even now, persist in believing that these black marks on white paper bear the greatest significance, that if I keep writing I might be able to catch the rainbow of consciousness in a jar."[74] Somewhat less convincing is the seemingly disingenuous claim, "I don't care if I write a great book anymore, but just one which, whatever its flaws, will leave a record of my impossible life"—after all, the novel did win a Pulitzer prize—but even this line speaks to the importance of writing as a means of honestly unveiling, both for the narrator and the novel itself.[75]

The record Cal wishes to leave is one more true to emotional reality than strict facts. The novel has a tenuous connection to realism in any event, moving fluidly as it does from biological facticity to the purely fantastical. In discussing the novel's more realistic aspects, Shostak cautiously counters the slew of critiques regarding the novel's traditional heteronormative conclusion, which "does not imply a failure of imagination on Eugenides's part. Rather, it is an effect of the social discourse itself: the conservatism lies not in the messenger but in the materials."[76] While the novel does not ignore the limited options of our society (Cal notes that he must choose one of two restrooms), it also revels in the more open possibilities of its fictional form. We all may be limited to our biological genders, but the novel can contain multitudes. In this space we can see a world in which no one must pass because everyone has a fluid identity. The novel helps us ask what truth is for individual identities of all types and to question the assumptions that they must remain fixed. Just as Callie, forced to write a proto-autobiography for Luce's evaluation, "quickly discovered that telling the truth wasn't nearly as much fun as making things up,"[77] Eugenides can use the fictive space to create a narrator who is simultaneously male and female, Greek and American, homo- and heterosexual. The novel contains both the feminine "*jouissance*" and the masculine "linearity" that Luce attempts to quantify,[78] and the fact that both derive from a male author demonstrates the folly of such characterizations. The novel is, for Cal, a full disclosure, a photograph with the dehumanizing black box removed.[79]

Society may not be ready to abandon all categories of race, gender, and sexuality, but *Middlesex*'s fictional space enables Cal to be the multigendered subject with no false façade: a person who does not have to pass. Michele Elam suggests in her article "Passing in the Post-Race Era" that we may eventually "dismiss two of the most common charges against or for passing: either that it makes fake or that it makes brave—that is, that it cynically violates one's 'true' essential identity or heroically refutes social ascriptions of identity."[80] The novel shifts the discourse on the topic of passing in just this way: neither fake nor brave, *Middlesex*'s acts of neo-passing interrogate the categorizations we so often take for granted. Presenting myriad characters who, voluntarily or not, pass in some form, the novel questions what it would mean to jettison all the categorizations that render passing enticing or necessary. Perhaps we may popularize the use of the *ze* pronoun, make *cisgendered* a household term, and cease considering "white" the default race and any other in need of classification. Perhaps novels like this one can help put passing in the past.

Notes

1. I follow convention in shifting the pronouns in accordance with when the narrator is Calliope (female) versus Cal (male). Gender neutral pronouns, such as *ze* or singular *they* (= *s/he*) and *zir* or singular *them* (= *him/her*), are gaining popularity, but to avoid confusion I use the terms Calliope/Cal uses in the novel.

2. Sollors, *Neither Black nor White*, 250.

3. Sollors discusses the myths that supposedly "prove" one's race, specifically the idea that bluish half-moons at the base of the fingernails indicate blackness.

4. Pfeiffer, *Race Passing*, 150.

5. Jackson and Jones, "Pass*ed Performances," 14.

6. Butler, "Performative Acts," 272.

7. O'Nan, "New and Noteworthy."

8. Miller, "My Big Fat Greek Gender Identity Crisis."

9. One of the most delightful tragicomic moments involves Cal's grandmother Desdemona's response to the Turkish massacres via a "collector's set" of "atrocity fans" that she employs with such vigor that "the whole house seemed to be hyperventilating." Another concerns Cal's description of the night of her father's death; she's hoping for a "noirish mood," but "the sky wasn't cooperating. We were having one of our pink nights" when the sky resembles "cotton candy," "Pepto-Bismol," or "a muted, a fabric-softener color." Her father then dies in "a car chase between a Greek Orthodox priest and a middle-aged Republican." *Middlesex*, 219, 502, 505.

10. Specifically, from Smyrna to Detroit, the siblings Desdemona and Lefty pass for lovers; from Detroit to Grosse Pointe, the poor immigrant Stephanides clan passes as well-off Americans; from New York to California, our narrator, raised female, begins passing for male; from America to Germany, he passes as heterosexual and (until the end) traditionally cisgendered.

11. Griffith, "Siblings," 216.

12. Brodkin, *How Jews Became*.

13. Brodkin's argument explicitly counters the persistent myth (oft-repeated in my own Jewish family) that work ethic and the value placed on education cause Jewish success, demonstrating instead how Jewish "passing" is possible only due to our generally Caucasian appearance.

14. Eugenides, *Middlesex*, 258.

15. Leyshon, "This Week."

16. To offer just a few examples: an Islamic prophet is a clandestine bootlegger, an innocuous priest plays a vengeful kidnapper, an aquatic porn star is really midwestern schoolgirl Callie, and her stripper friend is in fact an erudite author.

17. Miller, "My Big Fat Greek Gender Identity Crisis."

18. Eugenides, *Middlesex*, 374.

19. Ibid., 218.

20. Ibid., 266.

21. Ibid., 267.

22. The novel emphasizes Callie's sense of shame by the allusions in the Clementine section to Vladimir Nabokov's *Lolita*, wherein the narrator implies that his interrupted childhood love for a young girl who abruptly vanishes causes his brutal pedophilic obsession with Lolita. These scenes are linked by aquatic imagery; Humbert's love for Annabel Lee takes place on the Riviera and consistently evokes the "kingdom by the sea" of Edgar Allan Poe's poem, while Cal's involves the bathhouse pool. By these links to the abusive pedophilia in Nabokov's novel, adult Cal, who knows his literary allusions, seems to highlight young Callie's deep shame over her childhood lesbian attraction.

23. Cal notes that after Lina's death in 1979, her lesbianism was "posthumously declassified" but that it was in any case a "secret kept . . . only by the loosest definition." Eugenides, *Middlesex*, 86.

24. Eugenides, *Middlesex*, 280.

25. Lillian Hellman's radical 1934 play *The Children's Hour* depicts a similar girls' school plagued by malicious and false accusations of its founders' lesbian conduct that tragically destroy both the school and the lives of the main characters.

26. Eugenides, *Middlesex*, 388.

27. Ibid., 341.

28. Ibid., 327.

29. Harper, "Nobody Likes a Gay Guy."

30. One relevant example of this is seen in the way both The Object and her brother Jerome are attracted to Callie. Jerome seems drawn to the fact that she appears so masculine but has the "acceptable" guise of a women. Similarly, The Object can spend so much time alone, and even in bed with, Callie because of her female appearance, even though she may be drawn to Callie's masculinity, as well.

31. Eugenides, *Middlesex*, 386.

32. Genetic disorders like Cal's are very rare (and notably different from transsexualism). "Disorders of sexual differentiation" as a whole number 1:5,500, according to *Medscape*; Cal's specific condition is less common. Isfort, "5-Alpha-Reductase Deficiency."

33. Witterick, "Dancing," 22.

34. Botelho-Urbanski, "Baby Storm."

35. Landrum Shettles's book *Baby's Sex: Now You Can Choose* describes that male sperm are faster but female sperm are stronger, so parents trying to conceive a girl should have intercourse a few days before ovulation and then abstain. Milton obtains a basal body thermometer to determine Tessie's optimal time for conceiving a girl. Shettles's book was not released until 1970; but as Calliope requests in a different context, "Allow me an anachronism." *Middlesex*, 325.

36. This is in contrast to "true hermaphroditism," in which both genital tissues are present at birth.

37. Imperato-McGinley, Guerrero, Gautier, and Peterson, "Steroid 5 Alpha-Reductase Deficiency.

38. Eugenides, *Middlesex*, 312, 296, 361.

39. The pseudonym is fairly clear; John becomes Peter (both apostles, but Peter is the betrayer, as Callie views Dr. Luce), and Money becomes Luce, which, though meaning *light* (ironic, in this case?) and locally fitting as a county in Michigan, is close to a synonym for money: lucre. Money's unfortunate patient, David Reimer, finally found a sympathetic ear in a sexologist and intersex advocate named Milton Diamond, a longtime rival of Money; this, besides the obvious literary allusion, could have contributed to Milton Stephanides's name.

40. Money took a radical stance on most sexual matters, most notably by advocating showing pornography to children in his 1975 book *Sexual Signatures*: "Explicit sexual

pictures can and should be used as part of a child's sex education," and by defending pedophilia in *Time* magazine, April 14, 1980: "A childhood sexual experience, such as being the partner of a relative or of an older person, need not necessarily affect the child adversely." Both quoted in Colapinto, "True Story."

41. ISNA, "Who Was David Reimer?"

42. Colapinto, "True Story."

43. Eugenides, *Middlesex*, 437.

44. Desdemona, like her Shakespearean namesake, is haunted by a forbidden love.

45. Hillman, "Made-for-TV," 39.

46. Eugenides, *Middlesex*, 39.

47. Nor does Cal blame his parents, who are also closely related; they know they are cousins on their father's side but don't realize they are cousins on their mother's side as well.

48. Each of these seminal American novels uses incest for a specific purpose, not for mere shock value. In brief, Faulkner uses incest to parallel the South's inwardness and obsession with the past rather that the future; Morrison and Ellison both use pedophilic incest to demonstrate that nothing (not even that) is worse than the socially condoned structures of institutionalized racism; and Nabokov's novel is about an obsession with language, demonstrating the frightening power that words can have to exonerate even the irredeemable.

49. Eugenides, *Middlesex*, 72.

50. Ibid., 172; Shostak, "Theory Uncompromised," 395.

51. Eugenides, *Middlesex*, 529.

52. See for example Daniel Mendelsohn, who critiques the book by claiming that the immigrant narrative and intersex story don't cohere. Mendelsohn, "Mighty Hermaphrodite."

53. Eugenides, *Middlesex*, 312.

54. Ibid., 102.

55. Ibid., 323.

56. Ibid., 145, 88, 203, 250, 275, 298–99, 76.

57. Cohen, "Novel," 383.

58. Eugenides, *Middlesex*, 440.

59. Ibid., 174, 441, 450, 451, 462; 445, 469; 445.

60. Ibid., 455. Sal lives in Paterson, New Jersey, but his story with Dean begins in New York City, on the first page of the novel.

61. Ibid., 449.

62. Butler, "Performative Acts," 279.

63. Eugenides, *Middlesex*, 487, 445, 444.

64. Ibid., 515.

65. Carroll, "Retrospective Sex," 188. Some corrections to this article: Middlesex is the name of the house and street but not the neighborhood; the Stephanides business impacted by the riots is the Zebra Room, not Hercules Hot Dogs; Callie *is* phallically penetrated by Jerome (causing her intense pain due to her concealed testicles).

66. Cohen, "Novel," 371. See also Stephanie Hsu, who critiques the choice to leave Cal living as a "stealth" man, "certain of his manhood," noting that the novel might help enact "a biopolitical fantasy" that the intersex body "might then be cured of its heterogeneity." Merton Lee makes an analogous point, saying the novel "endorses a narrative of heteronormativity and ethnic assimilation" and that "to close the book with Cal as a stable, happy, heterosexual male is to enact the neutering of the queer." Hsu, "Ethnicity and the Biopolitics," 92, 88; Lee, "Why Jeffrey Eugenides's *Middlesex*," 32, 45.

67. Eugenides, *Middlesex*, 269.

68. Hsu, "Ethnicity and the Biopolitics," 102; Eugenides, *Middlesex*, 41–42.

69. Eugenides, *Middlesex*, 301.

70. Bem, "Measurement." Bem describes her methodology: "The Androgyny score is the difference between an individual's masculinity and femininity normalized with respect to the standard deviations of his or her masculinity and femininity scores." Ibid., 158.

71. Ibid., 162.

72. Eugenides, *Middlesex*, 20.

73. Athanassakis, "American Girl," 223.

74. Eugenides, *Middlesex*, 179, 297.

75. Ibid., 302.

76. Shostak, "Theory Uncompromised," 410. Although it is less the focus of their articles, see also Athanassakis's point that "Cal's 'troubling' decision to live as a male can be read not as a move to go 'straight' but as quarrying the classifications of what 'straight' has thus far signified," and Kristin Zeiler's that the conclusion need not be so negatively normative; using the lens of phenomenology, she observes, "This should not be seen as a matter of re-incorporation and return to a previous mode of being-in-the-world. Even though Cal may not explicitly question the idea of sexual difference, his way of refusing surgery and expressing his own body in new ways can be seen as embodied resistance to particular 'solutions' articulated by others." Athanassakis, "American Girl," 227; Zeiler, "Phenomenology," 81.

77. Eugenides, *Middlesex*, 418.

78. Ibid.

79. Hsu notes that Callie's face is "covered with a black rectangle after a practice of medical photography that many intersex activists have compared to child pornography." Hsu, "Ethnicity," 96.

80. Elam, "Passing," 750.

Bibliography

Athanassakis, Yanoula. "'The American girl I had once been': PsychosomaticTrauma and History in Jeffrey Eugenides's *Middlesex*." *European Journal of American Culture* 30, no. 3 (2011): 217–30.

Bem, Sandra L. "The Measurement of Psychological Androgyny." *Journal of Consulting and Clinical Psychology* 42, no. 2 (1974): 155–62.

Brodkin, Karen. *How Jews Became White Folks and What That Says about Race in America.* New Brunswick, NJ: Rutgers University Press, 1998.

Butler, Judith. "Performative Acts and Gender Constitution: An Essay in Phenomenology and Feminist Theory." In *Performing Feminisms: Feminist Critical Theory and Theatre,* edited by Sue-Ellen Case, 270–82. Baltimore: Johns Hopkins University Press, 1990.

Carroll, Rachel. "Retrospective Sex: Rewriting Intersexuality in Jeffrey Eugenides's *Middlesex.*" *Journal of American Studies* 44, no. 1 (2010): 187–201.

Cohen, Samuel. "The Novel in a Time of Terror: *Middlesex,* History, and Contemporary American Fiction." *Twentieth Century Literature* 53, no. 3 (2007): 371–93.

Colapinto, John. "The True Story of John / Joan." *Rolling Stone,* December 11, 1997, 54–97.

Elam, Michele. "Passing in the Post-Race Era: Danzy Senna, Philip Roth, and Colson Whitehead." *African American Review* 41, no. 4 (2007): 749–68.

Eugenides, Jeffrey. *Middlesex.* New York: Picador, 2002.

———. "Sex, Fate, and Zeus and Hera's Kinkiest Argument: Interview with Laura Miller." *Salon,* October 8, 2002. Accessed June 15, 2017. http://www.salon.com/2002/10/08/eugenides_3/.

Griffith, Michael. "'Siblings of the Genus Erroneous': New Fiction in Review." *Southern Review* 39, no. 1 (2003): 213–16.

Harper, Gabe. "Nobody Likes a Gay Guy, Especially Other Gay Guys (on 'Straight Acting')." *Thought Catalogue,* August 3, 2014. June 15, 2017. thoughtcatalog.com.

Hillman, Thea. "Made-for-TV Movie Version." *Lambda Book Report* 11 (October 2002): 38–39.

Hsu, Stephanie. "Ethnicity and the Biopolitics of Intersex in Jeffrey Eugenides's *Middlesex.*" *MELUS* 36, no. 3 (2011): 87–110.

Imperato-McGinley J., L. Guerrero, T. Gautier, and R. E. Peterson. "Steroid 5 Alpha-Reductase Deficiency in Man: An Inherited Form of Male Pseudohermaphroditism." *Science* 186, no. 4170 (1974): 1213–15.

Intersex Society of North America (ISNA). "Who Was David Reimer?" *ISNA,* June 15, 2017. http://www.isna.org/faq/reimer.

Isfort, Anna H. "5-Alpha-Reductase Deficiency." *Medscape,* November 11, 2016. Accessed June 15, 2017. http://emedicine.medscape.com.

Jackson, John L., and Martha S. Jones. "Pass*ed Performances: An Introduction." *Women and Performance: A Journal of Feminist Theory* 15, no. 1 (2005): 9–16.

Lee, Merton. "Why Jeffrey Eugenides's *Middlesex* Is So Inoffensive." *Critique* 51 (2010): 32–46.

Leyshon, Cressida. "This Week in Fiction: Jeffrey Eugenides." *New Yorker,* November 11, 2013. Accessed June 15, 2017. www.newyorker.com.

Mendelsohn, Daniel. "Mighty Hermaphrodite." *New York Review of Books,* November 7, 2002. Accessed June 15, 2017. www.nybooks.com.

Miller, Laura. "My Big Fat Greek Gender Identity Crisis." *New York Times,* September 15, 2002. Accessed June 15, 2017. http://www.nytimes.com.

Morrison, Toni. *Playing in the Dark: Whiteness and the Literary Imagination*. Cambridge, MA: Harvard University Press, 1992.

O'Nan, Stewart. "New and Noteworthy." *Atlantic Monthly*, September 2002. Accessed June 23, 2017. https://www.theatlantic.com.

Pfeiffer, Kathleen. *Race Passing and American Individualism*. Amherst: University of Massachusetts Press, 2003.

Shostak, Debra. "'Theory Uncompromised by Practicality': Hybridity in Jeffrey Eugenides's *Middlesex*." *Contemporary Literature* 49, no. 3 (2008): 383–412.

Sollors, Werner. *Neither Black nor White Yet Both: Thematic Explorations of Interracial Literature*. New York: Oxford University Press, 1997.

Witterick, Kathy. "Get Your Gender Binary Off My Childhood! Towards a Movement for Children's Gender Self-Determination." In *Chasing Rainbows: Exploring Gender Fluid Parenting Practices*, edited by Fiona Joy Green and May Friedman, 43–51. Ontario: Demeter, 2013.

Zeiler, Kristin. "A Phenomenology of Excorporation, Bodily Alienation, and Resistance: Rethinking Sexed and Racialized Embodiment." *Hypatia* 28, no. 1 (2013): 69–84.

Afterword

Why Neo Now?

MICHELE ELAM

> I always found half-lights more blinding than utter darkness, and my eyes didn't know which way to adjust.
>
> —Unnamed protagonist, Danzy Senna, *Symptomatic*

What *is it* about passing that lets it live so large and so long in the public imagination? Passing—both as literary trope and as lived experience—seems to have such an unlikely and extended historical and literary shelf life that, as this volume attests, it has apparently evolved into the neo-passing stage. The introduction to the current volume suggests that the neo-ness of contemporary cultural narratives about the phenomenon can be divined through a continuity of genre or themes or simply by awareness of its own obsolescence, "typified by direct engagement with the idea that . . . by now, passing should have passed." Of course, that passing *should* have passed by now gives it a time stamp that hoards a kind of wish fulfillment: the hope that old-timey pre–Civil Rights era passing would naturally have been rendered moot in a legislatively and socially enlightened mark-one-or-more world. Indeed, the assumption that multiple racial options, ipso facto, represent or effect social progress shadows many discussions about what the putative rise and fall of passing actually *means*—and it is precisely those narratives about passing's social meanings wherein lie, I think, the secret to both our profound fascination with it and its social potential. I suggest that, at its root, passing (of both the elder and neo varieties) is so compelling because of the kinds of stories we tell ourselves and each other about it—which is to say, passing makes for the kind of foundational storytelling that shapes human experience.

In order to fully appreciate what makes passing so renewable and anew, if you will, just consider the near-magical multipurposes to which the term *passing* is evoked: as an adjective, a noun, or a verb (a verb, by the way, that can be both transitive and intransitive, what linguists sometimes call ambi-transitive, a term I find particularly amusing given how racial ambiguity is so common to questions of passing).[1] The play on the term in the titles in this volume alone reflects its obliging adaptability; it was hard to resist invoking it myself for this afterword's title. In William Shakespeare's famous use of it, *passing* is used as a superlative: Othello's story is "passing strange" (roughly translating as "stranger than strange")—inspiring awe, pity, desire—to Desdemona.[2] Musician and raconteur Stew, in his award-wining Broadway rock musical *Passing Strange* (2006) reprises Shakespeare's meaning to suggest his protagonist's racial bildungsroman, too, is a most marvelous tale worthy of both dread and longing.[3] P*assing* so deliciously lends itself to the elastic colloquial that it is hard to pass up—such as, *passing on, passing by, passing out, passing time, passing the buck, passing over* (as in not getting that job promotion *or* transitioning into the afterlife), and *making a pass* (in *either* amorous or sports vernacular—which only proves my point: where else could these idioms meet?)—to name but a few.[4]

Central to all these "passings" is an emphasis on an action, a doing, foregrounding the performative nature of identity itself. Most important, this is never action in isolation—passing is always a social event: others are always implied and implicated, whether they are in the know or knowing nothing.[5] In that regard, passing highlights the nature of race as a process, and as Michael Omi and Howard Winant recognize, racial formation always acknowledges the way in which enactments of race, whether they occur at the level of the interpersonal or the institutional, are necessarily imbricated with questions of power and equity, linking "racial formation to the evolution of hegemony, the way in which society is organized and ruled."[6] In the same regard, to speak of the performative dimension of racial formation is not to suggest race is play without social consequence or that such a theorization evades the everyday of racism (both common canards); quite the contrary, the performance of passing can often best index the truth of the lie of race. As I argue in *The Souls of Mixed Folk* (2014), "those who can pass not only inherit the legacies of mixed race heritage; they put that heritage into practice in a way that marks the transgression of, and thus lays bare, the paradox of unequal entitlements in the land of equality. This is why passing creates such cultural anxiety and yet why, too, it holds so much progressive potential. . . . by understanding the performance of passing as always politically implicated in the larger possibilities for social change."[7] As a character in Lorraine Hansberry's play *Les Blancs* puts it, "Race—racism—is a *device*. No more. No less. It explains nothing at all. . . . It is simply a means. An invention to justify the rule of some men over others. [But] it also has consequences; once invented it takes on a life, a reality of its own. . . . And it is pointless to pretend that it doesn't exist—merely because it is a *lie*!"[8] Indeed, "analyzing race as a type of performance helps determine the social politics and cultural dynamics of the concept of race as well as more carefully explain in what ways and to what ends racialization processes occur."[9] In other words, appreciating passing as performance means shining a spotlight on not just the constructedness of but also the purposes to which race is put.

Arguably, then, what garners the neo status of many of the works examined in this thoughtful, provocative volume is their heightened attention to these means and ends, the possibilities and the losses—in short, to the social realities of race that passing can so uniquely plumb. Moreover, because they can often more fully illuminate the world as it is, these neo-passing narratives offer potential utility in imagining the world as it is not and in doing so make possible the realization of, hopefully, more equitable and more just futures that might be. Passing in Colson Whitehead's *The Intuitionist* (2000), for instance, is represented as sly preparation for a grand epistemological rupture that will "enable fresh conventions, unexpected normative subjects—and by implication, new societies organized with both at their center."[10] After all, the novel's passing figure, Fulton, is "not passing from what he 'is' to what he 'is not.' Rather, he is passing into [W. E. B.] Du Bois's projected dream in 'Of Our Spiritual Strivings' of 'the worlds I longed for,' passing from the present to an alternative future. Passing reflects Fulton's 'keen longing for the next [world], its next rules,' a way of living in '*another world beyond this one*.'"[11]

Whitehead's novel reminds us those aspirational worlds are neither "post-race nor "post-passing," to use Gayle Wald's terms in her foreword to the current volume—and that we might well be more cautious about urging the time of passing to hurry up and get to passé. After all, if we measure the contemporary relevance of passing in relation to its ability to index racial truths, then it surely warrants even more attention to what Danzy Senna's unnamed protagonist in *Symptomatic* calls those blinding "half lights" that force our eyes to search "which way to adjust." Perhaps, wishing too fervently for passing's "obsolescence"—to the degree we hope its end might self-evidently hail our arrival at an evolved social order—simply defers the responsibility to adjust our sight to see more fully the world we live in now.

Notes

1. Generally, transitive verbs have an object (e.g., I eat apples), and intransitive do not (e.g., I eat).

2. My story being done,
 She gave me for my pains a world of sighs;
 She swore, in faith 'twas strange, 'twas passing strange;
 'Twas pitiful. 'twas wondrous pitiful,
 She wish'd she had not heard it, yet she wish'd
 That heaven had made her such a man.

Othello in Shakespeare, *Othello*, act 1, scene 3, lines 158–63

3. Stew's *Passing Strange*—co-created with Heidi Rodewald—received the 2008 Tony Award for Best Book of a Musical and four other Tony nominations, including Best Musical. He is also a two-time Obie Award winner for *Passing Strange*. Spike Lee's feature film of the Broadway production of *Passing Strange* toured the United States before debuting on PBS's *Great Performances* in 2009.

4. My husband, an avid sports fan, reminds me of the various sports terminology also using *passing, for example, pass interception* and *pass interference*, already suggested in the word's history in the *Oxford English Dictionary*, which traces the term *pass* circa 1275 as "to go by (something)" and "to cross over." The intransitive sense of "to go on, to move forward, make one's way" is from around 1300. The figurative sense of "to experience, undergo" (as in pass the time) is first recorded in 1390. The meaning "to be thought to be something one is not" (especially in racial sense) is from 1935, from *pass oneself off (as)*, which is first found in 1809. The general verb sense of "to be accepted as equivalent" is from 1596. In football, hockey, soccer, and other sports, the meaning "to transfer the ball or puck to another player" is from about 1865. The colloquial *make a pass* or to *offer an amorous advance* is first recorded in 1928, perhaps from a sporting sense. *Pass the buck*, from 1865, the *OED* says, is from poker, a slang reference to the buck horn–handled knife that was passed around to signify whose turn it was to deal. *Oxford English Dictionary*.

5. For her discussion of the triangulated relationship among the passer, the dupe, and the one in the know, see Robinson, "It Takes One to Know One."

6. Omi and Winant, *Racial Formation*, 55.

7. Elam, *Souls of Mixed Folk*, 118.

8. Hansberry, *Les Blancs*, 92.

9. Elam and Elam, "Race and Racial Formation," 192.

10. Elam, *Souls of Mixed Folk*, 120.

11. Quoted in ibid., 121, original emphasis; Du Bois, "Of Our Spiritual Strivings," 694; Whitehead, *Intuitionist*.

Bibliography

Elam, Harry, and Michele Elam. "Race and Racial Formation." In *Sage Handbook of Identities*, edited by Chandra Mohanty and Margaret Wetherell, 186–200. Thousand Oaks, CA: Sage, 2010.

Elam, Michele. *The Souls of Mixed Folk: Race, Politics, and Aesthetics in the New Millennium*. Stanford, CA: Stanford University Press, 2011.

Hansberry, Lorraine. *Les Blancs: The Collected Last Plays*. New York: Vintage, 1994.

Omi, Michael, and Howard Winant. *Racial Formation in the United States*. 3rd ed. New York: Routledge, 2014.

Passing Strange. Directed by Spike Lee. New York: 40 Acres and a Mule Filmworks, 2009. DVD.

Passing Strange. By Stew. Music by Stew and Heidi Rodewald. Directed by Annie Dorsen. Berkeley Repertory Theatre, Berkeley, California, 2006.

Robinson, Amy. "It Takes One to Know One: Passing and Communities of Common Interest." *Critical Inquiry* 30, no. 4 (1994): 715–36.

Senna, Danzy. *Symptomatic: A Novel*. New York: Riverhead, 2005.

Contributors

DEREK ADAMS is assistant professor in the Ithaca College English department and specializes in literature of the Harlem Renaissance and narratives of racial passing, with a particular interest in the intersections among gender, sexuality, and race. His most recent research focuses on the constitution of racial subjectivity within a socially constructed, postracial ethos.

CHRISTOPHER M. BROWN is assistant professor of English at Wake Forest University. His research and teaching take up the often competing logics of law and race, exploring how legal and literary discourses alternately converge and diverge over the course of US history. His essays appear in *Law and Literature* and *Law, Culture, and the Humanities*, and his book-in-progress is called "'And There See Justice Done': The Problem of Law in the African American Literary Tradition." His research has been funded by several fellowships and grants, including support from the American Council of Learned Societies and the Ford Foundation.

MARTHA J. CUTTER is professor of English and Africana studies at the University of Connecticut. Her books include *Unruly Tongue: Language and Identity in American Women's Writing, 1850–1930* (1999), *Lost and Found in Translation: Contemporary Ethnic American Writing and the Politics of Language Diversity* (2005), and *The Illustrated Slave: Empathy, Graphic Narrative, and the Visual Culture of the Transatlantic Abolition Movement, 1800–1852* (2017). She is also the coeditor (with Cathy

Schlund-Vials) of *Redrawing the Historical Past: History, Memory, and Multi-Ethnic Graphic Novels* (2018). She is currently at work on a manuscript about the cultural and literary history of racial passing.

MARCIA ALESAN DAWKINS is professor of communication at Walden University and corporate educator at Performance Learning Concepts. She is author of *Clearly Invisible: Racial Passing and the Color of Cultural Identity* (2012), *Eminem: The Real Slim Shady* (2013), and *Mixed Race 3.0: Risk and Reward in the Digital Age* (2015). Dawkins speaks and writes frequently on diversity, media, technology, and politics. Her expertise has been sought out by BBC World, NPR, AOL Originals, TIME Magazine, Vox, Truthdig, HuffPo Live, the Mayo Clinic, the Minerva Project, and the Public Relations Society of America, among others.

MICHELE ELAM is Olivier Nomellini Family University Fellow in Undergraduate Education, professor of English, and director of the interdisciplinary graduate program, Modern Thought and Literature, at Stanford University. She is author of *Race, Work, and Desire in American Literature, 1860–1930* (2003) and *The Souls of Mixed Folk: Race, Politics, and Aesthetics in the New Millennium* (2011) and editor of the *Cambridge Companion to James Baldwin* (2015). Her work has appeared in *African American Review, American Literature, Theatre Journal,* and *Genre,* among others, and she is a national contributor for CNN, *Huffington Post,* and *Boston Review.*

ALISHA GAINES is assistant professor of English at Florida State University. From 2009 to 2011, she was a Carter G. Woodson postdoctoral fellow at the University of Virginia. Gaines's first book, *Black for a Day: White Fantasies of Race and Empathy* (2017), constructs a unique genealogy of white liberals who temporarily "become" black under the alibi of racial empathy. She is a lifelong fan of Michael Jackson.

JENNIFER GLASER is associate professor of English and comparative literature at the University of Cincinnati. Her published work includes *Borrowed Voices: Writing and Racial Ventriloquism in the Jewish American Imagination* (2016), articles in venues such as *PMLA, MELUS, Safundi, ImageText,* the *New York Times,* the *LA Review of Books,* and a chapter in an anthology of essays.

MOLLIE GODFREY is assistant professor of English at James Madison University, specializing in African American literature. Her book manuscript "Black Humanisms: Race, Gender, and the Fictions of Segregation" examines the ways in which African American women writers of that era transformed the supposedly universal but functionally exclusionary discourse of American humanism into one productively shaped by cultural, racial, and sexual particularities. Articles related to this topic have appeared in *MFS: Modern Fiction Studies, MELUS,* and *CLA Journal.* She has also participated in and organized several community-engaged public scholarship projects dedicated to preserving African American archives in Chicago, Maine, and Virginia.

ALLYSON HOBBS is associate professor in the History department and director of African and African American studies at Stanford University. Hobbs's work includes a TEDx talk at Stanford and appearances on C-Span, MSNBC, and National Public Radio. She is a contributor to the New Yorker.com. Her work has been featured on cnn.com and slate.com, and in the *New York Times, Los Angeles Times, Chronicle of Higher Education*, and *Christian Science Monitor*. Her first book, *A Chosen Exile: A History of Racial Passing in American Life* (2014), examines the phenomenon of racial passing in the United States from the late eighteenth century to the present. *A Chosen Exile* won two prizes from the Organization of American Historians: the Frederick Jackson Turner Prize for best first book in American history and the Lawrence Levine Prize for best book in American cultural history.

BRANDON J. MANNING is assistant professor of African American studies and gender and sexuality studies in the interdisciplinary, gender, and ethnic studies department at the University of Nevada, Las Vegas. He is a Woodrow Wilson Career Enhancement Fellow and has published book chapters in *Post-Soul Satire: Black Identity after Civil Rights* (2014) and *The Psychic Hold of Slavery: Legacies in American Expressive Culture* (2016) and an article in *Black Camera*. His current book project "At Wit's End: Black Men and Vulnerability in Post-Soul Satire" reflects his scholarly interests in contemporary African American literary and cultural studies, black popular culture, black feminist theory, masculinity studies, and humor studies.

LORAN MARSAN is a lecturer in the women's, gender, and sexuality studies program at Ohio University in Athens. Her current research focuses on queer pedagogy and the genealogy of LGBTQ+ pop-culture history, icons, and outing. She teaches multiple courses for the LGBTQ studies certificate, hybrid media classes, and research classes. She is currently working with her program to develop online gender-sexuality-intersectionality competency content for working professionals as well as an online platform for the LGBTQ studies certificate.

LARA NARCISI is associate professor of English at Regis University in Denver, Colorado. Her articles have been published in journals such as *MELUS* and *Southern Studies*, and her recent book chapters appeared in *American Indians and Popular Culture* (2012), *Critical Insights: Kurt Vonnegut* (2013), and *The Road to Tenure: Interviews, Rejections, and Other Humorous Experiences* (2014).

EDEN OSUCHA is associate professor of English at Bates College, where she also holds affiliations with the programs in African American and American Cultural

Studies (AAACS) and Gender and Sexuality Studies. Her research expertise is in American literature from 1865 to the present, African American literature, literature and law, critical race studies, gender and sexuality, and studies of passing. Her book manuscript "The Post-Racial Past: Race, Privacy, and Identity before the Obama Era" examines historical productions of postracial discourse in law, literature, and media, linking the evolution of postracial thought to the legal history of privacy in the United States. Her scholarship has appeared in journals such as *American Literary History* and *Camera Obscura* and in edited collections, and she is coeditor of the June 2017 special issue of *American Literature* on critical pedagogy in the field of American literary studies.

GAYLE WALD is professor of English and American studies at George Washington University. Her book *Crossing the Line* (2000) is a study of cultural narratives of passing and the instrumentality of the concept of a permeable color line in twentieth-century American racial discourse. She is also author of *Shout, Sister, Shout! The Untold Story of Rock-and-Roll Trailblazer Sister Rosetta Tharpe* (2007) and *It's Been Beautiful:* Soul! *and Black Power Television* (2015). Wald is a recipient of National Endowment for the Humanities and Guggenheim fellowships.

DEBORAH ELIZABETH WHALEY is professor of American studies and African American studies at the University of Iowa, where she teaches courses on comparative American cultural history, black cultural studies, film, music, and critical theory. Whaley's first book, *Disciplining Women: Alpha Kappa Alpha, Black Counterpublics, and the Cultural Politics of Black Sororities* (2010), examines the cultural practices, cultural work, and politics of the oldest historically black sorority. Her latest book, *Black Women in Sequence: Re-inking Comics, Graphic Novels, and Anime* (2015), explores graphic-novel production and comic-book fandom, looking in particular at African, African American, and multiethnic women as deployed in television, film, animation, gaming, and print representations of comic-book and graphic-novel characters.

VERSHAWN ASHANTI YOUNG is an associate professor at the University of Waterloo, Canada. He has also served on the faculties of the University of Iowa and the University of Kentucky. He teaches communication, English language and literature, and performance studies. He serves as a consultant to schools and organizations in the areas of cultural competency and diversity. He values collaboration and has authored and coauthored several books, including *Other People's English* (2014) and *The Routledge Reader of African American Rhetoric: The Longue Duree of Black Voices* (2018). For the past decade, he has been developing the concept of code-meshing, using multiple Englishes and dialects in formal written and oral communications in school and at work.

Index

abolitionism, xi, 77
accommodationism, 105
acting white, 3, 168
Acting White? (Carbado and Gulati), 93*nn*5–6
activism, antiracist, 90
Adams, Derek, 19–20, 190*n*15
advertising: marketing and, 140; psychological effects of, 190n21; for runaway slaves, 17, 49–50, 52–54
affect, 207
"Affect" (Puar and Pellegrini), 216*n*18
affective strategies: neo-passing and dissociative identities as, in *Frankie and Alice*, 193–215; sexual and intellectual, 197–207
The Affect Theory Reader (Gregg and Seigworth), 216*n*18
affirmative action, 21, 75
African American letters, 79
African American literature, 71–72, 79, 176–77; coherence of, 82*n*7
African American presidency, depiction of first, 100, 112n2. *See also* black president(s); Obama, Barack Hussein
African Americans: affirmative action and, 21; as interchangeable, 122; biracial, 50; contemporary women's identities and, 190; divide between gays and, 191n26; emancipation for 20th-century, 103; equality of opportunity and, 103, 104; failure of justice and equality for, 79; light-skinned, 12, 13, 122; mistrust of Bush, George W., 109–10; need to be adept in reading, 122; political aspirations of, 100; postbellum illustrations of, 128; postwar economic prosperity and, 44; race consciousness and, 44; racial stereotyping and, 179; recording of violence against bodies of, 125; recruitment for NASA program and, 111; slavery and, 50, 73; worldview from standpoint of, 179. *See also* black Americans; blacks; Negroes
African American satire, 92, 93, 112
"African American Women's History and the Metalanguage of Race" (Higginbotham), 48*n*11
Afrika Bambaataa, 84, 85, 93, 114*n*23
afrofuturism, 84, 93
Against Race (Gilroy), 21*n*4
agency, 194
age passing, 135–36

Albrittain, James, 22*n*19
Aldama, Frederick Luis, 130*n*1
Alexander, Michelle, x, xiii*n*5, 21*n*3
Alice (character in *Frankie and Alice*), 196–97, 201, 204, 207, 208–9, 210, 211–12, 213
Allen, Jodie, 22*n*19
Allen, Samantha, 22*n*24
Along This Way (Johnson), 6, 22*n*17
alpha-5 reductase deficiency (A5RD), 219, 225–26, 227, 236*n*32, 236*n*37
ambiguous sexuality, 183–84
"America" (Simon), 172*n*24
"'The American girl I had once been'" (Athanassakis), 238*n*73, 238*n*76
The American Health Empire (Ehrenreich), 215–16*n*9
American identity, 11, 44–45
American mass killings, centrality of white men in, 89–90
American-ness, 220
American Revolution, opposition of slavery and, 63n2
"America's Historical Newspapers," 64*n*13, 64*n*15
America's Next Top Model (TV show), 15
"Am I Blue?" (song), 113*n*12
Anderson, Tanisha, 15–16
androgyny, 232, 233
Angry Black White Boy (Mansbach), 17–18, 93*n*2, 93*nn*10–11, 94*n*19, 94*n*21, 94*nn*23–25, 94*nn*27–28, 94*n*31; postracial imaginary in, 84–93
Angry White Men (Kimmel), 89–90, 94*n*18
Another Country (Baldwin), 92
antebellum slave narratives, 3
anti-immigrant sentiments, xii
antiracist policies, 21, 90
Apel, Dora, 130*n*12, 131*n*13
Appelbaum, Yoni, 22*n*23
Appiah, Kwame Anthony, 21*n*4
The Apprentice (TV show), 165
Appropriating Blackness (Johnson), 24*n*49, 85, 93*n*3
appropriation: cultural, 13; problem of, 137
Armstrong, Louis, 113*n*12
"Army Man's Suicide Reveal He Is Negro" (*New York Times*), 47*nn*1–2
assassinations, ix; attempted, 110
assimilation, 123, 136; American melting pot and, 177; ethnic, 238n66; facilitating their, 183, 195; passing and, 19, 137, 139, 140; resisting, 188
"'As White as Most White Women'" (Cutter), 64*n*9
Athanassakis, Yanoula, 233, 238*n*73, 238*n*76
Atlanta World, 47*nn*1–2
authenticity, 15, 147, 149, 150; black, 91, 92; cultural, 60; deference, authority, and, 85, 86, 88; demands of racial and ethnic, 162; dissonance and, 148; emotive forms of, 144, 149; ethnic, 162; guido/guidette, 163; identity-immersion journalism and the experience of, 142–54; legitimacy and, 87; nature of, 154; notion of, 143, 160; objective and emotional, 144–46, 147; objectivity and, 154n2; obsessions with, 19, 139; of passing, 150, 151; perceived, 23n31, 147; racial, 5, 88, 162
authority, authenticity, and deference, 85, 86, 88
autobiographical narratives, 154n2
The Autobiography of an Ex-colored Man (Johnson), 4, 6–7, 22*n*13, 86, 131*n*18
autonomy, 194

Babe the Blue Ox, 230
Babo, 181
Baby Boy (movie), 109
Baby's Sex (Shettles), 236*n*35
The Bachelor (TV show), 15
Baker, Josephine, 159
Baldwin, James, 92
Bambaataa, Afrika, 84, 85, 93, 114*n*23
Bamboozled (movie), 59–60, 65*n*35
banana, as epithet, 173*n*29
Barack Obama, Post-Racialism, and the New Politics of Triangulation (Smith), 93*n*7
Baraka, Amiri, ix–x, xiii*n*3
Barber, William J., II, x, xiii*n*5
baseball umpire analogy, 74
Bassard, Katherine Clay, 82*n*19
Baysden, Matthew F., 64*n*17
Bear Swamp Recovery (TV show), 165
Beatty, Paul, 86, 92
Bell, Bernard, 2

Belluscio, Steven J., 63–64*n*5
Bem, Sandra L., 232–33, 238*nn*70–71
Benito Cereno (Melville), 181, 190*n*17
Bennett, Juda, 63–64*n*5
Bennett, William, 21*n*2
Berlant, Lauren, 214
Berlin, Ira, 63*n*2
Berry, Halle, 8, 196
Bessie Yellowhair (Halsell), 142, 155*n*43, 155*nn*47–48, 155*n*50, 156*n*51
Besson, Luc, 113*n*7
Between the World and Me (Coates), xiii*n*5
Beware of the Other Side(s) (Schwarz), 215*n*4
biculturalism, 195
Big Game (movie), 113*n*7
The Big Sea (Hughes), 93*n*1
binaristic systems, 221
binary categories, 64*n*10
binary racial identities, 44
biological essentialism, 123
biracials: African Americans as, 50; celebrities as, 114n26; fictional experiences of, 50; heritage and, x, 8, 10, 126; passing of, as ethnic Jews, 4; protagonists as, 4; sociological and cultural concepts of, 4
Birth of a Nation (movie), 100
bisexuality, 185, 195
Black, Daniel, 4–5, 22*n*11
black Americans: defining and negotiating identify and, 197; during the Jim Crow era, 118–19. *See also* African Americans; blacks; Negroes
Black and Blue (Hoberman), 215*n*8
"Black and White Both Cast Shadows" (Adams), 190*n*15
black artistic freedom, x
Black Arts Movement, ix–x
black authenticity, 91, 92
black-authored comedy, 107
"Black Bush," 18, 113*n*3; cultural blackness of, 109; as interpretation of George W. Bush, 96–112
black cultural production, 88
black culture: identity, as way of resisting white privilege, 87–88; jazz as metaphor for, 202
black diaspora, 202
Blacked Out (Fordham), 22*nn*8–9
blackface, 13
Blackface, White Noise (Rogin), 24*n*42
black female sexuality, 177, 179; in literature, 179; outlets for expression of, 189; self-affirmation of, 188
black feminine identities, affective dimensionalities of, 197
Black Feminist Criticism (Christian), 190*n*12
black gangsta-inflected films, 109
black hypermasculinity, 97, 101, 105, 107, 108
black hypersexuality, 200–201
"Blacklash?" (Gates), 191*n*26
Black Like Me (Griffin), 19, 119, 142, 143, 145, 148, 154*nn*10–11, 154*n*13, 154*n*16, 155*nn*21–22, 155*nn*43–45
Black Lives Matter, 162; Shaun King and, 10, 23*n*31; rise of, 2
Black Looks ("The Oppositional Gaze") (hooks), 131*n*19
black male body: identifying, in visual culture, 98; stereotypes and, 112
black masculinity. *See* masculinity
black men, self-identification of, 197
black/mulatto-becomes-white medium, 179
blackness, 59; acceptance of, 50, 90; adoption of, as neo-passing, 87; attempt to separate from whitemess, 51; as complication, 154; complication of, 54; cultural, 109; defined, 60; embodiment of, 85, 98; essential, 112; hostility to, x; identification of, with, 104; identity as president and, 98, 99; illusion of, 88; imagery of, 89; insufficiency of, 18; lower-class, 7; meaning of, 52; passing and, 13, 176–190; performance of, 180, 183, 231; performative, 60; post–Civil Rights, 107; poverty and, 61; privilege and, 90, 177, 178; proof of, 234n3; pseudo, 90; racial, 98, 101; racist ideologies of, 63n2; reclamation of, 50; satire and, 92; slavery and, 52; stereotypical modes of, 59; suppression of, 112; surrender of, to new postracial order, 70; transcendence of blackness and, 86; transcendence of whiteness into, 89; treatment of, in literature, 88; utilization of, 176; as viable social category, 177
Black No More (Schuyler), 18, 84–85, 92, 94*n*30, 138, 170, 173*n*32

"Black or White" (*Atlanta World*), 47*n*1
black owners, treatment of slaves by, 76
Black Panthers, 111
black passing: as distinct from passing as black, 180–81; limitations of, 188–90
black performance tropes: dialect as aural signifier of, 99–100; racial blackness as defining trait of, 101
black political masculinity, 107
Black Power Movement, xii
black president(s): as emblem of impossibility, 96; as figure of social critique, 97; lineage of fictional, 97; neo-passing narratives of, 47; as popular culture trope, 97; postracial fictions conception of, 102; racial identity and, 98; as sign of postracial in popular media, 96; symbolism of first, 162; trope, 97; *24*'s depiction of, 112*n*2
"The Black President Hokum" (Edwards), 113*n*7, 114*nn*19–20
black presidentialism, 18, 102, 106; historical reality of, 107; passing narrative and, 102; popular culture's discourse of, 97
black press: passing in the, 47; testimonials of light-skinned blacks in, 44
black racial identity, social currency of, 177
black rage, 88, 90, 91; public focus on, 89
blacks: attempts to escape slavery, 73; Civil War Amendments and, 74; enslaved, 73; free, 72, 73; light-skinned, 44; sociolegal political crisis for, 71; tanning by, 159. *See also* African Americans; black Americans; Negroes
"Blacks and Gays Healing the Great Divide" (Smith), 191*n*28
black sexuality, films and, 208
Black Skin, White Masks (Fanon), 131*n*21, 197, 215*n*6
Blacks See Growing Values Gap (Kohut et al.), 22*n*19
Blacks Who Pass for Indian and White (Pulley), 64*n*17
black-to-black racial passing, 1, 6–7
black Twitter, 23*n*33
black universalism, 107
Black. White. (TV show), 5, 142, 145, 146, 147, 148, 149, 151
Black, White, and Jewish (Walker), 155*n*31
"Black Women and Mental Health" (Wilson), 216*n*10
black women, 190, 197, 198; daily struggle of, 214; devaluation of, 214; disenfranchisement of, 182; exoticness of hair, 184; heteronormativity for, 179; potential of, 207; rape of, by white slavers, 209; reality of, 214–15; scientific assessment of, 202; self-identification of, 197; sexuality of, 179, 189; as writers, 179
Black Women in Sequence (Whaley), 215*n*1
Blair, Cynthia M., 216*n*15
Blake, John, 81*n*2
Blues Legacies and Black Feminism (Davis), 217*n*26
The Bluest Eye (Morrison), 228
Bonilla-Silva, Eduardo, 2, 21*nn*3–4
Booth, Zachariah, 52
Borden, Lizzie, 113*n*7
border crossings, 64*n*10
Born in Flames (movie), 113*n*7, 113*n*11
The Boundaries of Blackness (Cohen), xiii*n*5
boundary crossings, 148
Boyd, Rekia, 15–16
Bracco, Lorraine, 167–68
Bradley, Joseph P., 74–75, 76
Breitbart News, 10, 22*n*25
Brennan, Neal, 113*n*3
Bricks without Straw (Tourgée), 76, 82*n*18
Brodkin, Karen, 222, 235*nn*12–13
Brooks, Daphne, xii, xiii*n*9
Brothers on Call (TV show), 165
Brown, Alan E., 64*n*6, 64*n*12
Brown, Christopher M., 17
Brown, James, 84
Brown, Michael, 16; death of, 2
Brown v. Board of Education, ix, 71, 142
Broyard, Anatole, 58, 65n32
Broyard, Bliss, 4
brutality: history of, 183; police, 18. *See also* violence
Buchanan, Nicole T., 216*n*10
Buchanan, Rose Troup, 24*n*47
Buñuel, Luis, 224
Bunyan, Paul, 230

burden, 76, 120, 196
Bush, George H. W., failed assassination attempt on, 110
Bush, George W., 114*n*24; African American mistrust of, 109–10; Chappelle's satirical portrait of, 97, 98, 108–9; foreign-policy agenda of, 108; Iraq War policy of, 97; public image of, 110; racial coding of, 18; song-and-dance numbers in, 113*n*12; speech on Hussein, Saddam, 110
Buszek, Maria Elena, 216*n*14
Butler, Judith, 65*n*25, 179, 190*n*11, 220, 235*n*6, 237*n*62

"café au lait" complexion, 158
Cake Boss (TV show), 165
Callahan, Yesha, 23*n*33
Carbado, Devon W., 85–86, 93*nn*5–6
Carby, Hazel, 179, 190*n*13
Carroll, Rachel, 231, 237*n*65
Carter, Mandy, 186, 187, 191*n*27
category crisis, 52, 64*n*10. *See also* identity
Caucasia (Senna), 4, 50, 63*n*4, 73, 154*n*2
Caughie, Pamela, 11, 23*n*32
"Caught on Tape" (West), 154*n*8
Celebrities Undercover (TV show), 15
A Celebrity Apprentice (TV show), 171
census, 79; in 1840, 73; recognition of mixed-race people in 2000, 45
Century City (TV show), 113*n*7, 113*n*11
"Chameleon Changes" (Miville et al.), 64*n*17
Chanel, Coco, 159, 161
Chaney, Michael, 130*n*1
"Change the Joke and Slip the Yoke" (Ellison), 47*n*4
Chappelle, Dave, 18, 47, 96–112, 113*nn*3–4; burlesquing of presidential authority, 108–9; satirical portrait of George W. Bush, 97, 98, 108–9
chattel slavery, 179; education and, 181
Chauncey, George, 185, 191*n*23
Cheney, Dick, xi
Cherokee heritage, 9
Chesnutt, Charles, 8–9, 56, 57, 64*n*21
Chicago Defender, 47*n*3
child pornography, 238n79
children: alpha-5 reductase deficiency and, 219; of disobedience, 208; fear of deformation, 228; gender differences between American, 225; gender identity and, 226; inheritance of, 4; mixed race, 46, 73; showing pornography to, 236n40; wisdom of, 207
The Children's Hour (Hellman), 223, 236*n*25
A Chosen Exile (Hobbs), 23*n*28, 23*n*32, 47*nn*1–2, 64*n*17
Christian, Barbara, 179, 190*n*12
Christie, Chris, 165
Cillizza, Chris, 81*n*1
circumcision, botched, 226
cisgender, 22*n*16, 234
civil rights, passing between gay rights and, 185–88
Civil Rights Act (1964), 142, 143
civil rights activists, 176; and gay rights activists, 176
Civil Rights Cases (1883), 74–75, 82*n*12
Civil Rights Movement, ix, xii, 44, 86, 142, 186; Jim Crow legislation and, 1
Civil War Amendments, 74–75
Clark, April, 22*n*19
classism, 198, 214
class passing: depiction of, 219; invisibility of, 152; narratives of, 4; racial, 7, 8, 137
Class-Passing (Foster), 155*n*36, 155*n*38
Cleage, Pearl, 217*n*27
Clearly Invisible (Dawkins), 23*n*27, 23*n*30, 140*n*3, 140*n*7, 140*n*10
Clementi, Tyler, 14
Cliff (character in *Frankie and Alice*), 208
Clifford, James, 194, 215*n*2
closet racism, 209
Coates, Ta-Nehisi, x, xiii*n*5
coconut, as epithet, 173*n*29
Cohen, Cathy J., x, xiii*n*5
Cohen, Julie E., 140*n*11
Cohen, Samuel, 230, 231–32, 237*n*57, 238*n*66
Cohn, D'Vera, 22*n*19
Coker, Hillary Crosley, 22*n*23
Colapinto, John, 237*n*40, 237*n*42
colonialism, 13
color, association of, with inferiority, 177–78
Colorblind (Wise), 21*nn*3–4

colorblindness, xii, 68–81, 130n3; as aesthetic, 69; in America, 21; attitudes in, 177; debate over, 75; identity-immersion journalism and, 151; ideological framework of, 103; jurisprudence and, 71, 72; justice and, 72–81; laws and, 76, 79; postracial discourse and, 16; rhetoric on, 74, 75; tension between color-consciousness and, 2, 23n5; thesis of, 46; value of and/or problems with, 21*n*4
Color Conscious (Appiah and Gutmann), 21*n*4
color-consciousness, tension between colorblindness and, 2, 23n5
"Coloring America" (Royal), 130*n*1
colorism: life stressors associated with, 198; racial passing and, 60–61
color line, 180; American identity and, 11; Du Bois on, 14, 180, 190n14; entrenchment of, 101–2; establishment and dismantling of, 8–9; operations of, 8–9; problem of, 14, 71, 97, 101, 190n14; subversion and reinforcement of, 102
Colossians 3:5, 208–9
Columbia University, racial diversity at, 185
comedy, 109; black-authored, 107; crossover, 109; crude, 102; dark, 166; musical, 102; sketches, 16, 97
comics, 18, 19, 29; high vs. low, 130n4; race in, 117–30, 130n1
Comics and Sequential Art (Eisner), 131*n*15
comic strips, passing in, 215n1
commensurability, 80
commodity: authenticity, deference, and authority, 85, 86, 88; self as, 136
The Complete Maus (Spiegelman), 131*n*22
Confessions of a Guidette (Polizzi), 171, 173*n*33
Configuring the Networked Self (Cohen), 140*n*11
Constantine, Madonna G., 64*n*17
"Consuming Performances" (McCarroll), 65*n*36
contemporary American society, 11, 17, 46
Contested Closets (Gross), 140*n*18
Cornyn, John, 110
Coronado, Marc, 155*n*31
Cortese, Deena Nicole, 161
Costa, Thomas, 64*n*16
counterburlesque, 110, 114n25
Covering (Yoshino), 177, 190*n*3
Crane, Helga, 8
Crenshaw, Kimberlé, 86–87, 93*nn*8–9
Criss, Doug, 23*n*31
critical race theory (CRT), 123, 130*n*3
Crossing Lines (Coronado et al.), 155*n*31
Crossing the Line (Wald), 23*n*32, 24*n*41, 113*n*5, 154*nn*1–2, 154*n*4, 155*n*45
crossover comedy, 109
cross-racial identification, 15–16; racial violence and, 16
Cruz, Jon, xiii*n*7
Cully, Joe, as runaway, 53–54
cultural appropriation, 13
cultural authenticity, 60
cultural blackness, 109
cultural difference, racial difference in, 80
cultural mulattos, 60
Culture and Authenticity (Lindholm), 143, 154*n*7, 154*nn*19–20
Culture on the Margins (Cruz), xiii*n*7
Cundieff, Rusty, 113*n*3
Curnutt, Hugh, 165
Cut Chemist, 84, 86, 93
Cutter, Martha J., 17, 64*n*9, 65*n*24
Cvetkovich, Ann, 214, 216*n*18, 216*n*24

DaCosta, Kimberly McClain, 47*n*6, 48*n*10
dago, as epithet, 169
Daily Beast (news site), 9, 22*n*24, 24*n*47
Dancing with the Stars (TV show), 171
dandyism, 101
Dangerous Liaisons (Gates), 191*n*26, 191*n*28
Daniel, G. Reginald, 155*n*31
Danquah, Meri, 214–15, 216*n*11, 216*n*25
dark comedy, 166
Davis, Angela, 217*n*26
Davis, David Brion, 63*n*2
Davis, F. James, 22*n*10
Davis, Lennard J., 214, 216*n*23
Davis, Miles, 215, 217*n*27
Davis, Sammy, Jr., 99, 101, 113*n*12
Davis, Sean, 23*n*34
Davis, Thaddious, 177, 178, 190*n*5
Dawkins, Marcia Alesan, 11, 18–19, 23*n*27, 23*n*30, 140*n*3, 140*n*7

"Days of Outrage, Operation Snatchback" (song), 87
de Beauvoir, Simone, 130*n*10
Deep Impact (movie), 99, 107, 113*n*7
Def, Mos, 60
deference, authenticity, and authority, 85, 86, 88
Delacroix, Pierre, 59
Delano, Amasa, 181
DelVecchio, Paul "Pauly D," 161, 163
denaturalization of whiteness, 105, 123
Depression (Cvetkovich), 216*n*18, 216*n*24
depression, whiteness as cause of, 209
desegregation, 142
Desiring Whiteness (Sheshadri-Crooks), 190*n*4
Detornay, Macon (fictional character), 85. See also *Angry Black White Boy* (Mansbach)
Detroit, violence in, 221–22
dialect, and blackface performance tropes, 99–100
Diamond, Milton, 236*n*39
DID. *See* dissociative identity disorder (DID)
Dilman, Douglas (fictional character), 99, 102–6, 108
Dimock, Wai Chi, 80
Dina (fictional character). *See* "Drinking Coffee Elsewhere" (Packer)
Dineen-Wimberly, Ingrid, 64*n*17
Ding Dongs, 201
disability studies, 213
discriminatory laws, 2
disguise, as aspect of American identity, 44–45
"Displacing Desire" (Rohy), 155*n*27
dissociation, 214
dissociative identity disorder (DID), 20, 194–95, 215; attack on, as diagnosis, 196; contemporary narratives of, 196, 216n22; examples of, 196; in *Frankie and Alice*, 193–215; skepticism of, 195
DJ Shadow, 84, 86, 93, 94*n*33
DNA, 144
Doane, Mary Ann, 140*n*6
"docusoap," 161
Dolezal, Rachel, reverse passing by, 9–10, 11, 12, 13, 15, 21, 22*n*22, 24n47
domestic violence, 139
Donnell, Chandra M., 216*n*10
Don't Ask, Don't Tell (policy), 186
Douglass, Frederick, 75–76, 82*nn*14–15, 181, 190*n*16
Dr. Oswald (character in *Frankie and Alice*), 201–2, 203, 204–7
drag-queen controversy, 138–39
"Drawing Blood" (Spiegelman), 131*n*23
Dreisinger, Baz, 11, 23*n*29, 23*n*39, 24*n*41, 63–64*n*5, 143, 154*nn*1–2
"Drinking Coffee Elsewhere" (Packer), 20, 175–90, 190*n*1, 190*nn*18–20, 191*n*25
drug users, passing of, as sober, 14
dual invisibility, 129
Du Bois, W. E. B., 14, 24*n*45, 180, 190*n*14, 197, 215*n*7, 243, 244*n*11

Ebony, 111
edited self, passing of an, 135–36
Edna (character in *Frankie and Alice*), 209, 212
education, 150; *Brown v. Board of Education* and, ix, 71, 142; chattel status and, 181; earning access to better, 136; Harvard, 59; higher, 153; Jewish success and, 235n13; medical industrial complex and, 215n9; passing and, 178; racism and, 2, 114n17; sex, 237n40; upper-class status and, 59, 60
Edwards, Erica, 98, 99, 107–8, 113*n*7, 114*nn*19–20
Edwards, Leigh, 164, 165, 172*n*3, 172*n*13
Ehrenreich, Barbara, 142, 145, 146, 150–51, 152
Eisner, Will, 131*n*15
Elam, Harry, 244*n*9
Elam, Michele, 11, 20–21, 64*n*6, 234, 244*n*7, 244*nn*9–10
Elder, Larry, 21, 24*n*51
elections: of 2008, x, 2, 68, 96; of 2016, xii
Ellington, Duke, 193
Ellison, Ralph, 8, 44–45, 197, 228
Ellison, Thelonious "Monk" (fictional character), 8
emancipation, 75
embodiment of blackness, 85, 98
Emmerich, Roland, 113*n*7

emotional intimacy, 147
"The Emperor's New Clothes" (Carter), 191*n*27
employment: passing and, 178; racial barriers to, ix
enslavement, racial difference and, 50
epithets, 169, 173*n*29
Erasure (Everett), 8, 22*n*21
Erb, Kelly Phillips, 172*n*5
essentialism, 123, 193
ethics: purview of, 127; of representation, 123; witnessing and, 130
ethnic assimilation, 238*n*66
ethnic authenticity, 162
ethnicity: MTV marketing of, 162; Snooki and the grotesque reality of, 158–72; whiteness and, 167, 168
"Ethnicity and the Biopolitics of Intersex in Jeffrey Eugenides's *Middlesex*" (Hsu), 238*n*66, 238*n*68, 238*n*79
ethnic Jews, passing of biracial protagonists as, 4
ethnic passing, 227–30
ethnographic framework, 194
eugenics, racialized, x–xi
Eugenides, Jeffrey, 219–34
Eurocentric ideology, 178
The Event (TV show), 113*n*7
Everett, Percival, 8, 22*n*21, 81*n*3, 86
Evers, Medgar, assassination of, ix
Expulsion Act (1806), 73

Facebook, 23–24*n*39, 24*n*47, 139; drag-queen controversy in, 138–39
FaceTime, 139
Faking It (TV show), 15
Falco, Edie, 166
familial belonging, 165
families, 129, 220; multiracial, 114n26; in reality television, 165
Fanny (runaway slave), description of, as white, 49–50
Fanon, Frantz, 131*n*21, 197, 215*n*6
Farley, Jenni "JWoww," 161
Faulkner, Michel, 186
Faulkner, William, 45, 228
Fauset, Jessie, 190*n*7
Federal Bureau of Investigation (FBI), ix
Federalist, 23*n*34
Feeling Italian (Ferraro), 172*n*25
Felix the Cat, 230
fellatio, 201
female-to-male transgender individuals, 24n40
femininity, 238n70
Femme Fatales (Doane), 140*n*6
Ferguson, Mo., racial violence in, 123
Ferraro, Thomas J., 167, 172*n*25
fiction: dissociative identities in, 196; experiences of biracials, 50; lineage of black presidents, 97; as popular culture, 196; postracial, conception of black presidents, 102; potential of space, 20; promise and ambivalence of, 69
fictional narratives, 154n2
Fields, Barbara Jeanne, 51–52, 63*n*2
The Fifth Element (movie), 113*n*7
film noir, 119, 120
films: acceptance as objective evidence, 145; archetypal mammies and, 99; black gangsta-inflected, 109; black sexuality and, 208; dissociative identities in, 196; iconic, 166; jazz as metaphor in, 202; as popular culture, 196; racism and, 99, 100, 101, 102, 105, 106, 128, 194; televised, 104. *See also specific films*
"5-alpha-Reductase Deficiency" (Isfort), 236*n*32
The Five Percenters concept, 94*n*14
Flight to Canada (Reed), 92
Flower Drum Song (musical), 223
Ford, Briggett C., 216*n*17
Ford, Dana, 23*n*31
Ford, Zack, 23*n*34
Fordham, Signithia, 3, 22*nn*8–9
Foster, Gwendolyn, 152, 155*n*36, 155*n*38
Fourteenth Amendment, 74
Fox & Friends (TV show), 24*n*51
Fox News, 24*n*51
Francine (character in *Frankie and Alice*): as black female trickster, 200; car crash of, 198–199, 204; in-group and out-group perceptions of culture and, 200; IQ of, 204; sexuality and, 200, 201; skin color of, 210; splintering of, into multiples, 205, 207, 213; third personality of, 211

Frankie (character in *Frankie and Alice*), 196–97, 200, 201, 202, 203–4, 207, 208–9
Frankie and Alice (film), 8–9, 20; neo-passing and dissociative identities as affective strategies in, 193–215
Franklin, Benjamin, 45, 168
free blacks, 72, 73
French, William J.: car crash of, 43; marriage of, 44; mental breakdown of, 43–44; racial identity of, 43; relationship with McEnroe, Gertrude and, 43–44; suicide of, 43–44
Frey, Shelly, 16
Friedman, James, 154*n*9
From Bourgeois to Boojie (Young), 140*n*12
From Jim Crow to Jay-Z (White), 94*n*20
Funk, Cary, 22*n*19

Gaines, Alisha, 19
Gallego, Mar, 178–79, 190*n*6, 190*n*9
Gandolfini, James, 166
Garber, Marjorie, 52, 64*n*10
Garie, Emily and Clarence, 55
The Garies and Their Friends (Webb), 55, 64*n*18
Garner, Eric, 15–16
Gates, Henry Louis, Jr., 58, 65*n*33, 92, 94*n*29, 191*n*26
Gautier, T., 236*n*37
"Gay at Yale" (Chauncey), 185, 191*n*23
Gaye, Marvin, 216*nn*12–13
gay rights, xii; activists, 176; passing as straight, 45; passing between civil rights and, 185–88
gays, divide between African Americans and, 191n26
gender, 129, 136, 139–40, 142–43, 148, 151, 153; reassignment of, 226
Gender and Race in Antebellum Popular Culture (Roth), 64*n*20
gender binary system, 130*n*10
gender dimorphism, racial passing and, 59
gender egalitarianism, 225
gender identity, 5, 226; in *Middlesex*, 225; racialized, 110. *See also* transgender identities
gender-neutral pronouns, 234*n*1
gender normativity, 23n37
gender passing, 14, 225–27, 228, 231
genderqueer people, 148
Gender Trouble (Butler), 65*n*25
generic passing, 178
Genius (character in *Frankie and Alice*), 196–97, 201, 202–7, 209, 210, 211, 213
"The Geography of Slavery in Virginia" (Costa), 64*n*16
Gerber, Jeff, 154*n*2
"Get Your Gender Binary Off My Childhood!" (Witterick), 236*n*33
Giancola, Sammi "Sweetheart," 161, 163
Giles, Eulelie (fictional character), 7
Gillespie, Angus Kress, 166, 172*nn*21–23
Gilman, Sander, 131*n*20
Gilroy, Paul, 21*n*4
Ginsberg, Elaine K., 24*n*43
Glam Fairy (TV show), 165
Glaser, Jennifer, 18, 19
Glass, Ira, 24*n*44
The Godfather trilogy (movies), 166
Godfrey, Mollie, ix, 194
God Help the Child (Morrison), 60–61, 65*n*37
Gold, Meta, 165–66, 172*nn*17–18
Golden, Jamie Nesbitt, 137, 140*nn*13–14
Google Books, 63*n*3
Gournelos, Ted, 140*n*17
Graham, Lawrence Otis, 171, 173*n*34
Grant, Oscar, 16
graphic narratives, 130n4
graphic novels, 29, 130, 130n4; passing narratives in, 119
Graphic Subjects (Chaney), 130*n*1
Gray, Freddie, 15–16
Green, Kai M., 23*n*35
Gregg, Melissa, 216*n*18
Griffin, John Howard, 24*n*41, 142, 145–47, 152, 153
Griffith, Michael, 221, 235*n*11
Grimes, Rick (fictional character), 68
Gross, Larry P., 140*n*18
Grosse Pointe, MI, white flight and, 222, 235n10
Grutter v. Bollinger, 75–76, 82*n*13, 82*n*16
Guadagnino, Vinny, 161, 163
Gubar, Susan, 114*n*18
Guenther, Lisa, 23–24*n*39
Guerrero, L., 236*n*37

Guevarra, Rudy P., Jr., 155*n*31
guevedoces, 226. *See also* alpha-5 reductase deficiency (A5RD)
guidettes, 161
Guidice, Joe, 167
Guidice, Teresa, 167
guido, 169; as an ethnic slur, 161; defining, 163
Gulati, Mitu, 85–86
Gunkel, David J., 140*n*17
Gunn, Sakia, 14
Gurdjieff, Georges, 45
Gutmann, Amy, 21*n*4

hacktivists, 137
Haggins, Bambi, 108–9, 113*n*4, 114*nn*21–22
Haizlip, Ellis, x, xiii*n*2
Halberstam, Judith (Jack), 12, 23*n*37
"halfed" masculinity, 106
"halfman," metaphor of, 106
Hall, Stuart, 216*n*16
Halsell, Grace, 142, 145, 146, 147, 151
Hamilton (musical), xi–xii; nontraditional racial casting of, xi
Hamilton, Alexander, xi
Hamilton, George, 161
Haney López, Ian, 64*n*8, 130*n*2
Hansberry, Lorraine, 243, 244*n*8
Hargraves, Hunter, 162, 172*n*10
Harlan, John M., *Plessy* dissent of, 74, 76
Harper, Frances, 4, 22*n*13
Harper, Gabe, 224, 236*n*29
Harris, Cheryl I., 140*n*9
Harris-Perry, Melissa, 23*n*33
Hartman, Saidiya, 131*n*16
Harvard University, racial diversity at, 185
Hawkins, Yusef, 87
Haysbert, Dennis, 98
HBO, 166
Head of State (movie), 107, 108, 113*n*7
Healy, Patrick, xiii*n*8
Helander, Jalmari, 113*n*7
Hellman, Lillian, 236*n*25
Hemingway, Ernest, 45
hermaphroditism, true, 236n36
heteronormativity, 179, 188, 190; white, 178
heterosexuality, 175, 188
heterosexual passing, 188
Higginbotham, Evelyn Brooks, 47, 48*n*11
"Higher Ground" (song), 210, 216*n*20
Hillman, Thea, 227, 237*n*45
hip-hop, 84, 87, 88; as antiracist mechanism, 93
hip-hop masculinity, 90
"A Hit Is a Hit" (episode of *The Sopranos*), 167
Hobbs, Allyson, 11–12, 15–16, 17, 23*n*28, 23*n*32, 24*n*50, 47*nn*1–2, 64*n*17
Hoberman, John, 197–98, 215*n*8
Hodges, Graham R., 64*n*6, 64*n*12
"Homonationalism as Assemblage" (Puar), 215*n*3
homonormative identity, 187
homonormativity, 188
homophobia, 176, 185–86
homosexuality, 175, 176, 188, 191n26, 223–24; cover-up for, 184
hooks, bell, 87, 89, 93*n*12, 94*n*17, 131*n*19
Horowitz, Juliana, 22*n*19
The House behind the Cedars (Chesnutt), 8–9, 56, 64*n*21
Howard, Sheena, 131*n*14
"How #BlackLivesMatter Started a Musical Revolution" (Brooks), xiii*n*9
How Jews Became White Folks (Brodkin), 222, 235*nn*12–13
"How Negroes Are Gaining in the U.S." (*U.S. News & World Report*), 47*n*3
"How Passing Passed Out" (*Sepia* article), 154*n*2
"How to Build Black Pride" (Kelley), 47*n*3
Hsu, Stephanie, 238*n*66, 238*n*68, 238*n*79
Huggins, Nathan Irving, 63–64*n*5
Hughes, Langston, x, 5, 8–9, 85, 93*n*1
Human Rights Campaign, 186
The Human Stain (Roth), 4, 58–59, 65*nn*28–29, 65*n*34
Hussein, Saddam, 110
hybridity, 46
Hypatia (journal), 23*n*39
hyperfemininity, 216n14
hypermasculinity, 98; black, 97, 101, 105, 107, 108
hyperreligious ranting, 204
hypersexuality. *See* sexuality
hypodescent, laws of, xi

identity: American, 11, 44–45; black cultural, 87–88; dualism, myth of, 138; homonormative, 187; invention, 230–33; other, taking new name for, 153; passing as mode of finding, 56–57; performance of, 5–6, 12, 189, 194, 211; policing of categories, 12, 15; politics, postracial, 176–90; and presidents, 98, 99, 161–62; in social media–driven marketplace, 136–37. *See also* category crisis; gender identity; racial identity
identity-immersion journalism, 145; and the experience of authenticity, 142–54
identity thieves, 137
Idiocracy (movie), 113*n*7
The Illegals (Halsell), 142
illicit identifications, 223–25
"Imagining Other Worlds" (Bassard), 82*n*19
Imitation of Life (film), 209
immigrants, 166, 219; dark-skinned African, 198; heritage of, 230; memoirs of, 221; narratives of, 229, 230; as scapegoats, xii; whitening of, by money, 222
immigration, incest and, 227–30
Imperato-McGinley, J., 236*n*37
inauthenticity, 148, 149
incest, 226, 227, 228, 237n48; immigration and, 227–30
Incognegro (Johnson and Pleece), 18, 130*n*5, 130*nn*7–9, 130*n*11, 131*n*17
incommensurability, 73–74, 101
"In Defense of Transracialism" (Tuvel), 23–24*n*39
Infants of the Spring (Thurman), 93, 94*n*32
inferiority, association of color with, 177–78
In Full Color (Dolezal), 22*n*22
Instagram, 139
institutional passing, 182
institutional racism, 137
intellectual affective strategies, 197–207
interracial conflict, 105
Interracial Intimacies (Kennedy), 65*n*27
interracial marriage, 46
interrogation in passing, 193
Intersex, for Lack of a Better Word (Hillman), 227
Intersex Society of North America (ISNA), 226, 237*n*41
intersexuality, 219, 221, 225–27, 228, 229, 230, 232, 238*n*66
In Their Shoes (Halsell), 154*n*11, 154*n*17, 155*n*40
"In the Wake of the 'Nigger Pixie'" (Haggins), 113*n*4, 114*nn*21–22
intimacy, emotional, 147
intraracial conflict, 7, 105, 180, 181
intraracial self-reflexivity, 86
The Intuitionist (Whitehead), 243
invisibility: of class passing, 152; dual, 129
The Invisible Man (Ellison), 8, 71, 215*n*7, 228
Iola Leroy (Harper), 4, 22*n*13
Iraq war, linking to 9/11 terrorist attacks, 108
"I Refuse to Pass" (Kingslow), 47*n*3
"Irony and Symbolic Action" (Skerrett), 22*n*17
Irony in the Age of Empire (Willett), 113*n*4
Isfort, Anna H., 236*n*32
Islam, Five Percenters in, 94*n*14
Italian Americans, 160, 162, 166
Italians, whiteness of, 168
It's Been Beautiful (Wald), xiii*n*2
"'It's not that simple'" (Dineen-Wimberly and Spickard), 64*n*17
"It Takes One to Know One" (Robinson), 155*n*37, 244*n*5
I've Gotta Make My Livin' (Blair), 216*n*15
"I Was So High" (Glass), 24*n*44

Jackson, John L., 5, 23*n*30, 220
Jacobson, Matthew Frye, 168, 216*n*19
jazz, as metaphor for black culture, 202
Jenner, Caitlyn, 12, 23*n*36
Jersey Couture (TV show), 165
Jerseylicious (TV show), 165
Jersey Shore (TV show), 8–9, 19, 158–72, 172*n*12, 173*n*31
Jet magazine, xiii*n*1, 21*n*1, 47*n*3
Jews: education and, 235n13; Nazi depiction of, 128; passing as Gentiles, 45; passing of biracial protagonists as ethnic, 4
The Jew's Body (Gilman), 131*n*20
Jim Crow: anticipation of dismantling legislation, 1; Black Americans during the, 118–19; Civil Rights Movement and, 1; governing logic of, 189; legal context of, 3; racism and, 45, 160; South, 168

Joe Millionaire (TV show), 5, 15
John Henry Days (Whitehead), 73
Johnson, E. Patrick, 24*n*49, 85, 93*n*3
Johnson, James Weldon, 4, 6–7, 18, 45, 86, 131*n*18
Johnson, Lyndon B., 114*n*17; on equality of opportunity for African Americans, 103, 104
Johnson, Mat, 18, 130*n*5, 130*nn*7–9, 130*n*11, 131*n*17
Jones, Edward, 72–74, 80–81
Jones, Martha S., 5, 22*n*14, 23*n*30, 220, 235*n*5
Jones, Patricia, 7, 22*n*18
Joyce, James, 221
Judge, Mike, 113*n*7

Kapital Volume One (Marx), 140*n*5
Kaufman, Gil, 172*n*4
Kaufman, Gunnar (fictional character), 92
Keeter, Scott, 22*n*19
Kelley, Don Quinn, 47*n*3
Kennedy, Randall, 58, 65*n*27
Kerouac, Jack, 230–31
Kilbourne, Jean, 184, 190*n*21
Killing Rage (hooks), 93*n*12, 94*n*17
Killing Us Softly 4 (Kilbourne), 190*n*21
Kimmel, Michael S., 89–90, 94*n*18
King, Martin Luther, Jr., 2, 91; assassination of, ix; I Have a Dream speech of, x, 74
King, Shaun, 11, 13, 15, 23*n*31, 24*n*46; pretending to be biracial, 10; Yiannopoulos on, 22*n*25
Kingslow, Janice, 47*n*3
The Known World (Jones), 17, 72–74, 78, 79, 81; colorblindness of law in, 76
Kohut, Andrew, 22*n*19
Kossuth, Louis, 63*n*1
Kroeger, Brooke, 58, 64*n*17, 65*n*30
Kuhn, Thomas S., 79, 82*nn*25–27
Ku Klux Klan, 129

La Ferla, Ruth, 48*n*7
Larsen, Nella, 7, 8, 56–57, 64*n*22, 65*n*23, 86, 177
laws, 52, 56, 72–73, 74, 75, 79; black literature and, 72; as color blind, 76; discriminatory, 2; fairness of, 77; of hypodescent, xi; institutional blindness of, 73; literature and, 80; perceptual slavery and, 63n2; race and, 71, 76, 78; separating God's from Caesar's, 77; slavery and, 63n2
Lean In (Sandberg), 14
Leder, Mimi, 113*n*7
Lee, Anthony W., 130*n*12, 131*n*13
Lee, Kalvin, 113*n*11
Lee, Merton, 238*n*66
Lee, Spike, 59–60, 65*n*35, 244*n*3
legitimacy, authenticity and, 87
lesbian and gay movement, 186–87
lesbianism, 175, 186
Les Blancs (Hansberry), 243, 244*n*8
"Let's Get It On" (song), 216*nn*12–13
"Letter from a Birmingham Bus" (prologue of *Angry Black White Boy*), 91
Letter to Louis Kossuth ([Garrison]), 63*n*1
Lewis, Bradley, 216*n*21
Leyshon, Cressida, 235*n*15
LGBT+ lifestyles, 185, 186, 187
"Life History and Narrative Analysis" (Sosulski, Buchanan, and Donnell), 216*n*10
Life magazine, 47*n*3
Life on the Color Line (Williams), 4, 61, 65*n*38
life stressors associated with racism, 198
Lincoln, Abe, 45
Lindholm, Charles, 143, 147, 154*n*7, 154*nn*19–20
literature, 139; African American, 71–72, 79, 82n7, 176–77; black, 72; black female sexuality in, 179; law and, 80; passing and, 143, 181, 209; treatment of blackness in, 88. *See also specific books*
Lolita (Nabokov), 228, 235*n*22
Looking for America on the New Jersey Turnpike (Gillespie and Rockland), 166, 172*nn*21–23
"Looking for the Perfect Beat" (song), 85
López, Ian Haney, 51
Lorde, Audre, 93
Lott, Eric, 24*n*42, 85, 93*n*4, 114*n*25, 154*n*2
Love and Theft (Lott), 24*n*42, 85, 93*n*4, 114*n*25
Luce, Peter, 226, 227
lynching, 118; early 20th-century, 124; epidemic of, 118; images of, 18, 123–24,

125, 126; interwar, 18, 117; participants at, 125, 126; race and, 117; reporting on, 128, 129; sexually motivated, as accepted practice in the South, 101; victim of, 125; vigilante justice and, 123. *See also* violence
lynching party, 124
Lynching Photographs (Lee), 130*n*12, 131*n*13
"Lynchings to Walter Scott" (Howard), 131*n*14

Mack, Roy, 113*n*7, 113*n*12
"Mad at Miles" (Cleage), 217*n*27
Made (TV show), 15
"Made-for-TV Movie Version" (Hillman), 237*n*45
"A Mad Fight" (Lewis), 216*n*21
Mad Pride, 213
make-believe performances, 5
Making Multiracials (DaCosta), 47*n*6, 48*n*10
Malcolm X, assassination of, ix
male-to-female transgender individuals, 24n40
The Man (made-for-TV movie), 96, 99, 102–7, 113*n*7, 113*n*13, 113*n*15, 114*nn*16–17
The Man (novel, Wallace), 96, 102–3, 105
Man & Woman, Boy & Girl (Money), 226
Man Caves, 165
Manning, Brandon J., 17–18
Mansbach, Adam, 17–18, 84–93
Many Thousands Gone (Berlin), 63*n*2
marketing, advertising and, 140
marriage: of incest and intersex, 227; interracial, 46; miscegenational, 56
The Marriage Plot (Carroll), 231
Marsan, Loran, 19
Martin, Trayvon, death of, 2
Marwick, Alice E., 140*n*2
Marx, Karl, 140*n*5
masculinity, 238n70; black, 90, 99, 101, 110; black political, 107, 108; codes of, 98; contemporary white, 89; crisis of, 103, 108; halfed, 106; hip-hop, 90; mask of, 147; as naturalized sign of presidentialism, 99; perceived, 14; white, 108, 110. *See also* black hypermasculinity
mass killings, centrality of white men in, 89–90
mass violence, racial minorities and, 14
Mathis-Lilley, Ben, 22*n*23
Matilda (Matt Sycamore), 155*n*31
Mau Mau (fictional rap group), 59–60
Maxine (character in *Frankie and Alice*), 209
McCarroll, Meredith, 60, 65*n*36
McCloud, Scott, 130*n*6, 131*n*15
McCright, Aaron M., 172*n*1
McDowell, Deborah, 179, 190*n*10
McEnroe, Gertrude, 43–44; relationship with French and William, 43–44
McGruder, Aaron, 113*n*11
McKee, Kimberly, et al., 23*n*34
McWhorter, John, 21*n*2
"The Measurement of Psychological Androgyny" (Bem), 238*nn*70–71
medical industrial complex (MIC), 198, 201, 213, 215–16*n*9
medical photography, 238n79
medical racism, 197, 213
Medley, Keith Weldon, 140*n*8
Melfi, Jennifer (fictional character), 167–68, 169
Melville, Herman, 181, 190*n*17
"The Memphis Blues" (song), 100
Menace II Society, 109
Mendelsohn, Daniel, 237*n*52
mental illness, 202, 213, 214
mental wellness, 213, 214
metalanguage, race as a, 47
Method & Red (TV show), 165
Mezzrow, Mezz, 24*n*41, 154*n*2
Michaels, Walter Benn, 21*n*4
Michigan, University of, Law School, 75
Mickey Mouse, 230
Middlesex (Eugenides), 21, 219–34
"Mighty Hermaphrodite" (Mendelsohn), 237*n*52
Millennium March on Washington, D.C. (2000), 186, 191n26
Miller, Laura, 235*n*17
Miller, Linda, 221
Miller, Monica L., 113*n*10
minstrelsy, legacy of, 85
Miranda, Lin-Manuel, xi
The Misadventures of Awkward Black Girl (Rae), 135, 140*n*1
miscegenation, 56, 98
"The Missing Link" (Spates), 216*n*10

Miville, Marie L., 64*n*17
Mixed Blood (Spickard), 63–64*n*5
mixed-race children, 46, 73
mixed-race identity, 45, 46; acceptance of, 17, 50
Money, John, 226, 227
Moniz, Jeffrey, 155*n*31
Montgomery bus boycott, ix
Moore, Kayla, 15–16
More Than Black? (Daniel), 155*n*31
Morin, Richard, 22*n*19
Morrison, Toni, 60–61, 65*n*37, 69, 73, 220, 228, 237*n*47
Mos Def, 60
"'A Most Disagreeable Mirror'" (Wald), 154*nn*14–15, 155*n*45
most-racial, 162
movies. *See* films
MTV, 161; marketing of ethnicity, 162
Muhammed, Fard, in *Middlesex*, 229
The Mulatta and the Politics of Race (Zackodnik), 63–64*n*5
mulatto, 46, 52, 53, 60, 64, 177, 179; passing and, 64n6
"The Mulatto Millennium" (Senna), 46, 48*nn*8–9
"The Mulatto Motif in Black Fiction" (Stetson), 65*n*31
Mulatto Muslim, 229
Multicultural Comics (Aldama), 130*n*1
multinational identities, 195
multiple personality disorder, 195
multiracial families, 114n26
multiracialism, 195
multiraciality, sociological and cultural concepts of, 4
Murdoch, Francine Lucinda (fictional character). See *Frankie and Alice* (film)
musical comedy, 102
"My Statement on the Current Media Controversy" (Smith), 24*n*46

Nabokov, Vladimir, 228, 235*n*22
Narcisi, Lara, 20–21
The Narrative of Arthur Gordon Pym of Nantucket (Poe), 130*n*5
Narrative of the Life of Frederick Douglass, an American Slave (Douglass), 190*n*16
National Aeronautics and Space Administration (NASA), 111
National Association for the Advancement of Colored People (NAACP), Dolezal as president of, 9
National Manhood (Nelson), 113*n*9
Native American ancestry, xiii, 9, 53, 54, 118, 144; slave connections to, 53
Native Son (Wright), 8, 91, 94*n*26
Neal, Mark Anthony, x, xiii*n*5
Near Black (Dreisinger), 23*n*29, 23*n*39, 24*n*41, 63–64*n*5, 154*nn*1–2
negation of difference, 70
Negro Digest, 47*n*3
Negroes, 85, 103, 104, 129; acculturation and, 122; freed, 73; living as, 145, 146; need to compete, 1; opportunities for, 1; passing by, ix, 7, 135; Toomer as great writer, 45. *See also* African Americans; black Americans; blacks
"Negroes: Big Advances in Jobs, Wealth, and Status" *(U.S. News & World Report)*, 47*n*3
"Negro eyes," 57
Negro-ness, 147
Neidorf, Shawn, 22*n*19
Neighbor Jackwood (Trowbridge), 55–56, 64*n*19
Neither Black nor White Yet Both (Sollors), 23*n*32, 63–64*n*5, 220, 234*nn*2–3, 240*n*2
Nelson, Dana, 99, 106, 113*n*9
neo-passing: adoption of blackness as, 87; as an analytic, 194; dangers of, 88; defining, 194; in *Frankie and Alice*, 193–215
neo-passing narratives: contemporary injustices and, 3; defined, 85; fictional black presidents in, 97–98; passing in, 16–17, 51–52; racial categories in, 47; rebuttals in, 71; reflection of racial politics and, 16; whiteness and, 63
neo-segregation narratives, 3, 9
Neo-Segregation Narratives (Norman), 22*n*6
neo-slave narratives, 3, 9
Neo-Slave Narratives (Rushdy), 22*n*5
Nerad, Julie Cary, 23*n*28, 23*n*30, 23*n*32, 64*n*6, 161, 172*nn*6–7

Nettles, Islan, 14
Newark, NJ, political struggles in, ix–x
Newark (NJ) Star-Ledger, 165–66
New Horizon Church of New York, 186
New Jersey: as favorite state in reality television, 165–67; as stage for white ethnic identity, 160–61
The New Jim Crow (Alexander), xiii*n*5, 21*n*3
New Left Review, 63*n*2
new millennium, 61; complexities of, 86; marketplace of, 15, 136; passing in the, 14, 17; racial dynamics of, 45; racial politics of, 16
"A New, 'Post-Racial' Political Era in America" (Schorr), 21*n*2
news media, use of "postracial" in, 114*n*26
newspaper advertisements, runaway slaves passing for white in, 49–50, 52–54
New York Royal Gazette, 64*n*12
New York Times, 24*n*50, 47*nn*1–2, 48*n*7
New York Weekly Journal, 64*n*6
Nickel and Dimed (Ehrenreich), 142, 150–51
9/11 attacks, link of Iraq War to, 108
nineteenth century, passing in, 55, 56, 86
"Nobody Likes a Gay Guy, Especially Other Gay Guys" (Harper), 236*n*29
Nobody Passes (Matilda [Matt Sycamore]), 155*n*31
nonwhites as scapegoats, xii
"Normality, Power, Culture" (Davis), 216*n*23
Norman, Brian, 3, 22*n*6
norms, performance of, 188
Not Just Race, Not Just Gender (Smith), 190*n*8
"The Novel in a Time of Terror" (Cohen), 237*n*57, 238*n*66
Nowatzki, Robert, 55
n-word, use of, 89

Obama, Barack Hussein, 23*n*31, 81*n*1; blackness of, 98; election of, in 2008, 68; inauguration of, 161; legitimacy of, xii; media treatments of, 97; polarization of racial attitudes, 162–63; post-racial promise of 2008 election of, x, 2; presidency of, 86–87, 97, 110; public image of, 96; racialization of, in media coverage, 113n8; racist "whitelash" to administration of, 162; significance of racial identity for, 161–62
Obama, Michelle, xi
Obama's Race (Tesler and Sears), 113*n*8
objectivity, authenticity and, 154n2
"Of Our Spiritual Strivings" (Du Bois), 244*n*11
Oluo, Ijeoma, 138, 140*n*16
Omi, Michael, x, xii, xiii*n*4, xiii*n*10, 21*n*4, 242, 244*n*6
O'Nan, Stewart, 221
One Drop (Broyard), 4
one-drop rule, 13, 97; in classic narratives of passing, x–xi, 4–5; multiracial activist challenge of, 45
O'Neil, Erin, 172*n*16
On the Road (Kerouac), 231
"An Open Letter to Wikipedia" (Roth), 65*n*32
Operation Snatchback, 87
oreo, as epithet, 173*n*29
orientation: sexual, 20, 136, 140, 175–90, 195; social conventions of, 176
orientation games, 175
Ortiz-Magro, Ronnie, 161, 164
Osucha, Eden, 18, 47
Oswald, Dr. (character in *Frankie and Alice*), 201–2, 203, 204–7
other identity, taking new name for, 153
otherness, 214
Our America (Michaels), 21*n*4
Our Kind of People (Graham), 171, 173*n*34
Ovid, 8

Packer, ZZ, 19–20, 175, 176, 190
Paige (character in *Frankie and Alice*), 207, 209, 210, 211–12
Palmer, David (fictional character), racial identity of, 96–97
Paradise (Morrison), 69, 73
Parker, Charlie, 111
Parker Royal, Derek, 130*n*1
"Pass•ed Performances" (Jackson and Jones), 22*n*14, 23*n*30, 235*n*5

passing: as act of duping the looker, 194; age, 135; as an accusation, 194; authenticity of, 150, 151; black (*See* black passing); blackness and, 13, 176–90; class (*See* class passing); in comic strips, 215n1; as concept of essentialist artifice, 194; connotations of, 55; defining, x–xi, 49, 51, 57, 85–86; education and, 178; employment opportunities and, 178; ethnic, 227–30; expansion of, 1–2; between gay rights and civil rights, 185–88; gender, 225–27, 228, 231; generic, 178; inauthenticity of, 150; journalistic, 19; language and grammars of, 193; literature and, 143, 181, 209; neo (*See* neo-passing; neo-passing narratives); New Jersey as geography of, 166; one drop-rule in classic narratives of, x–xi, 4–5; paradoxical nature of, 11; as passé, 63–64*n*5; persistence of, 2, 62–63; in a postracial world, 57–62; racial (*See* racial passing); racial-class, 7–8; racial identity and, 13; relationship between neo-passing and, 17; reverse (*See* reverse passing); shelf life of, 241–42; as social construction, 193; as social phenomenon, 1, 3, 242; straight, 223–25; as synonymous with performance, 11; for tan, 158–72; as term, 244n4; visual cues in, 105; whiteness and, 120, 123; wish for obsolescence of, 243–44

Passing (Jones), 7, 8, 22*n*18

Passing (Larsen), 56–57, 64*n*22, 65*n*23, 86, 177, 179, 180

Passing: Identity and Interpretation in Sexuality, Race, and Religion (Sanchez and Schlossberg), 23*n*32, 24*n*43, 154*n*5, 155*n*31

Passing: When People Can't Be Who They Are (Kroeger), 64*n*17, 65*n*30

Passing and the Fictions of Identity (Ginsberg), 24*n*43

"Passing and the Problematic of Multiracial Pride" (Senna), 24*n*48

The Passing Figure (Bennett), 63–64*n*5

"Passing for White, Passing for Black" (Piper), 24*n*48, 154*n*2

Passing Interest (Nerad), 23*n*28, 23*n*30, 23*n*32, 64*n*6, 172*nn*6–7

passing in sports, 244n4

"Passing in the Post-Race Era" (Elam), 234, 238*n*80

passing narratives: conventional, 142; lessons learned from traditional, 19; popularity of, with white audience, 178; reveal as essential in, 150–51; thematic possibilities and concerns in, 5

Passing Novels in the Harlem Renaissance (Gallego), 178–79, 190*n*6, 190*n*9

"Passing, Queering" (Butler), 179, 190*n*11

Passing Strange (Stew), 7–8, 22*n*20, 242, 244*n*3

Paulson, Michael, xiii*n*6

Peace, Emma Jean, 4–5

pedophilia, abusive, 235*n*22

Pellegrini, Ann, 216*n*18

Pence, Mike, xi–xii

Penn, Matthew, 172*n*20

Perfect Peace (Black), 4–5, 8, 22*n*11

performance, 188, 197; of blackness, 180, 183, 231; hyperfeminine, 216*n*14; of identity, 189, 194, 211; of norms, 188; racial, 178; of sexuality, 200; straightness as, 231

performance studies, 5

Performance Studies: An Introduction (Schechner), 22*n*15

"Performative Acts and Gender Constitution" (Butler), 235*n*6, 237*n*62

"Performing Citizenship" (Young), 22*n*17

Periscope (social-media app), 139

perpetual slavery, 63n2

Pete (character in *Frankie and Alice*), 209, 211

Peterson, R. E., 236*n*37

Pfeiffer, Kathleen, 143, 154*n*3, 220, 240*n*4

"A Phenomenology of Excorporation, Bodily Alienation, and Resistance" (Zeiler), 238*n*76

photography: acceptance as objective evidence, 145; differences between comics and, 125; medical, 238*n*79; as objective evidence, 145; in recording violence, 125

PhotoShop, 139

Pickens, Theri, 216*n*21

Pinchback, Zane. See *Incognegro* (Johnson and Pleece)

Pinky (film), 209

Pin-Up Grrrls (Buszek), 216*n*14
Piper, Adrian, 24*n*48, 154*n*2
Pivarnick, Angelina, 161
Planet Rock: The Album, 85
plantocracy, 76
Playing in the Dark (Morrison), 220, 237*n*47
Pleece, Warren, 18, 130*n*5, 130*nn*7–9, 130*n*11, 131*n*17
Plessy, Homer, racial passing of, 137
Plessy v. Ferguson, 137; Harlan, John's dissent in, 74, 76
"*Plessy v. Ferguson* and the Literary Imagination" (Thomas), 82*n*17
Plum Bun (Fauset), 190*n*7
Poe, Edgar Allan, 130*n*5, 235*n*22
police brutality, 18
police violence, 117, 118, 125, 127
political authority, 102–3
Polizzi, Nicole "Snooki," 158–72, 173*n*33
Pond, Allison, 22*n*19
poor, passing as rich, 45
pornography, 236n40, 238*n*79
Post Black (Womack), 190, 191*n*29
postblack fiction, promise and ambivalence of, 69
post–Civil Rights America, race in, 86
post–Civil Rights blackness, 107
post–Civil Rights ironies, xii
post–Jim Crow era: black-white color line in, 11; passing in, 7; racism in the, 2
post-race, xiii
postracial, use of, in news media, 114*n*26
postracial aesthetic, 68
Postracial America, x
postracial discourse, colorblindness and, 16
postracial identity politics, blackness, passing, and, 176–90
postracial imaginary: in *Angry Black White Boy*, 84–93; success of, 17–18
postracialism, 90; defined, 86, 87; reality of, 2
The Post-Racial Mystique (Squires), 114*n*26
Post-Racial or Most-Racial? (Tesla), 172*nn*8–9, 172*n*11
postracial world, passing in a, 57–62
poverty: blackness and, 61; passing for tan in disguising, 172
Powers, Richard, 73
presidency: of Obama, Barack Hussein, 86–87, 97, 110; whiteness of the, 104, 105, 106, 110. *See also* black president(s); black presidentialism; Bush, George W.
presidential authority, Chappelle's burlesquing of, 108–9
presidentialism: masculinity as naturalized sign of, 99; public discourse of, 98–99; race-neutral, 110
The Presidents We Imagine (Smith), 113*n*14
"Pretends to Be Free" (Hodges and Brown), 64*n*6, 64*n*12
privacy, 136; passing and, 19, 136–37, 139, 140
privacy pirates, 137
privilege, white. *See* white privilege
The Problem of Slavery in the Age of Revolution, 1770–1823 (Davis), 63*n*2
Proctor, William G., 64*n*11
proposition 8, 186
Pryor, Richard, 47, 110, 111–12
pseudoblackness, 89, 90
Puar, Jasbir K., 195–96, 215*n*3, 216*n*18
Pudd'nhead Wilson (Twain), 50
Pulley, Clyde, 64*n*17
Pym (Johnson), 130*n*5

quadroons, 52, 60
Quakers, 77
queer community, 14
Quicksand (Larsen), 8, 179
Quickskill, Raven (fictional character), 92

race, 51; in comics, 117–30, 130*n*1; contemporary vitality of, 71; as illusion, 50; lynching and, 117; as a metalanguage, 47; relevance of, 177
"Race, Love, Hate, and Me" (King), 24*n*46
"'Race and Gender Are Not the Same!' Is Not a Good Response" (Green), 23*n*35
"Race and Racial Formation" (Elam and Elam), 244*n*9
Racechanges (Gubar), 114*n*18
race consciousness, 44
race neutrality, 108, 112
race-neutral presidentialism, 110
Race Passing and American Individualism (Pfeiffer), 154*n*3, 220, 240*n*4
race riots, 87

"Rachel Dolezal's Unintended Gift to America" (Hobbs), 24*n*50
racial ambiguity, 45, 46, 51, 242
racial apocalypse, 87
racial attitudes, polarization of, 162–63
racial authenticity, 5, 88, 162
racial barriers to employment, ix
racial binaries, significance of, 61
racial blackness, 98, 101
racial categories: in neo-passing narratives, 47; salience of, 61. *See also* category crisis
racial-class passing, 7–8, 137
racial construction, 51, 61
racial difference: enslavement and, 50; representation in cultural production, 80
racial discrimination, 61
racial epistemologies, 70, 71
racial epithets, 173*n*29
racial equality, 11, 185
racial essence: affirmation of, 62–63; racial identity and, 60
racial essentialism, 92
"Racial Etiquette" (Thaggert), 23*n*38
racial formation, 242
Racial Formation in the United States (Omi and Winant), xii, xiii*n*4, xiii*n*10, 21*n*4, 244*n*6
racial hegemony, 103
racial hierarchy, property rules and, 76
racial hybridity, 17
racial identity: binary, 44; black, 177; categories of, 13–14, 54; loss of, 69; passing and, 13; racial essence and, 60; significance of, for Obama, 161–62; view of, as choice, 56; white ethnic, 160–61; whiteness as, 58. *See also* identity; transracial identity
racial ideologies, 17, 47
racial inequalities, enforcement of, 2
racial inferiority, 198
racialization, 50
racialized eugenics, x–xi
racialized subjectivity, 79
racial justice, realization of, 71
racial knowledge, effacement of, 70–71
racial markedness, 70
racial masquerade, 18, 97, 100, 109, 111
racial minorities, mass violence and, 14
racial nativism, x
racial passing, 13, 179; in the American context, 44–45; colorism and, 60–61; early references to, 64*n*6; epistemological ambiguity and, 148; history of, 50–54; link to gender dimorphism, 59; as mode of finding identity, 56–57; origins of concept, 17; parallel between closeted, gay lifestyles and, 14; persistence of, 1; in post–Jim Crow world, 189
racial performances, 178
racial performativity, 59–60, 61
racial politics, reflection of, 16
racial profiling, 122
racial remediation, 207–15
racial self-determination, 58
racial state, x
racial stereotyping, 179
racial "syndrome," 169
racial tension, privileging of, 176
racial trauma, 197
racial violence, 16, 18, 117, 125, 130; cross-racial identification and, 16; racial visibility and, 18
"Racing to Post-Racialism" (Crenshaw), 93*nn*8–9
racism: closet, 209; de facto, 92; films and, 99, 100, 101, 102, 105, 106, 128, 194; institutional, 137, 237*n*48; Jim Crow and, 2, 45, 160; life stressors associated with, 198; medical, 197, 213; segregation and, 2; trauma of, 210
Racism without Racists (Bonilla-Silva), 21*nn*3–4
racist anxiety, satire of, 110–11
Rae, Issa, 135, 140*n*1
Rapaport, Michael, 59
rape of black women, 209
rapping, xi
Rawlings, Donnell, 109
Ray, Billy (alter ego of Bruno Wurgel in *Black. White.*), 153
"Reading the Intersection of Race and Gender in Narratives of Passing" (Smith), 113*n*6
Real Housewives franchise, 165
The Real Housewives of New Jersey, 165, 167
Reality Squared (Friedman), 154*n*9

reality television, 5, 16, 19, 142, 160–62, 170, 172; defined, 164; fondness of families in, 165; New Jersey as favorite state in, 165–67; rhetorical devices of, 144–45

Really the Blues (Mezzrow), 154*n*2

The Real World (TV show), 161

rearticulation, 207

"Recitatif" (Morrison), 69

Reconstructing Womanhood (Carby), 179, 190*n*13

Redfield, Irene (fictional character), 179

Reed, Ishmael, 86, 92, 186

Reimer, Brenda, 226

Reimer, Brian, 226–27

Reimer, Bruce, 226

Reimer, David, 226–27, 236*n*39

"Re-inking the Nation" (Whaley), 215*n*1

remediation, 207

Renegades of Rhythm concert, 84

"Retrospective Sex" (Carroll), 237*n*65

"Return of the King" (episode of *The Boondocks*), 113*n*11

reveal, as essential in passing narratives, 150–51

Revelations: American History, American Myths (Huggins), 63–64*n*5

revenge, violence and, 12

reverse passing, 9–10, 11, 12, 13, 15, 21, 22*n*23, 24*n*47

rhetorical devices of reality television, 144–45

Rhinelander, Alice, 12–13

Rhinelander case (1925), 12–13

Rice, Tamir, 15–16

The Richard Pryor Show (TV show), 110

Rivers, Eugene, 21*n*2

Robbins, William, 73, 74, 76, 77, 81

Roberts, John G., Jr., 74

Robinson, Amy, 140*n*15, 140*n*19, 150, 155*n*37, 244*n*5

Robinson, Angelo Rich, 22*n*7

Rock, Chris, 107, 108, 113*n*7

Rockland, Michael Aaron, 165, 166, 172*nn*21–23

Rodewald, Heidi, 244*n*3

Roediger, David, 169, 173*n*30, 216*n*19

Rogin, Michael, 24*n*42

Rohy, Valerie, 148, 155*n*27

Rollins, Lisa Marie, 23*n*34

Ronell, Ann, 217*n*28; unrequited love for man, 217*n*28

Ronson, Jon, 24*n*47

The Root (website), 23*n*33

Rose, Lisa, 165, 167, 172*nn*14–15, 172*n*19, 173*n*26

Ross, Fran, 86

Roth, Philip, 4, 58, 65*nn*28–29, 65*n*32, 65*n*34

Roth, Sarah N., 64*n*20

Rufus Jones for President (movie), 96, 99–102, 104, 107, 113*n*7, 113*n*12; laughter at the election of a black president, 101

Runaway Slave Advertisements (Windley), 64*n*14

runaway slaves: passing for white, in newspaper advertisements, 17, 49–50, 52–54; as problem, 78

Rushdy, Ashraf H. A., 2–3, 22*n*5

Russian roulette, as metaphor, 182, 183

Rust, Marion, 143, 154*n*6

Sag Harbor (Whitehead), 69

Sanchez, Maria, 23*n*32, 24*n*43, 155*n*31

Sandberg, Sheryl, 14

Sargent, Joseph, 113*n*7

satire, 18, 59, 91, 92, 136; African American, 92, 93, 112; neo-passing narratives as, 138; passing and, 19, 137–38, 139, 140; television, 113n4

Sax, Geoffrey, 194

Scalia, Antonin, 76

Scandal (TV show), 68–69

scapegoats, xii

Scarface (movie), 166

Scenes of Subjection (Hartman), 131*n*16

Schechner, Richard, 5, 22*n*15

Schlossberg, Linda, 23*n*32, 24*n*43, 143, 154*n*5, 155*n*31

Schorr, Daniel, 21*n*2

Schuyler, George, 18, 84–85, 86, 92, 94*n*30, 138, 170, 173*n*32

Schwarz, Heike, 215*n*4

Sears, David O., 113*n*8

segregation: legal, 2, 3; racism and, 2; school, xi; US Supreme Court ruling on, 45

Seigworth, Gregory J., 216*n*18

selective disclosure, obsessions with, 139
self, splitting the, 151–54
self-identifications, 197
Self-Made Man (Vincent), 142, 146–49, 151, 152
self-transformation, 229
Senna, Danzy, 4, 24*n*48, 46, 50, 61–62, 73, 154*n*2, 241, 243–44
"separate but equal" doctrine, 137
Serch, M. C., 60
"Sex, Fate, and Zeus and Hera's Kinkiest Argument" (Eugenides), 235*n*8
sex education, 237*n*40
sex-role inventory, 232–33
sexual affective strategies, 197–207
sexual gratification, 184
sexuality, 148; ambiguous, 183–84; black, films and, 208; black female (*see* black female sexuality); performance of, 200. *See also* black hypersexuality
sexual orientation, 20, 136, 140, 175–90, 179, 195; centrality of, 175; illegibility of, 177, 189
sexual projection, life stressors associated with, 198
sexual promiscuity, 198
sexual trauma, 195, 197, 202
sexual violence, 81, 123
sex work, 200
Shadow and Act (Ellison), 47*n*4
Shakespeare, William, 221, 242
Shank, Barry, 216*n*26, 217*n*26
The Shank Force of Musical Beauty (Shank), 217*n*26
Shepard, Matthew, 14
Sheshadri-Crooks, Kalpana, 177, 190*n*4
Shettles, Landrum, 236*n*35
A Shore Thing (TV show), 165, 171
Shostak, Debra, 228, 233, 238*n*76
The Signifying Monkey (Gates), 94*n*29
Signs (journal), 48*n*11
Silk, Coleman (fictional character), 65*n*32
Simon, Paul, 172*n*24
Simon and Garfunkel, 167
Simone, Nina, 214–15, 216*n*26
Skarsgård, Stellan, 201
Skerrett, Joseph, 6–7, 22*n*17
Skiffington, John, 77, 78
Slate magazine, 22*n*23
slavery, 50, 73; African Americans and, 50; blackness and, 52; chattel, 179, 181; historical legacy of, 209; perceptual, 63*n*2; visual spectacle in, 131*n*16
"Slavery, Race, and Ideology in the United States of America" (Fields), 63*n*2
"Slavery in Southwest Georgia" (Proctor), 64*n*11
slaves: African-descended, 63*n*2; antebellum narratives of, 3; black owner treatment of, 76; Native American ancestry and, 53; passing of runaway as white, 49–50, 52–54; stereotypes about black, 181; whippings of, 131
Slaves to Fashion (Miller), 113*n*10
Sleepy Hollow (TV show), 68–69
"Sliding Significations" (Cutter), 65*n*24
Smith, Andrea, 13, 15, 24*n*46; outing of, 9–11
Smith, Barbara, 187, 191*n*28
Smith, Jeff, 103, 113*n*14
Smith, Shawn Michelle, 130*n*12, 131*n*13
Smith, Terry, 86, 93*n*7
Smith, Valerie, 98, 113*n*6, 178, 190*n*8
Smith, Zadie, 81*n*3
Smyrna, Turkey, 221
Snapchat, 139
Snooki. *See* Polizzi, Nicole "Snooki"
social construction, 213, 216*n*19, 225; passing as a, 193
"The Social Construction of Race" (Haney-López), 64*n*8, 130*n*2
social descriptions, conformity to, 194
social justice, 11, 16, 87
social media: abuse of, 15; identity in marketplace, 136–37; tools of, 19
social segregation, 210
social whiteness, 168
socioeconomic status, 198, 202
socio-legal-political crisis for blacks, 71
sociopolitical dimension, 160, 162, 182, 185
Sollors, Werner, 63–64*n*5, 220, 234*nn*2–3, 240*n*2
So-Lloyd, Gloria, 64*n*17
Sonner, Scott, 112*n*2
Soprano, Tony (fictional character), 167–68, 169
The Sopranos (TV show), 166, 167, 173*n*27

Sorrentino, Mike "the Situation," 161, 163
Sosulski, Marya R., 216*n*10
Soul! (TV show), xiii*n*2
Soul Babies (Neal), xiii*n*5
"The Soul Brother" (Baraka), xiii*n*3
Soul Sister (Halsell), 142, 147, 148, 151, 152, 155*nn*43–44
The Souls of Black Folks (Du Bois), 24*n*45, 190*n*14, 215*n*7
The Souls of Mixed Folk (Elam), 22*n*26, 64*n*6, 242–43, 244*n*10
Soulsonic Force, 85
The Sound and the Fury (Faulkner), 228
Sparks, Brian (fictional character), 151, 153
Sparks, Renee (fictional character), 153
Spates, Kamesha, 216*n*10
Spickard, Paul, 64*n*5, 64*n*17
Spiegelman, Art, 131*nn*22–23
Spitz, Mark (fictional character), 70
Split Ends (TV show), 165
Squires, Catherine, 114*n*26
Stankonia, 114*n*23
Stark, Clementine (fictional character), 223
state violence, xi
Status Update (Marwick), 140*n*2
Steele, Shelby, 21*n*2
Stephanides, Calliope (fictional character), 219–34
Stephanides, Desdemona (fictional character), 227
Stephanides, Lefty (fictional character), 227
Stephanides, Milton (fictional character), 236*n*39
stereotypes: about black slaves, 181; black male body and, 112; racial, 179
Stetson, Earlene, 58, 65*n*31
Stew (musician), 7–8, 22*n*20, 242
Stocker, David, 225
Storde, 64*n*6
straightness as performance, 231
straight passing, 223–25
The Structure of Scientific Revolutions (Kuhn), 82*nn*25–27
"The Subaltern as Imperialist" (Rust), 154*n*6
subjectivity, racialized, 79
Suls, Robert, 22*n*19
Summer Share (TV show), 165
"Sun-Tan Addicts" (*Collier* editorial), 159–60, 172*n*2
Supreme Court: *Brown* decision and, ix, 71, 142; *Grutter* decision and, 75–76, 82*n*13, 82*n*16; *Plessy* decision and, 74, 75, 82*n*17, 94, 137
surveillance, passing and, 19, 138, 139, 140
Sybil (TV show), 196
Symptomatic (Senna), 243–44
Szanto, Laura, 155*n*31

"Taking Identity Politics Seriously" (Clifford), 215*n*2
"Talking to Strangers" (Wang), 140*n*4
Talusan, Meredith, 23*n*36
tan, passing for, 158–72
"Tan TV" (Hargraves), 162, 172*n*10
Taylor, Paul, 22*n*19
Taylor, Yamara, 113*n*11
Teena, Brandon, 12, 14, 23*n*37
television: dissociative identities in, 196; as popular culture, 196. *See also* reality television; *and names of specific shows*
"Telling Tales" (Halberstam), 23*n*37
Tesler, Michael, 113*n*8, 162–63
Thaggert, Miriam, 23*n*38
"'Theory Uncompromised by Practicality'" (Shostak), 238*n*76
The Third Reconstruction (Barber), xiii*n*5
Thirteen Ways of Looking at a Black Man (Gates), 65*n*33
This American Life (radio show), 14
This Is What a Lesbian Looks Like (Carter), 191*n*27
Thomas, Brook, 82*n*17
Thomas, Clarence, 75–76
Thomas, J., 82*n*13, 82*n*16
Thoreau, Henry David, 193
Thought Catalog (Harper), 224
The Three Faces of Eve (film), 196
Thurman, Wallace, 93, 94*n*32
The Time of Our Singing (Powers), 73
Tiresias, 221
To Be Suddenly White (Belluscio), 63–64*n*5
"To Die For" (McCright and Vannini), 172*n*1
Toomer, Jean, 45, 46, 47*n*5

"To Pass//In Drag" (Robinson), 140*n*15, 140*n*19
Touré, 81*n*3
Tourgée, Albion W., 76, 82*n*18
Towards the Abolition of Whiteness (Roediger), 173*n*30
Townsend, Augustus (fictional character), 76, 78
Townsend, Henry (fictional character), 72–73, 78, 81
traditional narratives of passing: assimilation and, 137, 139, 140; privacy and, 136–37, 139, 140; satire and, 137–38, 139, 140; surveillance and, 138, 139, 140
The Tragedy of Pudd'nhead Wilson (Twain), 63*n*3
transgender identities, 12, 13, 23*n*39, 185, 229; connections between transracial identities and, 14
transgenderism, 23*n*39
Transgression 2.0 (Gunkel and Gournelos), 140*n*17
transracial identity, 23*n*34, 23–24*n*39, 229; acceptance of, 5–6, 12–13; connections between transgender identities and, 14
transracialism, 23*n*39
transsexuals, 231
transvestism, 64*n*10
trauma, 20, 195; racial, 197, 210; sexual, 195, 197, 202; violent, 202. *See also* violence
The Triumph of Reality TV (Edwards), 164, 172*n*3, 172*n*13
Trowbridge, J. T., 55, 56, 57, 64*n*19
"The True Story of John/Joan" (Colapinto), 237*n*40, 237*n*42
Trump, Donald J.: *Apprentice* show of, 14; election of, 162; use of Twitter by, xii
Tumblr, 139
Tuvel, Rebecca, 23–24*n*39
Twain, Mark, x, 50, 63*n*3
twentieth century: color line in, 190*n*14; lynchings in, 124; neo-passing in, 194; passing in, 50–51, 55, 56, 57, 86, 101, 120; postracial narratives in, 68
twenty-first century: civil rights activists in, 176; gay rights activists in, 176; neo-passing in, 194; passing in, 2, 14–15, 17, 19, 43–47, 101
24 (TV show), 96, 98, 99, 107, 112*n*2
Twitter, 24*n*47, 139, 140*nn*13–14; Trump's use of, xii
2012 (movie), 107, 113*n*7

unconscious thoughts, exposure of, 16
Undercover Boss (TV show), 5, 15
"Underneath a Harlem Moon" (song), 113*n*12
Understanding Comics (McCloud), 130*n*6, 131*n*15
Unico National, 161
United States of Tana (TV show), 196
Utne Reader, 48*nn*8–9

Vannini, Phillip, 172*n*1
Vested Interests (Garber), 64*n*10
vigilante justice, lynching and, 123
Vincent, Norah, 142, 145, 146, 147–48, 153
violence: casual, 127; circus-like atmosphere at, 125; Civil Rights and, 143; conviction of his actions and, 109; Detroit's eruption into, 221; domestic, 139; history of, 183; images of, 125, 126; in *Jersey Shore*, 164; mass, 14; police, 117, 118, 125, 127; racial, 16, 18, 117, 125, 130; reporting on, 129; resolution of dispute and, 78; revenge and, 12; sexual, 81, 123; *Sopranos* and, 166; spectacular, 124; state, xi; state-sanctioned, 124; trauma, 202; turning blind eye to, 71; visual representations of, 123; white acts of, 15; white masculine, 90; white-supremacist, 105; witnessing of, 127. *See also* brutality, lynchings; police brutality
"Violence and Trauma" (Ford), 216*n*17
"Visible Young Man" (Touré), 81*n*3
visual cues in passing, 105
visual spectacle in slavery, 131*n*16
Vivaldo, Daniel (fictional character), 92
Voting Rights Act, 71

The Wages of Whiteness (Roediger), 216*n*19
Wald, Gayle, 143, 145, 155*n*45; *Crossing the Line*, 23*n*32, 24*n*41, 113*n*5, 154*n*2; foreword to this book, 23*n*39, 243; *It's Been Beautiful*, xiii*n*2; preface to *Passing Interest*, 23*n*30
Walker, Rebecca, 155*n*31

Walker-Hoover, Carl, 14
The Walking Dead (TV show), 68–69, 70–71
Wallace, Irving, 96, 102, 103, 106
Wang, Tricia, 140*n*4
Warner, Michael, 99
Warren, Kenneth, 21*n*4, 71–72, 82*n*7, 176–77, 190*n*2
Washington, D.C., march on, 186, 191*n*26
WASPy homogeneity, 230
Watermelon Man (Gerber), 154*n*2
Waters, Ethel, 113*n*12
Wauters, Nick, 113*n*7
We as Freedmen (Medley), 140*n*8
Webb, Frank, 55, 64*n*18
Weber, Bruce, 82*n*11
WeChat, 139
Wells, Linda, 45, 46
West, Amy, 144
Whaley, Deborah Elizabeth, 20, 215*n*1
"What Is This 'Black' in Black Popular Culture" (Hall), 216*n*16
"What the Black Man Wants" (Douglass), 82*nn*14–15
What Was African American Literature? (Warren), 21*n*4, 71–72, 82*n*7, 176–77, 190*n*2
Where Did You Sleep Last Night? (Senna), 61–62, 65*nn*39–40
whippings, of slaves, 131
White, Barbara (alter ego of Renee Sparks in *Black. White.*), 153
White, Brian (alter ego of Brian Sparks in *Black. White.*), 153
White, Miles, 94*n*20
The White Boy Shuffle (Beatty), 92
white ethnic identity, 160; New Jersey as stage for, 160–61
white flight, 222
Whitehead, Colson, 69–71, 73, 81*nn*3–4, 243
white heteronormativity, 178
White House Down (movie), 107, 113*n*7
"White Like Me" (Lott), 154*n*2
white masculine violence, 90
white masculinity, 108, 110
white men, centrality of, in American mass killings, 89–90
whiteness, 50; as absence of culture, 169; acknowledgment of, 50; of the astronaut program, 111; as cause of depression, 209; claiming of "other" and, 169; defining, 52, 53, 54, 60, 220; denaturalization of, 105, 123, 129; description of, 49–50; desire for, 20, 187, 189; destabilization of, 87; ethnicity and, 167, 168; hegemony of, 124; heteronormative, 190; link to education and upper-class status, 59; neo-passing and, 63; normative, 180; one-drop ideology and, 117; passing and, 120, 123; of the presidency, 104, 105, 106, 110; as privilege, 90, 160, 197, 210; problem of, 88, 91; questioning of, 126; racial differences and, 184; as racial identity, 58, 61; rebranding of, 162; refusing, 168; social, 168; as social construction, 216*n*19; systemic nature of, 91; tanning and, 160, 167, 169, 170; values associated with, 61, 63; violence and, 183 "Whiteness as Property" (Harris), 140*n*9
Whiteness of a Different Color (Jacobson), 168, 173*n*28, 216*n*19
whiteness studies, 123
"Whiteness Visible" (Mansbach), 94*nn*15–16, 94*n*22
white paternalism, 13, 184
white privilege, 13; black cultural identity in resisting, 87–88; blackness and, 90; dismantling of, 90–91
white racial-identity politics, expansion of, x
whites, passing as black, 45, 154*n*2
white slavers, rape of black women by, 209
white supremacy, 2, 85, 89, 168; violence and, 105; witnessing of, xii
Who Is Black? (Davis), 22*n*10
"Who's Passing for Who?" (Hughes), 5, 8–9
"Why Does the Slave Ever Love?" (Robinson), 22*n*7
"Why I'm Masquerading as a White Bearded Hipster Guy on Twitter" (Golden), 140*nn*13–14
"Why 'Passing' Is Passing Out" (*Jet* magazine), ix, xiii*n*1, 1, 21*n*1, 47*n*3
Willett, Cynthia, 113*n*4
Williams, Gregory Howard, 4, 61, 65*n*38
Williams, Richard L., 47*n*3
Willow Weep for Me (Danquah), 198, 214–15

"Willow Weep for Me" (song), 215, 216*n*26, 217*n*28
Wilson, Melba, 216*n*10
Winant, Howard, x, xii, xiii*n*4, xiii*n*10, 21*n*4, 242, 244*n*6
Windley, Lathan A., 64*n*14
Winfrey, Oprah, 22*n*25, 113*n*11
The Wire (TV show), 172*n*20
Wise, Tim, 21*nn*3–4
Without Guarantees (Clifford), 215*n*2
witnessing: ethics and, 124, 130; of lynchings, 126; of violence, 118, 126, 127; of white supremacy, xii
Witterick, Kathy, 225, 236*n*33
The Wizard of Oz (movie), 213
Womack, Ytasha L., 190, 191*n*29
women: passing as men, 45. *See also* black women
women's movement, xii
Wonder, Stevie, 210, 216*n*20
work ethic, 136
workplace discrimination, erosion of, ix
World War I, 43
World War II, 44, 221, 222
Wright, Richard, 91, 94*n*26
Wurgel, Bruno (fictional character), 153

X-Clan, 87

Yale University, 180, 182, 185; Coming Out Day at, 185, 186, 187; institutional resistance to nonheteronormative lifestyles, 185; orientation games at, 175; racial diversity at, 185
"The Year of Living Postracially" (Colson), 81*nn*3–4
Yiannopoulos, Milo, 22*n*25
Yoshino, Kenji, 177, 190*n*3
Young, Vershawn Ashanti, ix, 22*n*17, 140*n*12, 194
Youngblood, Peter, 53
Younge, Gary, 24*n*47
"You Rascal, You" (song), 113*n*12
"You're Supposed to Be a Tall, Handsome, Fully Grown White Man" (Pickens), 216*n*21

Zackodnik, Teresa C., 63–64*n*5
Zavadski, Katie, 24*n*47
Zeiler, Kristin, 238*n*76
ze pronoun, 234
Zeus, 230
Zizmo, Jimmy, 229
zombies, 17, 68–72
Zone One (Whitehead), 69–71
Zuckerman, Ed, 113*n*7
Zulu Nation, 114*n*23

The University of Illinois Press
is a founding member of the
Association of American University Presses.

Composed in 10.75/13 Arno Pro
with Adrianna Extended Pro display
by Kirsten Dennison
at the University of Illinois Press
Cover designed by Jennifer S. Fisher
Cover illustration: Byron Kim, *Synecdoche*, 1991–present, oil and wax on wood, each panel: 10 × 8 inches (25.4 × 20.32 cm), overall installed: 120¼ × 350¼ inches (305.44 × 889.64 cm). Collection of the National Gallery of Art, Washington, Installed at the 1993 Whitney Museum of American Art Biennial, New York. Photographer: Dennis Cowley. © Byron Kim. Courtesy James Cohan, New York.

University of Illinois Press
1325 South Oak Street
Champaign, IL 61820-6903
www.press.uillinois.edu